When They *Weren't* Doing
Shakespeare

When They *Weren't* Doing *Shakespeare*

ESSAYS ON
*Nineteenth-Century British
and American Theatre*

EDITED BY
Judith L. Fisher
AND
Stephen Watt

THE UNIVERSITY OF GEORGIA PRESS
Athens and London

Paperback edition, 2011
© 1989 by the University of Georgia Press
Preface to the 2010 Edition © 2011 by the University of Georgia Press
Athens, Georgia 30602
www.ugapress.org
All rights reserved
Designed by Debby Jay
Set in Linotron 202 Garamond No. 3
Printed digitally in the United States of America

The Library of Congress has cataloged the
hardcover edition of this book as follows:
Library of Congress Cataloging-in-Publication Data
LCCN Permalink: http://lccn.loc.gov/88022044

When they weren't doing Shakespeare : essays on nineteenth-century
British and American theatre / edited by Judith L. Fisher and Stephen Watt.
xxii, 345 p. : ill. ; 25 cm.
ISBN 0-8203-1108-1 (alk. paper)
Includes bibliographies and index.
1. Theater—English-speaking countries—History—19th century. 2. English drama—19th century—History and criticism. 3. American drama—19th century—History and criticism.
I. Fisher, Judith Law, 1952– II. Watt, Stephen, 1951–
PN2594 .W47 1989
792'.0941—dc19   88-22044

PAPERBACK ISBN-13: 978-0-8203-3692-3
ISBN-10: 0-8203-3692-0

British Library Cataloging-in-Publication Data available

To Charles H. Shattuck and James Hurt

Contents

List of Illustrations	ix
List of Abbreviations	x
Preface to the 2011 Edition	xi
Acknowledgments	xv
Introduction	xvii

PART ONE: ACTORS AND THEIR ROLES

The Theatre of Edwin Forrest and Jacksonian Hero Worship — 3
   Bruce A. McConachie

Guy Mannering and Charlotte Cushman's Meg Merrilies:
Gothic Novel, Play, and Performance — 19
   Gary Jay Williams

A Picturesque Interpretation of History: William Charles
Macready's *Richelieu*, 1839–1850 — 39
   Denis Salter

Edwin Booth's Bertuccio: Tom Taylor's Fool Revised — 64
   Lorraine Commeret

James O'Neill's Launching of *Monte Cristo* — 88
   Myron Matlaw

A Forgotten "Fallen Woman": Olga Nethersole's *Sapho* — 106
   Joy Harriman Reilly

PART TWO: PLAYWRIGHTS AND GENRES

In the Shadow of the Bard: James Nelson Barker's Republican
Drama and the Shakespearean Legacy — 123
   Gary A. Richardson

Nautical "Docudrama" in the Age of the Kembles — 137
   George D. Glenn

Lofty Tragedy for Mundane Audiences: John Westland
Marston's *The Patrician's Daughter* and *Strathmore*   152
   Carol J. Carlisle

"Helpless and Unfriended": Nineteenth-Century Domestic
Melodrama   174
   Martha Vicinus

Historical Drama and the "Legitimate" Theatre: Tom Taylor
and W. G. Wills in the 1870s   187
   Stephen Watt

"A House Choked with Gunpowder and Wild with Excitement":
Augustus Harris and Drury Lane's Spectacular Melodrama   212
   James Stottlar

Edwardian London West End Christmas Entertainments,
1900–1914   230
   J. P. Wearing

PART THREE: COMEDY AND SOCIAL DRAMA

The Image of Fashionable Society in American Comedy,
1840–1870   243
   Tice L. Miller

Dion Boucicault's Comic Myths   253
   James Hurt

Society in Transition: From Manuscript to Performance   266
   Daniel Barrett

W. S. Gilbert: The Comedic Alternative   280
   Judith L. Fisher

Charles Wyndham in *Mrs. Dane's Defence*   299
   George Rowell

Works Cited   313
Contributors   327
Index   331

Illustrations

Charlotte Cushman as Meg Merrilies in *Guy Mannering*	31
William Charles Macready as Cardinal Richelieu and Samuel Phelps as Father Joseph	50
Richelieu's study in the Palais Cardinal, 1.2 and 2.2. Drawing in the 1850 promptbook	52
Richelieu's study in the Palais Cardinal, 1.2 and 2.2	52
The gardens of the Louvre. *Richelieu*, act 4 Blocking plan	54
King Louis XIII's apartment of state. *Richelieu*, 5.2 Blocking plan	54
King Louis XIII's apartment of state. *Richelieu*, 5.2	57
Playbill for *The Fool's Revenge*	65
Playbill for *The Fool's Revenge*	66
Edwin Booth as "Bertuccio"	75
James O'Neill about the time of the launching of *Monte Cristo*	89
James O'Neill as Edmund Dantes at the Château d'If	97
The magnificent ballroom scene. *The Count of Monte Cristo*	100
Olga Nethersole as "Sapho"	110
Scene from *The Patrician's Daughter*	157
Scene from *Strathmore*	164
Harold Kyrle as "Belvawney." *Engaged*, act 1	293
The end of act 1 and a collage of scenes. *Engaged*	294
Scene from *Mrs. Dane's Defence*, act 2	305
Scene from *Mrs. Dane's Defence*, act 3	306

Abbreviations

	London		United States
ILN	*Illustrated London News*	DT	*Daily Telegraph*
ISD	*Illustrated Sporting and Dramatic News*	EP	*Evening Post*
		NYE	*New York Empire*
LDT	*London Daily Telegraph*	NYH	*New York Herald*
LSR	*London Saturday Review*	NYDM	*New York Dramatic Mirror*
MP	*Morning Post*	NYDT	*New York Dramatic Times*
T	*London Times*	PES	*Philadelphia Evening Star*
		SR	*Saturday Review*
		Trib	*New York Tribune*

Preface to the 2011 Edition

It is difficult to describe adequately our surprise and profound pleasure at learning that the University of Georgia Press was interested in reissuing *When They Weren't Doing Shakespeare*. First published in 1989, this collection was offered as a *festschrift* to celebrate the distinguished career of Charles H. Shattuck of the University of Illinois, a scholar whom all eighteen contributors to the volume admired greatly and whom most called a friend or mentor. Fortunately, he lived to see the publication of this volume and wrote admiringly to us soon thereafter: "I don't know what possessed you to persuade all these good people to write these swell essays for me, but for that delightful idea, and for all the months of labor you've put into bringing it to so fine a finish, my sincere and everlasting thanks." Coming from Chuck, a careful reader, to say the least, who at times could be parsimonious in commending intellectual work that did not meet his high level of expectation, such praise was welcome indeed.

Much has happened in the more than two decades that separate the hardcover edition of these essays and the present paperback edition. Inevitably, some of these are deeply personal events that have caused great sadness. Like Samuel Beckett's Pozzo, who complains in act 2 of *Waiting for Godot* of being tormented by "accursed" time, the scholars whose work is assembled here are no more impervious to the maw of Time than anyone else. Chuck Shattuck died in the fall of 1992, more than two years after the passing of Myron Matlaw, whose fine essay on James O'Neill appears in the pages that follow. The distinguished Victorianist George Rowell died in 2001 and, as we write this brief essay, several contributors to *When They Weren't Doing Shakespeare* languish in ill health. That such a course is inevitable neither makes it less difficult nor renders voracious Time no less "abominable," as Beckett's suddenly blinded character laments.

There is, however, much to celebrate as well in the myriad of accomplishments of the scholars who contributed to this anthology, as after the publication of this book they continued to advance knowledge in a variety of areas, most of which, but certainly not all, pertain to the nineteenth-century British and American theatres. Even as a more broadly based performance studies emerged at about this time—and even as performance study challenges the centrality of the performed drama, or the privilege of any scrivened text, for that matter—many contributors to this volume helped cultivate a revised and intellectually robust sense of theatre history and its operations. Bruce A. McConachie's *Engaging Audiences: A Cognitive Approach to Spectating in the Theatre* (2008) epitomizes the work of scholars, such as Lisa Zunshine, Rhonda Blair, and Amy Cook, who bring a finely tuned scientific approach to the theatre event and the activity of spectatorship. McConachie and Gary Jay Williams have joined colleagues in writing the recent textbook *Theatre Histories: An Introduction* (2006), a text that demonstrates how traditions of performance combine with specific dramatic texts to perform a wide variety of cultural work within discourses of nationalism, imperialism, and others.

Many of the essayists in this volume have continued to enhance our understanding of specific national dramas, economies, or the conditions of women. Tice L. Miller's books *Entertaining the Nation: American Drama in the Eighteenth and Nineteenth Centuries* (2007) and *The American Stage* (2006), Gary A. Richardson's *American Drama: From the Colonial Period through World War One* (1993), and Stephen Watt and Richardson's *American Drama: Colonial to Contemporary* (1995) have endeavored to expand our sense of the theatrical event in America and the plays that contributed so vitally to it. An appreciable element in the expansion of the dramatic canon and of studies of the ascendant theatre in the later nineteenth century concerns the role of women in the theatre and in nineteenth-century culture more generally, topics Martha Vicinus and Judith L. Fisher have discussed with great incisiveness. And, in the years following the publication of *When They Weren't Doing Shakespeare,* those two distinguished historians of the British theatre, J. P. Wearing and George Rowell, continued to produce major volumes and editions, including new installments of Wearing's seven-volume history *The London Stage,* his critical editions of Bernard Shaw's *Arms and the Man* (2008) and Sir Arthur Wing Pinero's *The Second Mrs. Tanqueray* (2007), and Rowell's *The Old Vic Theatre: A History* (1993). Denis Salter has continued over the past two decades to be one of the most influential critics of the Canadian and postcolonial theatres. And taking a narrower, more specifically local approach, James

Hurt's *Writing Illinois: The Prairie, Lincoln, and Chicago* (1992) makes an eloquent case for the distinct formative relationship between writing and location.

Contributors to *When They Weren't Doing Shakespeare* were obviously unaware of some of the directions their discipline would take in the decades following the publication of this anthology. In his fine study *The Cambridge Introduction to Theatre Historiography* (2009), for example, Thomas Postelwait—a good friend of Professor Shattuck's, by the way—outlines the methods historians need to follow in their excavatory labors: determine the authenticity of sources and the reliability of witnesses, place historical events in appropriate contexts, construct arguments "based upon principles of possibility and plausibility," and so on. Such procedures are surely adhered to in the essays that follow, undiminished by the passage of time. Whether the topic is Jacksonian democracy or American fashionable society of the mid-nineteenth century, representations of gender and sexuality on the *fin de siècle* stage or popular entertainments during Christmas holiday season in London, contributors to this anthology advance "plausible" and often powerful arguments about the political and social contexts in which the theatre event occurred. It is also the case that while most of the principles of "historiography" Postelwait delineates are strongly in evidence in these essays, his capacious definition of "theatre" is not. In *The Cambridge Introduction to Theatre Historiography* Postelwait includes parades, processions, festivals, circuses, public conventions, and other performance events as the proper objects of study for theatre historians. By contrast, the contributors to this volume focus on actors, influential playwrights, and popular dramatic genres. That some of the latter might resemble performance events rather than well-wrought dramas—nautical docudrama, for example, and the more "open" textuality of pantomime—draws *When They Weren't Doing Shakespeare* more closely to the concerns of contemporary performance studies than one might initially expect.

We hope, then, that readers of this paperback edition will find the chapters of this book evocative and fresh in ways that belie their age—and judge them able and incisive examples of the writing of theatre history. Another way of saying this, perhaps, is that all of the contributors to this volume hope for little more from their readers than the simple, but powerful, headline of adulation that accompanied Chuck Shattuck's obituary in the *New York Times* on September 23, 1992: "Charles H. Shattuck, 81, Shakespearean Scholar." We write here, however, not to mourn a passing but to celebrate the birth of a new edition through an equally incisive headline: "*When They Weren't Doing Shakespeare*—nineteenth-century theatre scholarship."

Judith L. Fisher and Stephen Watt

Acknowledgments

The editors of this volume wish to express their gratitude to Beth Staggs and Brad Stiles, who typed the manuscript; to Paula Krebs, who helped proofread the book; to Kelly Lowe, who assisted with the writing of the index; to Nona Watt of the Indiana University library, who provided bibliographical assistance; and to Angela Ray of the University of Georgia Press. Any errors we have made here are certainly not their responsibility. Also, we wish to acknowledge the support of the Office of Research and Graduate Development, Indiana University, and of Associate Dean Albert Wertheim.

Introduction

Both the scope and substance of *When They Weren't Doing Shakespeare* mirror the broad interests of the scholar to whom it is dedicated, Charles H. Shattuck of the University of Illinois at Urbana-Champaign. For over fifty years, he has offered keen insights into authors ranging from William Shakespeare to Bertolt Brecht, into texts as diverse as *Othello* and James Joyce's *Dubliners*, into issues as different as the Romantic acting style of Junius Brutus Booth and the social comedy of Bernard Shaw. Professor Shattuck's best-known work, however, is in nineteenth-century theatre history and in the study of Shakespeare's plays as interpreted by major actors like John Philip Kemble, William Charles Macready, and Edwin Booth. This interest has led most recently to his two-volume *Shakespeare on the American Stage*, published by the Folger Shakespeare Library. (Volume two has been awarded both the Barnard Hewitt and the George Freedley Memorial awards for 1988.) We intend *When They Weren't Doing Shakespeare* to complement this fine scholarship and carry on its formidable precedent.

Throughout his distinguished career, Professor Shattuck has balanced his reverence for Shakespeare with his curiosity about the theatrical conventions used to lift Shakespeare's plays off the printed page and place them before the footlights. This curiosity has resulted in, among numerous other contributions to our knowledge of nineteenth-century theatre, *Bulwer and Macready: A Chronicle of the Early Victorian Theatre* (1958) and *The Hamlet of Edwin Booth* (1969)—and, in a sense, has led to this volume as well. The essays in this anthology, however, shift the balance toward the actors, playwrights, and tastes of nineteenth-century America and Victorian London which formed a context for productions of Shakespeare. *When They Weren't Doing Shakespeare*, as the title implies, addresses the often-ignored nineteenth-century plays and genres which either competed with Shakespeare for audiences or complemented revivals of Shakespeare's plays in the repertories of well-known actor-managers. In what follows, we shall try to outline briefly the organization and structure of this volume, our gift to Professor Shattuck.

Actors and Their Roles

The book's first section contains six studies of nineteenth-century actors and some of their most celebrated roles. "Ensemble" acting is a product of the late nineteenth century; before this, even the term theatrical "company," as it is used today with its connotation of humble anonymity, would have been unthinkable to star-actors. The phenomenon of the actor-manager—where the star actually leased the theatre, procured the text, directed its production, and often served as his own publicity agent—made the actor the "auteur" of the play, much as film directors like Alfred Hitchcock, François Truffaut, or Ingmar Bergman are accorded authorial status by one variety of film theory. Not until T. W. Robertson in 1865 did a playwright presume to exert creative control over his work. Consequently, prominent actors such as Charles Kean, Edmund Kean, Edwin Forrest, William Charles Macready, Henry Irving, and Charles Wyndham enjoyed enormous control not just over their roles, but over the direction of nineteenth-century theatre.

A successful actor created a unique reading of a character which could then become "his" (or "hers") and, in the cases of Macready and Irving for instance, presented productions which defined for their times what good theatre was. Success demanded a repertory both of original roles, defined by the actor and never played before, and adaptations of more traditional (often Shakespearean) roles. In some instances, as with Edwin Forrest, whom Bruce McConachie discusses in a more expansive historical context in this section, the actor commissioned a play with a role designed to suit his specific physical gifts and histrionic style. Often, however, the actor adapted roles in original plays. Macready, who produced several original plays by Sheridan Knowles, felt free to adapt lines and scenes from the tragedy *Virginius* (1820) to reflect more fully his talents and his concept of the dignity of the drama. In this regard, Denis Salter traces in his essay the negotiations between Macready and Edward Bulwer-Lytton over the former's production of *Richelieu*. Later in the century, Irving continued this process of adaptation with, among others, Lord Tennyson's *Becket* (1893). Such artistic license often created conflict between author and actor, with the actor usually winning. This state of affairs prompted Bernard Shaw, never an admirer of Irving, to remark that the great tragedian "took no interest in the drama as such: a play was to him a length of stuff necessary to his appearance on the stage, but so entirely subordinate to that consummation that it could be cut to his measure like a roll of cloth."[1] Shaw's objections aside, the actor's power could create a more positive result: Macready, for instance, restored the original texts of such plays as Shakespeare's *King Lear* and *Richard III* from their "improvements" by Nahum Tate and Colley Cibber.

Actors throughout the century discovered an enormous repository of starring roles in contemporary novels; Sir Walter Scott and Charles Dickens were two novelists whose work was employed in this way. Scott created perfect "character parts" in grotesques such as Meg Merrilies from *Old Mortality*—whom Gary Jay Williams describes as played by Charlotte Cushman—and romance heroes such as Rob Roy. Dickens' novels, among other attractions, included both spectacular effects like the shipwreck in *David Copperfield* and terrifying or heart-rending scenes of immediate theatrical interest, such as Bill Sykes' murder of Nancy in *Oliver Twist*. Both writers built readily identifiable visual or verbal traits into their characters which gave an actor or actress a foundation from which to build an impersonation. Moreover, the Dramatic Copyright Act of 1833 encouraged hack dramatists to become literary pirates because only printed plays were protected. *Oliver Twist*, for example, was on the stage before Dickens had completed its serial publication in *Bentley's Miscellany* in 1838.

But real success in the "legitimate" theatre—as opposed to that earned by popular comic actors such as John Liston and William Dowton, or music-hall performers—required an actor to excel in at least some of the traditional roles, especially Shakespearean ones. Macready's Shylock gave him lasting fame because he elevated the character from buffoon-like villainy to tragic dignity; similarly, Irving's Hamlet became *the* melancholy Dane of the late-Victorian stage. Not that every role met with acclaim: both actors realized less success with Romeo and the comedies (*Much Ado About Nothing* being a prominent exception in Irving's repertory, in part due to Ellen Terry's Beatrice); and Irving had tremendous difficulty with Macbeth in 1875, so much so that the "Captious Critic's" review in *The Illustrated Sporting and Dramatic News* was accompanied by an unflattering caricature of Irving entitled "Mr. Digby Grant [a character in James Albery's *Two Roses* that Irving played frequently] as Macbeth" (2 October 1875). In addition to playing leading parts in Shakespeare, an actor earned his or her reputation by succeeding in standard repertoire favorites, many adapted from French sources. Dion Boucicault's *The Corsican Brothers* (1852) was one of these, mainly because it allowed the star-actor to display his virtuosity by playing two parts, the twins, Fabian and Louis de Franchi. Somewhat less popularly performed but, as Lorraine Commeret explains, a staple in Edwin Booth's repertory, was Tom Taylor's *The Fool's Revenge* (1859). In some cases, however, a particularly successful impersonation such as James O'Neill's Count of Monte Cristo, recounted in this section by Myron Matlaw, could entrap the actor, the audience demanding it yearly. Such celebrity could limit the variety of roles the audience would accept from an actor, as well as inhibit the actor's own development.

One consequence of the emphasis on "star-actors" and its connection to theatrical management was the male dominance of the English stage. A few women, to be sure, managed their own companies—Madame Vestris early in the century and Olga Nethersole much later. But many well-known actresses became identified with specific male stars—Helen Faucit with Macready, Ellen Terry with Irving—and in the process were dominated by them in the sense that their roles and sometimes their interpretations were chosen by the actor with an eye to his own performance. One curious variation of this domination, in Shaw's eyes, was Augustin Daly's over Ada Rehan: while reviewing a production of *A Midsummer Night's Dream*, Shaw opined that "With Grandfather Daly to choose her plays for her, there is no future for Ada Rehan" (*LSR* 13 July 1895). On occasion later in the century, when Henry Arthur Jones and Arthur Wing Pinero produced their "Fallen Women" plays, actresses such as Mrs. Patrick Campbell achieved new levels of professional independence. And Ibsen's plays provided opportunities for striking performances by Janet Achurch. Sarah Bernhardt played male roles and, like Eleonora Duse, also developed her own vehicles; lesser-known actresses such as Olga Nethersole won fame somewhat notoriously in the United States in her sexy *Sapho*, as Joy Harriman Reilly describes in this section's last essay.

A second consequence of an actor-dominated system is intimated by all the essays in this section and in the volume's second part, "Playwrights and Genres." The power of actors and actresses over their roles—and their prominence as public figures—made many of them acutely aware of their social responsibilities. The didactic function of all art—painting, literature, and drama—placed a particular burden upon performers because they were, in a unique way, self-created works of art. Thus, they chose their roles not only for the artistic possibilities but also with an eye to the role's cultural value. While this self-consciousness contributed to making the major actors reluctant to revolutionize the theatre, it also created an era of memorable revivals of Shakespeare. These revivals are etched in the background of several of the essays in this opening section, "Actors and Their Roles."

A third, and from a literary perspective perhaps most significant, aspect of the star-actor system is the ascendance of the actor over the playwright. Other ramifications devolving from this devaluation of the writer—hence, of language as well—are discussed in the second part of *When They Weren't Doing Shakespeare*, "Playwrights and Genres."

Playwrights and Genres

The status of the dramatist in the nineteenth century was uncertain, to say the least. In the first half of the century, especially, playwrights tended to be "hacks," technicians who upon request could create almost any variety of dramatic entertainment: adaptations of Shakespeare; "original" plays constructed from topical events, as George Glenn outlines in this part of the volume in his essay on "Nautical 'Docudrama' in the Age of the Kembles"; plays designed to feature a particular performer or effect, and so on. Some dramatists of more lofty literary ambition such as John Westland Marston, whose attempts to write tragedy Carol J. Carlisle documents in this section, lost control over their work once the actor-manager accepted it; while others, as Gary Richardson explains, could never quite overcome the monumental legacy of Shakespeare. And, although this volume endeavors to treat some of these more literary playwrights, it inevitably contains examples of the more vulgarly popular playwright as well. Many of this latter variety, like John Baldwin Buckstone, made no pretense of being literary "artists." Buckstone wrote entertainments ranging from a favorite melodrama, *Luke the Labourer* (1826), to farces like *A Husband at Sight* (1830), as well as comedies and operettas. Altogether, Buckstone wrote eighty pieces staged between 1825 and 1849, and some of his plays, like *Green Bushes* (1845), attracted consistently large crowds (particularly in Dublin) throughout the Victorian era and on past the first decade of the present century. But he was not unusual. The now-forgotten Edward Towers wrote fifty-one plays, including such blood-curdling gems as *The Demon Doctor* (1867). The relative unimportance of the dramatist is confirmed by the fact that the original edition of Allardyce Nicoll's "Handlist of Plays" in *History of English Drama in the Nineteenth Century* from 1800 to

1850 includes 135 pages of plays by "Unknown Authors," and 134 pages of "Unknowns" for 1850–1900.²

This ambiguous position contains several implications. First, it is at times difficult to distinguish playwrights from other literati and theatrical laborers. Theatre manager Alfred Bunn, for instance, entrepreneur and businessman, also wrote a libretto for Rossini's *Guillaume Tell* (1838), and W. C. Macready adapted Walter Scott's *Marmion* (1814). Two of *Punch*'s contributors, Mark Lemon and Gilbert à Beckett, wrote extravaganzas such as *Open Sesame* (1844). Even the venerable essayist George Henry Lewes wrote plays, including five farces. Both Browning and Tennyson, as is well known, aspired to careers as dramatists; and Benjamin Disraeli, Prime Minister and Earl of Beaconsfield, tried his hand at tragedy with *The Tragedy of Count Alarcos* (written in 1839, though not produced until 1868). Further, in many productions of even the most elevated drama, attentiveness to language was superseded by attention to scenic detail. As Shaw complained consistently in his reviews of Irving's productions, the "art of literature is left shabby and ashamed amid the triumph of the arts of the painter and the actor" (*LSR* 19 January 1895). As both James Stottlar and J. P. Wearing discuss, in very different ways, managers were well aware that stage effects created a full house, satisfying Victorians' voracious appetites for visual stimulation. Pieces with broad humor and exciting effects—farce, burlesque, pantomime, and extravaganzas which were staples of this theatre—did not generate much opportunity for the writer of literary aspiration. Skillful dramatists like Boucicault shaped dramatic action around shipwrecks, fires, boat races, avalanches, volcanic eruptions, and other similar phenomena, developing narratives which climaxed in a so-called "sensation scene." But Boucicault's careful integration of story with spectacle might be regarded as exceptional, as managers thoughtlessly mangled plays and sources in search of increasingly sensational excitement. In short, even in productions of Shakespeare, the literary was frequently sacrificed to the scenic as the audience came to see, not always to hear.

The contest for effect and thus audiences left traditional dramatic categories impossible to sustain, as orthodox conceptions of genre fell by the wayside. Tragedies often included song; comedies included suspense; opera and ballet became part of other genres as well as texts in their own right. Individual plays such as Marston's *Strathmore* can be identified as tragedy, but is W. S. Gilbert's *Engaged* a comedy or farce? Is *Metamora* a melodrama or tragedy? It is quite telling, in this regard, that in his "Handlist" Nicoll identifies *sixty-six* "types" of plays (5:230). By contrast,

Introduction

Michael Booth in *Prefaces to English Nineteenth-Century Theatre* advances a narrower conception of genre: drama, comedy, and farce; pantomime, extravaganza, and burlesque.[3] For Booth, the distinction between comedy and drama rests finally upon the degree of seriousness in a play; and, as Stephen Watt maintains in his study of W. G. Wills and Tom Taylor, pretensions to the authorship of tragedy are usually indicated by historical settings, lofty rhetoric, and restrained dramatic action. Still, "drama" frequently drifted into melodrama as the latter's definition was no longer reducible to the amount of musical entertainment it included. As drama came to deal with the problems of contemporary life—something which, as Martha Vicinus observes in her essay, melodrama addressed—it began to exert appeals which melodrama possessed earlier in the century. Taylor's *The Ticket-of-Leave Man* (1863), to cite one last example, might be regarded as "drama" on the basis of its relatively unexaggerated rhetoric, but the play's villain shares much with counterparts in melodrama.

Much more than broadly descriptive definitions of comedy were equally difficult to formulate. "Low" comedy's thin plot was typically constructed around opportunities for physical, slapstick business; but low comedy often ran into farce, which itself contained the verbal humor—the puns and witticisms—characteristic of "high" comedy. As discussed in the book's final section, the primary development in higher comedy was a movement toward social realism. And this movement was accompanied by the ascendancy of the playwright. By the 1880s, dramatists like Jones and Pinero controlled their plays in production, following Robertson's lead. Jones extended Robertson's assumption of authorial dignity by designing his plays for publication, plays which he defined as "pieces of literature" which represented human life realistically.[4] His attitude reflects the newly privileged position of social relevance in the late-Victorian theatre and the comparatively complex psychological construction of characters such a shift necessitated. By the end of the century, plays seemed most aptly divided into either comedies or dramas with literary ambition or, alternatively, entertainments: music hall performances, pantomimes, and extravaganzas. Drama as "literary art" was making headway on the stage.

Comedy and Social Drama

This last section of *When They Weren't Doing Shakespeare* concerns developments in American comedy early in the century, as described by Tice L.

Miller and James Hurt, and the progress of a more sophisticated comedy on the later Victorian stage as charted by Daniel Barrett, Judith L. Fisher, and George Rowell. Comedy after 1850 and social drama, as Fisher and Rowell describe, are developmentally related, social drama evolving from comedy of the 1860s and 1870s. The closeness of their interrelationship, moreover, meant that, like other varieties of drama, comedy and social drama are generically quite similar: they share both thematic and stylistic affinities. And, while much late-Victorian historical and tragic drama looked backwards to the Elizabethan theatre, the comedies of Robertson, Pinero, and Jones ultimately were rooted in their own time even as they were at times constituted of conventions and techniques appropriated from earlier comic drama. These plays were, in short, modern.

Physical changes in theatres and differences in theatregoing contribute to this increased sense of modernism. By the 1850s, the typical theatre bill of five or six hours of various entertainments (farce, mainpiece, afterpiece, and ballet) had been trimmed to two items, then to one full-length play (Booth, *Prefaces*, 32). Also, during midcentury, seating and theatre interiors changed; stalls gradually replaced the pit, the décor became more luxurious, and seats could be reserved.[5] Theatres such as the Prince of Wales, where the Bancrofts produced most of Robertson's plays, were smaller and more comfortably appointed than most older houses. These developments, among other causes, encouraged increasing numbers of middle- and upper-class patrons to attend plays with the result that later in the century audiences were generally less rambunctious, less participatory than earlier in the century, and the plays themselves grew quieter. A key term for comedy and social drama of the period, therefore, is "restraint." Acting styles became more naturalistic as well: less exaggerated in movement and gesture, and more directed toward a coherent expression of character. More plays were produced without the grandiose effects of spectacular drama and, more important, contained subject matter which originated in contemporary social life: marriage, domestic problems, and social maladies.

Particularly influential on comedy and social drama were midcentury novelists such as Dickens, Mary Elizabeth Braddon, William Harrison Ainsworth, Mrs. Henry Wood, and William Makepeace Thackeray. All these writers concentrated on contemporary life and the myriad relationships between marriage, social class, and capital. Dramatists like Robertson not only reiterated the social themes of these novelists, but also borrowed dramatic techniques from them as well. Robertson was greatly influenced by Thackeray, for example, whose "domestication" became characteristic of Robertsonian comedy. Just as Thackeray in *Vanity Fair* refused to take his reader onto the battlefield of Waterloo, instead saying "our place is with the noncombatants," so Robertson in *Ours* (1866), his drama of the Crimean War, never dramatized a battle, although act three is set in a hut behind the battle lines.

Robertson crystallized the modernizing tendencies of Victorian comedy. His plays avoided physical comedy, had no outlandish costumes or cheap physical gags, and, as *Ours* exemplifies, were restrained, dealing as *Caste* (1867) does with issues such as class mobility in an unexaggerated way. Robertson emphasized the tradition of nineteenth-century comedy that included serious, albeit comedic, plots and themes. To be sure, his treatment of love was often sentimental, and his serious plots were lightened by comic subplots which echoed the thematic concerns of the main plots. Unlike melodrama, though, Robertson's comedies posited few moral absolutes: heroes and villains existed, for the most part, in the minds of other characters, who learned to correct their often immoderate perceptions during the course of the play. And Robertson personifies the newly empowered modern playwright; like Jones, Gilbert, and Pinero, Robertson controlled all aspects of theatrical production: rehearsal, staging, and acting style.

Following Robertson's development of a modern comedy were dramatists such as H. J. Byron and Sydney Grundy, yet their work is not nearly so important as Robertson's, in part because of their reluctance to pursue meaningful social issues with vigor. Indeed, other aspects of late-Victorian drama have more consequence for twentieth-century drama. One is the influence of the French *pièce bien faite*; another is that of the "problem plays" of Jones and Pinero, which are distinguishable from pure comedy in their emphasis on the serious issues underlying their plots and the false compromise a happy ending requires. Social matters such as class status, so important in Robertsonian comedy, are refocused into analyses of the "Woman Question" for Jones and Pinero. Plays such as Pinero's *The Second Mrs. Tanqueray* (1893) and *The Notorious Mrs. Ebbsmith* (1895) and Jones' *Mrs. Dane's Defence* (1900), discussed here by George Rowell, present women "with a past" and, in the process, expose an insidious double standard concerning female sexuality. This choice of dramatic topic, as opposed to that of class-crossing in marriage (Robertson's *Society* and *Ours*), of necessity results in a noncomedic ending as neither dramatic nor social convention would permit fallen women to rise in society. Ibsen and Shaw deal with such issues in an even less conventional manner than Jones or Pinero. So, in one sense, what might be termed "modern" drama is built on a foundation of Victorian social drama: quiet, realistic, and tightly focused on characters and issues.

Comedy without broad physical gags, comedy emphasizing character, meant perforce comedy in which dialogue became increasingly important. Throughout the century, some comedies of language did exist on the English stage. Early nineteenth-century comedy exaggerated "wit" the same way it exaggerated situations and low-comic routines. Outrageous punning and joking overwhelmed the more sophisticated repartée and wordplay characteristic of urbane dramas of wit. This florid comedy found its way onto the music hall stage and eventually to vaudeville. But the comedies of Gilbert, as Judith Fisher describes in her essay on *Engaged*, and those of his follower Oscar Wilde, mix the restraint of Robertsonian comedy with their own brand of witticism: puns, Gilbertian "topsyturvydom," and social satire. This line of comedy grows into the so-called "Screwball Comedies" of the 1930s and 1940s, and the sparkling, if self-conscious, wit of Noël Coward in England and writers like S. N. Behrman in the United States.

Fin de siècle drama and comedy were, to be sure, not all that the Bernard Shaws and William Archers of the theatrical world desired, but even Shaw acknowledged that the restraint and social dimension of the Robertson-Pinero-Jones drama were an "advance" (*Autobiography*, 239). English drama advanced to meet the times just as those times were changing rapidly, an historical development that made theatrical matters at the end of the century lively and especially socially relevant—when actors weren't doing Shakespeare.

NOTES

1. Bernard Shaw, *Autobiography, 1856–98*, sel. by Stanley Weintraub (London: Max Reinhardt, 1969), 231.

2. Allardyce Nicoll, *A History of English Drama, 1660–1900*, 6 vols. (Cambridge: Cambridge University Press, 1940–59), vols. 4, 5. The statistics about Buckstone and Towers also come from Nicoll.

3. Michael Booth, *Prefaces to English Nineteenth-Century Theatre* (Manchester: Manchester University Press, 1980), passim.

4. Henry Arthur Jones, "On Playmaking," in *The Renascence of English Drama* (1895; reprint, Essay Index Reprint Series [Freeport, N. Y.: Books for Libraries Press, 1929]), 227.

5. See also Allardyce Nicoll, *History of English Drama*, vol. 5, and Michael R. Booth et al., *The Revels History of Drama in English, 1750–1880* (London: Methuen, 1975), p. 4 for specific details about the changing nature of the theatre and audience.

PART ONE
Actors and Their Roles

The Theatre of Edwin Forrest and Jacksonian Hero Worship

Bruce A. McConachie

On 22 November 1828 the following announcement appeared in *The Critic*, a New York journal of theatre and the arts:

> To the author of the best Tragedy, in five acts, in which the hero or principal character shall be an aboriginal of this country, the sum of five hundred dollars, and half of the proceeds of representation, with my own gratuitous services on that occasion. The award to be made by a committee of literary and theatrical gentlemen.
>
> Edwin Forrest[1]

Forrest's playwriting contest netted him *Metamora, or The Last of the Wampanoags* by John Augustus Stone, a vehicle he performed throughout his long career in the American theatre. In the eight contests which followed, Forrest dropped his specification for an Indian play and raised the stakes to a thousand dollars. All except one of these prize plays were performed, several more than once, but only *The Gladiator*, by Robert Montgomery Bird, and *Jack Cade*, by Robert T. Conrad, gained success of the magnitude of *Metamora*.[2] Although Forrest appeared in many other roles until his retirement in 1872, he made the heroes of these three romantic tragedies the basis of his immense popularity with the American public, especially from the mid 1830s through the early 1850s when he was at the height of his powers. By the Civil War, it is likely that over three million people had seen Forrest in one of these vehicles.

Most scholarship on the popularity of the prize plays has focused either on Forrest's suitability for the starring roles or on the political subjects historians have detected in the dramas. *Jack Cade* and *The Gladiator*, for instance, have been viewed as antislavery tracts, while the popularity of

Metamora, a play presenting a conflict between Indians and white settlers, has been attributed to public interest in this issue in the antebellum era.[3] It is more probable, however, that the American public expected a drama far removed from contemporary social problems when they lined up to see Forrest in one his vehicles. Exotic costumes, scenery representing faraway lands, and stirring rhetoric affirming liberal political values were the stock-in-trade of romantic tragedy. Indeed, audiences would likely have been disappointed in a poetic drama which descended from the realm of the ideal to grapple realistically with mundane social issues. To locate these heroic plays within their historical context, then, the critic-historian needs to look beyond the popularity of their star or the contemporaneity of their subject matter to the rhetoric of American romantic tragedy.[4]

In England, audience enthusiasm for romantic tragedy was fulfilled by William Macready who, like Forrest, commissioned and adapted several verse dramas to suit public taste and his own talents. His performances of Knowles' *Virginius*, Mitford's *Rienzi*, and several of Byron's later plays, among others, proclaimed the justice of striving for political freedom in the midst of such idealized settings as ancient Rome and Renaissance Italy.[5] Similarly, Forrest's vehicles tapped the wellspring of American hopes and fears regarding political democracy in the United States. The cultural values and heroic images apparent in *Metamora, The Gladiator*, and *Jack Cade* bear a striking similarity to those of the president and political party that dominated the American scene from the mid-1820s to the 1850s—Andrew Jackson and the Democrats. Forrest's prize plays rode the coattails of American enthusiasm for "Old Hickory" and for the Democratic attack on aristocratic privilege in defense of "natural" rights. Though related in form and content to the romantic tragedies of Byron and Knowles, these uniquely American plays might more appropriately be termed Jacksonian melodramas.

Forrest's preference for plays expressing Democratic sentiments and embodying the public image of General Jackson is not surprising. A life-long Democrat and contributor to the party, Forrest was once asked to run for national office as a Democratic representative from New York City. The star had many political friends, among them William Leggett, the Jacksonian advocate of hard money and free trade, who also served as one of the judges in Forrest's playwriting contests. Leggett and Forrest corresponded often, with the Democratic journalist occasionally advising the actor on plays suited to their political views. Regarding Shakespeare's *Coriolanus*, for example, Leggett wrote, "He was not so much of a democrat as you and I are: but that is no reason why we should not use him if he can do us a service."[6] As theatre historian Montrose Moses states, "When [Forrest] became patron of the American drama, those who wrote new plays for him caught from his likes and detestations. . . . He used the dramatists for his own purposes."[7] Whatever the political inclinations of his playwrights—and there is some indication that Bird and Conrad were Whigs—Forrest, by demanding rewrites and cuts, made sure *his* plays reflected his Jacksonian beliefs.[8]

Democratic values were widely disseminated in antebellum America through campaign speeches, magazine and newspaper articles, and presidential proclamations. Jacksonian leaders and theorists often drew inspiration from Jefferson's vision of the United States as a sparsely-settled Arcadia in which sturdy yeoman farmers lived economically simple lives. According to historian Marvin Meyers, Jacksonian democracy involved "an appeal to an idealized ancestral way. . . . One sees a countryside of flocks and herds and cultivated farms, worked in a seasonal rhythm and linked in a republican community."[9] From the Jacksonian point of view, a Lockean "state of nature" involving minimal interference from the government was the best guarantee of equality of opportunity for "the people." But "the people"—those farmers, mechanics, and small businessmen whose livelihood depended upon their own hard work and frugality—were beset by "the aristocrats"—those drones of society protected by monopolies and other legal privileges who fed on the labor of "the people" and threatened to overwhelm their "natural" rights. To ensure the personal freedom and material happiness of "the people," Democrats mounted a moralistic attack on what were perceived to be the bastions of aristocratic power: privileged corporations, professional organizations, and, especially, the national bank. For the Democrats, the Second Bank of the United States came to symbolize all that was unnatural and aristocratic in the present economic and political order. When President Jackson slew "the Monster" in 1832, fellow Democrats applauded him like a stage hero in a melodrama. According to Meyers, "the effort to destroy the Monster Bank and its vicious brood . . . enlisted moral passions in a drama of social justice and self-justification."[10]

A similar drama was enacted on stage when Forrest attacked aristocratic villainy in his Jacksonian melodramas. As in other nineteenth-century melodramas, the machinations of the villain motivate the plots of *Jack Cade*, *Metamora*, and *The Gladiator*. In each, aristocrats oppress "the people," seducing innocent maidens, striking down helpless mothers, and greedily robbing the virtuous of the fruits of their labors. Jack Cade, for instance, tells his followers: "We toil to feed their lusts; we bleed / To back their quarrels; coin our sweat and blood / To feed their wassail and maintain their pomp" (2.3). In *Metamora*, Lord Fitzarnold and his Puritan cohorts overtax the white settlers and steal Indian land. Spartacus in *The Gladiator* taunts his Roman captors with their exploitation of "the people": "Look ye Roman—there is not a palace upon these hills that cost not the lives of a thousand innocent men; there is no deed of greatness ye can boast, but it was achieved upon the ruin of a nation; there is no joy ye can feel, but its ingredients are blood and tears" (1.1). The plots of these plays center on honest work versus idleness, freedom versus bondage, and natural rights versus unnatural privilege—themes dear to the hearts of fervent Jacksonians.

Metamora, Spartacus, and Cade, like General Jackson himself, lead "the people" in revolt against these decadent aristocrats. "Our lands! Our nation's freedom! Or the grave" (5.3), shouts Metamora, in a battle cry that echoes the hero's demands in the two other plays. Like a good Democrat, the Indian chief lives in harmony with nature—"The war and the chase are the red man's brother and sister; the storm cloud in its fury frights him not. . .; the Great Spirit hears his evening prayers and he sleeps amidst the roar of a mighty cataract" (1.1). But the coming of aristocratic privilege and Puritan government to American shores threatens his Lockean freedom, forcing Metamora and his warriors to battle for traditional ways and "natural" rights: "Never will Metamora forsake the home of his fathers, and let the plough of the strangers disturb the bones of his kindred" (2.3), proclaims the Indian Chief.

Unlike Metamora, Spartacus and Jack Cade have been uprooted from their ties to the land, but they yearn to regain their lost Edens. Before being dragged off to Rome and slavery, Spartacus lived in Thrace "among the hills piping to his father's flocks" (1.1). Images of Thrace as a land of pastoral bliss tug at Spartacus' memory throughout the play:

> But oh, the hills of our own native land!
> The brooks and forests . . .
> Where we fed sheep and laughed
> To think there could be sorrow in the world.
> (1.1)

Risking torture, the melodramatic hero refuses to fight a Thracian in the gladiatorial arena and later keeps his rebellion alive by the hope of returning to the land of his father. With his dying breath Spartacus exclaims, "There are green valleys in our mountains yet. Set forth the sails. We'll be in Thrace anon" (5.3). In *The Gladiator* as in the Democratic conception of the United States, virtuous free men might live in paradise were it not for the machinations of aristocratic villains.

Jack Cade leaves a Lockean state of nature in Italy to fight for similar freedom in England. Regarding Italy, Cade tells his fellow peasants,

> In that blest land the tiller is a Prince
> No ruffian lords break Spring's fair promises,
> And Summer's toils—for freedom watches over them—
> Are safe and happy.
> There are no poor where freedom is
> For Nature's wealth is affluence for all.
>
> (1.4)

This melodrama enshrines two other virtues prized by the Jacksonians: respect for private property and a negative definition of freedom. In hiding with his family after the initial failure of his peasant rebellion, Cade stops a wealthy peer on the highway and demands gold so that he might save his starving child. The nobleman refuses and Cade threatens to kill him, but the rebel leader cannot bring himself to commit a robbery and finally kneels to beg for bread. Even against a brutal lord, Cade admits, "I would do no wrong" (3.4). Such scruples in the midst of revenge are the result of Cade's concept of freedom:

> Liberty gives nor light nor heat itself;
> It but permits us to be good and happy.
> It is to man what space is to the orbs,
> The medium where he may revolve and shine,
> Or, darkened by his vices, fall forever.
>
> (3.3)

Despite the muddiness of the metaphor, here was a sentiment that Democratic lovers of limited government could applaud.

As in the plays, heroic action in the political arena was necessary to save the American people from aristocratic persecution, according to Democratic spokesmen. There is ample evidence that many Americans saw Andrew Jackson in melodramatic terms. Here was a "man of destiny," believed many, who had crushed the British at New Orleans, routed the Indians in Florida, conquered the foes of democracy in the 1828 election, and triumphed over the enemies of free enterprise in the Bank War. In the eyes of the populace, these complex events tended to be reduced to a series of moral contests in which Jackson vanquished the villains. Historian John William Ward points out that the gentleman-planter from Tennessee was pictured by many as an ideal yeoman farmer, a man who avoided the decadence of Europe and the savagery of the frontier. Further, as the instrument of God, the hero could do no wrong on the stage of history, though his personal life might be tainted with sin. Finally, despite his divine connections, most Americans believed that this man of iron had forged his success through sheer willpower. At a time when optimism concerning man's potential for self-advancement was at its peak, Andrew Jackson seemed to embody dynamic individualism. Ward's triad of nature, providence, and will aptly captures the rough outline of Jackson's public image.[11]

This portrait of the Democratic hero is reflected in the heroes of Forrest's Jacksonian melodramas. Spartacus, Cade, and Metamora, defenders of "natural" rights, are also natural heroes in their dramas and symbols of idealized yeoman farmers. Jack Cade and Spartacus, the peasant and the shepherd, stand above the decadent pleasures of the aristocrats and the petty squabbling of their serf or slave followers. Though aligned with "the people" by birth and sentiment, they have a natural nobility which elevates them above those who depend upon their leadership. "He has that in him, Say, / Will breed you griefs. The flash of such an eye / Broke never from a bondman's heart" (2.2), comments one nobleman to the villain, concerning Jack Cade. Spartacus is similarly blessed, combining ruthless, barbarian qualities with a civilized concern for the well-being of his wife and son. The image of Metamora, despite his ties to the Indians, borrows heavily from the Jacksonian ideal of the frontier farmer. Between the degeneracy of the representatives of European culture (the aristocrats and Puritans) and the general savagery of the Indians, stands Metamora, "the grandest model of a mighty man" (1.1). During the course of the action, Metamora honors a chivalric pledge involving the white heroine and displays tenderness and sympathy for his Indian wife and child. A positive norm between two extremes, Metamora argues for peace with the Puritans and restrains the Indians from murder and torture.

Not only are these dramatic heroes representative American men, they are also, like Jackson, the agents of God. Metamora and Cade experience visions in which a God of Judgment calls upon them to save their people. Amidst stage effects of thunder and lightning, Metamora tells his warriors, "The high hills sent back the echo, and rock, hill and ocean, earth and air opened their giant throats and cried with me 'Red man, arouse! Freedom! Revenge or death!'" (3.3). Cade's conversion experience is equally inspiring:

> [The storm] broke as heaven's high masonry were crumbling.
> And the wide vault, in one unpausing peal,
> Throbbed with the angry pulse of Deity. . . .
> I heard the genius of my country shriek
> Amid the ruins, calling on her son—On me!
> (1.4)

Spartacus experiences no such epiphany, but there is little doubt that he, too, is among the Chosen, leading his people like a new Moses out of slavery toward the promised land of Thrace.

Other evidence links the missions of these heroes to the work of God. "Man is heaven's work," says Spartacus, "and beggar's brats may 'herit / A soul to mount them up the steps of fortune / With regal necks to be their stepping blocks" (4.3). Cade's presence in England answers the prayers of Father Lacy, "the peasants' priest," for God's deliverance of the serfs from the bond. When one of the whites in *Metamora* objects that the Indian chief is not a Christian, another answers that "his worship, though untaught and rude, flows from the heart and Heaven alone must judge of it" (1.1). Heaven's judgment is soon known. The white heroine, draped over the tomb of her parents, calls on God to save her from the villain and Metamora's voice from within responds, "Hold! Touch her not!" (5.1). Then the hero bursts from the tomb (it contained a secret passage leading from the Puritan jail where Metamora had been imprisoned), rescues the maiden, and kills the villain. The God of Metamora is the Christian God of judgment, the same deity that has chosen Andrew Jackson to do His work on earth.

Regarding the third of Ward's triad, willpower, the heroes of these Jacksonian melodramas outdo the historical man of iron. Jack Cade glories in adversity:

> The wren is happy on its humble spray,
> But the fierce eagle revels in the storm.
> Terror and tempest darken in his path;
> He gambols 'mid the thunder; mocks the bolt
> That flashes by his red, unshrinking eye,

> And, sternly joyful, screams amid the din:
> Then shakes the torment from his vigorous wing,
> And soars above the storm, and looks and laughs
> Down on its struggling terrors. Safety still
> Reward ignoble ease:—be mine the storm.
>
> (2.1)

Facing the near impossibility of victory in the final battle with the Romans, Spartacus expresses the same sentiments:

> A cloud is on my path, but my ambition
> Sees glory in't: as travellers who stand
> On mountains, view upon some neighboring peak,
> Among the mists, a figure of themselves,
> Traced in sublimer characters; so I
> Here see the vapory image of myself
> Distant and dim, but giantlike—I'll make
> These perils glories.
>
> (5.1)

Like Spartacus and Cade, Metamora exhibits giantlike willpower, never troubled by hesitation or doubt. In one scene, he appears suddenly at the Puritan council with no bodyguard and only a knife and tomahawk to protect him. Throughout these plays, it is clear from the dialogue or stage directions that the hero is often alone, center stage, single-handedly imposing his will on groups of other characters—a stage picture perfectly suited to enshrining the power of these nineteenth-century supermen.

Indeed, the iron will of the hero is fired to such a point that it often wounds "the people" it is supposed to serve. Though battling for the Indian cause, Metamora must fight off laziness, cowardice, and even treachery within his own tribe. The aristocrats pursue Jack Cade but "the people," whose rights he defends, refuse to shelter him. As one sympathetic peasant comments, "The citizens own no God / But Mammon" (3.1). Slaves freed by Spartacus ape their former masters in their lust for glory and riches, joining the hero's brother in a disastrous attack on Rome. Though fifty thousand of his followers are slain, Spartacus steels himself through self-justification:

> Now, by the eternal fates,
> They did provoke high heaven deserting me. . . . Wretched fools!

> This was my vengeance, yea my best of vengeance,
> To leave them to themselves, that Roman praetors
> Might whip them for me.
>
> (5.1)

In both *The Gladiator* and *Metamora*, the hero has a moment of elemental anger in which he almost kills the captured daughter of his enemy. It is indicative of the lack of constraining social values in these plays that the hero's decision not to do away with the girl is presented as another example of his glory. These supermen apparently have the right to kill mortals who anger them, but achieve even greater grandeur by refusing to exercise their prerogative. Metamora, Cade, and Spartacus are Byronic heroes whose relation to "the people" in their plays is aptly summed up in Byron's *Childe Harold*: "Among them, but not of them."

Interestingly, however, the elevation of dynamic willpower over the values of community accord was the reverse of the effect most English romantic playwrights strove for in their tragedies, the precursors of Jacksonian melodrama. As Richard Fletcher in his *English Romantic Drama* notes, "The most important of the Romantic dramas in one way or another were directly concerned with this problem of the unbridled, unprincipled tyrant who must be won back within the fold of common humanity through the awakening of his conscience to the pangs of remorse.... The problem of how to deal with a Napoleon, after all, was still of pertinent concern to everyone."[12] Tragic remorse is conspicuously absent in Forrest's prize plays. Romantic tragedy and Jacksonian melodrama are similar in their advocacy of liberal ideals, but there is little sense of the need for the hero's social and moral rehabilitation in the American plays because he is presumed to be a law unto himself. Social order cannot be reaffirmed because society is the repressive order of the aristocrats. Partly for the same reason, the endings of the two types of plays differ. Though the Napoleonic heroes of both ultimately die, Forrest's supermen are overwhelmed by villains and traitors while the typical romantic hero is accorded major responsibility for his own downfall.

Forrest's acting style emphasized the iron will of his Jacksonian heroes and thus exacerbated the underlying tensions between leader and led apparent in the plays. Contemporary reviewers of the star's performances raved about his Byronic appearance, muscular physique, and thunderous voice. One awestruck but typical reporter, for example, exclaimed that acting the characters of Metamora and Spartacus requires "a physical energy, an almost awful power and vigor which we doubt if any actor on earth but himself can put forth."[13] Noting the personal qualities that Forrest brought to his roles, Rev. William R. Alger, the star's official biographer, concluded, "This imperial self-reliance and instinctive honesty, this unperverted and unterrified personality poised in the grandest natural virtues of humanity is the key note and common chord to the whole range of his conceptions. Fearless faithful manhood penetrates them all as the great elevating principle which makes the harmonies of one essential idea."[14] No doubt Forrest's "fearless, faithful manhood" was the distinguishing feature of his major roles, "penetrating," as the oblivious reverend would have it, the minds of his audience as well as his acting style.

In this regard, it is significant that Forrest avoided Shakespearean roles that required him to portray guilt and weakness. Despite Forrest's suitability for Macbeth, critics complained that his Scottish warrior lacked the "womanish" fear necessary to the part. In *Hamlet*, Forrest apparently muscled his way through the protagonist's moments of indecision and fear. A critic for the *Irish Shield* reported that Forrest, in the initial ghost scene of the tragedy, "instead of evincing the awful terror and appalled feeling which such an apparition would naturally produce . . . , *started* like a maniac after receiving a shock of electricity, and fell back into the arms of Horatio, bellowing with stentorian fury the solemn invocations, 'Angels and ministers of grace defend us!' "[15] Realizing, perhaps, his aversion to displaying vulnerability on the stage, Forrest rarely performed *Hamlet* or *Macbeth*. Although he did *King Lear* more frequently, it was his towering rage in the storm scene that critics liked best, not the moments of pathos later on. Theatre historian Garf B. Wilson, in a fine summary of Forrest's acting style, finds the star's lack of "spiritual insight and the highest type of creative imagination" to be his major flaw as a performer.[16] Forrest was fine when steeling himself against tears in the death scenes of Mariamne or Nahmeokee, even when pronouncing sentimental eulogies over their bodies. But opening himself up to reveal spiritual insights that arise through experiences of genuine terror, awe, or despair contradicted Forrest's image of himself as an invincible man of iron.

The parallels between the public images of Forrest and Jackson, especially as they relate to the problems created by the iron will of these heroes, go beyond similarities in content and style to the essential form of theatre and politics prevalent in antebellum America. Simply put, both theatrical performance and presidential politics involved a "star" system in which the leader exercised power hitherto unthinkable in theatrical and political history. Jackson's elevation of the presidency to what may be called star status is well enough known to require little elaboration. Contrary to the traditional conception of the power of the office, Jackson argued that the Constitution gave the president the right to veto any legislation he thought unwise and he exercised this prerogative on several occasions, vetoing bills for internal commercial improvements and a national bank. More significantly, perhaps, Jackson went directly to the American people on the key issues of rotation in office and the bank, arguing that he, rather than Congress, was the sole representative of all the people. Ironically, Jackson's revolutionary beliefs and the dramatic increase in presidential power witnessed during his administration resulted from his intention of stripping the Federal government of much of its authority so that the "natural" impulses of "the people" would be given freer reign.

The star system in the theatre involved a similar increase in the prerogatives of one individual over others with whom power had traditionally been shared. During the eighteenth and into the nineteenth century in England and America, actor-managers ran local stock companies in which they might achieve modest prestige and wealth, but their influence was generally confined to one city and further limited by their responsibility for the welfare of the company as a whole. The "transportation revolution" of the early nineteenth century began to alter the traditional pattern of producing theatre, allowing a popular performer to travel from one stock company to another with no permanent ties to any of them. The star's free-lance status undermined the older system. As Alfred Bernheim in *The Business of the Theatre* explains, "Playing limited engagements of from one night to two or three months a year, at the most, the star was better able to keep up the interest of the audience than could the stock actor who might be seen once a week or more in a season of forty weeks, and perhaps for many seasons."[17] As in the Jacksonian presidency, the theatrical star effectively bypassed traditional limitations to display his talents and reap his applause directly before the American people.

Edwin Forrest, the first American star to rival English competitors, was an eager, even greedy beneficiary of the new star system. He generally demanded half the gross receipts from the box office, lining his own pockets with thousands while leaving local managers with barely enough to cover expenses. In criticism similar to that leveled at President Jackson, Forrest was attacked for ruining the old stock system and lowering theatrical standards generally. But however much conservative critics might fume, they were powerless to alter Forrest's charismatic popularity with the American public. His demagogic role in the bloody Astor Place Riot of 1849, an instance of class warfare between supporters of the American star and others favoring Forrest's rival William Macready, merely confirmed Forrest's popularity as the preeminent tragedian of the nation. Despite a scandalous divorce trial three years later which went against the star, "the public reversed the judgment of the court and, while 'good society' applauded the clearance of the lady, the hard-handed democracy hailed their old favorite as 'martyr,' crowning him with a wreath of sorrow, only that they might worship him the more," reported a reliable witness.[18] One admirer wrote of Forrest after his death, "His personal magnetism was great and he could draw everything to him. Wherever he might be, men recognized him as a king, and he reigned without resistance."[19] Like his counterpart in politics (whom critics called "King Andrew"), Forrest became a living American myth, evoking the kind of blind hero-worship from a majority of Americans that easily erased his personal and public failings.

As often happens with star performers, the public tended to confuse Forrest's personal qualities with the characteristics of the heroes he represented on stage, with the result that Forrest himself was praised as a man of nature, Providence, and will—the qualities attributed to General Jackson. *The Democratic Review*, for instance, once lauded the actor as a man "struck out of the very heart of the soil," in spite of the fact that Forrest was born and raised in Philadelphia.[20] To link the star with the beneficence of the Almighty (and no doubt to blunt accusations of his greed), Forrest's occasional acts of philanthropy to orphans and down-and-out friends were widely noted and praised. With a bit more justification, newspaper reporters often applauded his personal energy and power, noting that he rose to the top of his profession with little formal training. When Forrest died in 1872, orators, poets, and journalists eulogized the star. One anonymous newspaper account effectively summarized the Jacksonian image Forrest had projected to his public:

> One thing must be said of Edwin Forrest, now that he lies cold in the tomb—he never courted popularity; he never flattered power. Importuned a thousand times to enter society, he rather avoided it. . . . He was essentially a self-made man. All the angularities that result from a culture confined by the very conditions of its existence to a few of the many directions

in which men need to grow were his. His genius developed itself irresistibly—even as a spire of corn will shoot up despite encumbering stones. . . . His art was acquired not in the scholar's closet or under the careful eye of learned tradition, but from demonstrative American audiences.[21]

Here is Forrest as a member of "the people" and a self-made man of democratic principles, spurning society and the hollow traditions of the past; never mind that much of the account is exaggerated, misleading, or wrong. Perhaps the most striking thing about this passage is its similarity to the eulogies of Andrew Jackson, even though the general died almost thirty years earlier. In this regard, Ward's triad seems less applicable to Jackson specifically than to the general qualities of heroism conventionally called upon to praise the hero in antebellum America. By squeezing Forrest into the conventional mold, the anonymous author, despite mention of Forrest's "angularities," elevates hero worship and its institutional cornerstone, the star system, over the unvarnished truth.

The rise of the star system in theatre and politics points up a central problem in Democratic ideology during the Jacksonian era. What was to stop an iron-willed, charismatic hero, in the real world of politics or the illusory world of the theatre, from confusing his own ambitions with the public good? Forrest's melodramatic vehicles, his thunderous acting style, and his kingly star qualities reduced "the people" in his performances to the status of theatrical extras. Forrest as Jack Cade may have led the peasants to victory, securing a charter of freedom from the king, but it was his triumph, not theirs. The stage was littered with the dead bodies of slaves and Indians at the end of *The Gladiator* and *Metamora*, but the audience wept only when Forrest's hero died. "The people," it seems, were expendable. This is not to accuse Forrest's heroes or, by extension, Forrest and Jackson themselves, of tyrannical intentions, but simply to note that the popular impulse for hero worship and the general conception of the hero as star leads, logically, to a kind of despotism in the name of "the people." If Forrest's melodramas and his preeminence as a star were representative of Democratic values during the period, Jacksonian democracy may have been less the era of the common man than the period of the man on horseback.

Or perhaps, by default, the age of the man on the make. Despite the glorification of heroic willpower evident in Forrest's performances of these dramas, the heroes of each play finally die, cut down by the villains they fail to vanquish. In *Metamora* and *The Gladiator*, though not in *Jack Cade*, their hope of freedom for "the people" dies with them. It may be, of course, that their deaths were simply conventional, part of the leftover baggage of English romantic tragedy in which heroes were expected to expire beautifully in the end. Yet these Jacksonian melodramas are so different from their predecessors in other ways, so congruent with the general outline of Democratic thought, that the failure of Forrest's heroes to restore a Lockean state of nature to "the people" (pictured in an idealized final tableau) raised an important question: Might the conclusion of these plays signal a covert fear on the part of the Democrats that their program of returning the country to an idealized past was doomed to failure? Perhaps the attempt to do so, the grand theatrical gesture toward a lost Eden, was subconsciously deemed enough. Certainly this covert fear would help to explain the contradictory nature of much Jacksonian behavior, with men proclaiming the ideals of a simple agrarian society while busily building the foundations of industrial capitalism. Uncompromising willpower was still the ideal, perhaps—an ideal glorified in ritualized public death—while behind the scenes men of unheroic cast made deals and counted their money.

NOTES

1. Quoted in Richard Moody, *Edwin Forrest: First Star of the American Stage* (New York: Alfred A. Knopf, 1960), 88.

2. These plays may be found in the following anthologies: *Metamora* and *The Gladiator* in *Dramas from the American Theatre*, ed. Richard Moody, New World Literature Series (1966; reprint, Boston: Houghton Mifflin, 1969), 205–27; 241–75; *Jack Cade* in *Representative Plays by American Dramatists*, 3 vols., ed. Montrose Moses (1918–25; reprint, New York: Benjamin Blom, 1964), 2:462–519. Act and scene numbers follow quotations in the text.

3. See Montrose Moses, "Introduction," *Jack Cade*, 432; Richard Moody, "Introduction," *The Gladiator*, 239–40; and Alan S. Downer, "Early American Professional Acting," *Theatre Survey* 12 (November 1971):89. For discussions of *Metamora* as it relates to public interest in American Indians, see Roy Harvey Pearce, *The Savages of America* (Baltimore: Johns Hopkins University Press, 1953), 196–235; L.M. Eich, "The American Indian Plays," *Quarterly Journal of Speech* 30 (1944):212–15; and B. Donald Grose, "Edwin Forrest, *Metamora*, and the Indian Removal Act of 1830," *Theatre Journal* 27 (May 1985):181–91.

4. Despite the playwright's belief that his *The Gladiator* was an antislavery play, for instance, Forrest performed the play before enthusiastic houses in

Mobile, Alabama, in 1839 (Moody, *Edwin Forrest*, 180). The only incident I have been able to discover in which the audience related the subject matter of one of these plays to an immediate social issue occurred in Augusta, Georgia, in 1831 when Forrest's performance of *Metamora* led to a near riot in the theatre. The audience apparently identified the Indians in the play with the Cherokees of the area whose land they wanted because of a recent gold strike. For more information on this unique incident, see James H. Dormon, *Theatre in the Antebellum South, 1815–1861* (Chapel Hill: University of North Carolina Press, 1967), 275 and Grose, cited above. Grose, however, pushes the relationship between the play and concern over Indian-white relations too hard. Doubtless some audience members occasionally made this connection, but *Metamora* achieved its greatest popularity in eastern seaboard cities where few spectators cared one way or the other about Indian removal.

5. For a good summary of the main themes of romantic tragedy, see Richard M. Fletcher, *English Romantic Drama, 1795–1843: A Critical History* (New York: Exposition Press, 1966).

6. Quoted in Montrose J. Moses, *The Fabulous Forrest: The Record of an American Actor* (Boston: Little, Brown and Company, 1929), 184.

7. *The Fabulous Forrest*, xi; "Introduction," *Jack Cade*, 430.

8. Bird attended Whig national conventions in 1844 and 1848 as a delegate and helped to edit *The North American and U.S. Gazette*, a Whig journal. Conrad also edited conservative literary magazines and was appointed a judge in Philadelphia by a Whig administration.

9. Marvin Meyers, *The Jacksonian Persuasion: Politics and Belief* (1960; reprint, Stanford: Stanford University Press, 1970), 24.

10. Meyers, 10.

11. John William Ward, *Andrew Jackson: Symbol for an Age* (1955; reprint, New York: Oxford University Press, 1971). Ward's article, "Jacksonian Democratic Thought: A Natural Charter of Privilege," in *The Development of an American Culture*, eds. Stanley Coben and Lorman Ratner (Englewood Cliffs, N.J.: Prentice-Hall, 1970), 44–63, has also been useful.

12. Fletcher, 106, 152.

13. A review from the *Courier and Enquirer* quoted in Moody, *Edwin Forrest*, 167–68.

14. Quoted in Downer, 89.

15. "Park Theater: Mr. Forrest's Hamlet," *Irish Shield and Monthly Milesian*, October 1829, 390.

16. Garf B. Wilson, *A History of American Acting* (Bloomington, Indiana: Indiana University Press, 1966), 28.

17. Alfred Bernheim, *The Business of the Theatre: An Economic History of the American Theatres, 1750–1932* (1932; reprint, New York: Benjamin Blom, 1964), 27.

18. Lawrence Barrett, *Edwin Forrest*, American Actor Series (Boston: James R. Osgood, 1881), 83.
19. Quoted in William R. Alger, *Life of Edwin Forrest, the American Tragedian* (Philadelphia: J. B. Lippincott, 1877), 2:841.
20. Quoted in Moses, *The Fabulous Forrest*, 216.
21. Quoted in Alger, 2:837.

Guy Mannering and Charlotte Cushman's Meg Merrilies

GOTHIC NOVEL, PLAY, AND PERFORMANCE

Gary Jay Williams

When a tribute by Sheridan Knowles called *The Vision of the Bard* was produced at Covent Garden on 22 October 1832, the bard of the title was not William Shakespeare but Sir Walter Scott. *The Vision* was Knowles's tribute to the immensely popular writer who had died one month before. It consisted of a pageant showing the dream vision of a mourning poet in Scottish garb (played by Knowles himself), in which appeared tableaux of eight scenes from Scott's novels. It concluded with a vision of a festival at Abbotsford in the year 3664 (1,832 years later), where many of Scott's characters were seen to be thriving still.[1] The piece ran for seventeen performances; Drury Lane produced a similar one.

It was fitting that the theatre should honor Scott; in the first half of the nineteenth century, it was greatly indebted to him. Between 1810 and 1849, at least 149 distinct plays or operas derived from Scott's poems and novels were produced in theatres in London, Edinburgh, New York, Paris, and elsewhere.[2] The novels most often capitalized upon were *Kenilworth*, *Ivanhoe*, *Guy Mannering*, *The Heart of Midlothian*, and *Rob Roy*. The stage versions followed fast upon the successes of the novels: *Guy Mannering, or The Astrologer* was published in 1815, and, between 1816 and 1827, at least nine plays or operas that borrowed from it were produced in theatres in England, France, and America.[3] The stage versions of Scott's story of the Scottish heir, especially Daniel Terry's version, held audiences well into the second half of the nineteenth century. The tale was by then familiar enough—and becoming old-fashioned enough—to be parodied in Robert Reece's *Guy Mannering in New Guise* (1866), J. Strachen's *Such a*

Guy Mannering (1868), and F. C. Burnand's *Here's Another Guy Mannering, or the Original Heir Restorer* (1874).[4]

This essay attempts to explain the central appeal of Scott's *Guy Mannering*, of the Terry stage version of it, and of Charlotte Cushman's remarkable portrait of Scott's sybilline, ancient gypsy, Meg Merrilies. In both Scott's character and Cushman's creation of her, which was one of the great performances in melodrama in the century, there is much to help us understand the appeal of gothic melodrama and the longings it satisfied, which must be described as essentially spiritual.

The Novel

The first portion of Scott's novel traces the decline of the ancient house of Ellangowan under its laird, Godfrey Bertram. The remaining three-quarters is devoted to the process by which Bertram's abducted son, Henry, is restored to his rightful heritage. The novel opens with the young traveler, Guy Mannering, lost at night on the dark and mossy moors of Dunfrieshire and being given lodging by Bertram, who presides, impoverished, over the ruins of Old Ellangowan. That night, a son, Henry, is born to the Bertrams. Mannering, schooled in the ancient divinations of astrology, reads the boy's future in the stars. Seeing a perilous youth in store for him, he declines to reveal all to the family. The next day, exploring the ruins of Ellangowan before he leaves, he sees through a crevice an old gypsy woman chanting over her spindle, reading young Henry Bertram's future in the threads.

The narrator then drops Mannering for a long stretch to focus on Godfrey Bertram, who rises to become a magistrate. He exercises his new power with untempered fervor, arresting poachers, prosecuting peddlers, and driving smugglers off the nearby coastline. He also drives from his own estate a band of gypsies long accustomed to dwelling on the largess of the ancient family. On the day that they depart, forlorn and bitter, Bertram encounters them on the road. As he turns to leave after watching the last of them pass, Meg Merrilies looms on a high bank before him. The old queen of the tribe, six feet tall, wearing a tattered red cloak and a red turban around her long, tangled black hair, is "a sibyl in a frenzy" silhouetted against the sky. Holding a tall sapling bough in her right hand, she cries out:

Ride your ways, Laird of Ellangowan—ride your ways, Godfrey Bertram!—This day have ye quenched seven smoking hearths—see if the fire in your ain parlor burn the blither for that. Ye have riven the tack [roof] off seven cottar houses—look if you ain roof-tree stand the faster. . . . Ride your ways, Godfrey Bertram—what do ye glower after our folk for?— There's thirty hearts there that wad hae wanted bread ere ye had wanted sunkets [delicacies]. . . . Ride your ways, Ellangowan—our bairns are hinging at our weary backs—look that your braw cradle at hame be the fairer spread up: not that I'm wishing ill to little Harry, or to the babe that's yet to be born—God forbid—and make them kind to the poor, and better folk than their father!—And now ride your ways.[5]

As if Bertram had, out of hubris, disturbed some natural order, had broken an ancient bond with the spirit world, violating its sanctuary in his faithless insistence upon the laws of man, his life turns tragic. His son Henry, now five, falls into the hands of smugglers who abduct him after a battle with the law officers whom Bertram has brought down upon them. The boy's disappearance and presumed death brings on the premature birth of Bertram's daughter and his wife's death in that childbirth. In the years that follow, Bertram and his daughter are increasingly threatened with dispossession of Ellangowan by Gilbert Glossin, a shrewd and greedy exploiter of such mean spirit as would shame the noble ruins. He would replace the motto of the Bertrams over the castle door, which reads "Right Makes Might," with "He Who Takes It, Makes It" (*GM*, 283). At a critical point in these affairs, the older Guy Mannering returns to Scotland, now a retired colonel who has served in India. He is widowed and intends to settle with his daughter in this area. He has no more than arrived when Godfrey Bertram, his benefactor of old, dies, and so Mannering takes a protective interest in his daughter, Lucy Bertram. He brings her and her beloved tutor, Dominie Sampson, into his care and into his home with his daughter, Julia.

In the years intervening between Mannering's visit to Scotland as a young man and his return, young Henry Bertram, having survived both his abduction and being carried off to Holland by the smugglers, has been adopted under the name of Vanbeest Brown and entered upon a promising military career in India. There he served under Colonel Mannering himself, with neither being aware of Brown's true identity. (Such coincidences were confirmations of the mysterious operations of destiny, the more so as they defied reason.) Young Henry also fell in love with the colonel's daughter, Julia. Although the colonel disapproved of his suit, Bertram comes to Scotland following her, a young traveler "on a blind path," unaware of his true parentage, with "a volume of Shakespeare in each pocket, a small bundle with a change of linen slung across his shoulders," and a terrier at his heels (*GM*, 145).

It is, to understate the matter, an eventful odyssey that brings Bertram to his rightful claim on Ellangowan and his Julia. He first stumbles into the lair of the smugglers and is saved from certain death by their associate of old, the wild-eyed Meg Merrilies, who hides him. Henry saves Dandie Dinmont from highwaymen and so wins the loyalty of this folk-honest sheep farmer. Late in the novel, Henry and Dandie find themselves being rescued from a burning jail at Portanferry by Meg's gypsies. In the novel's climax, Henry, Dandie, and his other supporters are led to the seaside cave at Derncleugh by Meg Merrilies, where they capture the smuggler and murderer, Dirk Hatteraick, the man who was child Harry's original abductor. Gilbert Glossin has conspired with Hatteraick to dispose of Bertram and gain Ellangowan; so the novel ends with a final dark justice being done when Hatteraick, locked in a midnight cell with Glossin, violently strangles him and then hangs himself. Between these dramatic events, there are elaborately detailed domestic scenes, such as that in the inn at Kippletringan when Mannering returns, colorful character portraits, such as that of Lucy's tutor, Dominie Sampson, and digressions on picturesque Scotland. The indefatigable narrator presides with baronial decorum.

Guy Mannering is the second of the so-called Waverley novels, with *Waverley* and *The Antiquary* on either side. Scott said the three illustrated the social history of their respective periods, from the mid-eighteenth century decline of the old clans and feudal society to the emergence by the 1790s of a significant middle class.[6] Though not tightly controlled thematically, *Guy Mannering* is morally purposeful and consistent in its tale of the passing of an old order and its vision of the establishment of the new, represented by a worthy future laird like Henry Bertram. Moral and compassionate, he wins the friendship of the honest sheep farmer, Dandie Dinmont, and so honorably pursues Julia that he wins the admiration of her skeptical father. Most importantly, he trusts his life to the intuitions of the unearthly old gypsy, Meg Merrilies, who weaves all the strands of his broken life together. By the end of the novel, Henry's right to his inheritance wants only those civil validations made possible by the city lawyer with a soul, Paul Pleydell, Mannering's friend.

More than anyone else, Meg facilitates the restoring of Henry Bertram, who was orphaned by an act of faithlessness and who, more than anyone else, trusts his intuition and her (perhaps having benefited from his years amid the mysterious spiritualism of India). Meg appears mysteriously at critical points of Henry's life, from the night of his birth to the day of his restoration, frequently a startling apparition at the edges of the glen, like the witches in *Macbeth* with whom Scott invites comparison. Her charismatic presence always compels attention. "The mixture of frenzy and enthusiasm in her manner seldom failed to produce the strongest impression upon those whom she addressed," Scott writes in the decorous style that is a foil to his subject. "Her words, though wild, were too plain and intelligible for actual madness, and yet too vehement and extravagant for sober minded communication. She seemed acting under the influence of an imagination rather strongly deranged. . . . This may account for the attention with which her strange and mysterious hints were heard and acted upon" (*GM*, 327). Her natural opposite is the comic pedant, Dominie Sampson, who places his faith in leatherbound and catalogued libraries. One of the most imaginative scenes in the novel is that in which Meg overpowers Dominie, fortifies him with stew from her cauldron, converts him to belief in her prophecy that Bertram shall be restored, and sends him on his way as her messenger. Once Bertram is restored, Meg dies, struck by Hatteraick's bullet during the struggle in the cave.

Meg Merrilies fascinated Scott's readers. He furnished elaborate "historical" notes on such "Galwegian figures" at the back of his novel, and, in his preface to the 1829 edition, he provided an account (which he had published earlier in *Blackwood's Magazine*) of Meg's prototype, one Jean Gordon, a gypsy queen of whom he had heard tales from his father. But the origins of Meg Merrilies run deeper than local history; she answers to a romantic longing for worlds beyond the reach of reason and for the play of the imagination. Early in the novel, Scott cites at length a passage from Coleridge's translation of Schiller's *Wallenstein* to give expression to a typical romantic nostalgia (ostensibly young Mannering's). In act two of this play, the young officer, Piccolomini, is in the strange astrological tower and speaks about the common world being too narrow for Love, which dwells in fables or among fays and spirits. He speaks longingly of divinities that once moved upon the earth:

> That had their haunts in dale or piney mountains
> Or forest, by slow stream, or pebbly spring
> Or chasms and wat'ry depths—all these have vanished—
> They live no longer in the faith of reason!
> But still the heart doeth need a language, still
> Doth the old instinct bring back the old names.[7]

The strange, tall figure of Meg Merrilies is a colloquial spirit answering to that longing to know that the cosmos includes such spirits. Residing in the shadows of the glen at the edges of the law and society, she is palpably accessible (the naturalistic details of her appearance are not accidental), far more so than classical deities or those disinterested planets whose influence the young Mannering interprets early in the novel with his ancient science. She presides over the passing of an old order and the establishing of a new, a charismatic figure who draws men's wonder and, in winning the assent of intuition and imagination, allows for something very much like faith.

The Play

The first stage adaptation of Scott's novel opened at Covent Garden on 12 March 1816.[8] Written by Daniel Terry with Scott's assistance, it was probably the adaptation most frequently produced in the century. Terry (1792–1829) was at the time an actor in John Philip Kemble's company and would later play Macduff to the Macbeth of William Charles Macready, who regarded him as a sure strength in any cast.[9] Terry had met Scott on the occasion of Henry Siddon's production in Edinburgh of *The Family Legend*, written by Scott's friend, Joanna Baillie. He became a lifelong admirer and friend of Scott, one of the few privileged to know the identity of "the Great Unknown," as the still anonymous author of the Waverly novels was described. Terry also adapted Scott's *The Heart of Midlothian* (1819) and *The Antiquary* (1820) for the stage.[10]

John Lockhart, Scott's son-in-law and first biographer, inferred from Scott's correspondence what Scott had never openly acknowledged—that he had assisted Terry with the adaptation, helping him modify the plot and rearrange dialogue.[11] At heart, Scott had misgivings about popular stage versions of his work. One of the earliest was a version of *The Lady of the Lake*; Scott wrote to Joanna Baillie in 1810 to say that two "play carpenters in ordinary to Covent Garden" were employed in "cutting her down into one of those new sloops called Melodrama." He tolerated it but told Baillie, "Entre nous, I wish them at the bottom of Lock Katrine with all my heart" (Lockhart, 1: 381). But the successes of adaptations of Scott continued. He once wrote, "I believe my Muse would be Terryfyed into treading the stage, even if I should write a sermon."[12]

The three-act *Guy Mannering* shows adroit selection and compression, excepting one or two crude seams, and included eleven songs, most of which were written or arranged by Sir Henry Rowley Bishop and Thomas Atwood.[13] It begins with Scott's eleventh chapter—the scene of Mrs.

McCandlish's inn in Kippletringan and Mannering's return to Scotland. At rise, a group of farmers sing a glee before a fire, "The winds whistle cold / And the stars glimmer red, / The flocks are in fold." The first act neatly compresses several episodes in the novel. At the inn, Mannering learns of the death of his old benefactor at Ellangowan, Godfrey Bertram, and of the disappearance of Bertram's young son, Henry. There he also meets Bertram's daughter, Lucy, now exiled from Ellangowan by Gilbert Glossin. Glossin, who is at the inn celebrating his imminent seizure of the estate, enters to offer Lucy a chance to marry him and recover Ellangowan. This provides dramatically efficient proof of Glossin's villainy (this is not in the novel), provides Lucy a dramatic show of virtue in her eloquently contemptuous refusal (both she and Julia Mannering are more assertive and interesting in the play), and provides Mannering a nice show of his manliness when he forcefully intervenes to protect her from Glossin. Mannering then offers Lucy a retreat in his new home at Woodburne, an arrangement made proper by Julia's presence. In the play, Guy Mannering is made a younger man than he is in the novel. He has been gone just sixteen years, and Julia is now not his daughter but his sister. This careful calculation makes possible a romantic match between him and Lucy at the end of the play. (The first act also introduces Dominie Sampson, Lucy's memorable tutor; Bailie Mucklethrift, a dealer in fire irons who mistakes Mannering for a rival salesman; and Mrs. McCandlish, who weeps easily still over the fateful day of young Bertram's disappearance.)

For her first appearance in the play, Lucy Bertram, exiled from Ellangowan, is given an air, an archetypal orphan's song written by Bishop, who would later give the world the melody for "Home, Sweet Home" (1823). Lucy sings:

> Ye dear paternal scenes, farewell!
> The home where early fortune smil'd!
> No longer there must Lucy dwell:—
> Of Fortune robb'd, from home exil'd,
> A wretched orphan child
> Now weeps her last farewell!
> Farewell!

Lucy's song of the friendless orphan, "doom'd to wander far and wide, / . . . With Heaven [her] innocence to guide" (Terry, 14), is one we know today only in parodies. But music in general has theatrical values intrinsic to melodrama. Lucy's song bypasses rational discourse and the elaborations of a cause-and-effect plot, inviting immediate emotional assent from the audience. As all such songs did for the many orphans of melodrama, it made her an archetype of wronged innocence and in so doing created an urgent occasion for providence (or any ordering force in nature) to show itself. The farmer's glee on a cold night that opens the play is no merry irrelevance; it sets the terms for the play, winning assent to sentiment, making the audience a community of believers at the outset.

This play itself confirms that there is a kind of divinity in music, since it speaks to the heart. For this reason, the villain Gilbert Glossin, so wholly of the material world, has forbidden singing at his Ellangowan. Early in the second act, Lucy sings, at Colonel Mannering's request, a lullaby contributed by the ballad-collecting Scott himself. Scott wrote the lyrics for the piece, "Lullaby of an Infant Chief," set it to an old Gaelic air, "*Cadul qu lo*," or "Sleep on till day" (Johnson, 1:514). Lucy says it was sung of old in her family "to soothe the slumbers of the infant heir," and that the old gypsy used to sing it to her vanished brother. Later in the play, Meg will use it to stir recognition in Henry Bertram's heart: heart speaks to heart. (The song corresponds to a similar use of musical motifs and recognition in the novel.) Also, the play uses from the novel a rhyming prophecy that Meg repeatedly chants, the last lines of which are, "The dark shall be light, / And the wrong made right, / And Bertram's right and Bertram's might, / Shall meet on Ellangowan's height!" Meg's verses have the conjuring power of incantation, of spirit over matter.

Bertram returns to Scotland in the second act, serenading Julia with a flute from his boat on a lake in the moonlight beneath her window at Woodburne. (The stage directions call for a boat to be seen passing at the back in the distance.) Julia responds and the two sing the "echo" duet (by Bishop). Bertram then enters and sings a love song to her (set to a Scottish folk ballad). Their love scene is interrupted by Dominie Sampson, blundering about in the adjacent library. Fearing Bertram's discovery, Julie and Lucy disguise Henry as a Brahmin pandit and set him among the mansion's many exotic furnishings of tiger skins and east Indian curiosities. Dominie enters, seeks conversation with this intriguing new mystic, and then Mannering enters to investigate the late night noise. Julia manages to get Bertram out and distract both Dominie and the Colonel. Alone, Julia wonders how she can move her brother to sympathy for her love for Bertram, and she sings a ballad (by Atwood) about a maiden whose tender tale moved the heart of a stern knight. This closes the scene.

Bertram is next discovered wandering "a desolate heath" at night. This is a clumsy but necessary contrivance (derived from the twenty-third chapter of the novel) that allows Bertram to meet up with the tipsy Dandie Dinmont. They sing a duet (by Whitaker) for friendship and bravery, beginning, "Without a companion, what's life but a heath." This scene also allows the lost pair to stumble into the gypsy camp in the next scene. There the gypsies talk of Dirk Hatteraick's plan to abduct Bertram once again to protect Glossin's claim on Ellangowan. The young gypsies fear old Meg, who has told them that fate has ordained otherwise. Then they sing a glee by the fire (a poem by Baillie set by Bishop) that describes the darkness of night as the heyday of the gypsy, beginning "The chough and crow to roost are gone. / The owl sits on the tree."

Bertram and Dinmont enter, lost and hungry, and have been given something to eat when Meg Merrilies makes her first appearance in the play. She enters from a cave to gaze intently upon Bertram. She has a young gypsy girl sing the cradle lullaby that she once sang to Henry; she reads his palm and prophesies that he will reclaim Ellangowan. She then exits, leaving Henry, who knew nothing of his past, and Dinmont stunned. Dinmont tells Bertram that, hearing her conjure, he was moved to muster a bit of prayer for her.

Two gypsy lads then lead Bertram and Dinmont off, ostensibly toward Kippletringan but instead into a glen where Hatteraick and his men set upon them. As they do so, Meg intervenes, commanding that the gypsies not assist Hatteraick. This allows Bertram and Dinmont to overcome and capture him. The scene concludes with a musical rite of justice triumphant: Sergeant M'Crae and his kilted soldiers happen by, marching to bagpipes, and take Hatteraick away, but not until after a song and a Scottish dance.

Hatteraick, however, escapes later. In act three, set on a seashore, Meg reappears and makes the reluctant Dominie her instrument, sending him to bring Mannering and aid to a nearby cave where Hatteraick is hiding, waiting to meet Glossin. From Julia and Lucy we then learn that Mannering's heart has melted; he is in love with Lucy. She sings a love song. The play moves then to the climactic cave scene. Meg leads Bertram and Dandie there, arranging for them to overhear Hatteraick confess his crimes. The dark is made light when she throws flax dipped in spirits on the fire in the cave, distracting Hatteraick. Bertram and Dinmont rush him and Glossin and subdue them, though not before Hatteraick wounds Meg with a pistol shot. Mannering and his rescue party rush in. Dominie

Sampson, now seeing Bertram for the first time, recognizes the man he tutored as a child and brings him into the arms of his sister, Lucy. (The confirmation of Henry's identity is thus dramatically swift, whereas in the novel it involves Bertram taking from a velvet bag around his neck the token of his identity—the astrological prophecy that Mannering made at his birth.) The wounded Meg calls for a shout of acclamation from the gathered villagers, and then faints and is carried off. The pairings of Julia and Henry, Lucy and Guy Mannering are then concluded with a finale based on a Scotch ballad (arranged by Bishop).

The premiere production of 1816 was well received, judging from its eighteen performances (Genest, 8: 550). It was played in New York in 1816 and 1818, in Edinburgh in 1817, and was revived at both Drury Lane and Covent Garden in 1819–1820. The American Oxberry edition of 1823 said the piece had been played "in almost every theatre throughout the country." The writer at first sniffed at it as a melodrama but noted that "if . . . popularity is a test of excellence, *Guy Mannering* stands in the first rank, for no drama has been a more universal favorite" (Oxberry, 1823, i). Its initial success was probably due to the popularity of Scott's novel, the swift flow of the adaptation, the music, and Scott's character roles. Dominie Sampson and Dandie Dinmont were well acted over the years by a number of major actors; for example, Dominie was played by Covent Garden's John Liston, Edinburgh's Charles Mackay (1817), and Drury Lane's William Oxberry (1819). The role of Meg Merrilies seems not to have had special prominence until Charlotte Cushman played it, although Terry and Scott clearly tried to imprint her image strongly on the adaptation, giving her six dramatic, if brief, appearances. The first Meg Merrilies was Mrs. Egerton and others in the role included Mrs. Yates (Covent Garden, 1820) and Mary Ann Duff (Baltimore, 1823). Later in the century, after Cushman had put her mark on the role, Meg was played by Genevieve Ward and Emma Waller, and men played the role at times,[14] not so unusual an arrangement when one remembers that men played the witches in *Macbeth* in Shakespeare's time and often after. Cushman's depiction of Meg attracted unprecedented attention to this character, and Meg was thereafter the centerpiece of the play.

Cushman's Meg Merrilies

By the time Cushman first played the role in 1837 in New York, the play was an old familiar.[15] She was twenty-one, in her first years as an actress, having changed course from an opera career after damaging her voice. She had debuted as Lady Macbeth in New Orleans in 1836 and toured thereafter. At five feet, six inches in height, she gave the impression of towering over some of the Macbeths she played opposite. She had a broad face with a high forehead, large blue-gray eyes set widely apart, and a thrusting jaw. She was well aware that she was not a pretty woman. When Thomas Sully painted a portrait of her, she wrote thanking him for his flattering rendering of "my unfortunate mug."[16] Her early training was under James Barton, an admirer of the Kemble-Siddons style, but the beautiful Sarah Siddons's classical poses were not for Cushman. Criticized once for her constant physical action in the role of Lady Macbeth, Cushman replied that, "unlike Siddons who could well be content to stand still and be gazed at, she must occupy the eye with acting and movement."[17] Her voice was distinctively low-toned (she had been a contralto), resonating, said a relative, from a throat "like the Arc de Triomphe" (Leach, 324). It had a slight aspirate edge, probably from the early strain on the vocal folds, and the effect was a woody, veiled quality. She was known for her distinctive articulation and intelligently selected emphasis. In performance, she executed a well-planned conception with purposefulness and emotional intensity. Her method and resolve often led male Victorian critics to pay backhand tributes to her "masculine" mind and powers. A *New York Times* critic wrote of her in 1871: "She pierces to the root of things, analyzes thought and motive, and holds up her work to the light with the assured wisdom of a deep-thinking man" (26 September). It was, in fact, not an actress but an actor who most influenced her; her careful preparation and control owed a debt to Macready, with whom she played Lady Macbeth in 1843 and who encouraged her. In any role, she was more apt to seize upon certain dominant emotions and facts than to be a passive vessel for genteel feelings. She was, said *Tallis's Dramatic Magazine*, "more vigorous than refined . . . she seeks rather to absorb you with the grand outline of a soul than to present it with a multitude of light and gentle shadings."[18] She also had a genius for creating striking visual images of a character. This, together with her emotional intensity, led critics to some revealing pictorial analogies. The London *Atlas* compared her acting to the vivid graphics of Gustave Doré (12 February 1854) and the *London Observer* critic was reminded of the new daguerreotypes (2 March 1845). Cushman herself, referring to her Meg Merrilies on one occasion, wrote of "the startling effects of our strong charcoal sketch."[19]

The role of Meg Merrilies came to the twenty-one-year-old Cushman on

8 May 1837, at New York's National Theatre, when the illness of Mrs. Chippendale thrust it upon her on the day of the performance. Studying the role for the first time, she made a discovery that led to a distinctive aspect of her portrayal. She reasoned that "if Bertram, the nursling of the old gypsy, is now a grown man, surely Meg will not be the hale, erect woman they all make her out to be. I must put more truth into my Meg."[20] "Hale and erect" is very much the image of the first Meg as Mrs. Egerton played her, judging from a sketch of Egerton's Meg published with the edition of the play in *Lacy's Acting Plays* (ca. 1855). Cushman's Meg was ancient, stooped, and haggard. The customary costume for the role, described in the costume lists of the pre-Cushman editions of the play, corresponds, in general, with Scott's descriptions in the novel: "Brown cloth petticoat and body, torn old red cloak, torn pieces of plaid, and old russet sandals." Cushman improved upon the image (perhaps in her debut but certainly as she repeated the role), with characteristic attention to naturalistic touches, including additional details from Scott. She aged her face and arms with make-up, added a gray wig, binding it with a loose red turban, such as Scott describes, and she carried a forked bough taller than she was.[21]

Cushman also brought to Meg Merrilies a distinctive doting, maternal fondness for the young man whom she had protected as a child. This insight, too, came when she first played the role, as she stood waiting for her entrance. She heard a gypsy express concern about what Meg might do if she knew of the plan to kidnap Bertram; another gypsy replies: "Why she dotes; she's no more what she was or ought to be. She's turned tenderhearted and swears she'll hinder us from lifting a finger against the lad Ellangowan."[22]

On her first appearance, she presented a startling image to John Braham, who was playing Henry Bertram. Braham had seen a line of Megs extending back to his performance as Bertram with Mrs. Egerton at Drury Lane in 1819. When he turned to confront the young Cushman's Meg, "cold chills ran all over [him]," and he went to her dressing room between acts to tell her so (Stebbins, 149). That entrance was memorable for many over the years. William Winter remembered that, "before any . . . could discern whence she came or how she got there," she had emerged from the cave opening and stood behind Bertram, who had not yet seen her. Actress Catherine Mary Reignolds-Winslow, who as a child acted in the play with Cushman, recalled that, "as her glance fell upon her foster child, she reminded you of a wave arrested at its very crest. She

Charlotte Cushman as Meg Merrilies in *Guy Mannering*. This undated photograph was taken by Mathew Brady's studio. (Courtesy of the Library of Congress.)

stood at her topmost height, as it seemed, without drawing her breath
. . . holding her position by aid of a forked bough she carried for a staff.
Though the attitude strained every muscle she was absolutely motionless."[23] Julian Hawthorne wrote: "That wonderful face, those awful eyes!
. . . when would the fellow turn and meet that appalling gaze? Not until
the suspense had grown intolerable and the two thousand spectators
choked for breath."[24] Theatre historian Barton Baker (whose father had
given Cushman her first thorough acting training) recalled the thrill of
this first appearance and also of her prophecy:

> [Meg] stood motionless, with one claw-like finger of a skeleton hand pointed
> at Henry Bertram; what a face! blanched and tanned and wrinkled and
> scarred, as it were, by the storms of centuries . . . with Medusa-like grey
> locks straggling from beneath a kind of turban. . . . Who that ever heard it
> can forget her delivery of the prophecy, more especially of the last two lines:
> "Till Bertram's might and Bertram's right / Shall meet on Ellangowan's
> height." The tall, weird figure on tiptoe, the withered arms thrown up, one
> holding the staff far above her head, the flashing eyes, the deep rough voice
> rising to the shriek of a bird of prey upon the final word—it was not mere
> acting, it was inspiration as great as anything Rachel ever achieved.[25]

She seems to have brought an emotional texture to the recognition
scene that went far beyond the text. In 1871, the *New York Herald* critic
wrote: "So intense a representation of the mingled feeling of joy, hope,
and surprise, struggling with the memories of wrongs done and suffered,
we have never seen" (24 October). Cushman herself sang the cradle lullaby
that Terry originally had assigned to a young gypsy girl, making Meg's
old voice tremble and break as she fitfully crooned the song.[26] As she read
Henry Bertram's palm, she had to stop to cry for joy over his return (*PES*,
2 April 1873). In all, the effect of the scene was apparently stunning; after
her prophecy and exit on "Fate calls you! Away! Away!" there was to be,
according to the promptbook, "a pause in the action, with no one moving
for perhaps half a minute."[27]

In the last scene of act two, where Meg intervenes to call her gypsies off
the attack on Bertram and Dinmont, Cushman struck an impressive pose
atop a rock; the promptbook calls here for "picture," a freeze-frame device,
as it were, common in melodrama to fix an image and maximize an
effect.[28] When Meg seeks out Dominie Sampson to run for aid, Julia and
Lucy are with him and, frightened by her, they pronounce her mad. Meg

replies, "I've been scourged for mad, and banished for mad, but mad I am not!" Cushman sent the first phrase whirling "like thongs striking"; the second she read with a keen cry of agony, and the last phrase was read with convincing conviction.[29] There was a typical piece of melodramatic acting in the scene in the cave. Hattaraick at one point pulls out his knife, seizes Meg and is about to kill her when, says the promptbook, Meg "looks at him, he trembles, and slowly lets his arm fall."[30]

With Cushman in the role of Meg, changes were effected in the end of the play. At the end of Scott's novel, Meg dies of her wound from Hatteraick's pistol in the scuffle in the cave. In Terry's adaptation, the wounded Meg is carried off after the villagers' shout of acclamation for Henry as heir of Ellangowan, with Mannering saying, "She may yet recover." Festive songs follow. But with Cushman in the role, Meg died on stage, and her passing required its moment. She raised herself to call for not one but three shouts of acclamation for Bertram and then collapsed. She then rose again, only to fall back into Dinmont's arms and there die.[31] The naturalistic details here were such that some critics objected. The New York *Empire* (10 February 1855) described Meg in her death throes, "her limbs now extended, then coiled together, the claw-like hook of the fingers, the eye glazed into horrible and lasting fixedness." Barton Baker wrote, "I have seen ladies in the theatre cover their faces with their hands, unable to endure the sight of the dying agonies of that awful face in the last fierce struggle" (Baker, 481). In the last years of Cushman's career, the curtain was brought down after Meg Merrilies' death, and the final songs were omitted.[32] (Such arrangements were not uncommon for star performances in the century; when Cushman played Queen Catherine in *Henry VIII*, the curtain fell on Catherine's death.)

There can be no doubt from the contemporary descriptions—and these are only a sample—that Cushman's Meg Merrilies was a compelling figure and close to the Meg of Scott's novel. Critics who knew the play's limitations were awed by her, and they often awarded her Meg the description "tragic." One wrote that her Meg "inspires not pity merely, but terror, awe, and a certain indescribable pride that any shape of human nature can be so grand."[33] Another wrote, "she stalks through the drama like the impersonation of Destiny, and in the very movement of her arm, the imagination might believe a decree of inexorable fate was made manifest" (*NYE*, 12 February 1854). For theatre historians lost amid seas of such superlatives in the nineteenth century, theatre critic and scholar Henry Morley is a reliable beacon light of discrimination. Morley wrote that

Cushman's Meg "had quite as indisputably the attributes of genius about it that any piece of poetry or tragedy could have." Moreover, "such were [Cushman's] powers in the role that the mere words of it become secondary. . . . She puts beauty and passion into language the most indifferent."[34]

A number of observers over the years were moved to try to describe what seemed to them a supernatural aura about Cushman's Meg. Actress Mary Anderson spoke of her as a creature not of this world, but "a mad majestic wanderer from the spirit-land."[35] A number of critics were especially affected by her reading of the line in which she speaks to Dominie Sampson of the glen at Ellangowan where she had once lived: "If ever the dead come back among the living, I will be seen in that glen many a-night after these crazed bones are whitened in the mouldering grave."[36]

Even in the 1870s, when the acting style had become more genteel and Cushman was seen as being of the older school of acting, with Forrest and the elder Booth, and when science was increasingly taming the supernatural, the gothic grandeur of her Meg Merrilies was scarcely to be resisted. Boston critic Henry Austin Clapp was a generation younger than Cushman when he saw her Meg in Cushman's later years. Clapp (1842–1904) found that she was at moments "merely a picturesque gypsy hag with a grim sense of humour," but at other times she was "of the order of the Scandinavian Nornae or of the Grecian fates." He does not seem to be puffing for a fellow Bostonian when he writes: "At the height of her passion she was a terrible being, glaring or glowering with eyes that reflected the past and penetrated the future, a weird presence dominating the dark woods and the cavernous hills, an inspired Prophetess and an avenging Fury. The wonder of wonders was that the performance was absolutely convincing. Miss Cushman, by the magic of her art, compelled the natural and the supernatural to fuse."[37]

Clapp's last line touches the heart of Cushman's art. She managed to bring to the stage what Scott had created in the novel, a colloquial spirit answering to a romantic longing for the supernatural. Her Meg Merrilies, at once physically decrepit and charismatic, aging but timeless, demonic but maternal, elemental but unearthly, was a creature of that realm where the boundaries between the natural and the supernatural might, to a willing imagination and an excited heart, seem to disappear. Her Meg, like Scott's, was at home among the gothic trappings of decaying castle ruins, graveyards, and secret caves of the banditti, for, like them, she was redolent of a world just behind, just under, or just beyond the apparent one.

It is remarkable that Cushman was able to embody her on stage, for Meg is well suited to the novel, where her mystery can thrive in the immaterial images of the mind's eye. But Cushman was able to do so within the language of the melodramatic theatre. In its swift-moving action, its emphasis upon the pictorial sequence, moments of emotional intensity, spectacle, heavy use of music, and in all its other means of addressing the senses and ready sentiment, its object was to excite the emotions and imagination to apprehend a world beyond the grasp of rational discourse.[38] It is helpful to think of it not as a naive or inferior theatre but as a theatre revivifying itself after the stagnation of neoclassicism, a theatre seeking a language beyond text to grasp a world beyond the ability of reason to comprehend, a theatre that science would soon tame. Antonin Artaud would cast a longing look back at it in his manifesto for a theatre to shock the twentieth century out of its well-ordered theatres of words, aestheticism, and psychology.

Within this theatre and with a sure grasp of its methods and powerful resources of her own, Charlotte Cushman made the extraordinary palpable in her Meg Merrilies. In the naturalistic, nearly grotesque details of her appearance, in the extravagance of her demonic intensity, in her maternal, broken crooning of the cradle lullaby, in the freeze-frame moments of her vivid pictorial imaging of Meg's exertion of unearthly powers, and in her Meg's radiant conviction that she was an instrument of otherworldly powers, she made masterful use of the language of the melodramatic theatre to storm the imagination by main force. Her gothic Meg won the assent of emotion and intuition and so made good the point of Schiller's line and of gothic melodrama itself: "But still the heart doth need a language."

NOTES

1. Leslie Howard Meeks, *Sheridan Knowles and the Theatre of His Time* (Bloomington, Indiana: Principia Press, 1933), 145–46.

2. This figure is based on the titles given in Allardyce Nicoll, *A History of English Drama, 1660–1900*, 6 vols. (Cambridge: Cambridge University Press, 1940–59), 4:92–95. This does not include Scott's own plays nor the burlesques of adaptations of his plays.

3. The figure represents my collation of apparently distinct works that were

derived solely or in some part from the novel as listed and described in: Richard Ford, *Dramatizations of Scott's Novels: A Catalogue* (Oxford: Oxford Bibliographical Society, 1979), 11–14; Henry A. White, *Sir Walter Scott's Novels on the Stage*, Yale Studies in English, no. 76 (New Haven: Yale University Press, 1927), 235–36; and Alfred Loewenberg, *Annals of the Opera, 1597–1940* (Cambridge: Cambridge University Press, 1943), 689–99.

4. Ford, 13; Nicoll, 5:537, 585, 290.

5. Sir Walter Scott, *Guy Mannering; or, The Astrologer* (Boston: DeWolfe, Fiske, n.d.), 65–66. Hereafter abbreviated as *GM* and cited in the text.

6. Edgar Johnson, *Sir Walter Scott: The Great Unknown*, 2 vols. (New York: Macmillan, 1970), 1:520–21.

7. *GM*, 327; the passage is from act 2.4 of *The Piccolomini*, the first part of Coleridge's *Wallenstein*.

8. John Genest, *Some Account of the English Stage from the Restoration in 1660 to 1830*, 10 vols. (Bath: H. E. Carrington, 1832), 8:550. Hereafter cited in the text.

9. Sir Frederick Pollock, ed., *Macready's Reminiscences and Selections from His Diaries and Letters*, 2 vols. (London: Macmillan, 1876), 1:214.

10. Johnson, 1:325; 2:896, 1050, 1082; Daniel Terry, *Guy Mannering* in *New English Drama*, ed. William Oxberry, 25 vols. (Boston: Wells and Lilly, 1823), i–ii.

11. John G. Lockhart, *Memoirs of the Life of Sir Walter Scott*, 2 vols. (Philadelphia: Carey, Lea, and Blanchard, 1838), 2:11.

12. Sir Walter Scott, Introductory Epistle, *The Fortunes of Nigel* (Edinburgh: A. Constable, 1822), 1:xxxiii.

13. Daniel Terry, *Guy Mannering; or, The Gipsey's Prophecy*, French's Standard Drama Series, no. 77 (New York, Samuel French, 186?), hereafter cited as Terry. Its text is the same, with minor variations, as that in the following editions that I have been able to examine (the page numbering does differ): *Guy Mannering* (New York: David Longworth, 1816); *Guy Mannering* in Oxberry's *New English Drama*, 12, 1 (Boston: Wells and Lilly, 1823), hereafter cited as Oxberry in the text; *Guy Mannering* (Baltimore: Joseph Robinson, 1839); *Guy Mannering* in *Lacy's Acting Plays*, vol. 18 (London: Thomas Hailes Lacy, ca. 1855); *Guy Mannering* (New York: Henry L. Hinton, 1871). A piano score of the play's eleven songs was published (London, n.d.), and the lyrics, from which my identification of the composers is taken, were published separately (London: John Miller, 1816).

14. The information on the performances and the roles is based on cast lists in the editions cited in note 13 and from Genest, 9: 29; W. Davenport Adams, *A Dictionary of the Drama* (London: Chatto and Windus, 1904), sub *Guy Mannering*; and George C. D. Odell, *Annals of the New York Stage*, 15 vols. (New York: Columbia University Press, 1927–1949), 2:465.

15. Odell, in *Annals*, 5:291, can refer to it as among the "hackneyed" pieces of

the 1845–1846 season at the Greenwich Village Theatre. (Cushman was not in the cast.)

16. Joseph Leach, *Bright Particular Star, The Life and Times of Charlotte Cushman* (New Haven: Yale University Press, 1970), 113.

17. Lawrence Barrett, *Charlotte Cushman* (New York: The Dunlap Society, 1889), 14.

18. February 1851, 132, cited in James Willis Yeater, "Charlotte Cushman: American Actress," Ph.D. diss., University of Illinois, 1959, 58.

19. Letter to Augustin Daly, 7 July 1873, in Joseph Francis Daly, *The Life of Augustin Daly* (New York: Macmillan, 1917), 134. See also Leach, 365.

20. Cushman's recounting of this was quoted in her obituary in the *New York Herald*, 19 February 1876.

21. The sketch of Egerton in *Lacy's Acting Plays* shows her wearing no wig, but a rather prim turban, and carrying no staff. Lacy probably published the play to coincide with its production, with Cushman, at the Haymarket in 1854.

22. Terry, 3; Cushman recounted her first night as Meg in an interview late in her career published in the *New York Dramatic Mirror*, cited without date in William C. Young, *Famous Actors and Actresses on the American Stage*, 2 vols. (New York: R. R. Bowker, 1975), 1:256–57. See also Emma C. Stebbins, *Charlotte Cushman: Her Letters and Memories of Her Life* (Boston: Houghton, Osgood, 1878), 147–48. Stebbins is hereafter cited in the text.

23. William Winter, *Other Days: Being Chronicles and Memories of the Stage* (New York: R. R. Bowker, 1975), 1:256–57. See also Emma C. Stebbins, *Charlotte Cushman: Her Letters and Memories of Her Life* (Boston: Houghton, Osgood, 1878),

24. Edith G. Hawthorne, ed., *Memoirs of Julian Hawthorne* (New York: Macmillan, 1938), 263.

25. Henry Barton Baker, *History of the London Stage* (1904; reprint, New York: Benjamin Blom, 1969), 481.

26. The song is marked for Cushman in the promptbooks for the productions at the Broadway Theatre, 1850, and the Booth Theatre, 1874 (?), 41–42 and 41, respectively, Cushman papers, Manuscript Division, Library of Congress. Her manner of singing is described by Winter, *Other Days*, 161.

27. Promptbook for an unidentified production with Cushman (well-marked French edition), 42, Cushman papers, LC.

28. Promptbook, Broadway Theatre production, 68.

29. Fugitive review, *Guy Mannering* reviews, Cushman papers, LC.

30. Promptbook, Broadway Theatre production, 82, Cushman papers, LC. An excellent survey of the vocal delivery and gestures common in melodrama is Michael R. Booth's "The Acting of Melodrama," *University of Toronto Quarterly* 34 (1964):31–48.

31. Promptbook, unidentified production with Cushman, 58, and promptbook for the Booth Theatre production, 58, Cushman papers, LC.

32. Promptbook, unidentified production (French edition), 58–59; promptbook, Booth Theatre production (1874?), 58–59, Cushman papers, LC.

33. Fugitive clipping, review of the 1871 production at Booth's Theatre, Cushman papers, LC.

34. Henry Morley, *The Journal of a London Playgoer* (London: George Routledge, 1891), 68, entry dated 11 February 1854.

35. Mary Anderson, *A Few Memories* (New York: Harper Brothers, 1869), 38, as cited in Leach, 381.

36. Examples are the London *Atlas*, 12 February 1854, and the New York *Herald* critic cited in Odell, *Annals*, 9:143.

37. Henry Austin Clapp, *Reminiscences of a Dramatic Critic* (Boston: Houghton Mifflin, 1902), 83–84.

38. I wish to acknowledge my general debt in this article to: Peter Brooks, *The Melodramatic Imagination* (New Haven: Yale University Press, 1976); Michael R. Booth, *English Melodrama* (London: Herbert Jenkins, 1965), and Booth's *English Plays of the Nineteenth Century*, 5 vols. (Oxford: Clarendon Press, 1969–1976); and David Grimsted, *Melodrama Unveiled: American Theatre and Culture, 1800–1850* (Chicago: Univ. of Chicago Press, 1968).

A Picturesque Interpretation of History
WILLIAM CHARLES MACREADY'S *RICHELIEU*, 1839–1850

Denis Salter

William Charles Macready's production of the five-act verse drama *Richelieu; or, The Conspiracy* by Edward Bulwer-Lytton at Covent Garden on 7 March 1839 made a noteworthy contribution to the development of the style of staging known as historical verisimilitude. Within the picture frame formed by the proscenium arch, Macready's production provided a series of such vivid and photographically accurate images that spectators were convinced they had been transported into the midst of court life in seventeenth-century France. The *mise-en-scène* established not merely a scenic backdrop to the on-stage action but rather an "actual" environment which seemed actually to be inhabited by the so-called real-life characters of the play. In this, as in many of his productions, Macready was guided by the artistic principle that the theatre should serve as a gallery of illustration or living museum where the imaginative and thoroughly researched pictorialization of the distant past allows the words of the dramatist to be understood as much through the eye as through the ear.[1] This was an important consideration in a theatre as large as Covent Garden which at that time had room for more than three thousand people.

The production of *Richelieu* is of interest not only for what it tells us about the intentions, methods, and distinctive features of this style of historical verisimilitude, but also for the light it sheds on Macready's characteristic approach to staging Shakespeare. During his two years' tenure as manager of Covent Garden from 1837 to 1839, Macready produced a number of Shakespeare's plays, including *Julius Caesar* and *Coriolanus*. In their preoccupation with period accuracy in settings and costumes and in their attention to lifelike or natural methods of acting and ensemble coordination, these productions contributed materially to Macready's efforts to refine the art of realistic stage-illusion and, in doing so, prepared the ground for the exemplary production of *Richelieu*. Comparing the *mise-en-scène* for *Richelieu* with those which had been devised for Macready's other productions, the *Morning Post* declared that it revealed an important step forward in the actor-manager's methods: "The getting-up is more superb than any other of his exhibitions upon the Covent-garden stage. The scenery is magnificent and gorgeous, and the costumes as rich, flaunting, and expensive as the extravagant taste of period could produce."[2] Inspired by a similar desire to place *Richelieu* in a contemporary context, the *Morning Herald* observed that "the costumes, *etc.*, were quite in keeping, so that the *tout ensemble* would have done credit to [Madame] Vestris." In turn, Macready's experience with *Richelieu* seems to have laid the foundations for some of his more important Shakespearean productions including *As You Like It*, *King John*, and *Henry V*.[3] It was on this last production that *Richelieu* exerted its most immediate stylistic influence, for Macready presented *Henry V* at Covent Garden on 10 June 1839, only a short time after the successful run of *Richelieu*. The kind of critical vocabulary which greeted *Henry V*—critics described it as being accurate, complete, picturesque, and splendid, as well as elaborate, animated, tangible, and realistic—could have been applied just as readily to *Richelieu*, and also provides a concise outline of the main features of this historically correct or antiquarian style of performance.[4]

The intention to create an illusion of everyday life in seventeenth-century France informed all revival productions of *Richelieu* during the eleven years it served as a mainstay of Macready's repertoire. By the time of his retirement in 1851, he had presented the play no fewer than seventy-one times in London alone, as well as in the British provinces and during his North American tour of 1843–1844.[5] Not surprisingly, the aspiration to reconstruct in painstaking detail the distinctive features of the France of Louis XIII also imparted artistic and lifelike truthfulness to Macready's acting of the title-character. He based his approach on the gradual integration of a wealth of "domestic" or familiar business and byplay, all of which fleshed out the salient aspects of the Cardinal's character. "Acted Cardinal Richelieu in my *very best* style; I quite moved the audience *out of* themselves," Macready wrote with much satisfaction in his diary after a performance in Boston on 17 November 1843. "I was very animated and real—very much in earnest" (*Diaries*, 2:236).

To create this kind of believable portrait, Macready had undertaken a great deal of scholarly research to discover what Cardinal Richelieu had really been like, intellectually, emotionally, and physically. Bulwer had written the part especially for Macready to capitalize on the actor's most admired qualities. Yet it is evident from their correspondence and from Macready's diary that author and actor often disagreed about which aspects of the cardinal's character to emphasize. Bulwer seems to have conceived of him as a man of many moods and attributes. But Macready believed that in searching for psychological complexity, Bulwer had been too cavalier in his treatment of French history, that he had toned down Richelieu's fundamental dignity and had substituted too much lowbrow nonsense. Eager to counteract Bulwer's notions, Macready read Alfred de Vigny's novel, *Cinq-Mars*, which brings into prominence, as Charles Shattuck has pointed out, those very qualities "of dryness, dignity, wily intellectuality, cruelty, and despotism" which Bulwer had in fact decided to downplay.[6] Macready also had instructive conversations with the French novelist who, as it turned out, was visiting London while Macready had the play in rehearsal. Macready confided to his diary that Bulwer's uncompromising approach to character had made the role "particularly difficult by its inconsistency" and that he was being forced to "resort to low jest, which outrages one's notions of the ideal of Cardinal Richelieu, with all his vanity, and suppleness, and craft." Since Macready liked to think of himself as a Victorian gentleman, he struggled throughout his diary accounts to be fair to Bulwer who was of course not merely a playwright and novelist but also a friend. On one occasion, for example, the actor wrote hopefully: "gave my attention to the inquiry as to the possibility of reconciling the character which Bulwer has drawn under the name of Cardinal Richelieu with the original, from which it so entirely differs"; then he added the despondent note: "Was not much cheered by the result of my investigation and experiment" (*Diaries*, 1:496–97).

Despite their differing attitudes towards the "real" character of the "real" Richelieu of French history, both men agreed on one point: they wanted the text to serve the art of the actor. Bulwer first proposed the subject of the play to Macready on 9 September 1838. In the early stages of the text's evolution, Macready worried that it lacked spirit. His suspicions were confirmed when, in reading it aloud on 25 November to a small gathering, his friend John Forster (on whose literary judgment the actor often relied) had the bad manners to fall asleep. Bulwer himself was present and, as Macready observes dryly in his diary, was "evidently hurt." However, with customary perseverance, Bulwer undertook more extensive revisions. On the auspicious date of New Year's day 1839, Macready received Bulwer's much altered and complete manuscript; on 5 January, Macready read the play to his actors "and was most agreeably surprised to find it excite them in a very extraordinary manner," and within a few days he resolved to present it "without further delay" (*Diaries*, 1:478, 486, and 488–89).

Yet the text still fell short of the actor-manager's exacting standard. It seems that both men, either independently or collaboratively, continued to make changes not only before and during rehearsals leading up to the premiere on 7 March, but also during the first run of thirty-seven performances. From their correspondence as well as from Macready's extant preparation copies, and from his diary entries concerning the changes he insisted on making to the developing text, we can determine the sorts of things which most concerned him. Bulwer, despite his considerable stage-writing experience, was essentially a literary man with a weakness for long passages of empurpled rhetoric. Macready, on the other hand, knew, as a practical man of the theatre, that too much unrelieved rhetoric—particularly when coupled with a great deal of repetitious and tortuous plotting—was apt to make audiences restless, or, as in Forster's case, was apt to put them to sleep! Macready therefore shortened the long speeches and lessened the amount of undigested historical data. He emphasized character-interaction achieved by means of pithy dialogue, the rapid development of plot and action, and the bringing of each scene, through rising emotional intensity, to an artful climax or strong curtain. Macready was, in fact, never completely satisfied with the play. The last extant promptbook, dating from 1850, shows him making numerous small but nonetheless important emendations with an eye, as always, to theatrical effectiveness.[7]

During rehearsals, the relationship between playwright and actor was sometimes strained, especially whenever Bulwer had the temerity to explain how Macready might improve his performance. For the most part, however, their exchanges remained cordial, despite the extreme anxieties they labored under. Yet they never managed to reach complete agreement about the distinguishing traits in Richelieu's character. Thus both expressed dissatisfaction, but for different reasons, with Macready's initial performance. After the premiere Macready recorded in his diary: "Acted Cardinal Richelieu very nervously; lost my self-possession, and was obliged to use too much effort; it did not satisfy me at all, there were no artist-like touches through the play." Bulwer meanwhile objected, as he had throughout rehearsals, to Macready's obsessive concern with Richelieu's intellectual and ecclesiastical dignity, and his neglect of the rich variety and bold contradictions in the cardinal's behavior. Bulwer thought in particular that Macready's subtle restraint was a mistake in judgment and attributed this problem as much to Vigny's unfortunate influence as to the actor himself. These and other tactless suggestions made the eminent tragedian very unhappy. Grumbling in the pages of his diary, he said of Bulwer: "he wishes me to substitute coarse and vulgar attempt at low farcical point in one instance, and melodramatic rant in another for the more delicate shadings of character that I endeavour to give. I have long had surmises about Bulwer's taste. . . . I am *sure* that his taste is not to be depended on." In brief, whereas Bulwer wished to impart large quantities of light and shade to the role, to secure a popular success while also being responsible to his own extensive reading in French history, Macready wished to make Richelieu into a somewhat idealized character based on sound historical research and yet also ennobled by stage conventions (*Diaries*, 1:500–503).

Macready's reservations about Bulwer's approach to character are relatively minor in contrast to the objections raised by the critics in their opening-night reviews. They pointed out that the incidents are ludicrously crowded together, that Bulwer's stagecraft was far too contrived to ensure a "willing suspension of disbelief," that the protracted passages of poetical fancy—made up of jumbled metaphors and sudden changes of tone from the sublime to the ridiculous—resembled the kind of bombastic hackwork found in transpontine melodrama, and that the so-called characterization amounted to nothing more than lackluster caricature weakened by the revisionist objective of showing Richelieu in a flattering light.[8] Yet, these strong doubts aside, some critics managed to say a few pleasant things about the playwright's achievement. *John Bull* declared that Bulwer had been remarkably successful in transforming the dryasdust facts of history into engaging, well-arranged drama: "Considered as a series of independent scenes and effects, the play is very ingeniously constructed. . . . Unexpected incidents, picturesque situations, and startling *coups de théâtre* course on each other's heels." However, this was essentially a backhanded compliment, for the critic also wished that Bulwer had been as successful in his character-drawing: "The memoirs of Cardinal Richelieu are copied into fair blank verse, and the writer imagines that he has called a human being into life."

Yet even on this last point consensus proved impossible. The critics, like Bulwer and Macready, did not really know how to turn history into drama. It is likely that most audience members and critics possessed little more than hazy knowledge of seventeenth-century French history, though it was incumbent on them to pretend otherwise. For the most part, however, they were inclined to believe that author and actor, like Shakespeare in his history plays, had done their responsible best in reconciling empirical research and histrionic effect, making the necessary sacrifices of historical truth.[9] The *Examiner*, for example, admired Bulwer's skill at characterization and lavished praise on "the vividness of poetical illustration which is given to almost every speaker in its scenes, and which seems to us to express to the life, and with fine effect of general truth and *keeping*, the ultra vivacity of the French character and the French country." Ultimately, however, the critics' reservations were not of much consequence, for as its enduring stage history proves, the play which Bulwer finally created with Macready's extensive assistance has provided, in the leading role of the cardinal, a first-rate vehicle for great and popular acting.

Macready believed, along with many other Victorians, that genius is the art of taking pains. The continuing success of his production did not occur haphazardly but was the result of thorough preparations and rehearsals as Macready made his influence felt in all quarters of the theatre. In an extant letter dated 12 January 1839 (probably written to Colonel Hamilton Smith, an antiquarian he frequently consulted on historical matters), he asks for portraits of figures such as Louis XIII and Cardinal Richelieu and for sketches of French domestic interiors and famous public places including the Louvre, the Bastille, and Luxembourg Palace. Not long afterwards Macready passed this pictorial material on to his staff to help them achieve an accurate yet evocative rendering of historical detail. Charles Marshall was responsible for the scenery, Mr. Head for the costumes, and Mr. Bradwell for the armor and pictorial accessories. To create an appropriately French atmosphere, Macready consulted with the music-arranger, Mr. T. Cooke, who provided an overture adapted from Gluck as well as entr'actes selected from Gluck, Martini, and Grétry. The production was thoroughly rehearsed from early February until the premiere just over a month later. Marshall had the painted and built-up settings ready for use by 25 February: in his dedicated efforts to achieve period accuracy and emotional authenticity, Macready could therefore concentrate, in the last ten days of the rehearsal-period, on the specific interactions between the "actual" characters and their "actual" environments.[10] The joint labors of the actor-manager and his staff were suitably rewarded. The *Morning*

Chronicle represented critical opinion in observing with pleasure that the "scenery, appointments, and costumes are replete with historical truth and artistical skill and beauty," and, as the *The Times* pointed out, "every successive change was followed by a burst of admiration."

Throughout rehearsals Macready insisted upon constant practice to ensure that all details came together in a disciplined, clearly focused, and harmonious style of production. He paid particular attention to the character-groupings, making them lively, natural, and historically convincing. Bulwer was much impressed by this part of the actor-manager's work. Thus when John William Calcraft produced the play in Dublin, Bulwer urged him to make certain that the courtiers express apparently real emotions including "dismay," "astonishment," and "alarm"; and during the hurried, breathtaking events of 5.2 he wanted the courtiers to be "turning to each other with surprise at each piece of news."[11] The extant promptbooks for Macready's production are full of references to exactly these kinds of effects, as in act four (located in the Louvre gardens) where the characters standing near Louis XIII are all required, at a key moment in the Harvard promptbook, to "express great delight and form a complete Circle round him." As this example also suggests, the carefully patterned movements and fluctuating emotions of these crowd-scenes placed maximum attention on the star performances: the concern with historical verisimilitude characterizing most of the production had not been carried so far as to overturn this venerable stage convention.

In doing the research and preparation for his own part, Macready gave much attention to the external minutiae of costume, make-up, and pose, so as to re-create, with subtle exactness, the well-known portraits of Richelieu by such artists as Philippe de Champaigne. Widely reproduced throughout the nineteenth century, these were of course familiar to English playgoers who had visited the Louvre. Indeed, since their knowledge of French history was mostly based on pictorial traditions, Macready's task in creating a convincing illusion was relatively straightforward. He wore a wig of "whitening hair" with straggling locks, a gray goatee, and a pencil-thin upturned mustache. Through the skillful application of make-up he succeeded in transforming his own somewhat thick face with its jutting jaw into a thin, elegant "fox-like face" as the *Examiner* called it, one that was unmistakably Gallic and unmistakably subtle and intelligent.[12] His costume was meant to be historically correct, though its effect somewhat misfired for the *Spectator*, which regretted that "the ermine cape over the red cloth robe gives him the appearance of a Judge of the Court of Queen's

Bench: the costume of Richelieu's portrait is much more picturesque and elegant." But, apart from this reservation, the overall impression was unquestionably authoritative and suitably ecclesiastical. The naturalness, exact physical realism, and forcefulness of this exquisitely wrought portrait created a classic instance of the art that conceals art: Macready the actor had managed to disappear from view and Cardinal Richelieu seemed to have magically taken his place.

The reviews are given to generalities, but we can nonetheless glean some concrete information about the realistic minutiae, the fine, carefully integrated pieces of byplay and business, which the actor relied on to impart a down-to-earth texture to the idealized form of his conception. Richelieu is only fifty-eight years old during the action of the play, but the weight of public office over many years has taken its toll. Macready therefore gave the character a "painful cough" and a walk that was "somewhat loose with age, but now quick and impulsive, [now] slow or suddenly arrested"; and throughout the play, particularly during the last scene, he emphasized the "struggle of the mind to conquer the weakness of the body."[13] All these features received subtle yet vivid expression during what became known, in stage tradition, as the famous sword-scene of 2.2 where Richelieu tries to lift a sword ("With this / I, at Rochelle, did hand to hand engage / The stalwart Englisher . . . .") but finds, to his regret, that he is no longer up to the challenge ("You see a child could / Slay Richelieu, now"). Some critics in fact took Macready to task for making the realism of old age too extreme and painful—they would have preferred a more dignified or elevated manner.[14] In this and many other scenes throughout the performance, Macready's mastery of his art and, above all, his disciplined intensity, meant that the diverse traits in the cardinal's character "seemed simultaneous rather than successive," to quote John Westland Marston's perceptive phrase (Marston, 1:52). This technique therefore contributed substantively to the main objective of making Richelieu appear a three-dimensional, "real" human being with a continuous existence: he was not merely a stage personality existing through a series of strong but essentially isolated moments or "points."

The variety of traits which Macready exhibited—collectively the critics refer to him as satirical, dignified, kindly, dry, and gay, as well as subtle, fervent, stern, haughty, and imperious—led to the creation of what today would be called a "psychological" study of character.[15] The critics of course did not use the word "psychological" but rather comparable terms and phrases drawn from the critical vocabulary of their own time. The critic for the *New York Albion* (7 October 1843), for example, admired how Macready carefully distinguished between Richelieu's outward public manner and his inner private nature:

> In the simple touches of feeling which the author has so ingeniously introduced into the character, as contrasted with the stoical indifference and concentrated ambition of Richelieu, Mr. Macready was inexpressibly beautiful—indeed, the whole of his scenes with Julie and with Mauprat where these natural ebullitions of the heart are exemplified, were the most perfect parts of the performance, and called forth repeated bursts of applause.

This kind of psychological emphasis is also evident in Macready's own musings on his performance: in this role (as in many others) he evidently judged his success by how much emotional and intellectual identification he managed to achieve (*Diaries*, 1:500–503). It was Marston's view that Richelieu in fact "touched some secret of his own personality" (1:107): if this is true, it might account in part for the psychological verisimilitude, together with the keen intelligence and deeply-felt emotions, which defined the entire performance.

Yet the actor's scrupulous attention to lifelike naturalness in every telling detail of the part should not lead us to overlook its idealized features. The critics also used words such as "elevated" and "sublime" to describe his predominant manner both here and in similar roles.[16] Macready's art, as his contemporary George Vandenhoff has pointed out, "was an amalgam of John Kemble and Edmund Kean. He tried to blend the classic art of the one with the impulsive intensity of the other; and he overlaid both with an outer plating of his own, highly artificial and elaborately formal."[17] Macready certainly believed in the aesthetic principle of the *beau idéal*; although a certain degree of realism was desirable, it had to be kept "within the limits of ideal truth."[18] In Richelieu, the sudden yet smooth transitions in vocal tone—from the solemn to the tender, or from the sarcastic to the pathetic—had to be made congruent with the innate dignity of his conception to provide consistency of effect and naturalness in the character-drawing. Again the popular scene with the sword offers an illuminating example of how the actor's attempts to create a picturesque style allowed both the ideal and the real to co-exist without descending into commonplace familiarity. After his embarrassing display of weakness with the sword, Richelieu resumed his authoritative manner and a few minutes later, in a speech which also became an important part of the role's tradition, spoke some words of encouragement ("Fail—fail? / In the lexicon of youth, which Fate reserves / For a bright manhood, there is no such word / As—*fail*!— . . . / . . . Farewell, boy! Never say / '*Fail*' again") to the page François with such awesome power that, in the words of John Coleman, the "speech thrilled through one like a trumpet-call."[19] William Archer summarized the mediate quality of the picturesque when he said the actor's overall performance "was a piece of what we now call character-acting, interspersed with magnificent passages of rhetoric."[20] Marston is also instructive on this theme when he observes in a general commentary on Macready's art: "There was something, in a word, Homeric in Macready's realism; it gave the force of truthful, simple detail to passion, but was not the substitute for it, nor its principal feature" (2:198).

The main characteristics of Macready's performance can be understood by comparing him with other actors in the original 1839 production. *The Sunday Times* spoke for several critics when it remarked of Helen Faucit in the role of Julie de Mortemar that "she exhibited the transition of sudden feelings in a manner that made her efforts apparently the result of actual nature, and not the efforts of art." Her acting therefore offered a telling example of the picturesque mode, being lifelike without being too idealized or too realistic. However, Bulwer, despite his professed interest in historical verisimilitude, evidently did not wish her to give too much emphasis to a lifelike manner: in a letter to Macready, he urged him "to *implore* Miss Faucit—to say I love *and* I am Woman—& with as much majestic swelling as she can—."[21] For the most part, however, she achieved the balance of qualities so essential to the picturesque style. The only reservations came from the *Idler; and Breakfast-Table Companion* ("[She] would have pleased us better, had she been more natural and less affected") and the *Satirist* ("Who, by-the-bye, has taught this young lady to drawl out her words so piteously?"). She herself did not care for the role and this might have accounted for a certain lack of ease and believability.[22]

Like her part, all the characters in the play are variations of well-known stage-types found in romantic melodrama. Count de Baradas is a villain, Father Joseph is a confidant, the Chevalier de Mauprat is a foppish gentleman, and Louis XIII is a vacillating king. Macready's actors worked hard to overcome these stereotypical characterizations by subduing crude and exaggerated traits to establish, instead, proportionate variety and credible motivations. James Warde (Count de Baradas) created "an orthodox stage villain" but did so by elaborating a number of interrelated traits "with masterly force."[23] Samuel Phelps (Father Joseph) seemed relatively "quiet, yet forcible," at least in contrast to Macready's more vigorous portrayal of the cardinal, yet he was not so natural as to be lackluster.[24] James R. Anderson (the Chevalier de Mauprat) sought, with Bulwer's approval, to be "ardent" and "gallant,"[25] but evidently he carried these qualities to an exaggerated extreme. The *Examiner* was the exception in finding him "earnest and most manly"; most other critics agreed with the *Idler* in calling him "too boisterous and impetuous," noting that "there was an absence of repose throughout his entire performance. His mode of making love . . . is highly ridiculous. He is, at such times, more like an affected school-girl than a manly suitor." These shortcomings troubled him most during the highflown speeches where, in the words of the *Spectator*, "his vehemence degenerates into rant." Edward Elton (Louis XIII) had to contend with similar stylistic problems, but as *John Bull* observed, he managed to make the King "bearable to the audience." Macready, of course, struggled diligently to achieve a high standard of ensemble acting. Yet he seems to have thought that his cast needed to be more (rather than less) vivid and passionate in creating a pervasive impression of graceful naturalness. In a letter written to Helen Faucit on 3 April 1840 about a revival production at the Haymarket Theatre in which she could not appear, he calls most of his actors "bad" (including, it seems, a number of those from the original production) and in particular censures Warde as Count de Baradas for being "now almost *effete*."[26]

The search for a heightened realism also informed Macready's approach to the *mise-en-scène*, which consisted of seemingly three-dimensional, built-up, and enclosed settings meant to replicate the kinds of private rooms, public gardens, palaces, and prisons commonly found in seventeenth-century France. These concrete scenic representations were mostly created from the venerable convention of painted wings and shutters.[27] This "rich and picturesque scenery" (as the *Morning Chronicle* succinctly described it) was therefore both pictorial and architectural in style; however, as with Macready's picturesque style of acting, such seemingly diverse or contrary elements were in fact made to appear complementary in reconstructing a specific social reality.

Cardinal Richelieu's own study in the Palais Cardinal (1.2 and 2.2) provides a case in point. According to the promptbooks, no labor was spared in making this room seem realistic in every single respect. Arms decorated the walls and a large painted screen was placed in one corner. Richelieu sat at a table covered with an elaborately decorated cloth

William Charles Macready as Cardinal Richelieu and Samuel Phelps as Father Joseph. (Drawing by Martha Sarah Rolls. From *Dramatic Recollections of the Years 1838-9* [London, 1839]. Courtesy of the Shakespeare Birthplace Trust: Shakespeare Centre Library.)

on which he had scattered his books, papers, and pens. Surrounding him, in various eye-catching places, were statues, busts, piles of swords and armor, and gaily colored banners and tapestries. Located entirely upstage of the proscenium arch, the room also had a number of practicable doors; and to establish a historically credible (rather than stagey) impression, it had been placed at an asymmetrical angle to the spectators. Moreover, from their vantage points, it seemed to have a real ceiling—this was yet another means of enhancing the illusion of actuality. As the *Morning Chronicle* expressed it, the whole atmosphere was "a combination of pontifical and regal splendour." Macready had certainly intended that the study should define not only the locale but also the cardinal's character: a note in one of the early preparation books in the Forster Collection explains that the setting should reveal "a Princely, but refined taste."

Macready also achieved a high degree of seventeenth-century *vraisemblance* in those settings fashioned merely from painted flats positioned in the first or second grooves of the stage floor. The first scene of the play discloses a number of courtiers who are gambling, eating, and drinking in a room in the home of the courtesan Marion de Lorme. As the curtain rose the audience could hear what the Stratford promptbook describes as the "Noise of betting etc. at L[eft] Table. and of Laughter and revelry at R[ight] Table," sounds which came from characters seated on chairs or standing around tables attractively laid out with fruit bowls and wine decanters. As one of the early Forster Collection promptbooks makes clear, here, too, the actor-manager intended that milieu should convey character in what we would now call subliminal ways: "The apartment should be gay and fanciful in decoration, like that of a rich Courtezan [sic]." This stylistic intention remained in effect throughout the eleven years the play remained in Macready's repertoire, for the 1850 promptbook describes it as a "Handsome Saloon 1st Grooves." As with Richelieu's study, Macready's intentions were well received: the *Morning Chronicle* called it "a splendid room" and was not the least bit troubled by its dependence upon painterly convention. The illusion was also strengthened by the ways the character related to it: "throws himself into chair R[ight]" is an apt instruction in the Harvard promptbook to the actor playing the gallant Mauprat.

This simulation of reality was not undermined by the use of an old-fashioned technique to bring the scene to a close. According to the detailed directions in the Harvard promptbook, as the servants entered to "clear the Stage," the painted backdrop was drawn away to reveal Richelieu's study in the Palais Cardinal, and then to complete this new setting

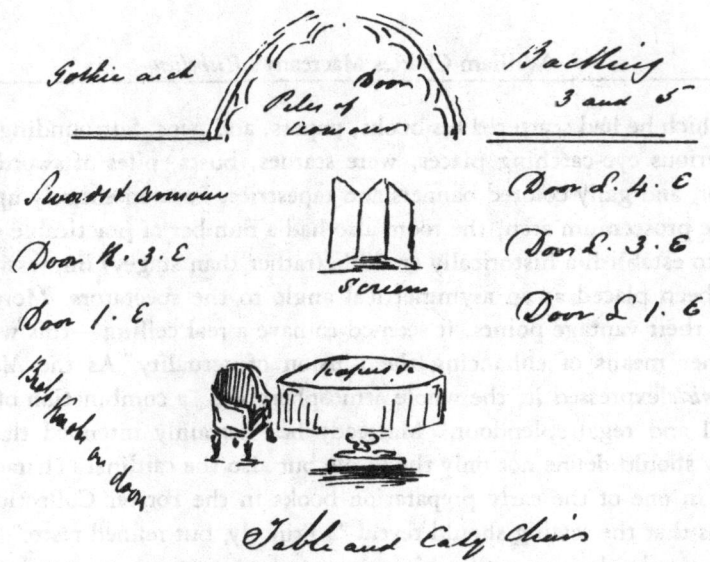

Richelieu's study in the Palais Cardinal, 1.2 and 2.2. Drawing in the 1850 promptbook. (Courtesy of the Special Collections Division, University of Calgary Libraries.)

Richelieu's study in the Palais Cardinal, 1.2 and 2.2. Richelieu (Macready), Julie De Mortemar (Helen Faucit), and Father Joseph (Samuel Phelps). (Drawing by George Scharf. From *Recollections of the Scenic Effects of Covent Garden Theatre During the Season 1838–1839* [London, 1839]. By permission of the British Library.)

the actor playing Father Joseph "wheels forward the Table—Chair & stool." Macready used this kind of *à vista* technique to change setting on several occasions and evidently it provided pleasure to the eye while harmonizing with the prevailing style.

Macready's objective in establishing a convincing historical illusion should not lead us to conclude that the *mise-en-scène* was only concerned with literal details at the expense of figurative evocations. On the contrary, some of the settings, while based on realistic minutiae, relied mostly on the power of suggestion to make the audience respond to the moral ideals which the cardinal is meant to represent. The setting of act four, set in the famous gardens of the Louvre, is a good instance of this representational yet also symbolical method. Taking up the full depth of the Covent Garden stage, it consisted of both painted flats and built-up pieces to create a three-dimensional impression of statues, shrubs, vases, and pathways, all laid out with symmetrical elegance. Beyond the gardens the audience could make out two famous Paris landmarks: the Bastille and Notre Dame. The distinguishing connotations which Macready's scene-painter, Charles Marshall, had given to each landmark not only defined locale but interpreted the moral pattern of Bulwer's drama. Critics and audiences alike seem to have realized, if only unwittingly, that, whereas Notre Dame was meant as a visual counterpart to the cardinal, the Bastille was meant, in marked contrast, as a visual counterpart to all his enemies considered as an entity. The *Morning Chronicle*, for example, referred to "the black walls of the Bastille, and the lowering clouds that seem as if they could cast their shadow upward on the heavens, while the towers and spire of Notre Dame are white and gladsome in the sunlight"; and the *Examiner* admired the scenic art which pictured "the Bastille under a threatening cloud and Notre Dame in the glittering sunshine."

This scene in the gardens also reveals how the picturesque acting style was supposed to interact with the picturesque style of the *mise-en-scène*. To excite interest, Richelieu's formal and climactic entrance was preceded by an impressive escort of two officers, four harquebusiers, and three pages: then the cardinal himself appeared, "leaning on Joseph" for support, as the Stratford promptbook carefully notes, and followed by six halberdiers. These figures gradually arranged themselves into a traditional semicircular blocking pattern; but Richelieu, in keeping with stage convention, assumed a strong central position: "When Rich[elieu] gets to C[enter], Joseph leaves him & goes straight down to R[ight] Corner," adds the promptbook. It was from this commanding position that somewhat later

*** Richelieu's escort begins to enter. (Pag. 70)

3 Inst. b., 1st & 2 officers.
4 Arquebusiers.
3 Pages.
Richelieu leaning on Joseph.
6 Halberdiers.

  ○   ○   ○ 6 Halberdiers. ○   ○   ○
      ○   ○ 4 Arquebusiers. ○   ○
          ○ 2 officers. ○
        ○   ○ 3 Pages ○   ○
2 Archers   Courtiers
 ○ ○ Capt. ○ Rich. Capt. ○   ○   ○   ○
     Arqr.   Louis   Louis
     DeMaur   ○ Bar.
Archer   When Rich. is to 4 C. Joseph   Orl. DeBer
 ○   leaves him & goes straight down
Joseph   to R. Corner.

The gardens of the Louvre, act 4, blocking plan in the Stratford promptbook. (Courtesy of the Shakespeare Birthplace Trust: Shakespeare Centre Library.)

(Page 82.)

※ At the same time the Cardinal is announced,
Louis, Orl., & Courtiers appear at R. opening, & after
a pause, advance.
                           Disposition
   3 Halberdiers.   when Rich. is in C.   3 Halberdiers.
   ○   ○   ○   ○   ○   ○

              ○   ○   ○ 3 Under Secretaries.
               ○   ○   ○ 3 Secretaries.
              ○ Courtiers.
Archers   ○   ○   ○   ○ 2 Pages
 ○ ○   ○   ○   ○   ○
    ○ Capt.   Bar.   Louis. Rich.   Jos.
              DeMaur.   ○ ○ 2 Priests.
                                                 ○ Gen.

King Louis XIII's apartment of state in the Louvre, 5.2, blocking plan in the Stratford promptbook. (Courtesy of the Shakespeare Birthplace Trust: Shakespeare Centre Library.)

in the scene Macready spoke one of the play's set speeches, the famous "Curse of Rome":

> Ay, is it so;—
> Then wakes the power which in the age of iron
> Burst forth to curb the great, and raise the low.
> Mark, where she stands!—around her form I draw
> The awful circle of our solemn church!
> Set but a foot within the holy ground,
> And on thy head—yea, though it wore a crown—
> I launch the curse of Rome!

At the start of this scene, Macready had made him seem feeble and abstracted; but, as Marston observes, during the speech itself "the might of Rome seemed to pass into the sick man's frame, as he sprang up, dominant and terrible, to shield Julie from the King with the aegis of the Church" (Marston, 1:49). The actor's boldly colored, elaborately detailed, and historically correct costume enhanced this impression of irresistible strength in the midst of apparent weakness: "his attitude assumed a dignity which was that of an immense power," recorded Lady Pollock, who added that as he spoke "his voice . . . gave out peals of thunder. It was no wonder that his enemies shrank away in terror, and that he stood alone in a charmed circle; no wonder that this man should have held the destinies of Europe within his grasp."

Not long afterwards, Count de Baradas taunts him ("His mind / And life are breaking fast!"); these words, too, had the unexpected effect of awakening the cardinal's dormant spirit: "The actor's passion," Lady Pollock explained, "rose to its noblest height as he stood looking down upon his foe, towering in his wrath" while speaking the climactic words, "Avaunt! my name is Richelieu—I defy thee! / Walk blindfold on; behind thee stalks the headsman. / Ha! ha!—how pale he is! Heaven save my country!"[28] However, the outburst had clearly drained his resources, and he fell back exhausted into Father Joseph's arms; "Pages advance & help him," instructs the Harvard promptbook. Julie de Mortemar stood on one side and Father Joseph stood on the other while the pages moved into position just behind him; it was on this vivid and touching tableau that the act-curtain came down. Weakness and strength had subtly followed each other in quick succession, deepened in their effectiveness by the highly contrasted "pictures" in the background of the Bastille and Notre Dame.

Similar stylistic qualities characterized Macready's approach, in both acting and design, to the last scene (5.2) located in the King's apartment of state in the Louvre. This setting made such a strong impression that, as the *Examiner* remarked, it "elicited frequent cheering" from the audience. The entrance of Louis XIII was grand and ceremonial. He was accompanied by four pages and eleven courtiers who distributed themselves, in a lifelike and graceful manner, into several picturesque groups along the traditional semicircular line of blocking. To mark his authority, Louis placed himself just in front of this line so that all attention was directed towards him. As before, the crowd was meant to react in ways which were psychologically and historically convincing; when at one moment Louis passes by a group of courtiers, they are instructed (in the Stratford promptbook) to "bow to him, cringingly."

This striking entrance prepared the way for the even more impressive entrance of the cardinal: he was accompanied by a large, gorgeously dressed retinue including four gentlemen, two pages, and two priests, along with three secretaries and six subsecretaries carrying portfolios and bags. Macready placed the emphasis, as he had throughout, on physical realism: Richelieu walked with difficulty and once he had reached the main position of authority at the center of the semicircle, Joseph and Julie had to help him sit down on a chair where he sank back exhausted.

This was merely the first stage of a series of thoroughly detailed, ever-fluctuating emotions which provided the main impetus for the scene. Remaining in the chair, the cardinal seemed to be dying. As ever, characterization was expressed through low-key, verisimilar details; Marston drew special attention to "the uneasy movements of the head," "the restless play of the wan fingers," and the way "his face now grew vacant" (1:50). The reversal of dramatic action in this scene occurs when François arrives with a packet of documents proving that the conspirators have been trying to overthrow the king. At this key moment Macready's Richelieu underwent a sudden change of manner arising directly from the characterization and therefore perfectly natural rather than forced or stagey. After Louis had beseeched him repeatedly to be of assistance ("—Oh! live!— / If not for me—for France!"), he seemed a man transformed from the sickness of old age into the vigor of youth. He took the packet from François, put it on the floor, rose up, and placing his foot down on it, answered Louis's anxious question ("Oh! this treason!— / The army—Orleans—Bouillon—Heavens!—the Spaniard!— / Where will they be next week?—") with the triumphant and culminating words: "There,—at my feet!" The critic

King Louis XIII's apartment of state in the Louvre, 5.2. (Drawing by George Scharf. From *Recollections of the Scenic Effects of Covent Garden Theatre During the Season 1838–1839* [London, 1839]. By permission of the British Library.)

for the *New York Albion* (7 October 1843) has left us with a vivid description of the extraordinary excitement created here:

> But the crowning triumph was reserved for the last scene—when he recovers his undisputed power—his trampling on the parchment which contains the disclosure of the conspiracy, and his rising from the chair Colossus like, renewed in vigour and in health—the all potent dictator of the destinies of his loved France—and hurls contempt and defiance on his enemies—was so electric in its effect, that we do not hesitate to place it among the highest efforts of histrionic excellence.

Several other commentators found themselves impressed by this kind of "Colossus-like" image: John Coleman, for instance, saw him "dilating to preternatural proportions," and the *Morning Chronicle* spoke in wonderment of his "sublime power," adding that as he trampled on the packet it seemed "as if the foot of a god were crushing a host of conspirators." These impressions of course received much support from the ceremonial splendor of the setting, with the king's throne dominating the background and the masses of richly dressed figures placing the cardinal in strong relief. According to the *Examiner*, Macready in fact made a showy display of the cardinal's resumption of authority "as he afterwards walked up and down the stage through crowds of bowing courtiers, laughing and receiving their supple cringings as if he sought, in that way, to fondle within his very arms the darling Power which, though absent but for a few short hours, had come back to him like a dear old stranger-friend." Here too the impression was of a god: "he always suggested to me the Divine image grown grey and ghastly through the efflux of the ages," Coleman observed with delight, "and once more gliding over the Sea of Galilee!"[29]

. The actor then provided a final mood-transition which in its physical realism counterbalanced the bias in the characterization towards the ideal. Evidently weakened by his exertion, he assumed a manner of "submissive reverence in striking contrast with this recent bearing as the proud and victorious minister" (Marston, 1:104) and in this expressive attitude delivered an apostrophe to God ("there is ONE above / Sways the harmonious mystery of the world / Ev'n better than prime ministers;—and so ends it!"). The disposition of the characters consisted of a traditional semicircle at the back, made up of the courtiers, pages, secretaries, subsecretaries, priests, and gentlemen; while at the front of the stage there was a relatively straight line formed by François, Father Joseph, and the king on one side of the cardinal and the lovers Julie de Mortemar and the Chevalier de Mauprat on the other. As the curtain slowly fell, these concluding moments offered a suitably picturesque resumé of all the moral and aesthetic values governing the production: in the telling words of the *Morning Chronicle*, "not only does 'the might of France seem to pervade his withered frame,' but the attributes of absolute justice are blended in the joys, the lightsomeness, the sympathies, the tenderness, and the reverence of humanity."

The cumulative emotional effect of the picturesque style is summed up by both the *Examiner* and the French writer Vigny whose knowledge of the life and times of Cardinal Richelieu had made such a deep impression on the actor's conception. Even when writing his notice a few days after the premiere, the critic for the *Examiner* discovered that he was still laboring under the pleasant delusion of having seen "the veritable mind (it was no violent fancy to imagine) of a living *Richelieu*." And then, in a sentence which briefly accounts for the objectives and techniques of this style of empirically-based *vraisemblance*, the critic declared: "Art never realized so perfect an identification with nature." In a similar spirit Vigny found himself much absorbed by the production's faithfulness to both the letter and the spirit of court life in seventeenth-century France. "Si jamais on perdait en France les portraits du C^{al} de Richelieu, il faudrait passer la mer et venir vous voir," he wrote in a note of praise to the English actor, "car vous lui ressemblez autant que la nature l'a rendu possible."[30]

The salient qualities of this picturesque style are also brought into focus by comparing Macready's performance with those of other major nineteenth-century actors in the role. Marston states that Edwin Booth "gives the character a more modern air—a greater air of *everyday* realism—than did Macready," though he hastens to add that Booth was by no means "deficient in the more heroic aspects of the character" (1: 53). John William Calcraft, however, seems to have been significantly more robust than Macready; so, too, was the powerful athletic actor, Edwin Forrest. Samuel Phelps, on the other hand, having played Father Joseph in Macready's original production, wanted to follow the example of the eminent tragedian in contrasting physical weakness with intellectual vigor to create a flesh-and-blood character of compelling psychological interest. Henry Irving, towards the end of the century, elaborated the physical minutiae to a greater degree than anyone, and, yet, like Macready, he also conveyed a large measure of uplifting dignity.[31] Thus, in his concern for a fundamentally picturesque rendering of Richelieu's character, Macready had laid down the essential stylistic features which served as theme and variation for all subsequent performers throughout the nineteenth century.

Macready, as noted in the summary of his disagreements with Bulwer, had wanted the characterization to occupy a stylistic middleground between the ideal, on the one hand, and the realistic, on the other. In this way he could create a mediate style which, as argued here, can best be described as picturesque. This kind of compromise is of course typical of Macready's acting career. In both the Shakespearean and non-Shakespearean repertoire he tended to strike a balance between the heroic and the ordinary and the tragic and the sentimental, as well as the generalized and the particular and "the lofty and the familiar."[32] This balance was intended to humanize or domesticate character while making it ample enough to suit the larger-than-life conventions of the stage. In his Shakespearean performances especially, Macready was often criticized for his attention to picturesque qualities, on the grounds that, since characters such as Macbeth, Lear, and Othello are heroic in conception, they are diminished when given even a partially realistic style of performance. But, in his non-Shakespearean roles such as Cardinal Richelieu, the admixture in the actual writing of widely diversified qualities—Richelieu's grandiloquence alternating, for instance, with his pithy colloquialisms—seemed perfectly suited to Macready's kind of picturesque treatment.[33] The most concise definition of the picturesque style came from the critic for *Saunder's Newsletter* (11 February 1850) in Dublin, who referred, in a suitably paradoxical phrase, to the "graphic reality" of the great actor's performance. In Macready's practiced hands, the picturesque seemed natural and artificial at once, and in this way remained just within the bounds of a typically nineteenth-century conception of artistic truthfulness.

NOTES

This is a revised version of a paper read to the Victorian Studies Association of Western Canada at the University of Lethbridge on 7 October 1983. The research was funded in part by a grant from the University of Calgary. I am grateful to Carol J. Carlisle, Stephen Johnson, Linda Peake, and John and Barbara Cavanagh of Motley Books, for assisting me with the research; William Appleton for allowing me to quote from Macready's letter to Colonel Hamilton Smith; and Dan Watermeier, Stephen Watt, and Charles Shattuck for helpful comments on various drafts.

1. *The Diaries of William Charles Macready, 1833–1851*, 2 vols, ed. William

Toynbee (London: Chapman and Hall, 1912), 2:18, hereafter abbreviated as *Diaries*. Quotations from Macready's *Diaries* will be cited in the text by volume and page number.

2. All London newspapers are dated 9 March 1839, except: 8 March (*Morning Chronicle*, *Times*), 10 March (*Bell's Life in London*, *Era*, *Examiner*, *John Bull*, *Satirist*, and *Sunday Times*), and 16 March (*Idler; and Breakfast-Table Companion*). The reviews in the *Examiner* and the *Morning Chronicle* might be written by John Forster and W. J. Fox respectively who, although close friends of Macready, were nonetheless prepared to criticize both Macready and Bulwer when criticism seemed warranted.

3. *Mr. Macready Produces* As You Like It; *A Prompt-Book Study*, ed. Charles H. Shattuck (Urbana, Ill.: Beta Phi Mu Chapbook Number Five/Six, 1962) and *William Charles Macready's King John, A facsimile prompt-book*, ed. Charles H. Shattuck (Urbana: University of Illinois Press, 1962).

4. Alan S. Downer, *The Eminent Tragedian: William Charles Macready* (Cambridge, Mass.: Harvard University Press, 1966), 247–50; *Spectator*, 15 June 1839; *Sunday Times*, 16 June 1839; and *Times*, 11 June 1839.

5. William Archer, *William Charles Macready* (London: Kegan Paul, Trench, Trübner, 1890), 204.

6. Charles H. Shattuck, ed., *Bulwer and Macready: A Chronicle of the Early Victorian Theatre* (Urbana: University of Illinois Press, 1958), 119.

7. This study is based on three preparatory promptbooks in the Forster Collection of the Victoria and Albert Museum; a promptbook in the Harvard Theatre Collection (TS 2587.100), annotated by Macready's prompter John Willmott; a promptbook in the Shakespeare Birthplace Trust, Stratford-upon-Avon (82.5 BUL Access No. 1727), "Marked from the arrangements & performance of Mr. Macready. By P. G. Lloyds, L'pool"; and a later promptbook, from 1850, in the Special Collections Division of the University of Calgary Library, "cut and marked from Macready's prompt book" by J. F. Spearing.

8. *Athenaeum*, *Bell's Life in London*, *Examiner*, *Morning Herald*, *Morning Post*, *Satirist*, and *Spectator*.

9. *John Bull*, *Sunday Times*, and *Times*.

10. *Diaries*, 1:496–500; *Macready's Reminiscences and Selections from His Diaries and Letters*, ed. Sir Frederick Pollock (New York: Harper & Brothers, 1875), 449–52; and Sir Theodore Martin, *Helena Faucit (Lady Martin)* (London: William Blackwood and Sons, 1900), 63–64.

11. John William Calcraft [John William Cole], "How The Theatre Royal in Hawkins'-Street Came To Be Built, With A Cursory Glance At What Has Been Done There During Thirty Years . . . ," *Dublin University Magazine* 39 (June 1852): 695–96. The original letter (from Bulwer to Calcraft) from which these observations are drawn is in the British Library (Add. MS. 33964). See Shattuck, ed., *Bulwer and Macready*, 145–46, n. 19. See also Christopher Murray, "*Richelieu* at the Theatre Royal, Dublin, 1839," *Theatre Notebook* 37 (1983):128–31.

12. *Diaries*, 2:419; illustration (artist unknown) in the Hoblitzelle Theatre Arts Library, University of Texas at Austin (7967.1546); sketches by James Sant in the Parrish Collection of Princeton University Library (AM 20799 and AM 21501); an anonymous wash drawing reproduced in Downer, *The Eminent Tragedian*, following 158, figure 8; and [John] Westland Marston, *Our Recent Actors: Being Recollections Critical, And, In Many Cases, Personal, Of Late Distinguished Performers of Both Sexes*, 2 vols. (Boston: Roberts Brothers, 1888), 1:39.

13. *Examiner*; Marston, 1:39–40; and *Liverpool Mercury*, 9 April 1847, respectively.

14. *Athenaeum*; *John Bull*; *Morning Herald*; *Morning Post*; *New York Albion*, 7 October 1843; and *The London Theatre 1811–1866: Selections from the Diary of Henry Crabb Robinson*, ed. Eluned Brown (London: The Society for Theatre Research, 1966), 161.

15. Marston, 1:39–53; *Examiner*, 7 February 1846; Lady Juliet Pollock, *Macready As I Knew Him*, 2nd ed. (London: Remington, 1885), 126–28; and letter from Alfred de Vigny to Macready, 10 March 1839, Huntington Library (HM 23638). The role was similar in many ways to his Richard III: see London Green, "'The Gaiety of Mediated Success': The Richard III of William Charles Macready," *Theatre Research International* 10 (Summer 1985):107–28.

16. *Bell's Life in London*; *Morning Chronicle*; *Cork Examiner*, 19 August 1850; and *Liverpool Mercury*, 9 April 1847.

17. George Vandenhoff, *Dramatic Reminiscences; or, Actors and Actresses in England and America*, ed. Henry Seymour Carleton (London: Thomas W. Cooper, 1860), 17. See also Marston, 1:106–107; *Athenaeum*, 1 March 1851; and *Glasgow Dramatic Review*, 16 April 1845.

18. John Foster Kirk, "Shakespeare's Tragedies on the Stage," *Lippincott's Magazine of Popular Literature and Science*, o.s. 35, n.s. 7 (June 1884): 613.

19. John Coleman, *Fifty Years of an Actor's Life*, 2 vols. (London: Hutchinson, 1904), 2:503.

20. Archer, 205.

21. Letter from Bulwer to Macready, dated [12 March 1839], Parrish Collection, Princeton University Library (Am 15520).

22. Sir Theodore Martin, 64. For a discerning analysis of the mixture of ideal and realistic qualities in her acting style, see Carol J. Carlisle, "Passion Framed by Art: Helen Faucit's Juliet," *Theatre Survey* 25 (November 1984):177–92.

23. *John Bull* and *Morning Chronicle* respectively.

24. *Idler* and *Times* respectively.

25. James R. Anderson, *An Actor's Life* (London: Walter Scott, 1902), 84.

26. This letter is in a grangerized copy of Helena Faucit, Lady Martin, *On Some of Shakespeare's Female Characters*, National Library of Scotland, Department of Manuscripts (MS 16433 f. 36–37 v.), following p. 202 of the printed text.

27. Hollis W. Huston, "Macready's *Richelieu* Promptbooks: Evolution of the Enclosed Setting," *Theatre Studies*, no. 21 (1974–75):41–51.
28. Lady Pollock, 127–28.
29. Coleman, 2:503–504.
30. Letter, dated 10 March 1839, in the Huntington Library (AM 23628).
31. Daniel J. Watermeier, "Edwin Booth's Richelieu," *Theatre History Studies* 1 (1981):1–19; W. May Phelps and John Forbes-Robertson, *The Life and Life-Work of Samuel Phelps* (London: Sampson Low, Marston, Searle and Rivington, 1886), 218; *The Times*, 19 June 1845; and *The Chicago Tribune*, 25 January 1885.
32. Alan S. Downer, "Players and Painted Stage: Nineteenth Century Acting," *PMLA* 61 (June 1946):544. See also his *The Eminent Tragedian*, 69–80.
33. George Henry Lewes, *On Actors and the Art of Acting* (1875; reprint, New York: Grove Press, [1957]), 40–43; *Illustrated London News*, 1 March 1851; and Kirk, "Shakespeare's Tragedies," 615–16.

Edwin Booth's Bertuccio
TOM TAYLOR'S FOOL REVISED

Lorraine Commeret

When they weren't doing Shakespeare, the great Shakespearean actors of the nineteenth century were thrilling their audiences with romantic heroes and villains of a lesser order—"actory" parts, Charles Shattuck has called them—which most playgoers thought as moving and fascinating as Hamlet or Iago.[1] Among Edwin Booth's most successful impersonations, mainstays of his repertoire throughout the years, were two such non-Shakespearean roles, the title role in Edward Bulwer's *Richelieu* and Bertuccio in Tom Taylor's *The Fool's Revenge*. Richelieu has been the first to draw significant scholarly attention, and expectably so, preferred as it was by Booth's critics and public and, from all indications, by the actor himself.[2] He assumed the role frequently, relishing its wit, its ease, its flashy theatricality as an actor's welcome antidote to heavy doses of Hamlet. As Shattuck concludes in *The Hamlet of Edwin Booth*, the success of *Richelieu* had partially been assured: fashioned by one of the most esteemed playwrights of the nineteenth century, it had been a jewel in the repertoire of many first-rate tragedians; and its central character, a remarkable amalgam of power, dignity, cleverness, and sentimentality, accorded perfectly with contemporary tastes. In contrast, *The Fool's Revenge* was virtually a new play and one of dubious standing among the critics, the product of a merely popular playwright, a jack-of-all-styles trying to refurbish a romantic drama in that genre's waning years. Booth succeeded as Bertuccio despite and not because of the play's reputation.

As a character which found its only great impersonator in Edwin Booth and as one of his most brilliant roles in the estimate of his contemporaries, Bertuccio lays claim to our attention.[3] This study chronicles Booth's early efforts with the play, examines both Taylor's script and Booth's acting

Playbill for *The Fool's Revenge*. (Courtesy of the Hampden-Booth Theatre Library, The Players.)

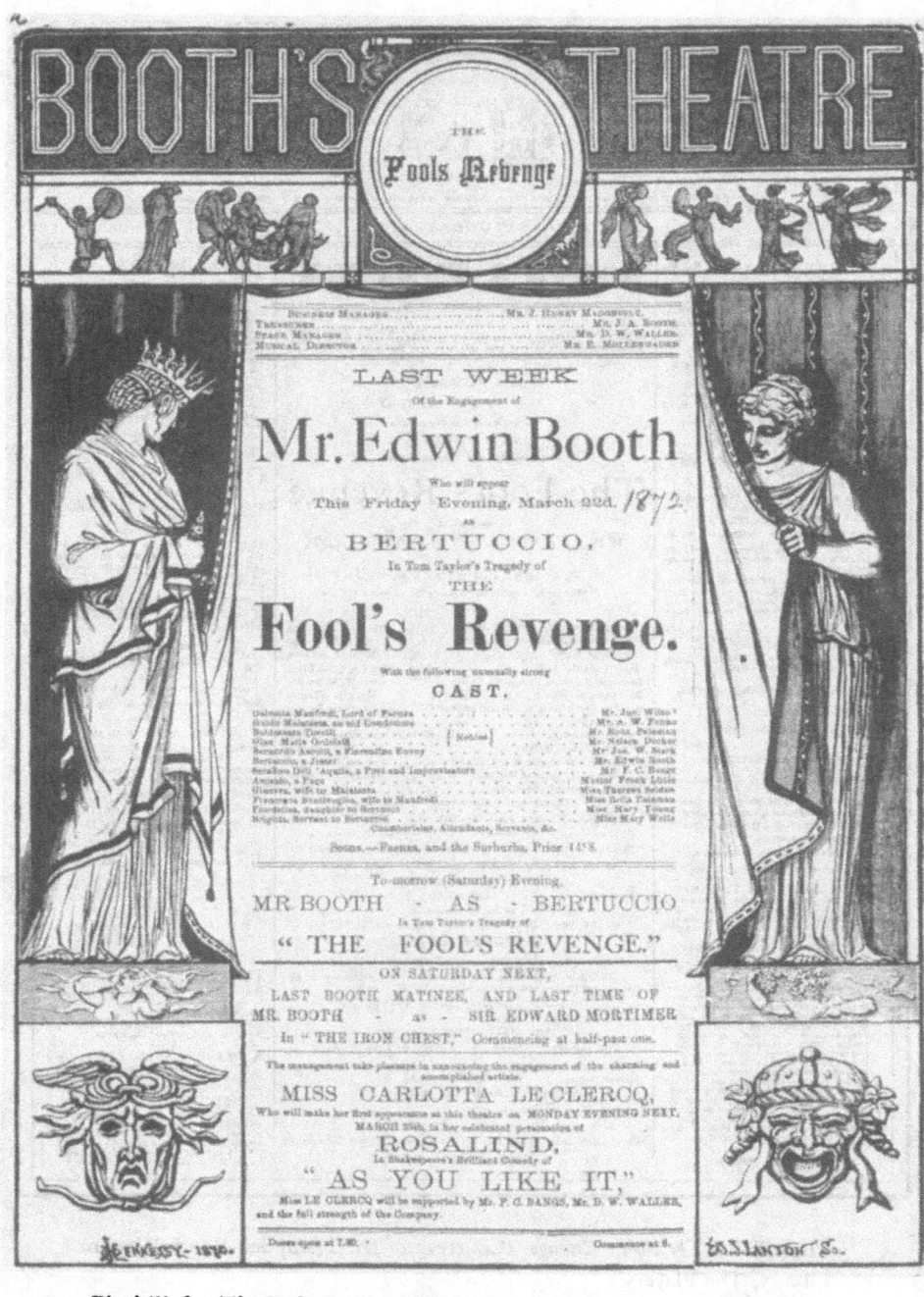

Playbill for *The Fool's Revenge*. (Courtesy of the Hampden-Booth Theatre Library, The Players.)

version, reconstructs Booth's performance from sources which date from the definitive production of 1871, assesses his critical reception, and attempts to "place" Bertuccio in Booth's repertoire.[4]

The Fool's Revenge was first mounted at Sadler's Wells on 18 October 1859 by Samuel Phelps, who, always eager for new scripts in the old blank-verse style, had snapped up the play after it was abandoned by Frederick Robson, the popular English comedian who had commissioned it.[5] In Phelps's able hands *The Fool's Revenge* shone brightly and briefly for a season after which it was given only occasional revivals by Phelps and lesser British actors.[6] The play came into Booth's hands within months of Phelps's successful run, through Joseph Jefferson via Booth's wife, Mary Devlin Booth. At her suggestion, Booth read it and in the fall of 1860 tried it out at the Arch Street Theatre in Philadelphia and at the Howard Atheneum in Boston.[7] He was pleased by audience reactions, but, being chary of his reputation as a Shakespearean actor, he hesitated to bring it out in New York, as he indicated in a letter to Lawrence Barrett, dated 21 November 1860: "*The Fool's Revenge* was a tremendous hit in Philadelphia—ran it a week to crowded houses—I'll make it 'howl' here—if I play it. I'm afraid though lest I get a sort of Metamoric or Meg Merrilic reputation instead of 'Shakes.'"[8]

Booth's comparison was an apt one. Like Edwin Forrest's noble savage and Charlotte Cushman's wild gypsy woman, Booth's Bertuccio was a powerful, romantic character who made "strong men shudder and women look pale."[9] The jester with his wild antics and licensed humor and the brooding hunchback with his grotesque deformity were popular romantic subjects, combined here in one compelling character. The role offered a smorgasbord of contrasting emotions which dazzled spectators and prompted critics in the decades to come to pronounce Booth's impersonation the most successful melodramatic acting on the contemporary stage. More than one critic ventured that if Booth had accomplished nothing else, he might have rested his reputation on Bertuccio.

Possibly, then, Booth's fears were well-founded, and they made him cautious, perhaps excessively so, about introducing the play to New York and including it regularly in his repertoire. Though the New York debut on 28 March 1864 at Niblo's Garden was undeniably successful, drawing "the highest encomium that criticism can bestow" from the *New York Times* (29 March 1864) and achieving a respectable run, the play nevertheless disappeared from New York for three years, emerged in a little-noted Winter Garden production in 1867, then vanished again for another four years.[10] On the circuit, however, Booth continued to perform *The Fool's Revenge* and experimented with it until he had arrived at a satisfactory acting version. Some time between 1867 and 1871, and not in 1860, as Asia Booth Clarke erroneously claims, Booth created the tragic ending, his most significant alteration of Tom Taylor's text, and presumably came to realize, as Clarke quaintly stated, "the perfect pathos and passion of the part."[11] From all appearances, Booth was still tentative about the play when he brought it out at Booth's Theatre on 3 April 1871, for he scheduled it for only one week at the end of the season during the notoriously slack Lenten period, and mounted it, though lavishly, with scenery recycled in part from *Romeo and Juliet*.[12] When press and public responded favorably, however, the run was extended for an additional week, and *The Fool's Revenge* became established finally and firmly in Booth's repertoire.

To understand Booth's Bertuccio, it is essential first to examine *The Fool's Revenge*, a less familiar script than Hugo's *Le Roi s'amuse* from which it was adapted.[13] It was, Taylor rightly argued, neither a mere translation of Hugo's drama nor a *rafacciamento* of the more popular operatic version, Verdi's *Rigoletto*, as some critics charged, but rather, in Taylor's parlance, a "new play," based on borrowed, but significantly reworked material.[14] What he did borrow, however, was singular enough to ensure constant comparison with *Le Roi s'amuse*. Both plays depict a misanthropic jester, abetting the debaucheries of his master and, through his vicious barbs, earning the enmity of his master's followers. And in both Hugo's and Taylor's versions, the courtiers avenge themselves by abducting for their master a beautiful woman, whom they assume to be the jester's mistress, but who is actually his daughter, contriving in their schemes to have the fool assist unwittingly in the abduction.

Taylor's reworking was considerable. He employed none of the original dialogue and replaced acts three through five with one compact act of entirely new material. Following Verdi, Taylor transported the play to fifteenth-century Italy, a more appropriate setting, he surmised, for the intriguing behavior of the characters, and added a touch of authenticity, he presumed, by using actual historical figures, Duke Galetto Manfredi and the wife who murdered him, Francesca Bentivoglio. Moreover, Taylor enhanced the play's domestic appeal by creating a more protracted, more pathetic scene between father and daughter in the second act. In more elemental ways too, such as obliterating the curse of St. Vallier, Taylor radically altered structure, characterization, and tone, creating out of Hugo's complex drama a pastiche of romantic tragedy, melodrama, and well-made play. In deference to contemporary English audiences, he aimed to remove what was "inadmissible," and to satisfy his own artistic standards, he aspired, with all due modesty, to correct what was "wanting in dramatic motive and cohesion" and "defective in that central aspect of stage effect, climax." The "inadmissible" included Hugo's all-too-human heroine, Blanche, who falls in love with a debauched prince, "submits" to him, and inexplicably sacrifices her life to save him. To remove her taint, Taylor redirected her affections to the more suitable Dell'Aquila, a modest and nearly mute poet, who never so much as kisses her throughout the play. Fiordelisa, as Taylor calls her, resists her seducer, Manfredi, vehemently. He for his part pursues a more gentlemanly seduction, not in his bedroom, but in a banquet hall, dying before he succeeds and leaving Fiordelisa uncompromised. The chaste lovers and the faithful Ginevra Malatesta remain unmistakably good, the courtiers unmistakably evil, and all flat and unquestionably melodramatic. Bertuccio alone, with his demoniacal hatred and tender love, retains the internal contradictions that enliven Hugo's romantic originals.

But even Bertuccio is softened somewhat into a character more comprehensible and more sympathetic than Hugo's Triboulet, for in Bertuccio envy and malevolence are subordinated to the one clear-cut motive that drives the play from the beginning: revenge for the abduction and death of his wife at the hands of Count Malatesta. Bertuccio's plan is to have his master, the Duke Manfredi, abduct the unwilling Ginevra, a plan which would make Bertuccio even with the count "wife for wife."[15] While Bertuccio's grief warrants pity, the injustice of his scheme, which would injure the innocent along with the evil, makes revenge a corrupting influence. When the plan recoils on Bertuccio and his daughter becomes victim, the moral is made clear: "Vengeance is not man's attribute—but Heaven's" (Taylor, 57). Redeemed by repentance, Bertuccio is preserved along with Fiordelisa, while the evil duke perishes.

Though characters, moral, and motive derive from melodrama, the plot with its remarkably intricate action owes more to the well-made play. The web of intrigue includes not only Bertuccio's scheme, but Francesca's plan to catch her husband "in the act," Malatesta's plan to thwart Manfredi by sending his wife to the country, the courtiers' plan to abduct Fiordelisa, and Dell'Aquila's counterplan to avert the abduction. Adorning these activities are such shopworn devices as a messenger's ring, poisoned wine, and a stolen key, and not one balcony to climb, but two. With singular regularity, the characters spy on each other in every scene, from behind statuary, bushes, curtains, walls, and doors. Despite such claptrap, Taylor's craft brings the play to a swift and powerful climax. Moreover, he replaces Hugo's clumsy devices in the abduction scene—the cloak of darkness and the mask as blindfold, which account for Triboulet's mistaking his own humble house for the nearby estate of Count de Cosse; instead he has Dell'Aquila hide Fiordelisa at the house of Malatesta, so that it is the identity, not of the house, but of the cloaked and unconscious woman which Bertuccio mistakes.

In most of the Booth reviews, intrigued and baffled critics gave abundant space to discussion of Taylor's unhappy hybrid. While old-school critics of a romantic bent naturally favored Hugo's play over Taylor's (a pale and watered-down imitation, they chided, with none of the force and vitality of the original) ironically, the most modern critics—all of them British—also favored Hugo, and disdained Taylor for a squeamishness which they found too old-fashioned. At the other end of the spectrum, the genteel critics lamented that Taylor had not done enough to remove what was offensive. Pittsburgh's *The Chronicle Telegraph*, for example, viewed the play as too grim and depraved and longed, after seeing it, "for a whiff of pure air" (28 January 1887). Among such critics the notion that drama should teach a moral purpose was axiomatic, and although the play did proclaim its moral blatantly, that was not enough to dispel the atmosphere of corruption which pervaded its world. William Winter, himself a critic of the genteel tradition, attempted to address such objections in his *New York Tribune* review of the 1871 production. His strategy was to compare the play with *Othello*, which had preceded *The Fool's Revenge*, and to claim its tragic impact as a social value: "The transition from 'Othello' to 'The Fool's Revenge'. . . . was, in one sense, a transition from gloom to gloom; but tragedy is tragedy, and the mission of it is to do good by hurting our feelings. It may make us sad, but it does not make us angry. . . .Dark and repellent themes occur, for instance, in both 'Othello' and 'The Fool's Revenge'; but, in each case, they are made tributary to an honest and lofty dramatic purpose. Therefore we endure them" (5 April 1871). Though questions of morality often muddied or displaced discussion of Taylor's craftsmanship, some critics appeared to have a clear-eyed view of the play itself. Henry Austin Clapp of the *Boston Advertiser* (10 May 1877) saw that despite its coherent and concise story and its vigorous movement toward a climax, *The Fool's Revenge* lacked the artistic unity of the original. And the critic for *Saturday Review* (29 July 1882) judged that Taylor's blank verse, while occasionally witty or fine, generally failed in the most dramatic moments of the script.

Except for its conclusion, Booth's acting version was quite faithful to Taylor's original.[16] Unlike his acting versions of Shakespeare's plays, which were shortened considerably and drastically rearranged for scenic convenience, it cut only some forty-odd lines and retained the original scenic order, for *The Fool's Revenge*, written as a star vehicle and already tailored for mid-century staging, required minimal revision. The modest alterations Booth did make, however, reflect his established practices. Over half his cuts were "objectionable" expressions—coarse language and sexual references of the sort Booth commonly excised, but which Taylor's tame script required to establish the depravity of his characters. Gone, therefore, is the reference to Bertuccio's "grinders" in the courtiers' "softer parts," gone the allusion to Fiordelisa as "meat" for Bertuccio's master (Taylor, 19, 18). Malatesta may climb into his sheets with his wife, but he may not be "warm" there (*HD* 1). And though the courtiers are permitted to imagine Bertuccio with a mistress, a dame with "matching hump," they no longer fantasize about the couple's progeny: "two-humped babes . . . like Bactrian camels" (*HD*, 16).

More fastidious than most in cleansing the language of his scripts, Booth was perhaps unique in purifying the motives of his characters as well. As he had with Richelieu, King Lear, and Iago, Booth sought to ennoble Bertuccio by simply removing his less savory impulses.[17] The first instance occurs at the end of act one, where Bertuccio sneers at the departed courtiers, whose jibes mean nothing to him now that his long-awaited vengeance is near. Here Booth cuts the line, "I am straight and fair and well-shaped as yourselves," thereby eliminating envy (a vestige of Hugo's Triboulet) and leaving only Bertuccio's thirst for vengeance.[18] Such an interpretation seems corroborated by a more lengthy cut at the end of act two where Bertuccio glories in thoughts of Malatesta's imminent grief. From this speech Booth excises the passage where Bertuccio explains why his involuted schemes are designed to ensnare Manfredi as well as Malatesta, and thereby expunges Bertuccio's last selfish motive:

> But I have private wrongs, too, to repay;
> This proud Manfredi—he you spat upon
> He you spurned such a day, set in the stocks,
> Whipped—he is even with your mightiness!
> Here is Francesca's ring; and here the letter,
> To tell her that her vengeance, too, is ripe.
> The blow shall come from her; but mine's the hand
> That guides the dagger's point straight to *his* heart!
>
> (*HD*, 39–40)

To strengthen the curtain at the end of the act, another of Booth's habitual motives for alteration, he rearranged the dialogue as well, the most significant alteration to come after the 1871 production. The long apostrophe to Malatesta, which anticlimactically follows the abductors' exit in the original, in Booth's final version is spoken by the jester as he still holds the ladder awaiting their descent. This change increases the irony of the speech and leaves Bertuccio after their departure with but a few spirited lines before his wild dance at the curtain's fall:

> Tis done!
> Now, murdered innocent, thou art avenged!
> I cannot sleep! I'll walk, I'll sing, I'll dance the night away!
> It is no night for me, my day has come![19]

All of these emendations are finally subordinate to Booth's tragic conclusion, a significant improvement over the insipid melodrama of the original. In Taylor's text, when Bertuccio learns that the wine destined to poison his daughter is already in the banquet hall, his cries to the courtiers draw them out, and he and Dell'Aquila gain access to the hall accidentally when the men rush back in to assist the duke. Bertuccio then hurries to Fiordelisa's still form, laments over her "death," and finding her alive, exults in her revival. Francesca and Bertuccio both confess their respective evil deeds, she adamantly unrepentant, he utterly contrite, and the play's moral is made unmistakably clear. Phelps set the entire conclusion in a kind of inner stage defined by the frame of the set of folding doors in the upstage wall of the anteroom, a device Booth himself employed before introducing the tragic ending.

With Bertuccio's death, Booth also introduced changes into the text, moving the play to a swifter and stronger conclusion and creating more visual excitement with a new *mise-en-scène*. He began with a distinctly more dramatic entrance—Bertuccio and Dell'Aquila breaking open the door—and followed that with what one critic called a genuine *trompe l'oeil*. The back wall of the anteroom suddenly disappeared, revealing a full view of the banquet hall behind with all its attendant horrors. The changing of scenery mid-scene in full view of the audience was no novel device, but a "transformation scene," frequently a high point of the pantomime, but used only rarely in legitimate drama. None of Booth's critics identified it as such, however, nor did they even give the change much notice. It was accomplished by removing the backing flats for the central archway right after Francesca came out of hiding there and by sinking or flying the back wall at the instant the men broke through the door. After the cries, "Do not drink. Your wine is poisoned!" were delivered from offstage, the two men reappeared again through a curtained entryway at the right rear of the banquet hall just as the duke was beginning to expire. Their exit from the anteroom and entrance into the banqueting hall thus occurred at two different points on the stage and demanded that the audience change perspective from the "outside" to the "inside," much in the manner of a modern film cut. This convention proved acceptable to the majority and raised objections only from one disgruntled British critic in the London *Reynolds* (2 January 1881).

Booth capped his entrance with a leap onto the table where he kicked over the flagon of wine and confessed that he was the murderer. Before the real murderer, Francesca, could intervene, Booth-Bertuccio was stabbed by the courtiers and crawled to his daughter's side. It was thus a dying Bertuccio who lamented and then rejoiced over his daughter, an episode now rendered more poignant, and in its briefer form, more effective than the original. Booth also cut a brief debate between Francesca and Bertuccio over justice and revenge and sent her off instead with a stormy exit, a change which tempered the high moral tone of the original and strengthened the focus on Bertuccio in the play's final moments. The point which Taylor made through rhetoric, Booth accomplished through action—in the penance which Bertuccio pays in forgiving Malatesta and in the penalty of his death.

In creating the tragic ending, Booth may have been prompted in part by negative critical responses to Taylor's original ending, which the *New York Herald*, for example, had compared to seeing "Lear revive . . . and dance a hornpipe" (29 March 1864). More likely, Booth was working for a theatrically more effective ending, one which would create more sympathy for Bertuccio and a more powerful impact on the audience. Most critics seemed mixed in their reactions to the change—pleased with the poetic justice of Bertuccio's fate, but unconvinced by his all-too-sudden forgiveness of Malatesta.

As with Hamlet, Richelieu, Iago, and his other finest creations, Booth seemed to identify with this character completely.[20] He lives the part, says one. "He is Bertuccio himself," says another (*NYH*, 6 February 1885). That Booth did identify with Bertuccio on occasion is the subject of a much-repeated anecdote, first published in a Pittsburgh paper in 1886 and prompted, the writer claims, by a discussion of Diderot's *Paradox of Acting*:

Mr. Booth told me that sometimes when he has been acting in "The Fool's Revenge," he has felt a singular sympathy with the character he was performing. On one occasion in particular the pathos of the poor jester's hard fate appealed to him more powerfully than it had been wont to do: he began to identify himself with the twisted and tortured Bertuccio; the tears rose to his eyes and streamed down his face; his voice was broken with honest emotion; he felt the part as never before; and it seemed to him that he had never played it so well. And yet, when the play was over and he left the theatre, his daughter, his surest critic, who had seen the performance from a stage box, asked him what had been the matter, as she had never seen him act the part so badly.[21]

The conclusion Booth would have the reader draw concerning the necessity of detachment is certainly corroborated elsewhere in Booth lore, but irrespective of his technique, the fact remains that for Booth admirers, he became the character who stood before them. Even more than in other roles, they insisted, his identity seemed "lost" in Bertuccio (*New York Democrat*, 9 April 1871). He was, one critic says in wonder, "transmogrified" (unidentified clipping, 4 April 1871, Booth Scrapbook, 1870–1872). Not Booth's affinity for the character, but rather the distance between Booth's own gentlemanly self and this "unnatural devil incarnate," this "gargoyle," made the transformation seem an act of genius (*Home Journal*, 12 April 1871; *The Stage* [London], 1 January 1881).

A significant aspect of that transformation was physical, both by reason of Bertuccio's profession as jester and because of his deformity, so that in makeup and movement, it was far removed from any other role in Booth's repertoire. He appeared in the motley of the late fifteenth-century Italian jester, a bright, though somewhat shabby, parti-color of red, yellow, and blue (*NYH*, 6 February 1885). His shoes with turned-up toes were decorated with bells, as were his coat, collar, waist, and the ear-like projections of his cap. The bauble, which became a living thing in his hands, was topped with a doll-sized jester's head, its features caught in a sardonic smile. In addition to the hump on his back, bosses of flesh hung from his calves and ankles and his legs were spread in an habitual wide-legged crouch (*The Stage* [London], 1 January 1881). The jester's cap pressed his hair close to his forehead, creating a low-browed effect which together with his grisly beard and mustache gave Booth's finely chiseled features and high brow a closed, pinched appearance—that "secretive" and "reticent" look which William Winter associated with the "physically deformed."[22]

Edwin Booth as "Bertuccio." (Courtesy of the Hampden-Booth Theatre Library, The Players.)

Booth created a Bertuccio so deformed that his legs were always bent beneath him, whether in rest or in motion. He did not walk in the usual sense, but moved on his haunches like a "crab" or a "misshaped top" or an "ape," by twisting, spinning, or pirouetting. Though disabled and aging, the character was full of feverish energy and incessant movement. Like Dagonet in Tennyson's "The Last Tournament," one critic stated, he "danced like the wither'd leaf before the hall" (*Stage* [London], 1 January 1881). He jumped and skipped and tumbled and sometimes sprawled at the feet of scene-mates, preventing their easy movement, hemming them in. Before his master and mistress he often cowered as if ready for the blow to come, only to fall in a picturesque attitude. Each action, though distorted, was exquisitely expressive. The acrobatics of the role, combined with its sustained intensity, made this one of Booth's most exhausting roles, a factor which may have accounted in part for the fact that Booth did not perform it more frequently.[23]

Though a Caliban or Quasimodo in appearance, some contended, he was keenly intelligent and full of wit, which he shot out "like a poisoned dart" or drove home "like a fine stiletto," looking into the faces of his prey with "affected simpleness or unaffected delight." He cringed and fawned, coaxed and wheedled, taunted and sneered, in a chain of infinite strategies that were startlingly distinct and real. And over his mobile features passed myriad shades of expression, subtle and swift, but utterly convincing. It was a role which Clapp thought ideally suited to the "vividness and intellectual rapidity" of Booth's style (*Boston Advertiser*, 10 May 1877).

Just as startling as his first-act entrance when he scuttled down the staircase, shaking his bauble and jingling his bells, was Bertuccio's quiet entrance in the second, as an ordinary man, dressed in street clothes, greeting his daughter with tender affection. He sat still for much of this scene, holding his daughter's hand and weeping, a relief from the unendurable life he refused to reveal to her. His voice was "ineffably touching" when he told her that her mother was dead, and as he questioned her of her movements, he riveted his attention on her and looked intensely into her eyes for an answer. It was a scene of unusual delicacy, "lacework," one New Orleans critic called it, "full of subtlety and tenderness."[24] Such was the reaction of admirers with Booth at his best, but "tenderness" was not Booth's strong suit, and in later years especially, critics would find the scene somewhat flat. Yet without the element of paternal love, critics like Winter protested, they could not have tolerated Bertuccio; it redeemed and turned the antipathy of the first act into profound sympathy in the second.

There was none of the fool in the father, just as there had been none of the father in the fool, and the contrast between these two disparate personae thoroughly impressed critics, especially in the third act, where they are placed in close juxtaposition, "drawing as it were alternate breaths" (*St. Louis Republican*, 14 October 1877). Still a third aspect of this fractured personality, Bertuccio the avenger existed, as it were, within the others, at the core of his personality. He revealed himself during act one in moments of by-play and in the monologues and asides where, Iago-like, he disclosed his dark secrets, and again in act two during a reluctant confession to his daughter when his long-nurtured hatred suddenly spilled forth. He seemed a demon at such moments, unnatural and repulsive, but utterly fascinating, as this susceptible critic reveals: "In pursuit of this phantom revenge, Bertuccio works himself up to a climax of concentrated hate, gloating with a demoniacal diabolism. . . . Subtle, scheming, fertile in resources, a stranger to the appeals of mercy, he turns his slimy, serpentlike coils about his victim, fancying his prey is secure. Joy, the terrible agonizing devilish joy of being soon able to crush his foe . . . gleams from his Dragon-like eyes, and animates his soul."[25]

Thus, the appeal of Booth's Bertuccio lay not just in the broad, contrasting roles or personae of the character, but in the boldness with which he rendered them and in the incredible variety of emotions that he portrayed—love, hate, irony, jealousy, revenge, disappointment, pathos, fierce joy, poignant grief—the critics' lists went on and on. It was Booth's best "emotional" acting, the best "melodramatic" acting to be seen on the contemporary stage. "His delineation was so full and flush," says the critic of the New York *Weekly Reviewer*, "so vigorous, pungent, animated, clear, bold, and flooded with bitter and deep feeling as carry all before its virulent, elastic, and restless power" (23 March 1872).

The scene which above all others drew such responses, and which some deemed the finest scene in all of Booth's impersonations, occurred toward the end of act three, and began with the moment when Bertuccio learns that it is his daughter who has been abducted and now sits in the banquet hall beyond the locked door, a prey to Manfredi's advances and in danger of being poisoned. The scene commenced with a bloodcurdling shriek, which was followed by Bertuccio's feverish explanations to Dell'Aquila; then came the episode with the servant when Bertuccio kicked over the flagon of wine, lest it prove to be the poisoned one, and finally the encounter with Torelli, the high point of the scene. At first he coaxed Torelli, flattering him in an unaccustomed tone; then came the wild assumption of the fool's manner, a false, strident gaiety, an "almost appalling" dance around the courtier ("The Theatres," *SR*, 29 July 1881). He fawned on Torelli and patted his knee. As one by one his strategies failed, his mask began to crumble, and only the pleading father remained, his "upturned face ghastly with its naked human pathos," his final words a barely audible whisper, "You'll take me in, Torelli?"[26]

Exhausted by his efforts, Bertuccio fell into a chair and, in an agony of grief, collapsed with his arms on the table and writhed convulsively. When Torelli reentered to thrust him rudely from the door with the news that the duke would have none of his ape's tricks, his despair was overwhelming. He fell weeping on the table and rolled on the floor, to be roused only by the poet's challenge to the duke's men within. Pushed too far, this scene might have fallen into bathos and become ridiculous, but again and again, it was affirmed, Booth kept just the right balance and struck no false notes. He expressed at once both the false joviality Bertuccio assumes before Torelli and the anguish underneath the antic disposition. "The breaking heart is audible in every tone," a San Francisco critic marveled, "visible in every lineament of his countenance."[27] By comparison, the conclusion of the play, where Bertuccio bursts into the hall, is attacked by the courtiers, and repents with his dying breath, appeared to the critics for all its bold action almost anticlimactic.

Whereas Taylor's jerry-built script and Booth's riveting characterization inspired lengthy analyses from reviewers, the *mise-en-scène* only rarely evoked comment—even the ingenious transformation scene in act three, which appears so remarkable in retrospect. If in 1871 the play had ranked in Booth's estimation with his other great creations, he might have given it the sumptuous mounting he had lavished on *Hamlet* or *Othello*. But then, as later, it was to survive on borrowed trappings. In the most detailed account available—the Benson Sherwood stage plan book listing the scenic arrangements for an 1878 production at the Fifth Avenue Theatre—*The Fool's Revenge* was mounted with an astonishing potpourri of scenic pieces: a garden platform from *Othello*, "Melnotte's kitchen flats," a set piece from *Camille*, "Rome's balcony," an Evadne street set, a Marion de Lorme drop, and a *Richelieu* drop, as well as a park drop, gothic flats, and other common stock pieces.[28] The fact that *The Fool's Revenge* was consistently drawn from stock is suggested, too, by Booth's promptbook floorplans, which are modestly scaled and nearly all symmetrical. For the Garden of Manfredi (act one) Booth employed a standard wing and drop set, the illuminated garden drop being fronted by a platform with central stairs and the garden "floor" being defined by four sets of wings and a pair of garden sets just left and right of center. Bertuccio's home in 2.1 was a simple, box-shaped room, punctured by many apertures and given strong central focus by Bertuccio's chair and Fiordelisa's footstool. Act two, scene two was a carpenter's scene, a street drop set in the first grooves, and act three shows a central arch, and—balancing each side of the stage—a door, a table, and a chair. The only setting to abandon practical classical symmetry for romantic off-center focus was 2.3, the exterior of Malatesta's house, which was placed stage left and angled up-center.

Romance and picturesqueness were nevertheless in evidence, thanks to some exotic scenic embellishments and to the many dramatic lighting effects and carefully orchestrated sound effects that are documented in the promptbooks. Music, in particular, was used to establish tone, to provide leitmotifs for certain characters, and to heighten climactic moments like Bertuccio's first entrance or the abduction. As the curtain rose on act one, the strains of "La donna e mobile" drifted across the garden and laughing maskers lingered among the statuary, lighted by streaming moonlight and the sparkle of "myriad colored lanterns." It was a scene Nym Crinkle (Andrew C. Wheeler) of the New York *World* found "especially chaste and delicate" (5 April 1871). In 2.1 violins signaled Fiordelisa's every entrance and a pair of lutes supplied an air of romance for the lovers. As in Phelps's production, Bertuccio's humble abode was enlivened by hanging tapestries and by "charming suggestions" of its young occupant. To build suspense in act three, Booth used, not music, which underscored only the poisoning of the wine and the final curtain, but the incessant clicking of locks, reminders of Fiordelisa's imprisonment, and the laughter of Manfredi and his band behind the scene, serving as counterpoint to Francesca's rage and Bertuccio's agony. Booth's skill in creating an effective *mise-en-scène*, so evident in his handling of the play's conclusion, was also demonstrated in 2.3, the abduction. Here, where an atmosphere of romance and danger are essential, where the action is swift and full of high tension, lighting and music were manipulated to create a rhythm of suspense and to carry the scene to an exhilarating climax. Music and moonlight accompanied the fearful lovers' entrance, and candlelight, deceptive in its warmth and promise of safe haven, lighted Fiordelisa's way to the house. During Dell'Aquila's exit speech, the moonlight gradually faded, there was a pause, and music rose again to usher in the abductors. As they gathered beneath the balcony, a light suddenly appeared in the window above, silhouetting a woman's form. Before they mounted, it was just as suddenly extinguished, plunging the stage into near darkness. The music started again as they climbed, played under Bertuccio's speech of triumph, and continued to the end. As they descended, the moonlight reappeared, and after their departure, Bertuccio burst into a frenzy of exultation and dancing, as the music rose to forte and the curtain quickly fell. Though the *mise-en-scène* itself attracted little notice, it was clearly calculated to reinforce Booth's remarkable performance.

In response to the 1871 production of *The Fool's Revenge*, critics were nearly unanimous in their approval of Booth's Bertuccio, though Nym Crinkle, never a staunch Booth ally, thought the appeal of the role lay in Bertuccio's "physical peculiarities" and not in Booth's singular characterization. Even the critic of the *New York Times* (8 April 1871), another Booth detractor, made grudging amends in his review of *The Fool's Revenge*, calling Bertuccio "one of the finest pieces of acting we have seen on any stage."

The spring of 1872 brought another run of *The Fool's Revenge* at Booth's Theatre, as splendid and well-received as the first. Thereafter came the loss of Booth's Theatre, bankruptcy, and a slow recovery from debt. Throughout the troubled seventies, Booth continued to play Bertuccio in his wide-ranging tours through the United States and Canada and, beginning in 1875, in New York again, at the Fifth Avenue Theatre, the Lyceum, and various other houses. In contrast to the long runs at the Winter Garden and at Booth's Theatre, he now offered such a wide array of roles during one engagement that critics became newly aware of his versatility. It became more apparent too, that in Bertuccio, Booth offered "a phase of his histrionic power and skill" that was separate from that he exhibited in other roles. The popularity of Bertuccio grew. The San Franciscans, who reluctantly took the play "on trust," sat spellbound and gave it ringing applause.[29] The Bostonians, who according to the *Boston Transcript* ("Edwin Booth in Boston," 16 April 1904), had not seen it for a decade, crowded the house. Booth's characterization was at its peak when Nym Crinkle (*Spirit of the Times*, 30 November 1878) gave it another nod of approval, even though Booth's energies were apparently diminished. "The great scene in the ante-chamber taxed, while it did not vanquish, the resources of the actor's art," he observed. But the performance still had "gained rather than lost with time." Even Stephen Ryder Fiske (*Spirit of the Times*, 10 April 1880), who had harped for years on the "mechanical precision of Booth's acting," maintained that, in *The Fool's Revenge*, he was "undoubtedly a great actor."

Not surprisingly, in London, which was raging with Irving fever at the time of Booth's visits in 1880 and 1882, there was none of the wholesale approval which had characterized American criticism of Bertuccio.[30] The claim Booth makes in letters to his friends—that while Irving's coterie was out to get him, audiences had welcomed him warmly—is confirmed by responses to *The Fool's Revenge*.[31] When he came on "grimacing and shaking his bauble," he received a double round of applause, an unusual honor, reviewers say, from London audiences. And as the curtain went down there were "calls and recalls and endless bursts of cheering" (*Stage Directory*, 1 January 1881). Here was an actor who knew how to "hold" an audience, Figaro exclaimed, and to "work his will with it" (*London Figaro*, 1 January 1881). Abundant tears and applause were reactions too strong to deny, so detractors explained them away instead as British politeness or admiration for Booth's craftsmanship.

In describing Booth-Bertuccio's faults, Irvingites reiterated what they had said of Hamlet and Richelieu—that he was careful, cold, and scholarly, mechanical and tricky, an accomplished actor merely and not a genius; that he failed in great moments of passion because he was not deep, powerful, or "tragic" enough, and that he lacked those all-important "touches of Nature." Booth supporters, to the contrary, found him spontaneous and sympathetic, natural and not at all pedantic. He reached the height of tragic force, they insisted, and brought tears to their eyes. His was "an art which concealed art" (*Morning Advertiser*, 1 January 1881). Thus, foes and friends among the London critics waged their ongoing debate, which precludes a clear London verdict, but sharpens our portraiture of Bertuccio.

That Booth still exerted himself in the acrobatics of the role is confirmed by the complaints of the London detractors. *The Times* (28 December 1880) found his cavorting and leaping about excessive for an older character, even a court jester, while the *Referee* (2 January 1881) thought such gamboling inappropriate for a dignified tragedian. Clement Scott, Irving's most ardent supporter, took the odd position of blaming Booth for being himself and not a court fool. "It was not a deformed creature, but a clever man imitating one; it was not a jester, but a facile actor reproducing the tricks of an eccentric" (*LDT*, 28 December 1880). Booth admirers thought his physicalization ingenious and exciting, and it spoke not only of his occupation and his deformity, but his state of mind: "The ambling gait of the crooked jester, too, so wondrously manipulated to express agony or mirth, a thrill of horror, or laughter. . . . Every antic, every twist of the gnarled body in passion or in glee, is a separate study.

The varied waving of the jester's wand is as full of meaning as a thing of life" (*ISD*, 15 January 1881). Physically, Booth was perfect for the jester, said the critic of the *Illustrated London News* (1 January 1881), neither too tall, like some "hulking Touchstones," nor so "comely" as some Rigolettos he had seen. His appearance as the misshapen jester was thoroughly realistic, and his endurance through three acts of grueling effort to simulate a cripple was astounding.

Bertuccio's tender encounter with his daughter in act two, a disputed scene among American critics, drew harsh responses from the British. *Pan* (1 January 1881) thought Booth vocally extravagant and shrill, more like Macbeth seeing Banquo than a grieving father, and Clement Scott, who obviously attended another night's performance, acknowledged Booth's "elocutionary grace" and rich voice, but failed to find him moving (*LDT*, 28 December 1880). Even critics who deemed Booth sufficiently artless and touching found this scene wanting.

Many Irvingites fairly pounced on the famous third scene, where, as the critic of the *Illustrated Sporting and Dramatic News* (29 July 1882) points out, "any actor of genius" would attain the "full standard of impressiveness." Booth, in his estimation, did not. The *Observer* (2 January 1881) found the scene merely interesting; the *Standard* (28 December 1880) complained of Booth's shrieking, and the *Stage* (1 January 1881) thought some of his transitions from hysterical laughter to a wail of pain were absolutely fine. All of a sudden, the artifice of the actor had disappeared. this critic protested—he created almost a mirror image of himself, thanks to the old-fashioned symmetrical furniture arrangement, which Booth ought to abandon.

The majority of the British critics, however, like their American counterparts, considered this scene the high point of Booth's performance. The *London Figaro* (1 January 1881) proclaimed it a bold *tour de force* of exceptional power and originality, and even Clement Scott abandoned his tone of indictment to give this "daringly eccentric" scene his full endorsement: "The hunchback danced and hopped about and screamed. He was more on wires than ever; he laughed and cried almost in the same breath; . . . and some of his transitions from hysterical laughter to a wail of pain were absolutely fine. All of a sudden, the artifice of the actor had disappeared. . . . We saw the man Bertuccio worked up to the passion and agony of the dramatic moment" (*LDT*, 28 December 1880).

After his second London engagement, Booth scheduled *The Fool's Revenge* for all the major stops on his tour of the English provinces, where attendance was given an unexpected boost by the flurry over a revival of *Le Roi s'amuse* in Paris, its first production there since its banning fifty years before. What Irvingites had denounced in London, Booth's "elocutionary grace" in particular, endeared him to the more conservative provincials. His Bertuccio, so powerful, so sympathetic, they contended, was the perfect answer to those carping critics who faulted Booth for coolness and "icy polish" (*Birmingham Daily*, 14 December 1882).

When Booth returned to America in 1883, he pleased Bostonians with several consecutive seasons which included Bertuccio, and in the years to follow, under Lawrence Barrett's management, *The Fool's Revenge* figured prominently in the repertoire, sharing a place on the bill in a curtailed version with *Yorick's Love*, *The King's Pleasure*, or *David Garrick*, when he co-starred with Barrett, and with *Donna Diana* in his season with Helena Modjeska. Although he continued to gather accolades for his characterization, by 1887 Booth was reportedly playing Bertuccio with "subdued force," and saving himself in the first two acts for the great climax of the third. In his last two seasons, when his powers were clearly failing, his voice became "light" and the "gymnastics" of the role understandably less impressive, although, it was insisted, none of the essential fine points of that portrait were missing.[32]

In retrospect, Booth-Bertuccio remains an anomaly. To be sure, he possessed certain traits in common with other Booth characters—subtlety and fiendishness like Iago or paternal affection like Shylock—but he was also the very antithesis of Booth's greatest character, Hamlet, for Bertuccio was without conscience, without doubts or reservations, a ruthless demon in his drive for vengeance, though his cause was no greater than the Dane's. Witty and mercurial in mood like Richelieu, he had none of that character's grandeur and stateliness. Compared to his other most popular creations, highborn and elegant, informed by the ideality which was at the center of Booth's aesthetic, Bertuccio remained a low-life creature, abnormal, but intensely real, and marked by a grotesqueness which set him apart from all others. The jester's profession made him a sanctioned role-player, inherently theatrical and eccentric, and Booth seized on this aspect of the character to re-create Bertuccio with an unaccustomed boldness and abandon.

A British critic audaciously suggested that Bertuccio was a role which "played itself," an odd conclusion when one considers that only Booth and Phelps ever succeeded in it. The kernel of truth in this assertion is that Bertuccio was immediately comprehensible and demanded no deep analysis of text, but was complex and difficult only in execution. The subtlety and force of Booth's flesh and blood creation owed but little to the slender frame Taylor provided. But to realize Booth's conception of the role—the versatility it demanded in those widely contrasting personae, the extraordinary intensity of feeling to be sustained, and the flexibility and sheer physical stamina required—took an actor of Booth's exceptional skills.

Bertuccio required virtuosity, but it was not virtuosity which burned the image of the wild dance around Torelli and the pathetic father's plea into so many memories. Whereas second-rate actors who essayed the role in the eighties intensified the grotesque aspects of Bertuccio, Booth always made audiences conscious of the injustices he had suffered. They could see the man beneath the motley. There was an undefinable "subjective element," one critic ventured, which lifted Booth's impersonation above the level of the written character (*Home Journal*, 12 April 1871). Booth's Bertuccio had a "soulful look," a British critic observed, a look which was a part of all his roles, "and it is this look which wins our sympathies."[33] When our hearts go out to him, another critic concluded, it is not because of Bertuccio's qualities, which repulse us, but because of the beauty of Booth's playing and the presence of Booth's own deeply hidden personality.

NOTES

1. Charles H. Shattuck, *The Hamlet of Edwin Booth* (Urbana: University of Illinois Press, 1970), 52.

2. In addition to Shattuck's perspective on the character in *The Hamlet of Edwin Booth*, 39–40, see Daniel J. Watermeier, "Edwin Booth's Richelieu," *Theatre History Studies* 1 (1981):1–19.

3. George C. D. Odell records single performances of *The Fool's Revenge* by three undistinguished actors during the period of Booth's career: Edwin Byron at the Broadway Theatre on 20 May 1878; Frederick Paulding ("an adolescent") at the Lyceum Theatre on 17 February 1879; and George C. Miln ("that clerical error turned actor") at the Academy of Music on 16 February 1884. *See* George C. D. Odell, *Annals of the New York Stage*, 15 vols. (New York: Columbia University Press, 1927–49), 10:405, 590 and 12:369.

4. Principal sources for this study include four Booth promptbooks and six scrapbooks of newspaper clippings and programs dating from 1861 to Booth's death from the Booth-Hampden Memorial Library, The Players, and miscellaneous unbound clippings and programs from the Booth Collection at the New York Public Library Theatre Collection, Lincoln Center (*NYPL*).

5. For a detailed account of the circumstances surrounding the writing and early reception of *The Fool's Revenge*, see Winton Tolles, *Tom Taylor and the Victorian Drama* (New York: Columbia University Press, 1940), 223–30.

6. For a description of Phelps's production and reception, see Shirley S. Allen, *Samuel Phelps and Sadler's Wells Theatre* (Middletown, Conn.: Wesleyan University Press, 1971), 290–92. Wybert Rousby, actor-manager from the Isle of Jersey, first appeared in *The Fool's Revenge* on 19 December 1869 at the Queen's Theatre. Taylor had more or less sponsored this London appearance on account of Rousby's lovely wife, Clara, for whom Taylor created the role of Elizabeth in *'Twixt Axe and Crown* (Tolles, 234–35). In the 1890s, E. S. Willard took his Bertuccio to America, presumably after showing it to his countrymen. For further information, see Montrose Moses, "History of Famous Plays: *The Fool's Revenge*," *Theatre Magazine* 8 (June 1908):169–70.

7. Asia Booth Clarke, *The Elder and the Younger Booth* (Boston: James R. Osgood, 1882), 152–53. Clarke establishes 1860 as the year of Booth's Philadelphia debut at the Arch Street Theatre under manager William Wheatley, while a review of the *Boston Transcript* for that same year reveals September 24 as the date of his first appearance as Bertuccio at the Howard Atheneum.

8. Edwin Booth to Lawrence Barrett, 21 November 1860, in Otis Skinner, *The Last Tragedian* (New York: Dodd Mead, 1939), 134–35.

9. Unidentified clipping, 1 January 1871, Booth Scrapbook, 1861–1873.

10. Beginning on 14 January 1867, Booth gave several performances of *The Fool's Revenge*, which subsequently eluded the memories of nearly all the critics of the 1871 production—William Winter included—who persistently recalled that the play had not been done for seven years.

11. Clarke, 153. The establishment of the late 1860s as the time of this revision is based on a comparison of the four Booth promptbooks housed at The Players. The earliest promptbook, which employs the Lacy Acting Edition, contains the time of the piece as performed in 1867 at the National Theatre, Cincinnati, Ohio, and shows some of the deletions of later acting versions, while still retaining the original ending. The tragic ending first emerges in promptbooks two and three, partly in pencil, partly in typescript, since the Booth-Hinton Acting Edition which they employed was first printed in 1868–1869 and still retained the original ending. Promptbook two includes a cast list from the 1871 production and number three, a playbill from the 1872 revival, so presumably these promptbooks were in use in the early 1870s. The fourth promptbook, a souvenir transcription by J. B. Pitman for Russ Whytal which uses the Booth-Winter Promptbook Edition (1878), contains the tragic ending.

12. The *Sun Times* reports that "many of the most beautiful scenes" of *Romeo and Juliet* were seen again in *The Fool's Revenge*, but were welcomed as "pleasing and realistic."

13. Hugo's play in translation had never been able to sustain the interest of American or English audiences. The *New York Times* of 29 March 1864 notes that

New Yorkers had seen it as a "Bowery drama" under the title of *The Court Jester*. Another translation, *The Court Fool*, which appeared in New York on 24 April 1852 and was believed to be W. E. Burton's version of the same title, first appeared in London at Sadler's Wells Theatre on 11 May 1840 (Ralph Hartmann Ware, "American Adaptations of French Plays on the New York and Philadelphia Stages" [Ph.D. diss., University of Pennsylvania, 1930], 20–21). Three other reportedly faithful translations were known to Londoners: *The King's Fool* (with Mr. Warde at the Victoria), *The Jester's Daughter*, and *The King's Buffoon* (*Dispatch* [London], 2 January 1881).

14. See Francesco Maria Piave, *Rigoletto*, in *Seven Verdi Librettos*, trans. William Weaver (New York: Norton, 1975), 7–77; Victor Hugo, *The King's Amusement*, trans. Frederick L. Slous, in *The Works of Victor Hugo* (Boston: Little, Brown, 1901), 1:276–356. Taylor defends his new play in the preface to the first edition of *The Fool's Revenge* in *Historical Dramas*, hereafter abbreviated *HD*, (London: Chatto & Windus, 1877), iii–iv. All further quotations from the play will be followed by page numbers in the text. For a discussion of Taylor's nomenclature, see Tolles, 20.

15. "Revenge in kind, to quit him—wife for wife" (Taylor, 31). Booth cut this line in the Booth-Winter Promptbook edition.

16. Except where otherwise indicated, statements regarding Booth's acting version are based on promptbook four, the Pitman promptbook, which employed the Booth-Winter Promptbook edition of the play.

17. Henry Austin Clapp refers to this practice in lamenting Booth's expurgation of lines which underscored the coarseness of Sir Giles Overreach and his readiness to sacrifice his daughter's honor (Clapp, "Edwin Booth in Some Non-Shakespearean Parts," *Outing* [June 1885], 349).

18. Compare Taylor, 21, and Hugo, 298–99.

19. Booth interpolates the words, "I'll sing, I'll dance" into the curtain speech to avoid contradiction between his exalted antics and Taylor's simple directive, "walk."

20. The notion that Booth "became" his characters, observed repeatedly by admiring critics, is discussed at length by Henry Austin Clapp in a retrospective on Booth's career in "Edwin Booth," *Atlantic Monthly* 72 (September, 1893):312.

21. Unidentified clipping, "Edwin Booth in 'The Fool's Revenge' at the Opera House," Pittsburgh, January 1887, Booth Scrapbook, 1886–1887. The anecdote is repeated in shorter form in Edwin Milton Royle, "Edwin Booth as I Knew Him," *Harpers* 132 (1916):839–49 and in Royle's book, which repeats the article title.

22. For a reprint of W. J. Hennessy's drawing of Booth as Bertuccio and an extensive discussion of deformity in the character, see William Winter, *The Life and Art of Edwin Booth* (New York: Macmillan, 1893), 228–31.

23. The most revealing descriptions of the jester could be found in London

reviews, among them: *Reynolds*, 2 January 1881; *Illustrated Sporting and Dramatic News*, 15 January 1881; *Bell's Weekly Messenger*, 3 January 1881; the *Globe*, 25 July 1882; *Society*, 29 July 1882. Odell notes in reference to an 1876 appearance by Booth that he brought out *The Stranger* "to relieve the strain of Bertuccio" (Odell, 10:204).

24. Unidentified clipping, New Orleans, 17 February 1887, Booth Scrapbook, 1886–1887.

25. Unidentified clipping, 4 April 1871, Booth Scrapbook, 1880–1882.

26. Unidentified clipping, "An Abrupt Transition," St. Louis, 1886, Booth Scrapbook, 1886–1887.

27. Unidentified clipping, "Footlight Flashes," San Francisco, 1876, NYPL.

28. "New York (City) Booth's Theatre Stage Plans and Settings of Scenery for Plays Performed at Booth's Theatre" on spine; Benson Sherwood's stage plan book for 191 performances (including 20 by Booth) during the 1873, 1874, 1878, 1881, 1882, 1883, and 1884 seasons at Booth's Theatre and the Fifth Avenue Theatre where he worked as stage manager and machinist.

29. Unidentified clippings, "Footlight Flashes" and "Amusements," San Francisco, 1876, NYPL.

30. During the 1880s Booth secured two London engagements, the first at the Princess's (6 November 1880–21 March 1881), under manager Walter Gooch, where he performed Bertuccio for three weeks (28 December 1880–16 January 1881); the second at the Adelphi Theatre (26 June–5 August 1882), where he presented four weeks of *Richelieu* and two of *The Fool's Revenge*. Charles Brooke, who had designed the new sets for the refurbished Princess's, was also responsible for the "entirely new" settings at the Adelphi and Samuel Mays designed costumes. A different company, assembled for the 1882 tour by Booth's manager, Wynn Miller, was better received than their predecessors at the Princess's. Since critical opinion about this role shifted little between engagements, I have drawn from reviews of both engagements in assessing the critical reception.

31. For one of many examples, see Edwin Booth to David C. Anderson, 14 November 1880, in Edwina Booth Grossman, *Edwin Booth: Recollections by his Daughter and Letters to his Friends* (London: Osgood, McIlvaine & Co., 1894), 214–15.

32. Unidentified clipping, Booth Scrapbook, 1888–1892.

33. "Plays and Players," *Society* (London), 29 July 1882.

James O'Neill's Launching of *Monte Cristo*

Myron Matlaw

For almost thirty years, beginning in 1883, James O'Neill toured *The Count of Monte Cristo* in virtually every city and town in the United States, crisscrossing the continent. According to one estimate, the play eventually was seen by well over fifteen million people and ultimately grossed O'Neill almost eleven million dollars—a phenomenal success for the age, even if the actual figures were to amount to only half this much.[1] *Monte Cristo*, as the play was usually featured on the billboards, was one of the nineteenth century's greatest hits. It was invariably associated with O'Neill, and "the world is mine," Edmund Dantes's exultant shout as he extricates himself from the sack in which he is hurled from the Château d'If prison fortress into the sea, became a household phrase.

Although O'Neill's repertoire included many Shakespearean as well as other roles, his stardom is inextricably identified with this melodrama. With his various companies, O'Neill reappeared in it night after night, for over four thousand performances. Not surprisingly, he himself thought it was over six thousand; it surely must have felt like it! Whenever he starred in other roles, audiences clamored for his return to the old warhorse, whose stage business and dialogue, especially the famous shout, became increasingly hateful to him. Again and again O'Neill attempted to extricate himself from the fetters of *Monte Cristo*. But unlike Edmund Dantes, he failed in his escape attempts. The aging and increasingly weary star kept "dripping with salt and sawdust, climbing a stool behind the swinging profile of the dashing waves," as his playwright-son Eugene many years later recalled the scene and the play that became traumatic to both father and son: "The calcium lights in the gallery played on his long

James O'Neill about the time of the launching of *Monte Cristo*. (Billy Rose Theatre Collection, The New York Public Library at Lincoln Center, Astor, Lenox and Tilden Foundations.)

beard and tattered clothes as with arms outstretched he declared that the world was his."[2]

It had all started innocuously enough. In the beginning of 1883, O'Neill was touring in upstate New York, alternating *A Celebrated Case*, "the greatest of all Union Square Successes," in the words of the program puffs, with C. T. Dazey's *The American King*. The latter did not, however, turn out to be the hit O'Neill had been hoping for.[3] This played right into the hands of John Stetson, the generally disliked and suddenly hard-pressed manager of Booth's Theatre in New York.

Though he was charitable and kind, Stetson had a rough exterior. He was contentious and considered foul-mouthed even in a milieu not particularly notable for its gentility. As O'Neill diplomatically put it, "I've met smoother-mannered men, and he sometimes thoughtlessly uses to his people the word that Senator Nye argued was a term of endearment in Nevada."[4] Yet to O'Neill, who never forgot having been left destitute early in his career by a manager who disappeared with the company coffers, Stetson was known to be a man who kept his word. "Stetson," O'Neill remarked to that San Francisco reporter, "always pays salaries down on the nail."

In the first days of 1883, John Stetson was facing major difficulties. His year at the theatre on the corner of Sixth Avenue and Twenty-third Street, the theatre Edwin Booth had so hopefully built—and soon lost—as a national showcase for great drama, had started out well. Following successful appearances by Madame Modjeska in two French hits, *Odette* and *Frou-Frou*, the ever-popular Charles Thorne, Jr., O'Neill's Union Square rival as a romantic lead, was to star in a series of melodramas. The first was Dion Boucicault's *The Corsican Brothers*, that curious psychological drama of ghosts and duels. Two nights after he opened at Booth's Theatre on January 6, however, Thorne succumbed to an attack of rheumatic gout. The attack was so severe that both Thorne and Stetson almost at once realized that any further appearances would be impossible.

Stetson, perhaps at the suggestion of Thorne himself, dashed off a telegram which was handed to O'Neill in the Rochester theatre on January 9: "Will you play the 'Corsican Brothers,' at Booth's theater, and when can you begin, and what salary, for balance of season? Thorne ill, and compelled to resign his position. If you will entertain it telegraph me quick. JOHN STETSON."

Valuing his independence, O'Neill sent a curt reply which, along with the text of Stetson's telegram, was duly publicized the next morning: "No."[5]

In the meantime, back in New York City, the aging understudy in Stetson's production, F. C. Bangs, was now playing the swashbuckling double leads of Fabian and Louis dei Franchi, the two Corsican brothers. But despite Stetson's puffs in newspaper advertisements that boasted of "crowded houses," the play's "continual success" and "perfect performances"—and "the greatest hit of the year"—the production merely hobbled along. Stetson was in a bind. No suitable replacement for Thorne seemed available, yet he simply had to find a star attraction to fill his house for the next scheduled play, *Monte Cristo*. Since James O'Neill was the obvious choice, the business manager of Booth's Theatre suggested that Stetson try again. They knew that O'Neill was scheduled to perform only five more days upstate before swinging his tour to various midwestern cities, beginning on the 25th. Why not take a train to Albany, where he was performing just then (January 18–20)?

And that's exactly what Stetson proceeded to do.

The two men had a long talk, and Stetson's final offer of $400 a week proved too tempting to resist.[6] In later years O'Neill recalled, in the fulsome public manner in which he invariably embellished past events, that Stetson made various proposals for a vehicle, all of which O'Neill considered unacceptable. "What will you do then?" Stetson is supposed to have asked him, impatiently. "'I will try to get Fechter's version of "Monte Cristo,"' I said, 'and manage myself.' 'I have a Fechter's version in my desk at Boston. I will have you open in that,'" he quotes Stetson as having said, whereupon O'Neill remembers replying, "Now you're talking business."[7]

The *Monte Cristo* version O'Neill referred to here was that of Charles Fechter, the renowned Anglo-French Shakespearean actor who was popular also in swashbuckling roles such as Monte Cristo. Although many, including Dumas himself, had attempted to transform the long, multiplotted work into a manageable evening's entertainment, Fechter alone really succeeded in this attempt. His first performance was panned, but Fechter further abridged and streamlined the play, whereupon it became a longplaying London hit.[8]

It was to remain one of Fechter's most successful productions. He continued to perform it, in England and America, until just four months before his death in 1879. Here he sold the play to his friend Arthur Cheney, one of the proprietors of Boston's Globe Theatre, where Fechter (as O'Neill was to do later) had repeatedly performed the play. When O'Neill waged his most desperate legal battle to retain exclusive rights to that version many years later, it was revealed that in 1877, Cheney had sold the script to another proprietor of that theatre, John Stetson.[9]

So while O'Neill's imaginative recollection of his agreement with Stetson may be true enough as far as the availability of the script and Stetson's desk are concerned, what had actually happened that January is somewhat different.

To O'Neill, his commitment to *Monte Cristo* was intended to be for only a few weeks, or at most until the end of the current season. That he had no inkling of what the play was to do to his subsequent career is evident from what transpired at another meeting, on Saturday (January 20), after he had seen Stetson. It was then that he and Dazey, the author of *The American King*, concluded and signed their contract under which, for a royalty fee of fifty dollars per week, O'Neill was to give that play preference in his repertoire.[10] Then the star took his company to the Academy of Music in his native Buffalo for two performances of *A Celebrated Case*, and then to Youngstown, Ohio, where the company opened on the twenty-fifth of January.

It was a busy two weeks for O'Neill: after Youngstown, he had two days in Akron, and only Sunday to get back to Chicago for his week's engagement, starting on the twenty-ninth at the Academy of Music. Although this was not one of Chicago's leading theatres, its manager was making every effort to make it one. Noting the excellence of the costumes and scenery as well as the crowded houses, the *Chicago Tribune* concluded that he was well on the way to succeeding in his attempt—with the help of James O'Neill. In *A Celebrated Case*, the play he gave throughout this engagement, O'Neill was highly praised by the *Chicago Tribune* for his "remarkable power and force": "he invests the character [of Jean Renaud] with power and pathos that stamp him a genuine and thorough actor" (30 January 1883, p. 6).

Even as O'Neill was completing this Chicago engagement, Stetson was in the midst of preparing "on a grand scale" for the mounting of *Monte Cristo* in New York.[11] Striving to rival the magnificent setting of *The Corsican Brothers*, which was now concluding its run, Stetson announced in his hyperbolic news releases that he hired the scene designer Joseph Clare to construct sets "made to fit closely the elaborate description of Dumas." These sets, as reviewers later agreed, were indeed grandiose—whether they considered them "gaudy" and "inappropriate" (*New York Daily Tribune*) or "fine" and "beautiful" (*New York Dramatic Mirror*). The company—excepting O'Neill himself—began rehearsing at the end of January, and the first advertisements of O'Neill's appearance as Monte Cristo appeared in the New York newspapers on Monday, February 5—exactly one week before the premiere, and the day on which O'Neill left Chicago after his very successful engagement there.

"Mr. O'Neill will appear as Edmund Dantes," the *New York Times* had reported the previous day in a news item (p. 5) that elaborated on the prominent Booth's Theatre advertisements. The item continued, with unintended ironies that emerge only in retrospect, that "this revival . . . ought to be interesting. Mr. O'Neill is an excellent actor who is too seldom seen here. He may be counted upon to do good work in a character like Dantes." The opening, it was announced, would take place on February 12—the very day that, after complications that culminated in an internal hemorrhage and death, Thorne's funeral took place.

The rush of events now was such that O'Neill had little time to prepare for the production. Precise information about his trip to New York is unavailable today. But we know that he was delayed by a snowstorm en route, and got to New York only on the Friday before Monday's opening. As soon as he arrived he started rehearsing with Stetson's company, all day long, throughout the weekend. Each night, after eight to nine hours of rehearsals with the company that ended at seven o'clock, he ate his supper and then retired to his rooms, fatigued but compelled to spend further hours studying the many long lines of Edmund Dantes, the later Count of Monte Cristo.

O'Neill was always handicapped by a congenital inability to learn lines quickly. Frantic, he now implored Stetson to postpone the premiere. But after four weeks of substitutions and crises, Stetson was intractable about facing any delays. Instead, he reassured O'Neill, who had reason to be even more jittery than actors customarily are about opening night reviewers. "I know all the newspaper boys," Stetson placated him, promising "to tell them that you had only three rehearsals" (Patterson, ix).

And so, a few moments after eight P.M. on 12 February 1883, a clear, bright day that, with a cheerful augury for our star, finally ended the earlier "threatening clouds and murky atmosphere," according to the *New-York Daily Tribune* weather report, the curtain rose, as planned and announced, on *Monte Cristo*.

Its opening that Monday night was far from the notable event it subsequently became in theatrical annals. In that week, it was but one of a number of tempting New York attractions. Some of these strangely foreshadowed O'Neill's own subsequent career and life. The internationally renowned Italian Tommaso Salvini, for example, who nine years later attempted to rival O'Neill's by-then long-established vehicle of *Monte Cristo* with one of his own, that week, in his "farewell season" at the Academy of Music, was starring as Othello and King Lear—both of whom O'Neill, as he grew older, frequently quoted and identified with as classical personifications of his own very private tragedies. Salvini's third play that week was Robert Montgomery Bird's then still-popular *The Gladiator*, which had been the great vehicle of Edwin Forrest—who, as O'Neill was frequently to recall in later years, had perceived a glorious future for him back when O'Neill, at the very beginning of his acting career, had a walk-on part with Forrest.

O'Neill's life and career are a pervasive and integral part of nineteenth-century American theatre history, and similarly ironic overtones are only now apparent in some of that night's other competing productions. At the Union Square Theatre, for example, just ten blocks from Booth's Theatre where O'Neill was making his appearance, an even greater actor was just making *his* equally epoch-making appearances in one of A. R. Cazauran's many adaptations, *A Parisian Romance*; acting the part of the "decrepit old rake" Baron Chevrial, young Richard Mansfield had just become a star overnight. A few years later, as a regular Connecticut summer resident accepted by New London's "higher society" as the O'Neills never were, the haughty Mansfield was to be a constant irritant to the O'Neills and particularly to James, who keenly perceived Mansfield as a living reproach to himself and his own circumscribed later career.

At the Grand Opera House, Denman Thomas played in the rural New England melodrama *Joshua Whitcomb*; its homespun title character, like O'Neill's Monte Cristo, was to become Thompson's virtually sole part and his trademark for the rest of his life in this vehicle, which he himself soon embellished as *The Old Homestead*.

New Yorkers crowded yet other notable competing productions that night. The renowned John Drew and Ada Rehan starred at Daly's Theatre "in their original creations" in *The Squire*. Haverley's Theatre presented Anson Pond's "new American play," *Her Atonement*, a lugubrious murder mystery whose advertisements boasted of a "sterling cast, splendid new scenery, 200 auxiliaries, military band—fife and drum corps." Among the "musicals," the D'Oyly Carte Opera Company was concluding its tour with Gilbert and Sullivan's newest hit, *Iolanthe*. With a touch of the Irish always so dear to O'Neill's heart, the long-popular team of Harrigan and Hart was delighting Théâtre Comique audiences with *McSorley's Inflation*.

And in another Irish offering, "the popular, original dialect comedian" J. K. Emmet, at the Cosmopolitan Theatre, was entertaining audiences with *Write in Ireland*.

At Booth's Theatre, that evening, a few minutes after eight, James O'Neill, as young Edmund Dantes, debarked in Marseilles and embraced his Mercedes.

Monte Cristo's popularity is easy to understand. Its story has the ageless appeal of sudden acquisition of immense riches and power, injustice avenged, suffering virtue rewarded. There is romantic passion, too, though its agonizing heartaches and ultimate resolution in the play, at least, are not clearly depicted. The story is long and full of suspense and excitement. It includes many heroes and villains, a great deal of action, and a series of subplots with poignant love stories that furnish the always popular tearful sentimentality.

It is a story that was very familiar to O'Neill's audiences. Dumas's novel had been read in America for almost half a century, and as early as 1848, long before Fechter's popular dramatization, it had been seen here in various other, often quite spectacular productions. O'Neill himself had played Edmund Dantes/Monte Cristo in 1875 during his Chicago stint, as had such once-prominent stars as the last and perhaps greatest of the Wallack dynasty, John Lester; the Bowery Theatre's favorite, Edward Eddy; and the distinguished E. L. Davenport, whom William Winter praised for his extraordinary "power and versatility."[12] The story was even more popular in Europe, particularly in France, where it was repeatedly staged, and where it had appeared in many editions and translations.

It has had countless numbers of readers, its great appeal continuing well into this century, right until World War II.[13] Of its many celluloid versions, the best known is the 1934 film starring Robert Donat and Elissa Landi. Performed, too, on radio and television, *Monte Cristo*, starring Richard Chamberlain, was presented as a two-hour NBC Bell System Family Hour Television Special in 1974, and rerun thereafter.

But though the enthralling adventures of Edmund Dantes are still seen and read today, the story is no longer as familiar as it was once. Those who read it as youngsters, or saw it on the screen, certainly will remember the climactic escape scene described earlier. They may remember, too, the machinations of two of Dantes's enemies as soon as this handsome young sailor lands in Marseilles: his shipmate, Danglars, jealous of Edmund's promotion to the captaincy by the kind-hearted shipowner Morel; and Dantes's rival for the hand of Mercedes, the shifty Fernand. While the lovers are joyously reunited and rush off to prepare for their marriage, Danglars and Fernand, drinking themselves into an ever greater anger in the inn of the already drunk Caderousse, write their anonymous denunciation of Dantes, who is unaware that the sealed letter he is about to deliver to one Noirtier is from Napoleon Bonaparte, plotting a return from his exile in Elba.

The remainder of O'Neill's version of *Monte Cristo*, like Fechter's, omitted much of the novel and camouflaged many of its more glaringly evident lapses in logic and credibility with theatrical thrills and suspense. It can be summarized quickly. Noirtier is a Napoleonic agent sought by the police—but turns out to be, as well, the stepbrother of the police chief, Villefort. To save his career, Villefort lets Noirtier escape and has Edmund arrested right in the midst of the latter's wedding. Though he knows Edmund to be completely innocent, he has him imprisoned in a dungeon in the notorious Château d'If.

Eighteen years later, when Noirtier reappears to demand Edmund's release, Villefort, so as not to jeopardize his imminent elevation to high state office, decides to murder both Noirtier (his stepbrother) and Dantes. He assures the faithful Mercedes that Edmund is dead, whereupon she finally agrees to marry Fernand, now Count de Morcerf, who in the many years of his courtship has supported both Mercedes and her son, Albert. Meanwhile, in the prison dungeon, Faria, the pious and apparently mad old prisoner in the adjoining cell with whom Edmund has been digging an escape tunnel, shrewdly deduces how and by whom Edmund was betrayed. Faria names Edmund sole heir to his hidden fortune and, realizing that he is about to die, instructs him on how to escape the prison fortress: he is to take Faria's place in the sack into which his corpse will be sewn.

After his escape, Edmund, now the Count of Monte Cristo and disguised as an abbé, learns from the repentant innkeeper Caderousse what had transpired during the eighteen years of his imprisonment at the Château d'If. Villefort fails in his attempt to murder Noirtier at this inn, and when Edmund appears, he kills himself. "One!" Edmund exclaims. (The "One!" "Two!" "Three!" exclamations that mark the fall of each of his enemies were another famous O'Neill–*Monte Cristo* trademark. O'Neill came to loathe them almost as much as "The Wor-r-r-l-d Is Mine!")

The newly arrived and fabulously rich but bitter Count of Monte Cristo mystifies all Paris except Mercedes, to whom he reveals himself. During a

James O'Neill as Edmund Dantes at the Château d'If. (Billy Rose Theatre Collection, The New York Public Library at Lincoln Center, Astor, Lenox and Tilden Foundations.)

grand ball, in one of the play's climactic scenes, he brings about Danglars's financial ruin and vows vengeance on Fernand through Albert. Then Mercedes reveals Albert to be not Fernand's but Edmund's own son (apparently conceived in sin, although that point is purposely left murky). Nonetheless, having "insulted" Albert with the public exposure of Fernand's (his putative father's) crimes, their duel is about to take place. Alone and conscience-stricken by his ruthless, unchristian vengeance, Edmund decides to let his son Albert kill him in the duel. But when he appears the youth apologizes: now he knows that Monte Cristo's charges against Fernand were indeed true.

The plot comes to a quick end: Edmund identifies himself to his remaining enemies. When Mercedes prevents Fernand's killing Edmund, Fernand shoots himself ("Two!"). Edmund then duels with Danglars and kills him ("Three!"). The curtain falls as Mercedes reveals to Albert "the secret of your birth," telling him to embrace Edmund: "You are his son!"

The play thus acted by O'Neill is considerably shorter and simpler than the novel. His typed acting script, bound in dark brown, well-worn, handsewn leather, gold-stamped "Property of James O'Neill," was donated by his son Eugene to the Museum of the City of New York, where it is now preserved. It is this same script that Fechter had used and sold to Cheney, the same script that was in Stetson's Boston desk that January day in 1883. Indeed the names Fechter, Cheney, and Stetson all appear on the typed title page, with their respective proprietary claims. James O'Neill's deletions, additions, and many changes in the script's dialogue and stage business are preserved in those typed pages; the last three pages are entirely in O'Neill's hand.

But that first night in 1883 he played Fechter's script exactly as it had been given him by Stetson. And just as had been true of Fechter's first London production in 1868, O'Neill's premiere was anything but a harbinger of the later success of *Monte Cristo*, nor did it indicate that O'Neill, like its young hero, was to gain such great wealth from it. As in Fechter's first performance, so in O'Neill's, the production ran far too long. Some of the more enterprising in the large audience, in fact, left the theatre during the intermission after 11 P.M. to make arrangements with neighboring caterers for an early morning breakfast. But actually the final curtain fell just about midnight.

The fault of the premiere's length lay not so much with the long script (later shortened) as with the stagehands' attempts to cope with the elaborate scenery. Stetson had been eager to dazzle the audience with lavish settings. And in that, as all accounts agree, he succeeded. The play opened to the cheers of the harbor crowds at the majestic arrival in Marseilles of the fully-rigged ship, bearing the young hero. Another colorful crowd scene followed almost immediately, at Edmund and Mercedes's wedding festivities. The Château d'If, its dungeons, and particularly the rolling ocean waves from which the drenched Edmund emerged, his hand brandishing the knife, his eyes blazing as his ringing voice proclaimed his triumph, seemed strikingly real in their menacing wetness. Again, during the Grand Fête when he exposes Fernand in the castle, a wide staircase that dominated the stage amply set off "the royal grace with which James O'Neill could walk down a staircase," according to George Tyler, his manager and later a major independent producer, in what became another of O'Neill's specialties in the play.[14] The only flaw in the otherwise "beautiful" settings was what supposedly represented the castle's tree archway: the use of box sets near the wings made the trees look curiously as if they lacked trunks. But in the impressively set finale in the forest, the tall trees and the little hut into which the various characters periodically retreated provided a striking background to the duel and the ultimate revelations.

Backstage, however, things were in a turmoil. The stagehands were not yet familiar with the many sets and props. Laboring amidst a bewildering conglomeration of primitive lighting fixtures, ropes, riggings, and heavy canvasses, some of which, for example, furnished the illusion of the rolling sea waves, they were slow in effecting the frequent set changes. As a result, the repeated delays between scenes and the four long intermissions separating the five acts seemed interminable to the impatient and thrill-seeking audiences. The more hardened newpaper reviewers were to be far more critical.

The supporting cast, although consisting of actors Stetson had chosen especially for this production, also left much to be desired. Although the exquisitely costumed Katherine Rogers was an established actress, she was not effective as Mercedes; a character critics readily conceded to be essentially stilted and colorless to begin with thus appeared even less interesting. H. Bradley's Villefort was, even in 1883, considered old-fashioned in his depiction of villainy, "talking as if the voice came from the region of the abdomen and . . . emitted with the acutest agony" (*NYDM*, 17 February 1883, p. 2). Some of the other actors were considered merely adequate; only Henry Lee, the Noirtier of the play, was really successful with

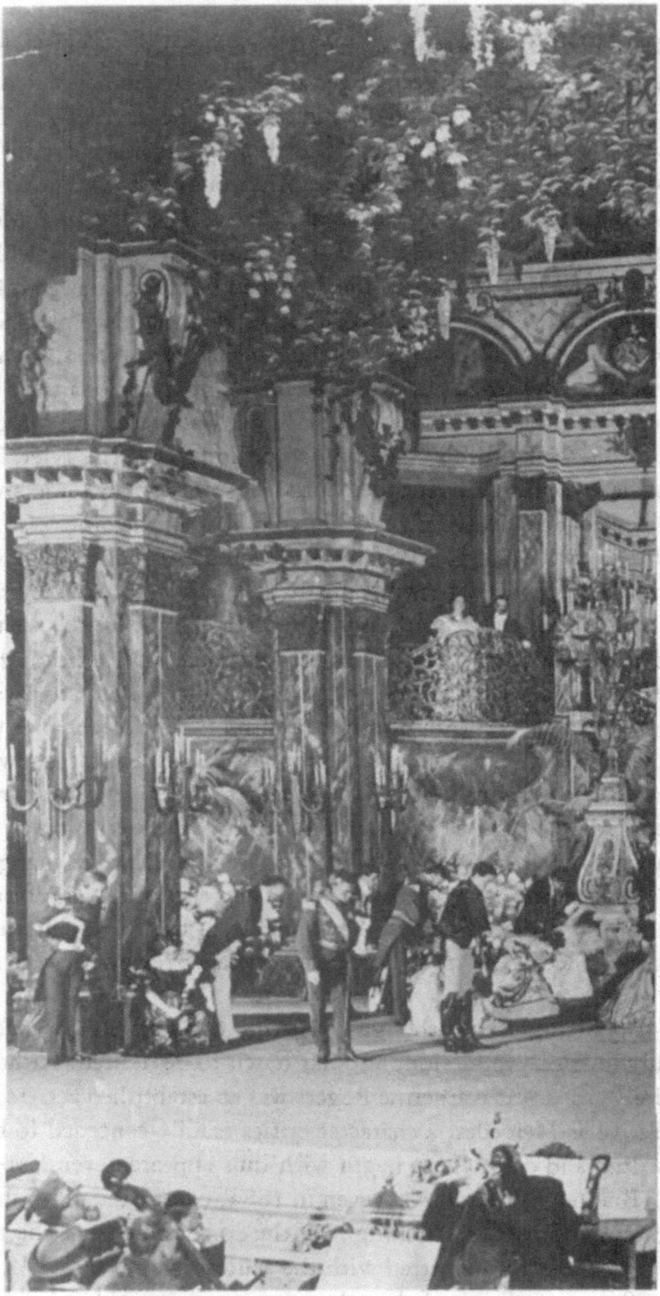

The magnificent ballroom scene. O'Neill (center) as the Count of Monte Cristo in his famous staircase descent. (By permission of the Theatre Collection, Museum of the City of New York.)

all the reviewers and the audience that night—especially in his many disguises, the most lustily applauded one being his appearance as a Jewish peddler.

The major problem was James O'Neill himself. His various costumes did indeed set off his figure to great advantage, and his renowned remarkable voice was as resonant as ever, at least much of the time. But his inadequate preparation, however frantically he had made use of every available minute of his limited rehearsal time, was painfully evident that night. He betrayed his insecurity in the role by his nervousness, stumbling over some of his lines and appearing unsure of some of the play's "business."

To make matters worse, Stetson in the rush of events had forgotten his promise to inform reviewers of O'Neill's inadequate rehearsal time. Thus the newspaper criticisms were ruthless. The play was "a failure, and . . . it deserved to fail," declared the *Spirit of the Times*, confidently predicting that it "will not run very long" (17 February 1883, p. 68). The *New York Daily Tribune* called it "a mechanical, business-like reproduction" (19 February 1883, p. 5), while the *New York Times* dismissed it as "tedious and awkward" (13 February 1883, p. 5). Many of the critics panned the elaborate ballet interpolated into the Grand Ball scene in act four, commenting on the near nudity and deficient art: "the clothing and accomplishments of the dancers were of the slightest," as the *Evening Post* put it succinctly (13 February 1883, p. 4).

It was O'Neill, however, who bore the brunt of the press criticisms, many of them laced with disappointment with the poor showing of this hitherto much-esteemed actor. Only the *New-York World* and the *Daily Graphic* found anything good to say about his acting, the former calling it "interesting and impressive" though not inspiring (13 February 1883, p. 5), and the latter finding his performance, if not as good as that of Fechter, "an excellent substitute" (13 February 1883, p. 717). The other critics were far less charitable: O'Neill was "fishing for his words, hesitating and stumbling," "quite ineffective" (*NYDM*, 17 February 1883, p. 2); "unsympathetic" and "inconsistent" (*NYDT*, 19 February 1883, p. 5); "especially disappointing" (*Sun*, 13 February 1883, p. 3); "uninteresting" (*EP*, 13 February 1883, p. 4); "tedious and awkward" (*NYT*, 13 February 1883, p. 5); lacking in "dash and romance" (NY *Clipper*, 17 February 1883, p. 778); and the unkindest cut of all, "without any Irish passion, sympathy, and magnetism" (*Spirit of the Times*, 17 February 1883, p. 68).

It should be noted, however, that at least some of these critics' disaffections were in fact unintentionally complimentary. Their invidious comparisons with Fechter and other earlier Monte Cristos focused on O'Neill's traces of the then-unfashionable mode of acting more congenial today. As in his other productions, O'Neill was an important precursor of the naturalistic style that was eventually to replace the flamboyant—what we would now consider excessively histrionic—style of the nineteenth century. The *New York Times* reviewer inadvertently made the point in a revealing comment: "Mr. O'Neill failed to make an impression of strength, because he applied to broad and dashing romantic action the restrained method of realism." And another witness later recalled O'Neill's performance as being "always picturesque, consistent in conception, surprisingly natural in view of the strained sentiment that he was called upon to speak. The characterization was not altogether wanting in superficial pathos, and the actor's skill in working up to and sustaining climaxes made the impersonation remarkably effective dramatically."[15]

Devastating though they were, O'Neill took these criticisms in stride and survived them. What is more, he readily acknowledged their validity. "The critics were right," he recalled in later years; "I was bad. I knew it" (Patterson, ix). And then, with characteristic tenacity, he devoted the next few days to many intensive hours of study in his rooms before he left for his evening performance. The very next morning, as the first newspaper reviews appeared, he sought and obtained important help: that of Lizzie Price, the widow of Charles Fechter. Having played Mercedes in some of her husband's productions, she was able to give O'Neill valuable information and pointers. James O'Neill learned quickly.

A number of reviewers had been perceptive enough to see that, as one of them emphasized, it was merely a matter of getting the stage machinery to work smoothly and the actors to become more familiar with and experienced in their parts before the play would "furnish a good evening's enjoyment." As far as the audience was concerned, however, even the flawed Monday production had already provided such an evening. "The public saved the life of the play," O'Neill later declared (Patterson, ix). Again, as had been true of Fechter's London production, notwithstanding critical rebuffs word of mouth had immediately made the play a hit: Tuesday's house, too, was packed.

Two weeks later, the newspapers reported that the production had "vastly improved." O'Neill "now gives a very satisfactory impersonation" (*NYDM*, 24 February 1883, p. 2). He was to refine it over the next few decades, and add many of the touches that characterized his Monte Cristo. His handsome and athletic appearance enhanced the swashbuckling heroics, and his magnificent bearing and voice—considered one of the finest ever heard on the American stage—contributed greatly to his success in the role. O'Neill's romantic scenes particularly affected the audiences. Amy Leslie, the well-known drama critic of the Chicago *Daily News*, gushed: "He could make love better than any man of his time and his airy grace, manliness and lovely voice . . . made him unique."[16] The stage machinery now worked smoothly, and even the ballet, which had been roundly criticized before, was praised once it acquired a much-needed premiere danseuse (Adele Cornalba). When the great Mary Anderson, "determined to have the best talent available for her English tour," invited O'Neill to join it as her leading man, he had already perceived the long-range possibilities of *Monte Cristo* and declined an offer he surely would have accepted eagerly only a few weeks earlier (*NYDM*, 3 March 1883, p. 6).

Booth's Theatre remained crowded during most of the run, enthusiastic audiences braving such still-familiar New York calamities as blizzards, public employee strikes, and even riots. It ended on March 17 only because the theater already had been slated for renovation—a mere month, it subsequently turned out, before its doors were to close forever.

But O'Neill's *Monte Cristo* had just begun its long career. It appropriately ended its first run in a blaze of Irish glory, with cheering audiences at a special matinee and then at the final evening performance making it a particularly festive Saint Patrick's Day for its chauvinistic star.

NOTES

1. Unidentified newspaper clipping, dated 12 August 1922, in the Theatre Collection of the New York Public Library.

2. Quoted in S. J. Woolf, "O'Neill Plots a Course for the Drama," *New York Times Magazine*, 4 October 1931:6.

3. A year later he is quoted as having found the play's construction faulty and asking Dazey, whose fame rests on his later play, *Old Kentucky*, to rewrite it. "I intend to bring it out the next season, perhaps," he remarked, according to the San Francisco *Morning Call*, 15 June 1884, "about the time the daisies bloom." See Patrick O'Neill, *James O'Neill*, Theatre Research Series, compiled by workers of the Writers' Program of the Work Projects Administration in Northern California (San Francisco, 1942), 20:93–94. *A Celebrated Case* (1878) is an adaptation of

Une Cause Célèbre, a popular French melodrama by Adolphe D'Ennery and Eugene Cormon. See also note 10, below.

4. San Francisco *Morning Call*, 16 June 1884; quoted in Patrick O'Neill, 97.

5. Rochester *Post Express*, 10 January 1883.

6. The meeting with Stetson is described in *New York Dramatic Mirror*, 3 February 1883, p. 6; the $400 figure, lower than the other publicized figure of $600 and therefore more likely to be accurate, is cited in *Chicago Tribune*, 6 February 1883, p. 7.

7. Quoted by Ada Patterson, "James O'Neill—the Actor and the Man," *Theatre Magazine* 8 (April 1908): ix. Hereafter cited in the text as Patterson.

8. For a detailed account of this and other versions of the play, see Myron Matlaw, "English and American Dramatizations of *Le Comte de Monte-Cristo*," *Nineteenth-Century Theatre Research* 7 (1979):39–53.

9. James O'Neill's copyright suit against the General Film Company appears in the *Reports* of the Supreme Court of the State of New York, Appellate Division, 171:854–69.

10. This meeting is described in the *New York Dramatic Mirror*, 27 January 1883, p. 8. See also note 3, above.

11. See *Daily Graphic*, 10 February 1883, p. 701.

12. William Winter, *The Life of David Belasco*, 2 vols. (New York: Moffatt, Yard, 1918), 1:197.

13. In the late nineteenth century it was among the most widely read books even in Russia. Turgenev immortalized it in the opening dialogue of *A Month in the Country*, when Natalya has her admirer Rakitin read it to her because a friend, amazed that she had not read *Monte Cristo*, urged her to do so. And in Samuel Beckett's 1951 novel *Molloy*, Moran says of his son: "Yes, he must have felt his soul the soul of a pocket Monte Cristo, with whose antics as adumbrated in the Schoolboys' Classics he was needless to say familiar" (Evergreen Black Cat edition of *Three Novels by Samuel Beckett: Molloy, Malone Dies, The Unnamable* [New York: Grove Press, 1965], 131). As recently as the 1980s the late Italian chemist and concentration camp survivor Primo Levi cited it as a socially influential work: "The concept of escape as a moral duty and the obligatory consequence of captivity is constantly reinforced by romantic (*The Count of Monte Cristo*) and popular literature" (*The Drowned and the Saved*, New York, 1988).

14. George C. Tyler and J. C. Furnas, *Whatever Goes Up—The Hazardous Fortunes of a Natural Born Gambler* (Indianapolis: Bobbs-Merrill, 1934), 150.

15. Lewis C. Strang, *Famous Actors of the Day*, 2d. ser. (Boston: L. C. Page, 1902), 173.

16. Unidentified newspaper clipping, the Beinecke Library, Yale University.

A Forgotten "Fallen Woman"
OLGA NETHERSOLE'S *SAPHO*

Joy Harriman Reilly

Olga Nethersole was an English actress-manager whose greatest triumphs were realized on the American stage. Her twenty-seven-year stage career began with her debut in Brighton in 1887; she made eleven major tours of America between 1894 and 1914 before she suddenly retired from the stage at the age of forty-four. For her efforts, America yielded the young entrepreneur a fortune, some real estate in the far west, and a reputation as one of the most exciting "emotional" actresses of her time.

At the height of her career, Olga Nethersole titillated *fin de siècle* audiences with her candid portrayals of scarlet women. Dressed in exquisite gowns and furs and exotic headpieces, and provocatively toying with "the decadent cigarette," she epitomized the Victorian view of the courtesan who entraps weak-willed young men with her serpentine charm. Nethersole made a career of playing Fallen Women, beginning with the Latin adventuress Lola Montez in *The Silver Falls* in London in 1888 when she was eighteen and ending with Maurice Maeterlinck's biblical *Mary Magdalene* in New York in 1910. The latter was a turning point in her career and precipitated her retirement from the stage. Her most famous "wicked women" were Alexandre Dumas's *Camille*, Henry Hamilton's *Carmen*, Arthur Wing Pinero's Paula in *The Second Mrs. Tanqueray*, and Fanny Legrand (alias Sapho) in Clyde Fitch's adaptation of Alphonse Daudet's novel *Sapho*. In the latter romantic melodrama she became for one brief moment in 1900 the most notorious actress on the American stage when her production at Wallack's Theatre in New York was closed down and she was arrested and hauled into court to answer a charge of lewd behavior.

It was not so much the plot (about a simple country boy seduced by a courtesan) which caused the uproar, but the Nethersole production. The lavish costumes and scenery were augmented by the use of a novel spiral staircase, which highlighted the dramatic ending to the first act, in which the young man is seen, in *tableau*, carrying the woman upstairs to a rendezvous in the bedchamber. This was enough to set off a storm of protest led by the evangelical fury of the daily newspaper, the *World*, which used the event and the sensational trial to boost its circulation. Conservative critic William Winter, in the *New York Tribune*, pronounced *Sapho* "a reeking compost of filth and folly," and a hotbed of "contemptible persons, gross proceedings, foul suggestion, impure pictures."[1] Despite such diatribes and the heated debate blown out of all proportion in the press, the court agreed with Nethersole's argument that the play taught a moral lesson—"As Ye Sow, So Shall Ye Reap"—and *Sapho* was allowed to continue. For the next few years the play's notoriety guaranteed huge profits at the box office.

The organized attacks on *Sapho* had a ripple effect, washing over other well-known performers in what were perceived to be suspect shows. Following "hundreds of letters" sent to police asking them to suppress Mrs. Leslie Carter in *Zaza*, Cleveland police raided the Euclid Avenue Opera House and found that the star was "indisposed," which kept her from finishing the engagement. Lillie Langtry, playing a woman of easy virtue in *The Degenerates*, ran into a hostile public at a Boston charity bazaar and was also the object of protest by the vigilant Women's Christian Temperance Union. Eventually her production was censored in New Jersey.[2] In the meantime, the Broadway Theatre featured its share of titillating shows, including *Coralie and Company, Dressmakers, Naughty Anthony, The Surprises of Love, Wheels Within Wheels, The Girl in the Barracks, Make Way for Ladies*, and *Mlle. 'Awkins*.[3] These had succeeded in infuriating the conservative element in the population to the point that the climate was ripe for a backlash against what was perceived as a new permissiveness. *Sapho* was merely the final straw that fueled a flame of moralistic fervor which had been building for some time.[4] When Nethersole found herself caught in this crossfire, she brought her own unerring professional instincts into play and eventually emerged victorious, and considerably richer, from a potentially disastrous confrontation with the press and her public.

Today, when Olga Nethersole is remembered, it is in that context, as Sapho, named for the legendary poetess of Lesbos. But Nethersole was an extraordinarily productive woman whose multi-faceted talents cannot be dismissed as culminating in one brief *cause célèbre*. She serves as an example of a self-made woman who rose to prominence as actress-manager in a profession dominated by men. She worked her way up from stagestruck neophyte with no theatrical background to become one of the most famous emotional actresses of the day.

Nethersole's performances left little to the imagination. Her powerful and passionate displays of emotional virtuosity were particularly suited to the mid-nineteenth-century Fallen Woman protagonist who typically went from chastely pure to sexually sinful, and various permutations of that role. This enabled the actress to demonstrate a wide range of emotions. The more psychologically complex and physically sophisticated New Woman of the emerging "modern drama" would not be so rewarding for a bravura array of passions. Nethersole's portrayals were characterized by such innovations as smoking a cigarette, blowing her nose, turning her back to the audience, crawling on hands and knees, showing bare feet, gruesome death scenes, fainting spells, and the "Nethersole Kiss."

As manager of her own company, Nethersole was a dynamic, forceful, and contentious woman at a time when the female equivalent of the autocratic actor-manager was practically nonexistent. She played a significant part in promoting young playwrights, while searching for new plays to showcase her talents. She had total artistic control over her productions, engaging her company, rehearsing the cast, and directing productions that featured spectacular scenery with antique furniture. Her designer-made gowns were purchased in Paris and London *haute couture* houses and, like those of other fashionable actresses, were responsible for setting fashion trends of the day.[5]

That her performances were also vigorously criticized by such influential drama critics as George Bernard Shaw in London and Edward A. Dithmar in New York for exaggerated mannerisms and old-fashioned acting technique did not stop their success at the box office. Nethersole was one of the international celebrities of the theatre who sipped tea at Buckingham Palace and dined at the White House. As a woman, she spoke out on such issues as emancipation and the divorce laws; as a fashion leader, she was admired for her sense of beauty and style. For at least six of her eleven American tours, Nethersole maintained her own personal railroad car, the "Iolanthe," at an annual cost of thirty-two thousand dollars, traveling an average of four hundred and eighty miles a week for thirty-eight weeks. On her first trip to the west coast in 1906, described somewhat extravagantly in the press as "the most important transcontinental tour ever undertaken by a foreign artist," she took with her a company of forty, to perform nine plays, requiring seven carloads of scenery and furniture (*Trib*, 12 December 1905). That she traveled across America in such grand style is an indication of her performing status and financial well-being. She regularly played the major cities for a week, sometimes two or four weeks, as well as three-days-plus-one-matinee in smaller cities and a grueling schedule of one-night stands at the less important stops. Thus, while not in the same class with Bernhardt or Duse, Nethersole was certainly as well known as Clara Morris and other contemporaries such as Mrs. Leslie Carter, Mrs. Patrick Campbell, and Ada Rehan. She was several notches above the journeymen actors who made a reasonable living on the regional circuits outside Manhattan.

Nethersole was a handsome woman who knew how to make the most of her hair, figure, and facial features, and used her sense of color and style to add excitement to her portrayals of Fallen Women. Although she gave the illusion of height on the stage, she was of medium build, with an excellent figure and a mass of chestnut hair with auburn highlights. Large eyes dominated a face which featured a Grecian nose and large mouth. *New York Times* correspondent Dithmar described her as an actress with a graceful figure, beautiful blue eyes, and a clear contralto voice (16 October 1894). Nethersole typified the Latin adulteress dressed in satins, furs, and precious jewels. There is a wonderful portrait of her in *Sapho*, lounging on a couch in a fur-trimmed embroidered red gown, with plumes and feathers in her hair. She gazes out at the world like an exotic bird of paradise, through heavy-lidded eyes, provocatively toying with a cigarette.[6]

Nethersole's image as the ultimate portrayer of Fallen Women received a major boost with her naturalism-inspired production of *Carmen*, which premiered at the Empire Theatre in New York on 24 December 1895 under the management of Daniel and Charles Frohman. She had commissioned her own version of the Prosper Merimée novel from Henry Hamilton, although the plot more closely followed Meilhac and Halévy's libretto for Bizet's *Carmen*. Nethersole's Carmen was a controversial, innovatively unromantic portrait of a calculating, streetwise trollop. The pretty gypsy of the opera version was replaced by a dirty cigarette girl. Nethersole's portrayal included an exit crawling off the stage, biting and scratching, a shrieking death scene, and the first prolonged "Nethersole Kiss." The notoriety of the kiss and the blatant sexuality of her feisty factory worker ensured sold-out houses on both sides of the Atlantic despite almost universal condemnation in the New York and London press. The

Olga Nethersole as "Sapho." (Courtesy of Joy Reilly.)

New York Dramatic Mirror exemplifies the tone of press reaction: "In view of the number and duration of the kisses she bestows it is not hard to understand why the men who impersonate the parts of her lovers have clean-shaven upper lips. An ordinary mustache subject to such treatment would soon be reduced to a shapeless hirsute mass. It is no exaggeration to assert that if Miss Nethersole were to reduce the duration of her kisses one-half, the performance would be over considerably more than a half hour before midnight" (4 January 1896). The kiss was a favorite topic in gossip columns, where it soon developed an identity of its own as "the Nethersole Kiss." It became the yardstick against which to measure how far an actress was prepared to take naturalistic detail, and as a hallmark of Nethersole's acting style, it naturally played its part in the *Sapho* controversy.

The *Sapho* affair began innocently enough as a promising vehicle for Nethersole, giving her a spectacular role created by a famous French writer and adapted by a popular American playwright to showcase her talents. She had such confidence in its success that she financed it entirely herself, providing it with lavish costumes and sets at a cost of four thousand pounds.[7] *Sapho* was given its world debut as part of Nethersole's fourth American tour in Chicago at the Powers Theatre on October 31. While the press reaction was mixed, less impressed with the play itself than with the costumes, setting, and displays of emotion by the star, the general public loved it. *Sapho* played to sold-out houses in Chicago and throughout the subsequent road tour to Milwaukee, Atlanta, Nashville, Louisville, New Orleans, Cincinnati, Cleveland, Detroit, and Pittsburgh, where local press criticism boomeranged into a colossal *cause célèbre*.

The effect of the *Sapho* controversy on ordinary people was startling, causing some of them to do most extraordinary things. In St. Louis, Jessaline Sweeter of the Hopkins Stock Company tried to commit suicide by swallowing carbolic acid rather than appear in the play (*NYDM*, 31 March 1900). In Chicago, two girls were sent to a house of correction for stealing copies of the book.[8] In Ann Arbor, a bookseller with a sense of drama publicly committed *Sapho* to the flames, while the Vandalia Railroad Company was moved to ban all copies of the offending volume from its newsstands (*NYDM*, 14 April 1900). Four hundred and fifty members of the Mormon Women's Christian Temperance Union marched in protest in Elizabeth, New Jersey, where two days later a couple of boys were arrested for selling copies of the book (*NYT*, 22 February 1900). Meanwhile, the mayor of Scranton, Pennsylvania, demanded his own personal full-dress rehearsal so that he could judge in private the extent of the depravity. Predictably, the clergy found in the topic of *Sapho* a wealth of material to warn against the temptations of the stage, one pristine preacher pronouncing publicly that "there is not a clean theatre on earth. Everyone [*sic*] of them is a pile of dirt" (*NYDM*, 5 May 1900).

Shortly before the company was due in New York, the *Dramatic Mirror* printed the following admonition to the actress:

> If Olga Nethersole will give us a *Sapho* that will not obtrude the voluptuousness of the part . . . if the too famous Nethersole Kiss could be done off the stage—if we could be allowed to imagine it instead of having it made the feature of the play—we ought to get one of the stage's most interesting heroines.
>
> But when you see Matinee Boys all about the house timing a kiss with their watches, as though it were some record-breaking feat in athletics, it gets you away from the thread of the plot. (14 October 1899)

In a blatant instance of the media hypocrisy which surrounded this production, a few months later (24 February 1900) the same newspaper carried an advertisement billing *Sapho* as "New York's Raging Sensation." *Sapho* had inevitably become one of the most controversial and widely publicized plays in the annals of the New York stage. Yet, according to Charles Burnham, manager of Wallack's Theatre writing in retrospect about the incident in 1925, this avalanche of public sentiment against "stage vileness" was sparked by an innocuous script "which could be read in Sunday-school today" (Burnham, 16).

Some of the *Sapho* controversy must be attributed to Nethersole's own publicity. Burnham postulates that, following "meretricious, obscene, and vulgar" criticism in the Pittsburgh press, Nethersole's manager Marcus Mayer got the idea of titillating prospective audiences with hints of sexual explicitness and sent out a steady stream of press releases "with many sly references to the risqué scenes in which the play abounded" (Burnham, 16). Burnham claimed to have unsuccessfully tried to have this kind of smutty advertising appeal stopped. The technique was so successful that by the time the tickets went on sale, every seat for the first four weeks was sold in one day. The play was supposed to have opened January 22 but owing to the actress's ill health was postponed to January 29 and again until February 5. Each delay served to heighten suspense, with reports that Nethersole's indisposition was due to emotional stress caused by hostile criticism. By opening night the distinguished gathering of social, artistic and literary celebrities, and a large press corps, waited expectantly for some display of risqué behavior. When nothing much happened, the audience overreacted to the avant-garde design of a new spiral staircase, according to Burnham, and became feverishly excited in the scene where Sapho's young lover picks her up to carry her up the staircase to the bedroom. The next day the generally negative press reaction ranged from bemused boredom to scathing indictment. The *World* newspaper launched into a yellow journalism crusade against *Sapho* with daily sensational headlines, thereby ensuring its notoriety.

Norman Hapgood not only provides an eyewitness account of the Wallack's Theatre production, but also offers an analysis of the original novel versus the new Clyde Fitch script. He insists that the play was inaccurately billed on the program as "a play by Clyde Fitch, founded on Daudet's story with scenes from the original play by Alphonse Daudet and Adolphe Belot."[9] Except for an expansion of act one, Hapgood claims it was a close copy of the French playscript with no fundamental changes of structure. Some minor changes suggested by the novel were incorporated in the Fitch version. Daudet's novel *Sapho*, subtitled *Parisian Manners*, was published in 1884. Daudet collaborated with Belot on a stage script which opened in Paris at the Gymnase on 18 December 1885, with Jane Hading in the title role, supported by Damala (Mason, 59). The French version was subsequently taken by Rejane to England and America. Daudet's novel is a lyrical and sensitive portrait of a young trainee diplomat who becomes hopelessly, emotionally enslaved by the sensual advances of an older woman. The author meant this as a warning to his sons, to whom he dedicated the work. Murray Sachs suggests that Daudet's own "long and painful liaison with Marie Rieu" was the model for the destructive relationship between Jean Gaussin and Fanny Legrand. It is, according to Sachs, the most detailed portrait that Daudet composed of the sexes: "man as the victim of woman," or the "weak-willed, gentle, and sensitive male, the domineering, coldly inconsiderate female."[10] The bond between Jean and Fanny is, therefore, clearly an intimidating one of sexual bondage rather than exalted love. As this is not the thrust of the Clyde Fitch script, Nethersole very likely requested a more sympathetic treatment of Fanny when providing the playwright with her own scenario.

In the Nethersole production, the drama begins at an ultra-Bohemian fancy dress ball in the home of Dechelette, a Parisian rake. Jean Gaussin, a young student from Provence who is studying to enter the consular service, comes to the ball with his Uncle Cesaire where he meets Fanny Legrand. She is the star of the gathering, making a dramatic entrance halfway though act one, draped in the flowing robes of Venus. He is filled with admiration for her wit, beauty, and flamboyance; and the two are soon dancing a waltz, as Fanny's former lover, Flamant, is being arrested. At the end of the party, Jean escorts Fanny to her home. He offers to carry her up to her room, and after a halfhearted protest, she consents with girlish frivolity. He does not come down. In the second act Fanny arrives at Jean's lodgings to care for him while he is sick and suggests that she move in with him. Their domestic bliss is threatened by several complications, some of them involving Jean's family. In the meantime, Dechelette and his friend the sculptor Caodal come to ask for Fanny's help for Flamant. It seems that not only was he arrested for committing forgery in an effort to pay for his mistress's extravagant tastes, but he is the father of Fanny's secret child. Jean is chagrined to find that Fanny is also Caodal's former model, the notorious Sapho, nicknamed after the legendary poetess of Lesbos because of her sensuality. To assure Jean that she is no longer the same woman who posed for the artists of Paris and to prove her love for him, Fanny fetches her casket of love letters, reads them to him, and burns them. She succeeds in placating him and they leave for a new life in a cottage on the outskirts of Paris.

However, their happiness is short-lived. In act three Jean begins to feel trapped and they quarrel frequently as he dreams of escape. The only contacts with the outside world are some rustic neighbors. In the meantime Fanny has persuaded Jean to adopt a child. When he finds out that the child is Fanny's by the forger, Flamant, they have a violent argument and he leaves. Fanny resolves to atone for her past by caring for the child. Act four opens the morning after Fanny has tried to poison herself. Flamant returns and offers to marry her and give the child a stable home. Fanny agrees and he goes on ahead to Paris with the child. In the meantime, Jean returns repentant and unable to live without his love. Purified by their love, and therefore nobler and wiser, Fanny makes the decision to return to Flamant and her child. While Jean is sleeping, she tells him of her love in a letter and then steals away. Curtain.

Nethersole's portrayal of the siren Fanny was a masterful combination of dramatic staging and emotional virtuosity. In Daudet's original, Fanny was a fading beauty, aware that her power to fascinate and entrap men was rapidly declining. Her advances to Jean were quiet and determined. As presented by Nethersole, Fanny was mistress of her domain, entering to musical accompaniment in a blaze of glory, and, according to Hapgood, "queen of everything in sight, a right royal star actress." Her version showed Jean as a country boy falling in love with a sympathetic temptress who made a halfhearted attempt to ward him off. The Nethersole Fanny was endowed with virtues to "soak the star with sympathy" (Hapgood, 356). In the original, an angry Jean forces a desperate Fanny to reveal the secrets of her past and then destroy them. In the Fitch version, Fanny voluntarily offered to show him the past and then burns the evidence to prove her love. Fanny's little boy is also given much more visibility in Fitch's third act, which enabled Nethersole to demonstrate twinges of conscience and maternal devotion. Her moment of parting from Jean was the high point of the Nethersole performance, earning the greatest applause. Hapgood writes that she played a range of emotions from wild pleading to utter despair "with a richness and justness that few actresses anywhere could equal." The actress's own innovations were the most hotly debated moments in the *Sapho fracasse*.[11] This included her first flamboyant entrance down a staircase, and Fanny reciting "Au Clair de la Lune" on a pedestal, crowned as Venus. At the end of the first act, Nethersole added the notorious staircase scene, which was presented in front of the main curtain. The scene in which Jean finds out that Fanny is the promiscuous Sapho was moved from the third to second act to separate it from Fanny's subsequent tour de force when Jean leaves. Fanny burns her keepsakes and stops Jean from leaving by seducing him and the two embrace passionately as the curtain falls. The scene in which Jean actually departs was so emotionally draining for Nethersole that she often fainted. The *World* reported that few people knew that she had actually fainted at the opening night performance. Although the curtain rose five times after the act, Nethersole made no move to receive the applause but lay inanimate on the floor until she was revived, with difficulty, behind the scenes.

Stage reviews document that the Nethersole performance also included violent, brutal moments, in which the actress showed Fanny as a survivor and streetfighter, a woman used to abuse in the seamy Parisian underworld, and quite accepting of being beaten up and thrown to the floor by her young lover. Given Nethersole's belief in stage *vérité*, her faithful adherence to naturalism, her unsqueamish acceptance of the "truth in life" together with its filth, disease, pain, and horror, her performance in this regard must have been riveting. Dithmar complained that she took her portrayal too far, it was "coarse, vulgar and violent" (*NYT*, 6 February 1900). The *New York Dramatic Mirror* reviewer described the Nethersole

Fanny as "a languorous, insinuating siren with a musical coaxing voice and wistful eyes" with "occasional moments of explosive emotion."

The same reviewer was quick to note the sensual nature of Nethersole's costumes: "The actress wore some gowns of amazing clingingness, her first act dress quite out-clinging anything yet seen here in its line" (6 February 1900). Indeed, Nethersole had four different costumes designed for the first-act gown alone, and the one she eventually selected caused a minor furor with a neckline "lowered to the apex of the heart." The *World* provided extensive coverage of all aspects of the production, including a series of reactions to the costumes by members of the public and society columnists such as Lavinia Hart, who was appalled that "she goes so far as to expose all of her limbs and most of her body above the waist" (6 February 1900). A careful description of her costume is provided by London's society and fashion magazines, upon *Sapho*'s debut there on 1 May 1902 at the Adelphi. They confirm that a salient characteristic of a Nethersole production was the detail of the costumes. The *Queen* (11 May 1902) describes the act-one costume as a "classic gown of soft white," which was embroidered with a border of flowers and worn with a scarf of the same diaphanous material, as well as a small green wreath and sandals. This was covered for a few minutes by a mauve-colored cloak embroidered in gold and steel. In act two she wore a low-cut cerise gown with white and gold embroidered bodice and hem. In act three she wore a simple black silk gown with a white lace collar, and then changed into "a soft clinging robe of white chiffon laid over faint colouring and bordered with tiny chiffon flowers in relief. This undescribable gown, soft and graceful, opens over lace. The sleeves have the new puff from the wrist to the elbow, and the under bodice is all cream lace" (*Queen*, 11 May 1902). While London society magazines emphasized the elegance and sophistication of Nethersole's designer gowns, the American press focused here, as everywhere, on the possibilities of excess sensuality, the potential for moral censure, and the profitable partnership of those factors in the noble endeavor of selling copy.

The public expectations of the trial were clearly inflated by excessive and inflammatory advance publicity. The *New York Times* ran a series of articles condemning the "hysterical" media coverage (26 January 1900) and deplored the relationship of morality to art which was being debated by newspapers throughout the country. It called these debates "futile" and suggested that for the good of the public *Sapho* should be banned from the theatre altogether. It is not surprising, therefore, that artistically the production itself was somewhat of a fiasco. Dithmar provided an unflattering appraisal of the opening night performance published under the headline, "A COARSE AND SUPERFLUOUS PLAY AND NOT WELL ACTED, EITHER" (*NYT*, 6 February 1900). Two days later the *World* published a report that the harsh press criticism had actually fueled the desire for tickets, as well as a flourishing side industry on the sale of the novel, under the headline "MOB FRANTIC TO SEE SAPHO STORMS DOORS OF THEATRE."[12] The paper reported that seats were hawked at four dollars apiece, double their normal price. It also provided a series of negative excerpts from the opening-night reviews of thirteen newspapers and charged that Nethersole had been convicted of hypocrisy in her claim that she presented *Sapho* as a moral lesson for the general good. Its sub-headline read: "OLGA NETHERSOLE CHARGED WITH ACTING ROLE OF SCARLET WOMAN TO GRATIFY MORBID DESIRES" (7 February 1900). Apparently, the gratification of its own desires to fuel this profitable scandal had blinded the press to its own hypocrisies.

While the theatrical press and the religious element were vociferously opposed to *Sapho*, the ordinary theatregoer was thrilled and impressed by the play and Nethersole's performance. The *World* continued to interview audience members as they emerged from the theatre and included their views in its daily coverage. A typical theatergoer responded: "I came prepared to hear much that was risqué and was agreeably disappointed. The third act is one of the strongest scenes ever enacted on a stage. Nethersole threw into the situation all her virility and flame of genius. The result was thrilling, wonderful, lasting" (6 February 1900). The *World* also reported that this "sin-stained" *Sapho* at the 1,600-seat Wallack's Theatre had taken over as the most popular entertainment ever on Broadway, surpassing *Ben Hur* and requiring police protection for theatre patrons (8 February 1900). The *Herald*, the only major newspaper whose theatre critic had been favorable to the play, provided the Nethersole viewpoint that *Sapho* taught a moral lesson by giving a "truthful picture of human life, its frailty, its weakness and the consequences that invariably follow the breach of moral law" (7 February 1900). It noted that a performance of *Sapho* was a much more effective conveyor of that message than a clergyman's sermon.

Despite these voices of moderation, on February 21 Olga Nethersole was arrested with her leading man, Hamilton Revelle, her manager, Mayer, and Theodore Moss, lessee of Wallack's Theatre. The production had been charged with being "a public nuisance" based on an affidavit submitted by a reporter for the *World*, who revealed a basic confusion between the character in the play and the actress's own character. The indictment accused Nethersole of "indecent postures, indecent suggestive language against good morals and indecent conduct" and went on to specify the "staircase scene" in which she permitted "an actor in the presence of an audience to carry her up a staircase in a vile and indecent manner" (*World*, 22 February 1900). A hearing was set for February 23. With superb showmanship, Nethersole performed *Sapho* that night in a house that could have been filled four times over. The crowds outside Wallack's were so huge that they blocked the sidewalk and stopped the cable cars until policemen cleared the street (*NYT*, 23 February 1900). There were demonstrations and curtain calls between the acts and, following the famous third-act curtain, which received ten calls, the actress was persuaded to respond to the audience. She asked: "Am I to understand that you are all with me?" To which she received a thunderous response and replied, "With you at my back I feel that my fight is won." The case was bound over for a full jury trial to the Court of General Sessions and the four defendants were released on bond after a payment of five hundred dollars each (*NYT*, 3 March 1900). In the meantime the controversy raged in the newspapers, and the *New York Dramatic Mirror* provided a weekly sample of editorials about *Sapho* which were being expressed throughout the country outside New York. By the time the court case was finally decided in Nethersole's favor, *Sapho* had become a household word. It starred in a series of legal maneuverings, colorful court testimony by the prosecution, and dramatic courtroom appearances by the actress; it also served as a source for editorials, cartoons, letters to the editor, denunciations from church pulpits, and violent demonstrations by the upstanding citizens of several concerned communities. It was the most famous play of the decade and assured Nethersole and her production of *Sapho* a prominent place in the columns of every major newspaper in the city.

Dramatic developments continued on March 5, when, without warning, *Sapho* was shut down by the police commissioner pending the trial. Nethersole announced that *The Second Mrs. Tanqueray* would be presented in the interim. On March 22, the grand jury returned a blanket indictment against the four defendants, charging them with being of "wicked and depraved mind and disposition" and of creating "lustful desires" in *Sapho* because of "lewd, indecent, obscene, filthy, scandalous, lascivious and disgusting motions" and "indecent postures and attitudes" (*NYT*, 23 March 1900).

Simultaneously, Nethersole's physicians announced that she had collapsed with "nervous prostration" and all performances would be canceled for two weeks. The trial began April 3 and ended April 5, right after the defense, in a dramatic gesture, waived the right to call any of its fifty witnesses. This move was at the actress's suggestion, according to the *New York Times* (5 April 1900), which noted the incredible excitement surrounding the actress's appearance in the courtroom. The spectators jostled to get a closer look at her magnificent gowns. Her attorney's closing summation for the defense was itself a masterpiece of dramatic rhetoric, worthy of a stage performance.[13] He ended by comparing Nethersole to Caesar's wife, a woman above suspicion, and asked: "Has there ever been a smirch on her pure womanhood? After fame and fortune are hers now comes a charge that she is trying to subvert public morality and forsooth she is dragged into a criminal court. Poor defenseless woman!" At this point he was overcome by the force of his own emotion while Nethersole fell forward on the table in front of her in a flood of tears. Suddenly he pointed dramatically to the sobbing prostrate figure and called out: "Why you libidinous creature, how did you dare do it?" (*NYT*, 6 April 1900). The trial judge then commented that in the United States Supreme Court every day you could see a statue of a woman with more exposed than Nethersole was said to have revealed. It took the jury only fifteen minutes to reach a verdict of innocent.

Cablegrams, greetings, and flowers poured into Wallack's Theatre from around the world once the verdict was known. Four road companies authorized by Nethersole, as well as two Yiddish versions and one in Japanese, immediately took to the boards, in addition to numerous "cheap" versions and the very popular burlesque *Sapolio*, which starred May Robson.[14] On April 7 Nethersole was back in business with *Sapho*, and was given what was described as one of the "most remarkable ovations" received by any actress in the city. Her tearful address to the audience acknowledged that she was still suffering from the strain but that she was proud to have borne "the brunt of this battle" when she remembered what had been done "for the freedom of art and literature" (*NYT*, 8 April 1900). The eighty-six-performance run played to full houses at Wallack's until May 29, when she sailed as usual for Europe. The battle was won and the spoils were sweet: *Sapho* would make her a fortune and continue to be popular for the rest of her career.

The role which Nethersole's own publicity played in the *Sapho* controversy casts this theatrical adventure in a different light today. Knowing the adroitness with which Nethersole handled the relationship between her public and her own actress persona, we can only speculate how much of the *Sapho* phenomenon was deliberately or unconsciously orchestrated. Nethersole would have been very aware of the moral climate of the time and would have known her American audience well by the time she made her fourth tour. Surely she realized that *Sapho*, particularly *her* Sapho, would contain the seeds of controversy. Regardless of who started the ripples which grew into a tidal wave of public and press overreaction, we can see how well Nethersole rode that wave as it crested. Her courtroom maneuvers were among the best-staged pieces of acting in her career and reveal how adept this actress was at comprehending and then subverting the forces in her society which might have become enormous obstacles. That she turned these to her own professional and financial advantage is belated testimony to her own artistic instincts. Nethersole's ability to construct and control a public persona between the contradictions of Victorian propriety and "Fallen Woman" gave her the edge she needed to maintain her competitive status as a star in a patriarchal world.

NOTES

1. William Winter, "The Sacred Labors of Olga Nethersole," in *The Wallet of Time*, 2 vols. (New York: Moffat, Yard, 1913), 2:313–14.
2. Anne Everal Callis, "Olga Nethersole and the Sapho Scandal," (Master's thesis, Ohio State University, 1974), 78.
3. Brooks Atkinson, *Broadway* (New York: Macmillan, 1974), 6.
4. Charles Burnham, "Stage Indecency Then and Now: A Play That Made Our Daddies Blush Could Be Read in Sunday School Today," *Theatre Magazine*, September 1925, p. 16. Hereafter cited in the text as Burnham.
5. *See* Karen Adele Recklies, "Fashion Behind the Footlights in England from 1878 to 1914," (Ph.D. diss., Ohio State University, 1982).
6. *See* frontispiece, Joy Harriman Reilly, "From Wicked Woman of the Stage to New Woman: The Career of Olga Nethersole (1870–1951); Actress-Manager, Suffragist, Health Pioneer" (Ph.D. diss., Ohio State University, 1984).
7. Olga Nethersole, letter to Clement Scott, 22 November 1894, Gabrielle Enthoven Collection, Victoria and Albert Museum.
8. Hamilton Mason, *French Theatre in New York: A List of Plays, 1899–1939* (New York: Columbia University Press, 1940), 23.
9. Norman Hapgood, *The Stage in America, 1897–1900* (New York: Macmillan, 1901), 356–57.
10. Murray Sachs, *The Career of Alphonse Daudet* (Cambridge, Mass.: Harvard University Press, 1965), 131.
11. *See* Anne Callis's reconstruction of the *Sapho* script.
12. Cited by Callis, 48.
13. *See* Reilly, chapter 4, for a detailed account of the trial.
14. Hapgood, 353–54.

PART TWO

Playwrights
and Genres

In the Shadow of the Bard
JAMES NELSON BARKER'S REPUBLICAN DRAMA
AND THE SHAKESPEAREAN LEGACY

Gary A. Richardson

The political and aesthetic paradoxes of America in the early years of the republic generate a remarkably contradictory cultural chronicle. Though the American Revolution had set the stage for a new political order, though the Constitution and Bill of Rights had institutionalized an unprecedented measure of political freedom, and though public pronouncements from lectern, pulpit, and stump enthusiastically embraced the "noble experiment," American culture remained staunchly, though quietly, Anglicized. The inconvenience of the Revolution ended, the flow of British material culture resumed to an America tired of the sacrifices of war. But calfskins and brocades were merely the most tangible evidence of Britain's continuing cultural hegemony. The assumption of English predominance in the arts, a proposition unquestioned before 1775, gradually reemerged unsettlingly intact as revolutionary fervor began to disappear. Thus, in the face of long-held and resilient cultural attitudes, the issue of a national culture was by no means a straightforward one. On the one hand, concerned citizens, politicians, critics of art and literature, and artists themselves stoutly demanded the development of a truly national culture. Indeed, when in 1837 Emerson optimistically announced that "our day of dependence, our long apprenticeship to the learning of other lands, draws to a close,"[1] his audience's enthusiastic response arose, at least in part, from its sense that a national effort was finally being crowned with success.

On the other hand, most of the artists of the early republic maintained their allegiance to English aesthetic models and, with few exceptions, reflected those prejudices in art. American painters such as Benjamin West, John Singleton Copley, and Gilbert Stuart chose to study and, in the case of West, to reside in London, even after the revolution. And though their canvases occasionally reflect the events of colonial or revolutionary America, their presentations consistently betray the influence of Reynolds and Gainsborough. In the related field of architecture, Americans continued to look to English models, belatedly adopting the Palladian and Adamesque styles only to follow in course European and English interest in Gothicism and, still later, Classicism. The American musical scene was similarly dominated by patriotic ditties and sentimental songs.

Not surprisingly, American literature, especially early republican drama, reflects the same conflicting impulses that characterized other American arts. For example, the prologue to Royall Tyler's *The Contrast* (1787), often cited as the "first wholly successful American play performed by professional actors,"[2] innocently applauds the author for having chosen to expose "the gay scenes—the circles of New York" rather than the follies of "foreign climes."[3] Despite claims for its native subject matter, however, a cursory reading of the play reveals its derivative nature. Colonel Manly's tattered Continental Army uniform and Jonathan's Yankee dialect cannot disguise a colonial Sheridan's first effort. Nevertheless, in the heady years immediately following the Revolution, contemporary commentators were obviously less interested in *The Contrast*'s structural similarities to the late Georgian comedy of manners than in its ideological perspective. Typical is Candour's comment in the *Daily Advertiser* on 18 April 1787 that whatever the play's faults, its sentiments "are the effusions of an honest patriotic heart expressed with energy and eloquence."[4] But when nationalistic ardor faded, as it did increasingly after the Revolution and again after the War of 1812, "the American theatre operated as if America was still an outpost of the mother country."[5]

In large measure the Anglicized character of American stage and drama sprang from two related cultural phenomena—the general reluctance of American managers, actors, and audiences to challenge a received dramatic canon dominated by British plays; and the steady procession through America's theatrical centers of touring English actors whose superior performances reinforced the public's prejudice for British plays. (Very few of these actors mounted any American efforts.) To create a national drama, an aspiring American dramatist would of necessity have to overcome the English grip on both the library and the stage. Unfortunately, from a nationalistic perspective, the bulwark for English theatrical and cultural ascendancy in early nineteenth-century America was Shakespeare.

Reevaluating Shakespeare

Shakespeare's work was part of the fabric of Anglo-American culture almost from the beginning, but because of significant antitheatrical and antidramatic biases and the lack of an organized theatre to spur interest, English colonists in the late seventeenth century knew Shakespeare first as a poet.[6] As the library catalogues of eighteenth-century American colleges testify, the public's estimation of his merit as a poet and moralist initially secured him a prominent place in the readings of educated and cultured colonials, even those who were at best dubious about his choice of genre.[7] The stage, the most appropriate vehicle of dissemination, finally became available at midcentury. Productions began, somewhat ironically, with Thomas Kean's 1750 New York production of Colley Cibber's adaptation of *Richard III*, but soon included thirteen other (mostly "improved") plays, predominantly the tragedies and histories.[8] By the end of the eighteenth century, audiences regularly saw productions of Shakespeare mounted by touring professional troupes in Charleston, Williamsburg, Richmond, Annapolis, Philadelphia, and New York.[9] In the early nineteenth century, Americans continued to flock to productions of Shakespeare, perceiving their admiration of him as an index of the growing civility of their society.[10] In fact, appreciation of Shakespeare had become such a touchstone of national refinement that Americans' rage with Edmund Kean during his first American tour stemmed as much from his arrogant assertion (in a letter to the *National Advocate* of 1 June 1821) that Americans did not sufficiently honor Shakespeare as from his affront in refusing to play before a small Boston audience.[11]

By the early nineteenth century, a cultural moment had arrived which forced Americans, like their European counterparts, to reevaluate Shakespeare. The general influence of romantic aesthetics made itself felt, not only in contemporary European literature, but also in the Shakespearean criticism of Lessing, Schlegel, Coleridge, Morgann, Goethe, Lamb, Hazlitt, and Carlyle. This torrent of romantic commentary was augmented in America by the writings of Emerson, Lowell, and Whitman. Though each of these critics approached Shakespeare from a slightly different perspective, their collective efforts had two overarching effects: the last vestiges of the "tyrannical" neoclassical rules were swept aside and replaced with a reliance upon refined sensibility of the "beauty" and "truth" of Shakespeare; and the central characters of the plays became the focal points of interest and of new aesthetic, psychological, and moral insights. Almost simultaneously, English actors, eager to augment their primacy over the text, further encouraged the transformation of Shakespeare by changing their acting styles. Ever responsive to shifts in public taste, actors such as Edmund Kean and Junius Brutus Booth supplanted the measured, intellectual style of John Philip Kemble with more emotionally charged characterizations. In the United States, Americans, prepared by a national cult of the individual, quickly embraced the romantic characterizations of Kean and Booth and the "new understanding" of Shakespeare on which they were grounded.

Despite the pervasive idolatry, however, much early dramatic commentary reveals an almost studied attempt to exempt Shakespeare's plays from the type of ideological critique imposed on other authors' works. Part of this reluctance derived, no doubt, from an unenunciated, commonsensical notion that the ideological perspective was inappropriate to the received canon. More important, perhaps, was the popular political affiliation between Shakespeare and the patriotic discourses on liberty that arose before and during the American Revolution and that seemed implicitly to nationalize part of the English poetic heritage. Initially a source of private and public wisdom, Shakespeare also provided support for the political arguments of many Americans. But for aspiring dramatists such as James Nelson Barker, Shakespeare constituted a formidable obstacle to the writing of serious American drama. In his criticism and plays, Barker provocatively explores the basis of a democratic national drama, the ambiguities attendant to America's aristocratic dramatic heritage, and the desirability of reconciling the two.

James Nelson Barker

James Nelson Barker (1784–1858) was the scion of a prominent Philadelphia family; his occupations ranged from poet to public servant. The son of General John Barker, a three-time mayor of Philadelphia, James Nelson Barker was formally educated in Philadelphia and politically schooled by a sojourn in Washington, D.C. (1809–1810). After serving on the Canadian border during the War of 1812, he continued in the army until 1817 when he resigned, having risen to the rank of major as an assistant adjutant-general. Following his father into Democratic party politics, Barker held a series of elected and appointed positions in local and national government: in 1819 he was elected mayor of Philadelphia;

he was appointed collector of the Port of Philadelphia (1829–1838), comptroller (1838–1841) and assistant comptroller of the United States Treasury (1841–1858).

Like most of the playwrights of his generation, Barker was more a talented amateur than a working professional, and he conceived of his dramatic writings as the diversions of his idle hours.[12] His theatrical endeavors, as he detailed them in an 1832 letter to William Dunlap, include seven mature efforts: *Tears and Smiles* (written 1806, produced 1807), *The Embargo* (1807), *The Indian Princess* (1808), *Marmion* (1812), *The Armourer's Escape* (1817), *How to Try a Lover* (written 1817; played in 1836 as *A Court of Love*), and *Superstition* (1824). The breadth of these efforts, which include drawing room comedies, overt propaganda pieces, historical dramas, and tragedies, indicates a serious interest in drama, an inference further sustained by Barker's consistent interest in the theatrical world of Philadelphia.[13] In addition to writing dramas and regularly attending the theatre, Barker found time to provide, through his prefaces, prologues, and newspaper articles, an insightful commentary on the history of the theatre and drama, the nature and merits of both the classic and contemporary canons, and the actors and acting techniques of the day. While Barker provides interesting accounts of the Philadelphia stage in the early nineteenth century, his early, forceful statements on cultural nationalism and his thoughts on the role of drama in perfecting democracy are his most significant contributions.

Barker's first important comments on the state of American drama were attached as a preface to the 1808 published version of *Tears and Smiles*. Using the fiction of a friend's comments on his play, Barker asserted one of his recurrent critical themes—that American critics are indisposed to recognize merit in American plays. In fact, he maintained through his friend's voice, "every delineation an American may attempt to make of American manners, customs, opinions, characters or scenery" is perceived as an aesthetically worthless, provincial self-indulgence, mere "Columbianisms."[14] Barker admitted that his play's favorable reception undermines his friend's complaints somewhat, but still insisted upon the accuracy of these assertions. The preface to *The Indian Princess* develops this point still further, asserting that American plays receive an inhospitable reception from their countrymen in part because the standards embodied in the received canon are inappropriate to an emerging national literature. Casting American drama as a child, Barker notes the unreasonable expectations of critics who chide American drama "because its unpracticed tongue cannot lisp the language of Shakspere [sic]."¹⁵ The evocation of Shakespeare, the symbol of British dramatic hegemony, not only personifies the narrow aesthetic model of the critics, but also casually defines an antithesis between the ideology of a revered British heritage and that emerging in the more "childish" American literature.

While Barker's plays reveal most fully his conception of what a national drama should be, at least one element of that ideal (and one that suggests a pivotal difference between British and American literature) forms a central topic in his preface to *Marmion*. After acknowledging that because his play follows Scott's poem of the same name it conforms to "no received dramatic rule," Barker attacked Scott's lack of dedication to his homeland, noting that "the cause of Scotland . . . had occasionally found less support in the fine poetry of her gifted son than from the simple relation, in homely prose, of the *suthron* Hollingshead."¹⁶ Specifically, Barker attacked Scott for choosing as his subject the historical moment in which Scotland effectively lost its national independence, and, in the process, Barker tellingly linked art and patriotism when he suggested that Bruce or Wallace would have been more appropriate heroes since their histories displayed "every object that might allure the poet or invite the patriot" (*M*, iv). In the same preface, Barker made an ominous prediction: the American playwright's failure to address such nationalistic concerns and his countrymen's failure to support him in his efforts will mean inevitably that Americans "must be content to continue the importation of our ideas and sentiments, like our woollen stuffs, from England" (*M*, vii). For Barker, clearly, national drama was nationalistic drama.

Notwithstanding the specific context of *Marmion*, the desirability of patriotic sentiment is not confined, in Barker's estimation, to periods of national crisis. Between 18 December 1816 and 19 February 1817, Barker wrote a series of eleven articles on theatrical topics for Philadelphia's *Democratic Press*. While these pieces range from general aesthetic discussions of the circus and the legitimate theater to theorizings on the essence of burlesque, they are, in the main, concerned with particular productions and individual actors' performances. Nevertheless, they tangentially provide some insight into the aesthetic which had informed Barker's previous plays. Barker's most important theoretical observations arise in the first number, in which he argues that desirable private and public effects justify drama's central place in the new democracy's arts. Echoing the classical justification that literature joins instruction to pleasure, Barker claimed that "Considered either as a school of Ethics or as a source of a rational and refined amusement, the Drama has always claimed the protection of the enlightened and the polished classes of society."[17] He then traced the didactic uses of drama from classical Athens to nineteenth-century Philadelphia, asserting that no one can doubt "the uniform and powerful tendency of a well regulated stage, to polish and improve manners, to chastise and correct vice, and to promote in various ways the best interests of mankind" (18 December 1816). But the supreme function of drama, a purpose that can only be achieved in a democracy, is "to keep alive the spirit of freedom; and to unite conflicting parties in a common love of liberty and devotedness to country" (18 December 1816). Here Barker stakes out an American dramatic aesthetic whose central tenet is antithetical to both British history and literature, at least as popularly conceived in republican America.[18] Barker's consistent use of this standard and its effects on his dramaturgy are best seen by examining two of his plays— *Marmion*, which precedes the *Democratic Press* articles by four years, and *Superstition*, which Barker was not to write until 1824.

Marmion and *Superstition*

Given the theatrical proclivities of early nineteenth-century American audiences, the success of *Marmion* was not difficult to forecast. An exotic setting complete with bloodthirsty prelates, spectacular court pageantry, imperiled maidens, ghostly personal combats, pitched battles and a compellingly evil protagonist might have well been expected to prove irresistible to audiences whose tastes had been formed by plays such as Cibber's adaptation of *Richard III*. In spite of its obvious appeals, as Barker relates in his letter to Dunlap, William Wood and Thomas Abthorpe Cooper sought to improve the play's reception by announcing that it was the work of an Englishman, Thomas Morton. The ruse was sufficient to guarantee the play a fair hearing, and the result was a play which "ran like wildfire" through the American theatres (Dunlap, 315). Significantly, Barker attributes much of the initial success of the play to the audience's belief that it was the work of an Englishman.

Barker's plot follows the Scott poem: before the play's action begins, Marmion, a fictitious noble, has decided to secure the body and fortune of Clara de Clare. To that end, he has accused her beloved, Ralph de Wilton, of treason and seemingly has killed him in mortal combat. Clara has fled and has taken refuge in the convent of St. Hilda at Whitby. The play opens with Marmion on his way to Scotland, having been sent as emissary by Henry VIII to the court of Scotland's James IV. On his procession north, he returns his cast-off mistress, the erstwhile nun, Constance de

Beverly, to the vengeance of the Roman Catholic Church. Following a combat in which he is defeated by the "ghost" of de Wilton, who has joined Marmion's train in the disguise of a palmer, Marmion arrives at the court of James. James is gathering his forces for a war with England, but his judgment is being clouded by his mistress, the Lady Heron, another ex-mistress of Marmion and an English agent. Marmion serendipitously gains Clara, whose ship has been forced ashore in Scotland, but before he can violate her, James attacks England and Marmion returns to the English army. James is lured from a strategically superior position by an English plot, and after great losses on both sides, the Scots are destroyed. Marmion dies in battle, forgiven by all because of his valor during the fighting.

Quite obviously, this play superficially shares many of the characters, situations, and devices of other "historical" plays of the period. However, while Barker's play is informed by the same conventions that produced a spate of romantic histories, they serve a much different end. Of course, Barker is intent upon producing the best historical play that he can engineer from Scott's poem. However, his main interest in the play, as both his comments in the play's preface and the play itself testify, is ideological rather than aesthetic. That a play set wholly in England and Scotland in the sixteenth century is part of an attempt to forge an American drama may seem a bit paradoxical. But, as Barker's critical writings make clear, he does *not* demand that the action of the play concern itself with Americans or American circumstances; rather, a play must endorse American ideals, a more complex project.

In *Marmion* Barker attempted to advance the development of a national drama on at least three fronts. First, he tried to free the materials of art by reexamining received history. He sought to expose the reality behind the chronicled glories of England, and, that accomplished, he argued for the necessity of a national perspective by indicating the dangers of adopting the English viewpoint. In order to understand the art, Americans must reexamine events from their new vantage point, unencumbered by English bias. In a nice bit of displacement, Scotland becomes America's precursor state and America's conflicts with Britain are metaphorically presented in the guise of the Scottish-British conflict in the sixteenth century. While a reconsideration of history is important to Barker, an examination of the chivalric values which ostensibly underpinned English actions in the Renaissance is even more imperative. Barker's contention, personified in the play's title character, is that those values are merely rationalizations for aristocratic privilege. The very word *chivalry* is so emptied of meaning by play's end that it is little more than what Falstaff calls it—a puff of air. Finally, for Barker, Scott was merely the last in a long line of artists who had forsaken liberty for profit, had become "the mercenary minstrel of a feudal lord" (*M*, iv). In this view, the literature of England had, in large measure, inculcated generations of readers with a set of aristocratic values whose moribund and corrupt nature had remained hidden behind a veil of art. If a new democratic art was to emerge and grow, the first order of business was to reveal the baseness of aristocratic life and, by implication, art.

Barker's tactics are easily illustrated by act four, scene four, the episode in which he develops the parallels between Scotland and America and places in the mouth of James IV a stinging indictment of England. The scene begins interestingly with James kindly guaranteeing the safety of Clara and her abbess. James then compliments Marmion, "the star of chivalry" (*M*, 50), and the focus shifts to Lady Heron who sings a song of Lochinvar's securing of "fair Ellen" (*M*, 51). The chivalrous action of James and the literary ideal evoked by Scott's song stand in ironic opposition to the evil and corrupt Marmion, whose true nature is known to the audience, if not to the king. Realizing that the audience may assume that Marmion is an anomaly, Barker quickly eradicates that comforting prospect by transcending personal concerns and moving to national politics. James's indictment of England's aggressive policies is all the more damning for the light it sheds on England's methods. First, says James, England "Professes but to fight for others' rights, / While she alone infringes upon every right" (*M*, 54). Next, England attempts to find justifications for her actions by suggesting that Scotland is partial to France, which insults the intelligence of the Scots who "know who wounds us and who gives us balm" (*M*, 54). Most significantly, James states impassionedly, England abrogates the rules of chivalry:

> It was then—
> Even in days of truce! I burn to speak it—
> Murder and pillage, England's constant agents,
> Roamed through our land, and harboured in our bays!
> (*M*, 55)

James concludes his speech with lines which literally brought the play to a halt in one of its early performances as the audience engaged in an impromptu patriotic rally:[19]

> My lord, my lord, under such injuries,
> How shall a free and gallant nation act?
> Still lay its sovereignty at England's feet—
> Still basely ask a boon from England's bounty—
> Still vainly hope redress from England's justice?
> No! by our martyred fathers' memories,
> The land may sink—but, like a glorious wreck,
> 'Twill keep its colours flying to the last.
>
> (M, 55)

The subsequent action of the play bears out all of James's assertions. Scotland is not defeated by a morally and politically superior country, but is lured to destruction through the policy of the English. Perhaps most important, the play ends with the preeminent figures of English arms and morality, Surrey and Wilton, able to excuse Marmion's failings because he has fought bravely—in the destruction of a liberty-loving Scotland. In sum, the play vindicates Barker's estimation of chivalric society and indicts the literature which has sustained it.

If *Marmion* provided a basis for an American drama, Barker's last play, *Superstition*, not only proved such a drama possible, but also gave it a large measure of artistic and ideological legitimacy by refusing to glorify an unflattering moment in colonial history. Set in New England during the late seventeenth century, *Superstition* tells the story of a fanatical Puritan minister's destruction of a woman and her son who refuse to conform to the minister's narrow-minded expectations. Isabella and Charles Fitzroy have fallen afoul of Ravensworth, whose implacable hatred is such that he attributes every disaster in the community to their sorcery. As the play begins, Charles is returning home, having been expelled for his supposed impertinence to his college's officials. Lost in the wilds, Charles meets the Unknown, a man living alone who refuses to divulge anything about himself to Charles. Charles arrives at home just in time to save his love, Mary Ravensworth, from the advances of George Egerton, an English courtier who has accompanied his uncle Sir Reginald on a secret mission to the New World. In a subsequent duel Charles wounds George in an honorable fight. The village is almost destroyed by an unexpected Indian attack, but is saved when the Unknown leads a counterattack. Ravensworth attributes both the Indian attack and the appearance of the Unknown, whom he regards as a demon, to Isabella's witchcraft, and has both mother and son charged with sorcery. Charles is also falsely charged with attempted murder and rape, for his sword and handkerchief have been found at the site of George Egerton's wounding and Mary has collapsed in Charles's arms when they are surprised by her father. Unwilling for Mary to appear in court and thereby ruin her reputation, Charles refuses to recognize the validity of the court. Ravensworth uses Charles's refusal to plead as a pretext for whipping the townspeople into such a frenzy that they lynch Charles. The Unknown arrives too late to stop Charles's murder, but he reveals that he is Isabella's father, a regicide who had fled to America at the Restoration. Sir Reginald discloses that Charles Fitzroy's father was none other than the king, Charles II, and that his mission has been to present Isabella's father with a royal pardon. A distraught Mary Ravensworth dies of grief, and the play ends in a tableau of despair as a storm rages outside.

Despite its melodramatic leanings, *Superstition* works effectively on the stage. Indeed, Arthur Hobson Quinn, who saw a revival of *Superstition* at Columbia University, justly deemed it the best play written to its day.[20] The characters, especially Ravensworth, Mary, Charles, and Isabella, are well drawn, the action is fast-paced, and the verse is well handled. Beyond these aesthetic considerations, however, the play provides evidence of Barker's durable ideological commitments and their effect on his treatment of American characters and situations. An opportunity for Barker to excoriate English literature's tendency to mythologize its national abuses, *Superstition* counters the literature of Scott and Shakespeare by educating a democratic citizenry rather than by glorifying the ruling class. In this play Barker emphasized drama's ability to unite factions and encourage freedom by metaphorically presenting the effects of factionalism and tyranny on both England and America.

The central figure in the drama and the chief exponent of a new variety of American tyranny is Ravensworth, a type of the grim Puritan who would figure so prominently in the works of Hawthorne a few years later. Ravensworth, as his name suggests, is a portent of death in the play. Unable to endure what he sees as the laxity of his fellow Puritans, he is determined to "root out" with an "unsparing hand" the "weeds that choke the soil."[21] The object of his resolve is Isabella Fitzroy, who "holds herself above her fellow creatures, / And scorns our church's discipline" (S, 117) and Charles, "a lewd libertine" (S, 118). Regardless of his ostensibly disinterested rationalizations, Ravensworth's moral authority is undercut by the sense of personal injury and animosity that informs his comment to Mary that Isabella is "a scoffer at things sacred / At me, and at my functions" (S, 118). Just as Marmion has sought to reject the rules of humane interaction through abuse of his position, so Ravensworth seeks to exploit his privileged standing in the community. By transforming the people's anxiety about anything alien into terror of witches and projecting that fear on the Fitzroys, Ravensworth is able to persecute them with seeming impunity. He has, in essence, found the way to reconstitute tyranny in a democratic environment—by making the tyranny collective, by making it appear to be the "will of the people." But Walford, the choric representative of tolerance and reasoned faith, points out that Ravensworth has failed in his responsibility to educate "The unthinking crowd, in whom credulity, / Is ever the first born of ignorance" (*S*, 130).

Placed in opposition to Ravensworth's new tyranny is the Old World despotism of the Stuart monarchy highlighted through three generations of the Fitzroy family's interaction with the crown. Isabella's father is presented as one of those who fought the Stuarts out of conscience and religious belief, but would have suffered death had he remained in an England which could not or would not tolerate dissent. Isabella's seduction suggests graphically the moral corruption associated with Charles II, an "execrable monarch" who "sanctioned every vice" (18 December 1816). Charles Fitzroy's death represents, from Barker's perspective, the culmination of monarchist history. For Barker the destruction of monarchy at the hands of forces that it has set in motion is inevitable. But the cost of freedom wrenched from monarchy can be very high indeed. This play ends, after all, with the best of the younger generation on a bier and the ability of the older generation to transform itself through this experience uncertain.

Like *Marmion*, *Superstition* argues persuasively for Barker's democratic ideology. While Americans had escaped the physical tyranny of the old world, they remained yoked to a set of attitudes which had consistently given rise to despotism. Many, like Ravensworth, seemed to have embraced the concept of freedom only superficially, wishing merely to exchange one hierarchy for another. But, Barker seems to suggest, such patterns of thought may be broken and freedom may finally triumph. For that to occur, the citizenry must be constantly vigilant, must strive for knowledge, and must not give up their freedom lightly to the will of another. And they must have an art that alerts them to the dangers that they confront both from without and from within.

Conclusion

The specter of Shakespeare and the English cultural tradition he epitomized loomed large in the minds of early republican authors. Audiences and artists alike had been educated by and to a literature which had, from an American ideological perspective, the goal of perpetuating a set of values diametrically opposed to the principles of freedom which had founded the country. To continue to utilize English forms, at least temporarily, seemed acceptable. To perpetuate the values which had informed them was unthinkable. In this sense, Barker was part of a broad cultural phenomenon whose participants included such writers as Brown, Irving, and Cooper. While using familiar, almost trite forms, all of these writers, to a greater or lesser degree, sought to find a method of embodying American ideals. Notwithstanding the similarities with other writers of the time, Barker performed a unique service in American literature by championing the cause of American drama both through his provocative criticism and through his intriguing plays.

NOTES

1. Ralph Waldo Emerson, "The American Scholar," in *The Collected Works of Ralph Waldo Emerson*, 4 vols. (Boston: Belknap Press, 1971–87), 1:52.

2. Richard Moody, ed., *Dramas from the American Theatre, 1762–1909* (Cleveland and New York: World Publishing, 1966), 27.

3. Royall Tyler, *The Contrast*, in *Representative American Plays*, ed. Arthur Hobson Quinn, 7th ed. (New York: Appleton-Century-Crofts, 1957), 48.

4. *The American Theatre as Seen by Its Critics, 1752–1934*, ed. Montrose J. Moses and John Mason Brown (New York: Norton, 1934), 24.

5. Charles H. Shattuck, *Shakespeare on the American Stage, from the Hallams to Edwin Booth* (Washington, D.C.: Folger Shakespeare Library, 1976), 31.

6. James G. McManaway, "Shakespeare in the United States," *PMLA* 79 (December 1964): 513.

7. Shakespeare's presence on these campuses is made even more remarkable considering that serious and widespread study of English literature was not initiated in American colleges until the 1880s.

8. While a production of *Romeo and Juliet* may have been mounted in New York in 1750, the Kean performance is the first for which we have definite evidence.

9. Robert Falk, "Shakespeare in America: A Survey to 1900," *Shakespeare Survey* 18 (1965):102; Norman Sanders, "American Criticism of Shakespeare's History Plays," *Shakespeare Studies* 9 (1976):11.

10. Hugh F. Rankin points out that despite the paucity of information from the period, 180 performances of fourteen plays can be documented. He suggests that "it would be reasonable to guess the total to be at least 500." *The Theater in Colonial America* (Chapel Hill: University of North Carolina Press, 1965), 191.

11. Raymond Fitzsimmons, *Edmund Kean: Fire from Heaven* (New York: The Dial, 1976), 151.

12. Indicative of this attitude is Barker's comment to William Dunlap in 1832 (eight years after Barker had written his last play), that since he is writing to Dunlap on Sunday the "work-day world cannot find fault, however I may deserve the censure of *holy-day* folks." William Dunlap, *History of the American Theatre* (1832; reprint New York: Burt Franklin, 1963), 308. Future references to this letter will be cited by page number in the text as *Dunlap*.

13. Barker's biographer cites, for example, Barker's going to the expense of securing passes in the 1820s to both the Olympic and Chestnut Street theatres in Philadelphia. Paul H. Musser, *James Nelson Barker* (Philadelphia: University of Pennsylvania Press, 1929), 83.

14. James Nelson Barker, *Tears and Smiles* in Musser, 141.

15. James Nelson Barker, *The Indian Princess* in *Representative Plays by American Dramatists*, 3 vols., ed. Montrose J. Moses (New York: E. P. Dutton, 1918–25), 1:576.

16. James Nelson Barker, *Marmion* (New York: Longworth, 1816), iii. Hereafter cited in the text as *M* followed by page number.

17. James Nelson Barker, "The Drama," *Democratic Press* [Philadelphia], 18 December 1816, p. 2. Further references to this series, all of which bear the same title and appear on page two, will be made parenthetically in the text by date.

18. It seems important to note that Barker is concerned not with ideas of individual liberty, but with styles of acting, preferring, as several of these articles make clear, the more vigorous interpretations of George Frederick Cooke to the more formal characterizations of America's premiere Kembleite, Thomas Abthorpe Cooper.

19. Musser, 46.

20. Arthur Hobson Quinn, *A History of the American Drama from the Beginnings to the Civil War*, 2nd ed. (New York: F. S. Crofts, 1943), 151.

21. James Nelson Barker, *Superstition* in *Representative American Plays From 1767 to the Present Day*, ed. Arthur Hobson Quinn, 7th ed. (New York: Appleton-Century-Crofts, 1957), 117. Hereafter abbreviated as *S* and cited by page number in the text.

Nautical "Docudrama" in the Age of the Kembles

George D. Glenn

In the twentieth century, the term "docudrama" is used to describe that category of drama which is based almost entirely on either historic or contemporary documentary materials. From the Federal Theatre Project's "Living Newspapers" to the dramas of Kipphardt, Weiss, Littlewood, et al., documentary materials have been used to explore and comment on complex social and political issues, presenting them in theatrically exciting ways.

The use of contemporary factual sources in the creation of drama is, of course, not unique to the twentieth century, although each age has differed both in the extent to which documentary materials were utilized and in the dramatic/theatrical function of such materials. In the late eighteenth and early nineteenth centuries, although there were numerous opportunities for employing documentary materials, their use was primarily for their potential as exciting entertainment and political, social, and moral self-aggrandizement.

The period of the French Revolution and the Napoleonic Wars (1792–1815) coincides almost exactly with the age of the Kembles. Because England had become a naval power, the popular imagination was always easily captured by plays which depicted nautical characters and events: the many successes of the dominant British Navy during the 1792–1815 period naturally resulted in the production of numerous nautical dramas and "operas" at Covent Garden, Drury Lane, and the minor theatres in London.

Three categories of naval events provided opportunities for theatrical adaptation: the great naval battles between the British and French fleets, land-based civilian celebrations commemorating British fleet victories, and battles between single British and enemy ships. A number of events of each type is represented in plays, typically hurried into production, whose timely dramatic content, coupled with numerous scenic displays and a spectacular conclusion, stimulated and reinforced patriotic sentiment in the audience.

Lord Howe's victory over the French fleet off Ushant on 1 June 1794 was the first fleet action to be dramatized during this period, and is typical of the timely connection between the contemporary event and the stage production based on it. The news of the "Glorious First of June," as the battle was called, reached London on 10 June, and was announced at the theatres that night: at Drury Lane, for example, "in the second half of 'No Song No Supper,' the audience was agreeably surprised by a formal declaration from Suett that Lord Howe HAD TAKEN SEVEN FRENCH SHIPS OF THE LINE" (*T*, 11 June 1794, p. 3).

Only three weeks later Drury Lane announced that a "new Entertainment," *The Glorious First of June*, by James Cobb and R. B. Sheridan, would be performed on 3 July as a benefit for the widows and orphans of men killed in the battle.[1] The play was "written so much on the spur of the occasion that the copy . . . was not delivered to the Prompter" until just three days before the performance (*T*, 3 July 1794, p. 2). *The Glorious First of June* opens with a "very spirited Prologue . . . most ably delivered by Mr. Kemble," and has a plot which revolves around two villagers who leave their sweethearts to join Lord Howe's fleet. Patriotic songs ("Hail happy Britain, favour's isle / Where Freedom, Arts and Commerce smile! / Long may thy George in glory prove, / The transports of a nation's love") (*T*, 4 July 1794, p. 3) and a sea fight, "the most complicated, as well as striking spectacle ever exhibited," were featured (*T*, 3 July 1794). Indeed, "the shipping was managed with so much skill, that an honest tar in the gallery, fired at the deception, exclaimed, 'Douse my lights, how I should like to be among them'" (*T*, 5 July 1794, p. 2). The piece ends with "Commander Broadside" hosting a celebration with a "superior resplendency" of fireworks for the returning heroes of the battle.

Aside from scenic spectacle, *The Glorious First of June* also illustrates some of the other conventions of this genre: the settings are on land and the characters are land-based, although they may go off to sea; the naval battles depicted are at a distance; and there is an extensive use of patriotic airs and sentimental ballads.

Thomas Dibdin used this device of land-based dramatic action culminating in the characters' (and audiences') observing the fleet battle in *The Mouth of the Nile*, produced at Covent Garden 25 October 1798. The battle Dibdin commemorated was Admiral Horatio Nelson's defeat of the French fleet in Abukir Bay (Egypt) in 1798, during which all but two of the French battleships were captured or destroyed; the French flagship, *L'Orient*, with 120 guns and 1,010 men, blew up, and Nelson was wounded by a splinter and lost an eye. In Dibdin's dramatization of this battle, the convention of having land-based characters observe the fight was based on reality: *The Times* reported that during the actual battle "the shores were lined with the natives, who shared in the joy of our brave countrymen in witnessing the total defeat of the enemy" (3 October 1798, p. 2).

The play opens on "An Egyptian Landscape—An Old Peasant enters meeting Michael, Adela, and a number of [other] Egyptian Villagers."[2] The old peasant informs the villagers that the French have landed and issued a proclamation "to tell us we are all slaves, and that they come to make us free whether we will or no." He then delivers a "Chaunt," which is the proclamation in verse:

> . . . we hereby proclaim, and ordain, and invite,
> That all the good folks of this Province unite,
> To make themselves free, of their chains we shall rid 'em,
> And permit them to do—just whatever we bid 'em.

No sooner does the old peasant finish reading the proclamation than an "outré" French officer enters. His behavior and language immediately reinforce the impression of the French as tyrannical hypocrites as is implied by the proclamation. The French officer "*goes up among the women*: . . . Dat is ver pret girl, come here, ma dear, you can love a Frenchman? . . . We make free all over the vorld . . . We are come to gain *laurels* by conquering the *Beys*."

The French officer is interrupted by the entrance of Jack Junk, Pat, and a group of English sailors, who inform him that the English fleet is coming. Jack Junk proposes a toast to the blue sea, but Pat argues that all the seas are green, even the Red Sea, the Black Sea, and the White Sea. Junk explains in a song that that is because the laurels of England, reflecting on the sea's surface, have turned it green, and the more laurels, the greener it becomes: "As the sea grew more green, why Monsieur grew more white: / And they never behold it, but vex'd at the view, / They scold at poor Neptune, and they cry out *Mor bleu*." As the song ends (with lines praising Admirals Howe, Duncan, St. Vincent, and Nelson), "The English fleet appears, heaving in sight; guns fire." More sailors enter, announcing that they have captured the French garrison and are going back to fight. Junk and Pat join them.

The third (and final) scene is "The Open Sea. The two fleets are seen preparing for battle. The Engagement commences, and having terminated in the discomfiture of the French fleet, the crews land and are met and congratulated by the Egyptian Peasants." The French officer is there, and is taunted, but Junk, displaying the traditional British sense of fair play, defends him: "Come, come, no hitting a man when he's down. Give us your hand, Mounseer, and I wish with all my heart, that the work of our brave Admiral to-day may lay the foundation of a general shaking hands throughout Europe." The French officer responds with "You are right, it will make all de hands in my country shake." The play ends with a final song in praise of Nelson.

Dibdin's dialogue characteristically relies on puns and quips: *The Times* felt that the dialogue and songs possessed "considerable merit," with the songs abounding "in humour and epigrammatic point." Although the best thing in the production was the representation of the fleet action, the *Times* reviewer averred that the explosion of the French Admiral's ship *L'Orient* "proved the most satisfactory thing in the piece" (26 October 1798, p. 2).

The Mouth of the Nile was revived 18 November 1800 for its most popular performance, when Nelson himself came to Covent Garden to see it performed. As the *Morning Post and Gazetteer* reported, his presence created hysterical outbursts of patriotic enthusiasm in the audience as he, in effect, became part of the spectacle. "On his entrance he was received with loud huzzas . . . and 'Rule Britannia' was called for and sung amidst the greatest applause. . . . Many illusions were applied to the gallant tar, and warmly applauded. In the last song, one of the verses says 'Nelson shall go and fight them again;' this excited particular enthusiasm; Lord Nelson and the whole audience rose, his Lordship bowing to the audience" (19 November 1800, p. 3).

The government and the populace in England celebrated major military victories with illuminations, processions, and mass gatherings. Plays depicting victory celebrations inspired by fleet actions were as popular as the plays about the actual fleet actions themselves. Typical of this kind of production are William Pearce's *Arrived at Portsmouth* and Andrew Franklin's *A Trip to the Nore*. *Arrived at Portsmouth* opened at Covent Garden 31 October 1794. An "operatic Drama in Two Acts," it begins with three sea captains—Pendant, Tropic, and Magnet—accompanied by a group of sailors and females, coming ashore at Portsmouth to celebrate their victory of the First of June: "We've bade the restless seas adieu / To toy dear girls, some hours with you."[3] The main plot concerns Captain Pendant's love affair with Louisa, whose sea-captain guardian has died in battle; the comic subplot revolves around Pendant's half brother, Wildfire, who wants nothing more than a military career, but who is prevented from one by the terms of his father's will. The play is full of the standard patriotic expressions and songs, but, like *The Mouth of the Nile*, also includes an expression of British fair play: when Magnet comments that the fleet's prisoners are "landed to hospitable treatment," Tropic responds with "Heaven forbid it should be otherwise:—the English nation will ever give proof to the world, that they consider an enemy in their power, as an enemy no longer. (*Impressively*)."[4]

The scenery was of the travelogue type: that is, it was representative of actual locations. The first scene, for example, is "The Platform and Battery, commanding the Entrance to Portsmouth Harbour, with a view of Spithead, and the Isle of Wight in the distance." Other scenes are "The Old Anchor Forge in Portsmouth Dock Yard" (with a chorus of singing blacksmiths), "A View of the Governor's House," and the concluding scene, "A View of High-street Illuminated, including the Market-Hall, taken from the extremity of the Parade near the Governor's House. Bells ringing, etc." This last scene was described by *The Times* as being the "*chef d'oeuvre* of scenic brilliancy and taste" (26 October 1798, p. 2).

A Trip to the Nore opened at Drury Lane on 9 November 1797. The play's inspiration was the celebration of Admiral Duncan's defeat of the Dutch fleet at Camperdown, and King George III's procession in his royal yacht from Greenwich to the Nore to inspect Duncan's fleet and the Dutch prizes. More than *The Glorious First of June*, *A Trip to the Nore* is a processional with each scene representing a stage on the road from Greenwich to the Nore. In each of six scenes, a group of representative characters finds the opportunity for a song and comic or patriotic dialogue.

The first scene is simply described as "Greenwich." The description for scene two is more particular: "Greenwich Hospital—Guns fire—Flags are hoisted on the vessels—The Royal Barge appears—the vessels sail—Martial music, which ceases when the vessels disappear." This scene is followed by "The Road-side beyond Greenwich," "A Landscape and Public-House on the Road to Sheerness," and "Sheerness." The last scene takes place at "The Nore." "The British Fleet reviewed, with the Dutch Prizes.

Enter Bowsprit and Sailors (huzzaing) meeting all the Characters and Mob."⁵

The British spirit of fair play is again exhibited in *A Trip to the Nore* through the character of Hokensloken, the "honest Dutchman, who behaved with the greatest humanity to one of our Countrymen in the late action, and who is on his parole to see the amusements of the day." Hokensloken is insulted by the chimney sweep, but is stoutly defended by the other characters:

> *Donald:* Haud [sic] your hand, Urchin—he's under our protection, and shan't be insulted while I wear a sword. None but a coward would crush a fallen enemy.
> *O'Thunder:* True, Donald, and shatter my timbers, you dirty little soot-bag, if you insult my honest Hocuspocus again, I'll cut you in two!
> *Bowsprit:* Bravo, bravo, damme!—the Mynheers fought bravely! The more valient they behaved, the more glorious, my boys, for those that beat them.

The British people—as well as the establishment—had to believe that Great Britain was presenting a "united front" to its enemies, especially as the war continued and Britain's allies were defeated by the French or retreated to a doubtful neutrality. In *A Trip to the Nore* the audience sees English, Irish, Scots, the lower and middle classes, and the civilian and military components of the British populace united in their support of the war effort, in their patriotism, and in their enthusiasm for British victories. The sentiments expressed in the plays mirrored and reinforced the attitudes of the audience.

The display of the peculiar idiosyncrasies of various social and economic classes was always popular with audiences. For example, Ben Bowsprit, a "Greenwich Pensioner, with a wooden leg" is the personification of the bluff, hearty, honest old salt. He is shown admiring the Dutch for their valor, but he is equally enthusiastic over England's victory. He first enters singing "Hearts of Oak," and when the boatswain complains of his being drunk, he responds:

> My brain has been boxing the compass ever since I heard of the late glorious Victory—Damme, Master, there is no use to disguise the fact—I've taken as many bumpers of Hollands as would float a Frigate, drinking success to brave Duncan and the British flag!

The irony of drinking to the defeat of the Dutch in Holland gin would not have been lost on the audience.

The lower classes are represented by such characters as the chimney sweep and Mr. and Mrs. Cockney. The best of the merchant middle class is depicted by Mr. Buckram, who behaves the way all wartime merchants ought to behave: Bowsprit accuses Buckram of war profiteering but forgives him when Buckram claims that not only did he subscribe to a relief fund at Lloyd's, but also he "was near breaking my neck in forcing my way into the Pit of Drury Lane Theatre to leave my mite for the relief of those poor Widows, whose brave Husbands fell on board ship in the *field* of battle."

Patriotic fervor is also expressed in the boatswain's song, "To Duncan and Glory the song let us raise," which contains the refrain: "To Duncan and Trollope now extend your throats / And defy the French and their flat-bottomed boats" (a reference to Napoleon's threatened invasion fleet). The third verse of the song pulls out all the emotional stops:

> Here's a health to our King—let the cannons roar, (cannons fire)
> Three cheers to King George, (cheers) and our friends at the Nore!
> To our Navy and Army the song let us close,
> With route and confusion to Old England's foes!

Even love must give way to patriotism and duty. When Donald and Mary finally find one another, after searching for each other for most of the play, Donald rejoices that "this is the greatest pleasure I have felt in my life, except when [I] saw the Dutch Admiral strike to the British flag." The pair sing a duet in which Donald's lyrics say that a sailor's primary duty is to the fleet, and Mary's aver that it is women's duty to support the sailors.

The last scene—the reviewing of the British fleet—is presented in a "Medly" of song which the boatswain, to the tune of "Rule Britannia," concludes with:

> While France remembers still the name of HOWE,
>   And Spanish triumphs grace ST. VINCENT'S brow,
> Fresh laurels deck another Victor's name,
>   And DUNCAN lustre adds to Britain's fame.

The production was well received by the press, more for its patriotic sentiment and humor than for any intrinsic dramatic merit. The *Morning Chronicle* pointed out that "if to cherish the opinion that British sailors are superior to all their rivals tends, as it undoubtedly does, to render them really superior, the object of this piece is highly commendable" (10

November 1797, p. 3). The *Morning Post and Gazetteer* agreed, calling the offering a "well-timed compliment to the British Navy," describing it as "highly gratifying to the feelings of the house [while] its humour excited incessant laughter, and it was received with thundering plaudits throughout" (10 November 1797, p. 2).

Fleet victories were of great military importance, and any such victory was enthusiastically celebrated in England, but public imagination was also greatly stimulated by any account of a victorious ship-to-ship duel. A number of plays had their sources in the accounts of such battles, and included the same spectacular elements and expressions of patriotic sentiment as did the plays commemorating fleet actions. An example is William Pearce's *The Death of Captain Faulknor; or, British Heroism*, produced for the actress Mrs. Martyr's benefit performance at Covent Garden, 6 May 1795.

The battle in question took place on 5 January 1795 in the West Indies when the English frigate *Blanche* defeated the thirty-eight-gun French frigate *La Pique* in a five-hour action. According to the "Minutes of the Proceedings" of the battle, as reprinted in *The Times* on 13 February 1795, the *Blanche*, under Captain Faulknor's command, had sighted a French frigate anchored under the protection of shore batteries, and after two or three days' effort finally lured the larger French ship out to fight. The English first sighted her at 8:30 P.M., but the first broadsides weren't fired until over four hours later. Finally:

> At One, A.M.—put our helm a starboard, and ran across her stern, and *lashed her bowsprit* to our capstern [*sic*]; . . . At this time our main and mizzen masts went overboard, and they *attempted to board us, but were repulsed*. At quarter before two, A.M.—She dropped astern, (at this time Captain Faulknor fell). We got a hawser up and made her well fast with her bowsprit abreast of our starboard quarter; the marines keeping a constant fire of musketry into her. Finding the carpenters could not make the ports large enough, we blew out as much of the upper transom beam as would admit the two aftermost guns on the main deck to be run out, and fired into her bows. At two, A.M. all her masts were shot away. In this situation we towed her before the wind, engaging til a quarter past five, when she called out that they had struck. The second lieutenant and ten more men then swam on board, and took possession of *La Pique*. (*T*, 13 February 1795, p. 3)

An addendum to the account noted that "*Captain Faulknor himself lashed the bowsprit of La Pique, to the capstern of the Blanche*, and was soon afterwards shot through the heart, by one of the people on the bowsprit of *La*

Pique." I have quoted extensively because Pearce used much of this account in forming not only the situation but also some of the dialogue of his play, thus making more extensive use of documentary material than any other similar play during this period.

The play opens with Captain Faulknor (the first time in these plays that a real person is portrayed), Lieutenants Steady, Oakley, and O'Cutter sitting at a table, drinking and singing, and toasting England and the navy.[6] After the last song, "all come forward," and we learn that they are glum because they are windbound in port. Faulknor expresses the hope that the wind will change and enable them to sail in pursuit of the French frigate which they have challenged to leave port and fight them. At this, the boatswain enters and reports that the wind has changed and the French frigate has been sighted. They all rush off to fight.

Since Pearce's "opera" was written and produced for Mrs. Martyr's benefit, Pearce had to include material for her. Mrs. Martyr's scene, the second in the play, has nothing to do with the ship duel or the death of Faulknor but does allow Pearce to present England as the one country where true liberty is to be found, French revolutionary assertions to the contrary. The scene presents Pounce, a freeborn and independent Englishman, setting the example for the rest of Europe to follow by bringing liberty to a West Indian slave, Mora, played by Mrs. Martyr in blackface. The scene, "Another part of the Island," opens with "negroes, men and women, discovered dancing.—After awhile enter Pounce, accompanied by one or two sailors, meeting Mora as she enters." Pounce is taken with Mora, and flirts with her, calling her "my little Dingey," "my pretty bit of ebony," and "my little black pepper-corn." He is surprised by her wit and good sense, and offers to take her back to London with him. Mora asks if she will have liberty in London. When Pounce asks what kind of liberty she wants, she replies: "Liberty to dance ven I please—sing ven I please—eat ven I please—and go nappy ven I please." This sensible answer so impresses Pounce that he exclaims, "By Temple-Bar, I swear, my sweet Mora, that 'tho thy face is black, thy heart is white—so I must have a kiss—(*kisses her*)." Mora then recounts in song how she was enslaved by a white man with a black heart: "In Africa once my heart beat chearly— / Chinka, chinka, chinka, cheero— / And Negro sweetheart loved me dearly— / Chinka, chinka, chinka, cheero." The song recounts how a white captain comes, captures her, and sells her. But now she is happy, because "Wid English man I'll happy be, // For Englishmans dey all be free // When to London you me bring // I will sing—'God Save the King!'"

As Pounce and Mora exit, the scene changes to a "View of the Sea. The

Firing of Guns heard.—English and French Frigates come in view in the act of Engagement—Action continues until the French flag is seen to strike."

The last scene is a sea port. The islanders come in rejoicing in the victory followed by Steady, Oakley, and O'Cutter, who land from a boat, sad in their victory because Faulknor has been killed. The islanders ask for an account of the battle, which O'Cutter delivers (in a speech that Pearce apparently took almost verbatim from the "Minutes of the Proceeding"):

> After exchanging a few broadsides within a short distance, our gallant Commander gave orders for the closest action— . . . we instantly put our helm astarboard—run across the Enemy's stern—lashed her bowsprit to our Capstan—the engagement now became furious on both sides—our main and mizzen masts soon went overboard—She attempted to board us—we repulsed her—she then dropped astern—but we instantly got out a hawser, and again made her fast to our Capstan—it was at this critical moment when our brave Captain, in the very act of strenuously assisting with his own hands to lash firmly her Bowsprit to us, that the glorious hero fell!—permit me, sir, to pause a moment,—(wipes his eyes, the other lieutenants and soldiers looking downcast)—well, Sir—the loss of our adored Commander raised fresh vigor and vengeance—we blew off part of our transom beam to get larger guns out astern—we fired into his bows for three hours. . . . she struck—we swam on board—and took possession.[7]

Minute guns are heard, Faulknor is praised, and then: "(Procession of Interment.) Dead March. Interment—Firing over the grave. Song. 'Rule Britannia,' etc. The End."

A different kind of single-ship action was the basis for Thomas Dibdin's *The Hermione; or, Retaliation*, performed at Covent Garden 5 April 1800. Dibdin based his play on the story of the frigate *Hermione*, which experienced a mutiny in August 1797 while she was stationed in the West Indies. Led by the master's mate, the mutineers chopped to pieces the captain and nine of his officers, and threw the Lieutenant of Marines overboard. The successful mutineers then sailed the ship to Spanish-held territory and surrendered her. The Spanish governor rewarded the mutineers and fitted the ship out to cruise for Spain, with the erstwhile master's mate as second captain (*T*, 8 March 1798, p. 3).

On 25 October 1799, Captain Edward Hamilton of H.M.S. *Surprize* undertook a successful cutting-out operation to re-take the *Hermione*, at anchor under the protection of a shore battery of two hundred guns.

Hamilton and a hundred of his officers and men in the ship's boats entered the harbor a little after midnight on the twenty-fifth. Fifty of the crew boarded the *Hermione* (which had a crew of over four hundred), while the remaining men in the boats cut her cables and took her in tow. After a fierce fight lasting two hours, they succeeded in capturing her and towing her out of the harbor while under the fire of the shore batteries (*T*, 22 January 1800, p. 3). The *Surprize* brought the *Hermione* into Kingston, where the commanding Admiral, Sir Peter Parker, recommissioned her as the *Retaliation*—thus providing the subtitle of Dibdin's play.

The *Hermione* is unique in that it contains a scene set on board ship, instead of having the entire action take place on shore.[8] This play also differs from the other plays examined in that it contains a scene typical of pure melodrama—the villain attempting to work his evil way with the heroine, but being foiled by a heroic sailor. Surprisingly, this appears to be the only nautical play of this period with such a scene.

The *Hermione*, a "Musical Interlude," opens "Inside of the Ship-Cabin. Captain and Officers discovered drinking, who open the piece with a Marine Glee and chorus." After the song, the Captain and his officers discuss the recapture of an English ship at anchor in a Spanish port. The boatswain implies that the *Hermione* wasn't captured by "fair play," an obvious reference to the original mutiny. The Captain and his men plan and describe the cutting-out expedition (it is an accurate description of the process) and end the scene with a song.

The scene changes to "A Spanish Landscape.—The Sea at a distance. Enter Corporal Flip and Sam Swig." Flip and Sam have escaped from a Spanish prison, and spot an English ship in the bay. They go down to the beach to signal to be taken aboard. After they exit, "Enter several Spanish soldiers." They discuss the *Hermione*, one of them referring to her as a "prize." In another oblique reference to the mutiny, the second soldier responds:

> A prize, do you call it? A robbery, a theft. The English are our Enemies, but they are brave ones, and I'd sooner lose a whole fleet of them at fair fighting, than be indebted for a single ship to a set of renegade rascals who having once broken the trust of their own country, are a disgrace to every other.

At this point a French officer enters, revealing that he is to be the real villain of the piece. He has been appointed to instruct the Spanish troops, whose reaction is: "We're sure to be well disciplined one way or other. The

Frenchmen lend us the Theory, and the English give us the practice." The Frenchman speaks with a heavy French accent and brags about what he is teaching the Spanish. The Spaniards don't like him and defend the English against his slurs. Finally, the Frenchman exhorts the Spaniards to guard their prisoners closely, for he has an English lady as his prisoner, and claims that he killed her husband in battle. The Spanish vow to be vigilant, "for a surprise might be fatal to us" (this is the only reference to the name of the ship which captured the *Hermione*).

The third scene takes place "Inside of an Indian House." Sam Swig enters, taking shelter from pursuit. Orora, described as "a black girl," enters; Sam shows her that his keg is empty and asks her for a drink. Orora questions him in several languages, and Sam humorously misunderstands her. They sing a comic duet, and at the end of the song Sam kisses her. They hear the drums of the pursuit, and Sam is afraid he will be captured. Orora "points to a recep [sic] with a door," and Sam hides inside as Orora leaves. The French officer enters with the English Captain's Lady. He tells her that her husband is not dead but his prisoner, and "If you are grateful, he may live." The Frenchman attempts to assault the Lady, who repulses him, crying "O mercy! help! has innocence no friend? Has heaven no power to strike?" At this point Sam "rushes out" and saves her. Sam locks the Officer in the "recep" as Corporal Flip enters. A boat has been sent from the English ship, and they all leave.

The final scene is set in "The Harbour":

> The *Hermione* at Anchor. The Spanish flag flying. The English boat approaches. They board the *Hermione*. The engagement to be represented as distinctly as possible, finishes with hoisting the British Colours, towing the ship out of port. The Band, Drums, Trumpets, etc. playing "Rule Britannia." The Captain and Boat's crew waving their hats and handkerchiefs and flags to the audience.

The Hermione was bound to be a success, having the emotional appeal that it did. Not only was a captured ship recaptured and returned in triumph, but a symbolic rape—that of the *Hermione* by the mutineers—was avenged. Similarly the symbolic rape of England, in the person of the Captain's Lady, by the French was prevented by English valor. All in all, the production must have been emotionally satisfying to the audience.

Even when little or no dramatic content is included, spectacle is still capable of arousing and reinforcing emotion, as is the case in the pieces that were produced following the death of Lord Nelson in the Battle of Trafalgar on 21 October 1805. The same issue of *The Times* (7 November 1805) that reported Nelson's death also recounted the initial reaction to the news at Covent Garden. When the curtain rose after the main piece, the audience was "surprised with the view of a superb naval scene" (*T*, p. 3). On the same day the *Morning Post* reported that the principal singers, costumed as naval officers and sailors, were "discovered supporting the flag of Great Britain, with the prostrate ensigns of France and Spain at their feet, and in the act of returning thanks to heaven." The *Post* described the scenery as consisting of downstage columns decorated with the names of England's foremost naval heroes; in the background was the English fleet, forming "a most pleasing *coup d'oeil*" (7 November 1805, p. 3). From the flies descended a half-length portrait of Nelson, inscribed with the words "*Horatio Nelson, Ob. 21st Oct*" (*T*, 7 November 1805, p. 3). "Rule Britannia" was sung by the company, with a new commemorative verse which produced "an universal and rapturous *encore*."

Covent Garden continued to develop this "little interlude," with "some alterations: . . . In the scenery there is a representation of the late glorious battle, and full length likeness of the immortal hero. . . . supported by *Mars*, while *Fame*, with her trump, proclaims to the world the heroic virtues of her beloved son" (*MP*, 8 November 1805, p. 3). By 8 November the interlude had acquired a title—*Nelson's Glory*—and "assumed a dramatic shape, and is as well adapted to the glorious, though melancholy event it is designed to celebrate, as anything got up on the spur of the occasion could possibly be" (*T*, 9 November 1805, p. 2).

Drury Lane got into the act the evening of 10 November: "After the Opera, a Naval Scene, in which a transparent portrait of the immortal Nelson, encircled with a laurel, was introduced" (*MP*, 11 November 1805, p. 3). The next night, a "little piece" no more than fifteen minutes long, by Cumberland, was brought forth. It consisted of a poem and some "appropriate music," and concluded with a representation of Fame descending from the flies, and a portrait of Nelson inscribed with his famous signal to the fleet: "England expects that every man will do his duty" (*MP*, 12 November 1805, p. 3). *The Times* called the piece a "Melodrama," describing it as beginning with a "grand Sea view, in which two Fleets are represented as towards the end of an engagement; a boat appears, from which Elliston and Braham, habited as Officers of the Navy, land. . . . After some pathetic lines, recited by Elliston, and a most affecting song by Braham, groups of volunteers and women are introduced, who join in lamenting their departed hero. An illuminated figure of Lord Nelson then rises from the stage" (12 November 1805, p. 3). The battle has been won but the hero was lost. England was torn between mourning Nelson's death and exulting over the defeat of the enemy fleet. The emotional reinforcement of *Nelson's Glory* and the "Melo-drama" were necessary for the English to convince themselves that all was not lost with Nelson's death—that victory over the French was still possible.

In addition to the interest inherent in the depiction of contemporary events, the immediate attraction in all these pieces was the scenic display they incorporated, particularly representations of the various naval battles. Drury Lane and Covent Garden must have had a large stock of naval scenery, since they were able to mount a naval battle at literally a day's notice. The naval scenery also must have been varied in type, for although a few wave machines would do for any ocean, the scripts called for every type of easily recognizable naval vessel from three-decker ships-of-the-line to ships' boats. For the most part, what documentary qualities these spectacles had was in the scenery, not in the dialogue or the characters. The reviews comment on the accuracy of the sea battles as well as on the accuracy of scenery representing locations familiar to the audience. If a reviewer mentioned the excellence of the representation of Greenwich Hospital, for example, one can trust that evaluation. One might not be so confident about the accuracy of a West Indian hut, but the scenery satisfied the audience's desire to experience the exotic and adventurous.

The nautical docudramas of the age of the Kembles became an important part of the national celebrations of victory, as well as being successful as pure entertainment. They reinforced patriotic fervor and encouraged positive virtues and attitudes in the English populace. In addition, the plays present the diversity of the English people as a positive asset: almost every nautical play demonstrates cooperation among English, Irish, and Scots; the Cockney gets along with the countryman, and the tar with the merchant, as Great Britain presents a united front to her enemies. England is the true land of liberty, despite France's boast of Liberty, Equality, and Fraternity. The English condemn slavery and allow other peoples to go their own way. France imposes her will on the Dutch and the Spanish, not the English. England hopes for peace and friendship among nations.

One could lament the lack of significant, serious nautical drama. No play treats of the appalling shipboard conditions that led to the fleet-wide mutinies at Spithead and the Nore in 1797, nor does any playwright depict the inequities and injustices of the press-gang. Such things are not even suggested. But what did England need? She was fighting for her existence, alone against the whole of Europe. She did not need or want moral or social introspection. She needed, and got, positive reinforcement, moral justification, spiritual uplift, and patriotic enthusiasm, in addition to the solid entertainment values of monumental scenery, fireworks, jokes, music, and song. Every production ended with an enthusiastic rendition of the one song audiences always demanded, and the people would leave the theatres humming "Rule Britannia," secure in the knowledge that "Britannia rules the waves."

NOTES

1. Advertisement in *The Times*, 2 July 1794: p. 2.
2. Thomas Dibdin, *The Mouth of the Nile; or, The Glorious First of August* (London: J. Barker, 1798), in *Three Centuries of Drama: English*, ed. Henry W. Wells (New York: Readex Microprint, 1953–).
3. William Pearce, *Arrived at Portsmouth* (London: Printed by G. Woodfall for T. N. Longman, 1794), 1, as reproduced in Wells.
4. Pearce, 5.
5. Andrew Franklin, *A Trip to the Nore: A Musical Entertainment in One Act* (London: British Library, 1797), as reproduced in Wells.
6. [William Pearce], *The Death of Captain Faulknor; or, British Heroism* (London: Glindon, 1795), as reproduced in Wells.
7. Pearce, *The Death of Captain Faulknor*, Larpent MSS. #1079, as reproduced in Wells.
8. Thomas Dibdin, *The Hermione; or, Retaliation*, Larpent MSS. #1288, as reproduced in Wells.

Lofty Tragedy for Mundane Audiences

JOHN WESTLAND MARSTON'S *THE PATRICIAN'S DAUGHTER* AND *STRATHMORE*

Carol J. Carlisle

Like a hero in one of his own dramas, John Westland Marston (1819–1890) had a streak of unconscious hubris. As a youthful member of the Syncretics, a society dedicated to the harmonizing of truths from all philosophies and creeds, he enthusiastically embraced their secondary aim of revitalizing poetic tragedy.[1] To endow the stage anew with legitimate dramas of the loftiest kind was an ambitious dream in an age of illegitimate and hybrid entertainments. But Marston outdid his colleagues in audacity. His first play, written with all the confidence of a twenty-two-year-old idealist, was designed to fulfill the ancient functions of tragedy while challenging some of its conventions. *The Patrician's Daughter* attracted wide attention when it was published (1841) and again when it was produced (1842). Critics disagreed about its merits, but they united in recognizing the author as a man of "no common mind."[2] Marston's innovative zeal soon subsided, but his idealism continued to make itself felt in some twenty plays—comedies and tragicomedies as well as other tragedies. Although he occasionally wrote in prose, he was best known as "the chief upholder of the poetic drama on the English stage." As the *Dictionary of National Biography* remarks, "His talents, indeed, were unequal to so arduous a task, but the mere fact of his having undertaken it singles him out from the crowd."[3] One imagines him as a half-grown Prometheus, waving a handful of sparklers against the gloom.

Any Prometheus commands a certain respect, of course, and this one, though his struggle against the gods of history was futile, deserved the admiration accorded him by many contemporaries. The remarkable thing about Westland Marston was that, while maintaining his commitment to the "higher drama," he constructed his plays with sufficient skill to get almost all of them performed—and by such well-known actors as William Charles Macready, Helen Faucit, Samuel Phelps, Barry Sullivan, Gustavus Vaughan Brooke, Charles and Ellen Kean, Charles Dillon, E. H. Sothern, and Adelaide Neilson. Although Marston's plays rarely achieved long-term popularity, a good half dozen—including his two most impressive tragedies, *Strathmore* (1849) and *Philip of France and Marie De Meranie* (1850)—were decidedly successful when first produced.

Nevertheless, even his best works promise more than they ultimately accomplish. They are always offering glimpses of what they could have been, both as literary creations and as practical pieces for the Victorian stage, if only—if only what? That elusive "what" teases one into a closer look at Marston's plays. Since the tragedies represent his strongest efforts to rejuvenate the drama, they call most insistently for critical attention. Their characteristic qualities, good and bad, can best be discovered by a combination of literary analysis and theatrical reconstruction. It will be particularly instructive, I think, to study in this double way a contrasting pair of Marston's dramas: *The Patrician's Daughter*, his most self-consciously innovative tragedy, and *Strathmore*, his most traditional one.

First, however, a brief reminder of the conditions from which Marston and his friends proposed to lift the drama. Nineteenth-century critics frequently discussed the drama's decline and adduced various reasons for its deplorable state. Since these have been echoed by later writers, the list is familiar: the depressed economic conditions, the democratization of the audience with consequent decline in taste, the monopoly of the patent theatres, the star system, the strict censorship of the drama, the undramatic character of the age, the dramatists' habit of imitating the Elizabethans, and so on.[4] There was plenty of theatrical activity, but few of the successful new plays would qualify by traditional standards as comedies or tragedies; most were farces, melodramas, or "dramas" (like the French *drames*, plays that treated a serious subject and involved semi-tragic events but usually ended happily). Although "dramas," like the earlier tragicomedies, might be accepted as "legitimate" (a word whose meaning shrank or expanded with the user), there was sometimes a thin line between these and melodramas. Numerous poetic dramas were written, but most remained unacted. The critics' laments concerned the paucity of contemporary works that were both commendable as literature and successful as theatre pieces. True, an occasional reviewer, preferring vital new plays to uninspired imitations of the classics, came close to the modern perception that the acted drama of that period "did not so much decline as, within new social and cultural contexts, radically change its nature."[5] But many of Marston's contemporaries longed for a rebirth of theatrically effective tragedy with all its traditional glories—its noble hero, its pitiable and terrible suffering, its grandeur of language and sentiment.

Certain contemporary attitudes, however, made it difficult to capture the essential qualities of tragedy while also presenting a meaningful view of life. Assuming that authentic tragedy conveys a "sense of ancient evil . . . of the permanence and mystery of human suffering,"[6] Marston's period was in many ways inhospitable to tragedy. As several critics have noted, the "triumph of rationalism" had long since reduced the mystery of man's natural and supernatural surroundings, and Rousseau's influential doctrine that the evils in man's life are due, not to some "immutable flaw in human nature," but to the remediable ills of society had left a heritage of optimistic thought that survived all social and political disappointments. A nineteenth-century outgrowth was the widespread belief in the inevitability of progress—hardly a promising basis for tragedy.[7] It is particularly unpromising if one defines tragedy so narrowly as to eliminate those dramas of suffering and death which hint of redemption "in some other dimension of place or time" and those in which the hero's death effects some worthy purpose;[8] but this, I think, is unduly restrictive. Perhaps the positive emotions that blend with and often transcend the grief at the end of tragedy—wonder at man's endurance, exultation in the sublimity of his spirit—came too easily to the Victorians, with their love of Gothic grandeur and poetic idealism, but such emotions were evidently genuine if not profound.[9]

A trend that affected the form of tragedy was a shift in interest from the public figure to the private individual. This trend is usually traced to the rise of the middle class, and one result had been the eighteenth-century experiments in "*bourgeois* tragedies."[10] The heroes of these plays were not kings or generals but weak-willed apprentices and compulsive gamblers, and their speech was not in blank verse, traditionally used to lift tragic heroes above the mundane level, but in commonplace prose. Although one such drama, Edward Moore's *The Gamester* (1753), was still moving audiences to tears, the experiment as a whole had been short-lived; domestic melodramas now served a similar purpose. The Romantic poets had made a determined, if unsuccessful, effort to "restore tragedy to its former honours,"[11] and the Syncretics were following in their train.

Though beset with difficulties, tragedy was not impossible in Victorian England. Human beings do not give up their deep-seated, intuitive feelings because of some change, however important, in their intellectual climate. Indeed one critic believes that when "[t]raditional certainties . . . failed to accommodate individual experience" a new crisis arose in that period, producing something like the old tragic fear of the irrational.[12] Here was a situation made for tragic treatment: the real-life conflict between creed and experience was directly analogous to a recurring motif which many critics consider basic to tragedy: the hero torn between two worlds or forced to choose between strong but opposing imperatives.[13] Victorian writers recognized the tragic nature of such conflicts: George Eliot found tragedy in the "irreparable collision between the individual and the general," Matthew Arnold in Lamennais's image of humanity with "one foot in the finite and the other in the infinite."[14] As Geoffrey Brereton points out, the idea of "divided personalities" permeated nineteeth-century thought and literature—except for drama. The failure of drama to "explore the forces internal to the individual" he attributes to the inadequate assumptions on which characterization was based at that time.[15] Richard Sewall thinks there was simply "no tragic theater at hand" to interpret the new crisis.[16] Yet there were fine tragic actors in that period, and, although most theatre managers, knowing a popular audience's preference for melodrama, were wary of producing new, untried tragedies, there were a few who took their intellectual responsibility seriously. Response to tragedy was not dead, at any rate. *Hamlet* and *King Lear* (with the tragic ending restored) still had power to move an audience, and, even allowing for the effects of spectacle and emotional acting, surely much of that power lay in the plays themselves.

Why, then, could not a modern dramatist find some way to touch the tragic chord in human nature, still present, if largely unused and out of tune? In 1841, Westland Marston, eager young champion of poetic drama, thought he had found a way. Since the tragic experience was universal, he believed, it was still to be found in the lives of people at all social levels.[17] He would engage the audience's sympathy with a hero from their own class, caught in a modern situation, but would endow him with tragic status through the magnitude of character, the symbolic value (as champion of all who suffer indignities on account of rank), and the impressive blank-verse speech usually reserved for the noble heroes of tragedies set in mythical or historical times. So he wrote *The Patrician's Daughter*.

The scene of the play is contemporary England; the hero is a man of working-class origin who has risen by his merits to a seat in the House of Commons; the theme is "the conflict between the pride of Aristocracy and that of Democracy, with the evils resulting from their collision."[18] Edgar Mordaunt, Marston's hero, is clearly superior in natural gifts and greatness of soul to his associates of higher social rank: he is a magnetic orator, a fine poet, a high-principled young statesman. But he has the classic flaw of excessive pride. At best it takes the form of an admirable, if rather pompous, self-respect ("Shall I tell God he has not made me great, / My soul within me telling me he has?"); at its worst, however, it is a morbid sensitivity to insult that makes him fear his own nature, knowing (as he admits in an early soliloquy) that if "stung" he would be spurred to vengeance regardless of consequences. His kind of pride is pitted against the arrogance of the Lynterne family, particularly the Earl and his sister, Lady Lydia. The title character, Lady Mabel, though she has her share of pride, recognizes and loves the greatness in Mordaunt. She is the victim of the conflict.

This is how Marston works out his theme: Lord Lynterne, always interested in rising politicians, invites Mordaunt to visit his estate. Mordaunt and Lady Mabel, Lynterne's daughter, fall in love; but, before any declaration can be made, Mabel's haughty aunt notices the mutual attraction and determines to forestall an engagement. She tricks the lovers into a misunderstanding that ends in hurt pride on both sides, Mabel denying that she loves Mordaunt and he denouncing her as shallow and heartless. Five years pass. Mordaunt, now Sir Edgar, has become a great man, accepted by Lynterne as a suitable match for his daughter. The engagement has been announced, but, just as the marriage settlement is to be signed, Mordaunt refuses Mabel's hand in the presence of the assembled guests, reminding the Lynternes that they had not thought him good enough for her in his humbler days. Mabel, shocked and heartbroken, goes into a decline, and Lady Lydia, equally ill from attacks of conscience, confesses her responsibility for the original problem. Seeing his daughter's pathetic condition, the Earl humbles himself to visit Mordaunt and reveal the truth. Mordaunt is appalled at what he has done, particularly when he sees Mabel's wasted form. The two declare their love; then, at Mabel's request, the men embrace as the Earl calls Mordaunt "son." Sighing, "I am happy— *very* happy," Mabel expires in Mordaunt's arms.

The Patrician's Daughter has many commendable features which cannot be adequately suggested in a brief summary. Although there is little action in the first half of the play, several powerful scenes enliven the latter

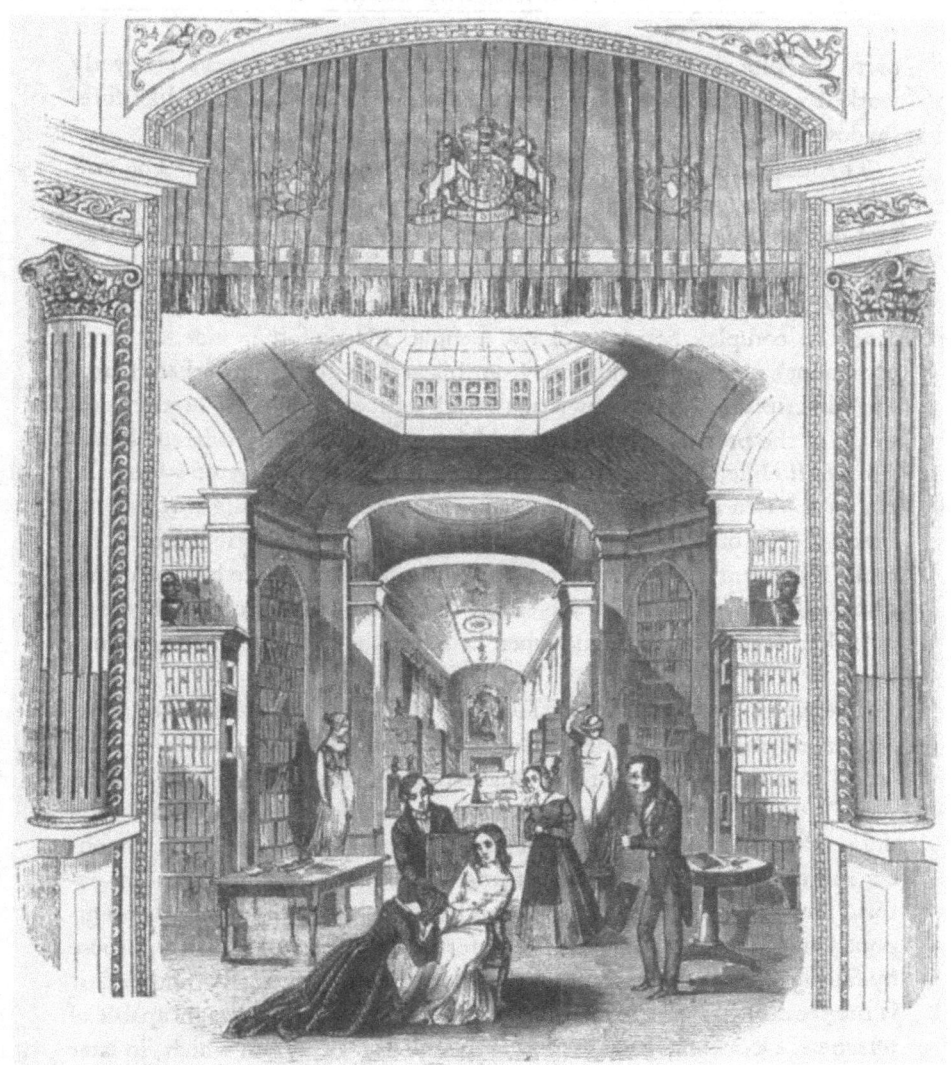

Lady Lydia's confession in *The Patrician's Daughter*, Drury Lane, December 1842. (By permission of the *Illustrated London News* Picture Library.)

part. The plot is carefully articulated, and some of the scenes are cleverly worked up; there are subtler evidences of dramatic skill, too, like foreshadowings and parallels.

The dramatic deficiencies, however, are more noticeable. The improbabilities are perhaps too obvious to mention, and some of them (like two psychosomatic illnesses in the same play) may not have worried Victorian audiences. More important is the thinness of both plot and character. What happens seems to be the demonstration of a proposition rather than the complex behavior of real people. Most of the evidence about Mordaunt's character comes not from his actions, but from other characters' descriptions and his own analytical soliloquies. When he does act, much of the previously accepted evidence seems to be invalidated. Mabel is more lifelike, but she, too, must keep her place in Marston's formula. An ideal Victorian woman, she accepts the prospect of living through her husband, but only if she can find a man worthy of her devotion. Except for rank, Mordaunt is the one man who fulfills her ideal. Once her "soul" has given him its "allegiance," she clings to his image emotionally, however tarnished it may become, and when he rejects her, life becomes meaningless.

The worst characteristics of *The Patrician's Daughter* are those of style. Most annoying is the frequent use of archaic language, not only "thee" and "thou" but many other words of Shakespearean vintage ("methinks," "forsooth") and some quaint constructions that belong to no period. In a drama designed to portray the "habits and spirit of the age," it is disconcerting to find the characters speaking such a self-consciously literary patois. Thus, while Marston wished, understandably, to dignify his contemporary theme with blank verse, he unfortunately defeated his own purpose by failing to divorce poetry from artificially poetic language. Another flaw is the tendency to overdevelop a point. Not that Marston was incapable of terseness. Occasional passages reveal the talent for epigram which, in later years, would make his *bons mots* admired in social gatherings.[19] There are deftly worded aphorisms, and brief and telling speeches of a more individualizing kind, like the dry, somewhat cynical remarks with which the Earl counters the emotional effusions of other characters. Too often, however, the give-and-take of dialogue is neglected in favor of thoughtful, attractively phrased speeches more suitable in a verse essay than in a drama.

For all its faults, *The Patrician's Daughter* deserves more respect than some recent historians of drama have accorded it.[20] It is, after all, the work of an inexperienced youth. But, whatever one thinks of it simply as a play, one must grant its inadequacy as tragedy, hence its failure to accomplish Marston's high purpose. The elements of tragedy are there, ingeniously adapted to new interests: the "tragic conflict" between classes (rather than centered in the hero) looks forward to the problem play, but it is not unworthy of tragic treatment; the "tragic flaw" shared among several characters, though rather schematic, has interesting possibilities; the heroine is a sacrificial victim who reconciles the two sides; the hero experiences a "tragic recognition." Yet there is something hollow and contrived about it all: one gets the impression that the gap between patrician and plebeian could have been easily bridged if not for Lady Lydia's scheming. When he was preparing to produce the play, Macready—reminded, perhaps, of his great success with Bulwer's *Lady of Lyons*, a highly popular "drama" with which *The Patrician's Daughter* has obvious affinities—suggested that a happy ending would enhance its appeal. Although he gave up this idea on the advice of friends, it was an understandable one.[21] Marston's first "tragedy" is essentially a "drama" with a sad ending.

The Patrician's Daughter aroused much excitement among reviewers because of its innovations. Some, like John Oxenford of *The Times*, acclaimed the daring choice of a contemporary theme and setting. A good many others, however, preferred a remote or historical setting for tragedy, arguing that the familiar trivia of everyday life interfered with the necessary ideality, that larger-than-life passions were out of place in the restrained atmosphere of a modern drawing-room, and that poetry (which most of them accepted as the proper language of tragedy) seemed incongruous with modern dress and manners. The most interesting reviewer, George Henry Lewes, took a very different view from the others: tragedies on contemporary subjects were indeed possible, but he asserted that they must be in prose and must be realistic rather than idealistic—must include, in fact, "all that is petty, mean, or ludicrous in modern life." The critical disagreement over *The Patrician's Daughter* reflects considerable confusion about tragedy, its essentials and its relevance to contemporary society.[22] More recently, Fred C. Thomson has suggested that Marston performed an unintentional service by demonstrating in this play that the old blank-verse drama was a dead-end street and by bringing into question "the entire concept of tragedy, and how its traditionally aristocratic, idealistic basis could be reconciled with the conditions and attitudes of a modern world."[23] Marston's contemporaries did not consciously subscribe to such ideas, but they were clearly uncomfortable with his attempt to pour new wine into old bottles. *The Patrician's Daughter*, by failing to live up to the expectations of tragedy, evidently confirmed some critics in their conviction that tragic form was incompatible with modern subject matter. They were not ready to accept as a corollary that traditional tragedy was incompatible with the modern spirit—not even Lewes went that far—but their uneasiness may have reflected some deep-seated fears about the future of tragedy.[24]

The Patrician's Daughter, auspiciously introduced with a prologue by Charles Dickens, had its first theatrical performance at Drury Lane on 10 December 1842 under Macready's management.[25] It gained immediate prestige from being presented at London's premier theatre by the most respected actor of that day, the only disadvantage being that the vastness of Drury Lane limited the effectiveness of facial acting. The staging was impressive, for Macready had lavished as much care on the scenery and appointments as if he had been mounting a new historical drama. Particularly striking scenes were the "library at Lynterne castle, with its pictures and statues, the sunset from the terrace shedding its illustrative radiance on the dialogue," and a room in Sir Edgar's house with its "glimpses of Richmond-hill through the windows." The cast was very strong: besides Macready as Mordaunt, there were Samuel Phelps as the Earl, Mary Amelia Warner as Lady Lydia, and Helen Faucit as Lady Mabel.

Macready received high praise for much of his portrayal. A few reviewers complained that his "heroic eccentricities" and "violence of tragic utterance" were inappropriate in a modern setting, but his exuberance must have been effectively contrasted with Phelps's quiet gentlemanliness. Favorable critics emphasized Macready's good judgment, his "dignity and feeling" (even when the author had withheld them), his "rare blending of the most delicate skill with the grandest force." The single incident that disturbed them all was, of course, Mordaunt's rejection of Mabel. Several reviewers thought Macready should have softened down this unpleasant passage in performance instead of playing it for all it was worth. The *Morning Post* said, for instance, that his "coarse vein of brutal triumph" was "abominably exact to the author's conception." The *Morning Herald* reported that Macready shouted "No!" in a startling manner, gave his justification in a pompously declamatory style, jerked out the words "though afterwards she gave herself the lie" as if in vulgar defiance, and even shook his hand in Mabel's face. These accounts by Tory critics, for whom Mordaunt's ringingly democratic speech was anathema, may well be exaggerated. According to the friendly *Morning Chronicle*, Mordaunt struggled with "suppressed tenderness" during the speech, as, with eyes averted from Mabel, he lashed himself on to vehemence. Whatever the critics thought, the audience responded with enthusiasm. As *The Times* reported, few parts of the play were more theatrically effective than the rejection scene.

But Helen Faucit drew the lion's share of critical notice. Her thorough identification with Mabel's character, her simple and natural impersonation, her combination of fervor and refinement—all were warmly admired. She was praised for her "sparkling animation" in the lighter scenes as well as her "strong emotion" in the more passionate ones. (Sometimes the emotions were subtly conveyed. Later, when she acted Mabel in Edinburgh, a critic declared that she created as fine an effect by her manner of shutting up a parasol as had ever been produced by the unsheathing of a dagger.)[26] Nearly every scene in which she appeared was approvingly described by one critic or another. In Mabel's opening scene with her father she laid "a charm upon the attention of the audience," imparting a sense of "social enjoyment." In later scenes she "finely marked" the development of Mabel's growing love for Mordaunt and convincingly portrayed her offended dignity when hearing Lydia's report of his unworthy conduct. Her repudiation of the man she really loved did not have the "repulsive character" a lesser actress might have given it but seemed "the honest rebellion of a woman's heart" at his taking her unconfessed love for granted, and her "quiet expression of despair as she sank down when Mordaunt left her" was "touchingly beautiful." She was evidently very restrained in the rejection scene; one critic even remarked that she did not make the most of her opportunities here. (One is inclined to respect her for that.) But in the fifth act, the high point in her performance, the "best criticism" of her acting was "the many tears it elicited." In the scene of Lady Lydia's confession, Mrs. Warner and Helen Faucit were effectively contrasted—the one, with an "appalling" look of agonized conscience, was "forcible and earnest"; the other, with her "shattered frame and broken spirit," was quietly touching. In the dying scene Helen Faucit "produced a painfully thrilling effect by the intensity of her feeling."[27]

The Patrician's Daughter was warmly applauded on the first night, the author and the principal actors receiving a call. It was acted for eleven nights, a respectable run at that time but nothing more.[28] Helen Faucit's personal success was so gratifying, however, that after she began traveling as a star, in 1843, she kept Mabel in her repertory for more than a decade (until 1857). Provincial critics often censured the play, but they could not say enough in admiration of Miss Faucit's distressing but intensely moving fifth act. Only in Manchester was the play as popular as the star: according to the *Manchester Courier* (8 May 1847), it was "more successful in drawing large audiences here than any modern production of a similar character." The reviewer's praise for its "noble sentiments," its vindication of the "dignity of man," suggests that Mordaunt's championship of common humanity struck a sympathetic chord here—not surprising in a city where merchants had rallied to the cause of free trade (idealistic in principle if also good for business) and working-class leaders agitated for Chartist reforms like universal manhood suffrage.[29] *The Patrician's Daughter* was not seen in London after Macready's production until Samuel Phelps revived it at Sadler's Wells in 1846. With Phelps as Mordaunt and Laura Addison as Mabel, the play ran successfully for thirteen nights, and it was revived briefly during several later seasons. As Shirley Allen points out, the democratic sentiments were much appreciated by the working-class audiences of Islington. The play was also acted occasionally in New York.[30] Marston's first tragedy, then, had a limited success, due largely to fine performances and, sometimes, to a partisan response somewhat at odds with the author's intentions.

The Patrician's Daughter did not offer an adequate test of Marston's new theory of tragedy; a better play might have encouraged other and more fruitful experiments. As it was, however, even Marston took no second step along the road he had supposedly opened up.[31] His next tragedy, *Strathmore*, written when he was thirty, was thoroughly traditional: it had a historical setting, Scotland in 1679, during the Covenanter troubles, and a long-familiar theme reminiscent of *Venice Preserved*. By this time (1849), the outlook for traditional drama was bleaker than ever: although the Theatres Act of 1843 had eliminated monopolies, the expected resurgence of legitimate drama had not occurred. Against all odds, however, Marston won a temporary victory for tragedy in the classic mode.

Strathmore owes its setting and situation to Scott's novel *Old Mortality*, but its characters and incidents are mostly original.[32] Marston's theme involves a love-honor conflict, but it is most precisely stated as the clash of moral principle and personal loyalty. Halbert Strathmore, only surviving member of a respected Loyalist family, is engaged to marry Katharine Lorn, daughter of his father's old friend Sir Rupert, a dedicated Loyalist. But, despite this background, his dismay over the persecution of the Covenanters and his conviction that justice is on their side force him to join them. Shortly afterwards the Covenant leaders, hearing that Sir Rupert has killed a Cameronian minister, order Strathmore to lead a stealthy invasion of Lorn Castle, capture it, and execute Sir Rupert. Though shocked by the proposed betrayal of his friends, Strathmore agrees, provided Sir Rupert is given a chance to prove his innocence. After a successful invasion, the Covenanters hold a trial, with Strathmore as judge, during which Sir Rupert, though previously conscience-stricken, becomes so enraged that he actually boasts of his deed. Strathmore has no choice but to condemn him. Katharine pleads with him to save her father, but, though he swoons from the pressure of his emotions, he does not relent. In a subplot, Isabel, spirited wife of Sir Rupert's absent son, Henry, exerts her arts to influence Brycefield, one of the invaders, and Fanchette, her maid, works on his man, Roland. The situation reverses when Henry Lorn, an officer in the Loyalist army, arrives with his men, recaptures the castle, and saves his father. Strathmore is now a prisoner to the Lorns, who do not realize he has been mortally wounded in the fight, and he is to be turned over to "fierce Dalzell," a merciless Loyalist leader. Sir Rupert promises to ask that Strathmore be spared if he will sign a recantation. When Katharine begs him to sign, he gives her the right to decide: shall he take the path through death to honor or through life to shame? She unselfishly urges him to "DIE!" Strathmore embraces her, rejoicing, "My wife! my Katharine! We are one forever!" When Sir Rupert and Henry rush in to report Dalzell's approach and to ask for the recantation, Katharine tells them they are too late. "No," Strathmore replies, "love is never too late," and he manages a brief reconciliation with his friends before falling dead at their feet.

Strathmore is a *psychomachia*, a Victorian version of the ancient war of the soul. When the play opens, the hero has just made the great decision of his life; what we see is a succession of inner conflicts arising from it. Although the plot is extremely simple, however, the question of right and wrong is not treated as one of black and white. There is no doubt that Strathmore's sympathy for the Covenanters is justified, but their intolerance and vengefulness are not overlooked. In the first scene of the play, we hear the fiery John Balfour of Burley, one of their most respected leaders, rejoicing in pseudo-biblical language over his part in the murder of the "godless Sharpe," Archbishop of St. Andrews. Thus, when the gentle Pastor Keith is killed by Sir Rupert, the fact, though shocking enough, does not make the Loyalists seem uniquely bloody. In this flawed world Strathmore, who insists on absolutes, must choose his "right" and be true to it.

What happens to the hero who is constantly forced to suppress his

The last scene of *Strathmore*, Haymarket Theatre, June 1842. (By permission of the *Illustrated London News* Picture Library.)

human feelings, detach himself from personal ties, and even abandon certain values in order to remain steadfast to a ruling principle? Marston shows us such a progress in Strathmore. Its result becomes apparent in the trial scene, when he suddenly feels that his human individuality is immobilized: his "heart is frozen," his "memory stifled"; he is "a pen in the great hand of Conscience / To write its bidding merely!" Entranced, he hears the shouts of the Covenanters for "Justice! Death!" as more than human: "The crash of some great sin performed / Hath wakened Fate, and space reverberates / Her doom in thunder! All the seas of sound / Dash it against my brain . . . Murder's doom is Death!" As he speaks the last line, he stands upright and rapt, as if possessed by some divine fury which decrees Sir Rupert's fate through him. Later his self-accusing thoughts confront him in visual form as the apparitions of Sir Rupert, Katharine, and his dead father. He wants to offer them his own life, but they only smile and fade. It is his "doom to live"—and to go on denying the people who have long meant the most to him. When Katharine is pleading for her father's life, she says it is not Strathmore who condemns him but his bloody companions that are forcing his hand. He replies, "No, 'tis not Strathmore! / That atom in all space of love, hope, grief— / Is ground to ashes; but its dust combines / In a dread form that shudders at itself, / And takes the name of Justice!" Not until the end of the play, when Katharine sympathetically enters into his concept of honor and agrees he must die for it, does he regain his feeling of shared humanity and claim her as his wife. Marston's concept of the hero who gives everything to a principle until he becomes first its automatic tool and then its monstrous incarnation is not only an original version of the "impossible dilemma" but, in my view, a genuinely tragic one.

Not that the tragic effect of the play is as pure as one would like. As in *The Patrician's Daughter*, Marston, while attempting to make a boldly unusual point, declines to risk its full consequences in audience response. I refer, of course, to his allowing Strathmore a conventionally honorable death from battle wounds instead of a conventionally shameful (but in his view honorable) death by execution for treason. Since Strathmore is a dying man when he lets Katharine decide his fate, her choice, though considered a moral victory, is actually a delusion. Nevertheless, Marston's conception and presentation of his tragic hero are sufficiently impressive to impart a sense of dignity to the play despite its contrived ending.

There are, admittedly, flaws in *Strathmore* besides those relating specifically to tragic effect. Most important is one it shares with *The Patrician's*

Daughter: thinness of plot and character. Since so much of the conflict occurs within Strathmore himself, it is difficult for Marston to objectify it; he can only show his hero becoming entranced, seeing apparitions, falling in a faint. A certain power does derive from the simplicity and concentration, but this is partially sacrificed to "variety" through the interruptions of a meaningless subplot. Even more than in the earlier play, the characters appear as figures in some giant equation. Too much complexity might have interfered with Marston's monumental conception of Strathmore, but further development was much to be desired in Katharine. Her passionate nature and her undying love are virtually her only characteristics. Isabel has a sprightly charm which, though stereotyped, could be effectively exploited by the actress. The other characters are hardly developed at all.

Even so, *Strathmore* is a much finer play than *The Patrician's Daughter*, not only in tragic stature but also in dramatic effectiveness. Most noticeable is the improvement in language and verse. There are fewer archaic words and awkward constructions than in the earlier play, and there is virtually none of Marston's former tendency to stretch the speeches beyond their dramatic requirements. Often the language conveys a sense of realism, sometimes of urgency and suspense. As in all Marston's plays, there are quotable aphorisms, like "He has no future who betrays his past." Even in the longer speeches, where the poetic quality is more evident, there is usually a kind of vigor too often missing in Marston's previous dramatic writing.[33] The more emotional passages are generally very effective, as witness those already quoted. The language may seem inflated for modern taste, but the inspired, yet controlled, hyperbole seems to me exactly right for this play.

Strathmore won considerable acclaim from the critics. Indeed the tone of the reviews suggests a surprised delight in the discovery that the highest type of legitimate drama was alive and well, after all.[34] *The Times* found "something really grand" in the conception of the hero as the embodiment of a fixed principle; the *Morning Chronicle* was impressed by the strong sense of an inescapable fate; the *Sun* described *Strathmore* as the best tragedy that had been produced in years. This drama, which Marston himself considered his masterpiece, deserved the praise it received in its own day, and, despite its imperfections, it deserves to be better known than it is today.

Strathmore was first performed on 20 June 1849 at the Haymarket Theatre under the management of Benjamin Webster. This relatively small theatre was ideal for a drama of inner conflict in which facial expression would be unusually important. Charles and Ellen Kean, who were in the midst of a long engagement there, played the roles of Strathmore and Katharine, and Kean himself undertook the planning and directing of the production.[35] The play was well staged, with completely new scenery and costumes and with considerable attention to detail. Several of the minor actors received good notices, particularly Miss Reynolds, who was charming and vivacious as Isabel, but the Keans themselves were largely responsible for the play's success.[36]

Charles Kean's Strathmore, "thoughtful, well studied," but "natural and impassioned," seemed to the *Sun* "what Hamlet would have been had Hamlet possessed Strathmore's stern sense of duty and decision of character." There was hardly any adverse criticism, though the *Examiner*, which praised Kean's acting at the beginning and end of the play, considered it too true to the author's conception in the "intermediate acts"—that is, too effeminate. Mrs. Kean's "exquisitely true, tender, and touching" delineation of Katharine was equally admired, despite the character's relative lack of prominence. Indeed some critics praised her performance even more than her husband's: the *Sun*, for example, rated it as "finer than anything we have seen on the stage in modern days" and declared that it had "all the impassioned intensity, all the overwhelming power of . . . Rachel in the *Horaces*, with more grace and infinitely greater truth to nature."

In the lovers' piquant farewell scene as Strathmore prepares to join the Covenanters, Mrs. Kean won sympathy for Katherine by the wild intensity of her pleading against his decision, but Kean's "frank and loyal bearing" and the "emphatic earnestness" of his arguments made Strathmore's sacrifice of love to duty seem entirely noble. Later, Strathmore's inner struggles over the proposed betrayal of his friends were depicted by Kean with "great force and truth." After the invasion of the castle, Mrs. Kean chillingly conveyed Katharine's "dreamy state" of mental desolation. Then suddenly she broke free with the joyous conviction that Strathmore was here, not to destroy her father, but to save him; this short-lived belief showed itself in one of the "flashes of energy" with which the actress occasionally lit up the gloom of doubt and despair. The trial scene was skillfully managed: the contrast between the "heart-crushed appearance of the judge" and the "haughty bearing of the prisoner" was very striking, and the "hoarse murmurs of the Covenanters" made an ominous chorus. In the apparition scene Kean was admirable, though his interpretation differed from the author's. According to Marston, "the phantoms . . . were meant in the end to be dispelled by Strathmore's sense of right and moral necessity. Charles Kean, on the contrary, abandoned himself to unresisted anguish. He suggested Orestes pursued by the furies."[37]

Both players were exceptionally fine in the last two acts. Kean was earnest, "eloquent, sometimes exceedingly touching," and entirely free of the stagey violence for which he had sometimes been censured. He impressively sustained the "rapt appearance of the individual absorbed in the idea." As Katharine pleaded for her father, Mrs. Kean's acting was "harrowing," and the pathos with which she reminded Strathmore of their childhood was "heartrending." During her emotional speech Strathmore seemed racked with the agony of conflicting passions, and when he collapsed from the pressure he could no longer bear, Kean received "universal plaudits." In the final scene Kean's deep earnestness and passionate pathos were very moving, but it was Mrs. Kean who made the greatest effect. When Katharine suddenly understood the worthlessness of life without honor, she rose above the tearful misery with which she had been urging Strathmore to recant and exclaimed with noble grandeur, "NO—DIE!" Mrs. Kean's "irresistible power" and "sublimity" at this high moment brought the play to a grand climax.

The performance was "vehemently applauded throughout," and at the end there were calls for the Keans, Miss Reynolds, and the author. Reviewer after reviewer proclaimed a triumphant success. The *Era* described *Strathmore* as "the most engaging serious piece upon the London boards, where it deserves to remain for some time to come." It did remain for twenty-two of the twenty-eight nights left in the Keans' engagement.[38]

Mr. and Mrs. Kean did not revive *Strathmore* during the next Haymarket engagement (December 1849–March 1850), but they did include it in the repertory during their provincial tours both before and after that engagement. John Cole reports that this play was a "deserved success" in Dublin and Cork, but he says nothing about its reception in Scotland, the country in which its scenes are located.[39] According to the *Edinburgh Evening Courant* (16 April 1850), *Strathmore*'s "representation here did not seem to equal the expectations of the audience," the reason being that the hero was "too metaphysical" to arouse their interest and sympathy. The fact that the play, though new to Edinburgh, was performed on only three of the Keans' nine nights does suggest that it was not a hit there. Even so, the receipts on the nights it was acted were comparable to or better than those on most other nights (benefits excepted). Its popularity was evidently greater in Glasgow, where it was offered on seven of the Keans' thirteen nights, again comparing favorably, financially, with their other plays.[40] All in all, though *Strathmore* was not of major importance in the Keans' careers, it undoubtedly "added," as Cole says, "to their established fame."

Marston was obviously fortunate in the production of his first two tragedies. Each was given an impressive mounting; each was brought out at a major theatre with eminent actors in the principal roles; each received, in general, enthusiastic reviews of the performances. Thus the plays were tested under highly favorable circumstances. The degree of success they enjoyed was probably commensurate with their theatrical worth, if not somewhat greater.

A close study of *The Patrician's Daughter* and *Strathmore* reveals that Marston had a certain skill in dramatic construction, though not much fertility in plot invention; that he managed to create at least two or three strong scenes in each play which could be effectively exploited in the theatre; that he displayed in the second tragedy a rapidly developing ability to write good dialogue; and that, despite an inclination toward artificial diction, he had a genuine poetic talent which he learned to sharpen and strengthen for the uses of drama. These two plays reveal an odd combination of originality and conventionalism, a wish to be daring yet a tendency to compromise for the sake of winning sympathy. Marston's attempts to create heroes whose impressiveness depended on strength of character rather than exalted position are both interesting, and Strathmore is, I think, successful. In neither hero, however, does the reader feel the presence of a fully realized human being, and the same can be said more emphatically about most of the other characters. One must stress "the reader," for, as we have seen, such idealized characters as Mabel and Katharine took on a convincing humanity in the theatre.

Perhaps the greatest lack in these two plays is texture. The little details of daily life, the suggestive allusions to "the other day" or "last year" casually thrown in, the eccentric but genuine-sounding speech of some minor character—such "unnecessary" but vital things are largely missing from these plays. Their omission might be deliberate—tragedy was supposed to be an idealization of life—but I suspect the answer lies elsewhere. Paradoxically, Marston needed to be either more extraordinary or more ordinary. His intellectual interests, his ideals, and his poetic talents might have enabled him to write some really distinguished dramas—whether timely or not is another matter—if his imagination, active as it was, had been richer and more various. Yet these same intellectual interests, ideals, and poetic talents often stood in the way of his writing plays that would make the best use of his dramatic assets and at the same time serve the needs of his contemporaries.

NOTES

1. [John] Westland Marston, *Our Recent Actors*, 2 vols. (London: Sampson Low, Marston, Searle, and Rivington, 1890), 1:195–99; Fred C. Thomson, "A Crisis in Early Victorian Drama: John Westland Marston and the Syncretics," *Victorian Studies* 9 (June 1966):377–88.

2. *The Times*, 12 December 1842, p. 5.

3. *Dictionary of National Biography*, s.v. "Marston, John Westland." The most extensive study of Marston's career is Lawrence Ashby Wood, Jr., "John Westland Marston, LL.D.: Neo-Elizabethan Dramatist in the Victorian Era" (Ph.D. diss., Case Western Reserve University, 1955).

4. See Ernest Bradlee Watson, *Sheridan to Robertson: A Study of the Nineteenth Century London Stage* (1926; reprint, New York: Benjamin Blom, 1963), chs. 1, 2, and 6; Ernest Reynolds, *Early Victorian Drama (1830–1870)* (1936; reprint, New York: Benjamin Blom, 1965), ch. 1; Allardyce Nicoll, *A History of English Drama, 1660–1900*, 6 vols. (Cambridge: Cambridge University Press, 1940–59), vol. 4, chs. 2 and 4.

5. Michael R. Booth, ed., *English Plays of the Nineteenth Century*, 5 vols. (Oxford: Clarendon Press, 1969–76), 1:6. For similar comments by a contemporary of Marston's, see the review of *The Lady of Lyons* in "The Theatres," *Spectator*, 17 February 1838, p. 160.

6. Richard B. Sewall, *The Vision of Tragedy* (New Haven: Yale University Press, 1959), 6; for fuller discussion, 4–6. Compare George Steiner, *The Death of Tragedy* (London: Faber and Faber, 1961), 5–7.

7. Steiner, *Death of Tragedy*, 193–94 (rationalism), 125–28 (Rousseauism, progress); Sewall, *Vision of Tragedy*, 84–85 (Rousseau, optimism, Victorianism); Herbert J. Muller, *The Spirit of Tragedy* (New York: Alfred Knopf, 1956), 242–43 (rationalism).

8. Steiner, *Death of Tragedy*, 8, 129; Geoffrey Brereton, *Principles of Tragedy: A Rational Examination of the Tragic Concept of Life and Literature* (Coral Gables, Fla.: University of Miami Press, 1968), 51, 108. The much-discussed question of whether Christianity is inimical to tragedy is relevant here, of course.

9. Sewall, *Vision of Tragedy*, 32, 48; Steiner, *Death of Tragedy*, 10; D. D. Raphael, *The Paradox of Tragedy* (Bloomington: Indiana University Press, 1960), 28, 36.

10. Steiner, *Death of Tragedy*, 194–95; Muller, *Spirit of Tragedy*, 241–42. There were, of course, a few domestic tragedies with common-life characters in

the late sixteenth and early seventeenth centuries—*Arden of Feversham*, for example.

11. Steiner, *Death of Tragedy*, 121–22.
12. Sewall, *Vision of Tragedy*, 85.
13. For the importance of this theme to tragedy, see Robert Bechtold Heilman, *Tragedy and Melodrama: Versions of Experience* (Seattle and London: University of Washington Press, 1968), 7–16, 291–92, 296; also Sewall, *Vision of Tragedy*, 6–7, 10, 19, 47. Many other critics emphasize this. Brereton, in *Principles of Tragedy*, denies that the agonizing dilemma is basic to tragedy, arguing that the concept did not become important in European thought until the Romantics. See chaps. 4, 8, 9; also pp. 110–15, 271.
14. For George Eliot, see Heilman, *Tragedy and Melodrama*, 11; for Matthew Arnold, see Brereton, *Principles of Tragedy*, 139–40.
15. Brereton, *Principles of Tragedy*, 182–83, 187.
16. Sewall, *Vision of Tragedy*, 85.
17. Marston, preface to *The Patrician's Daughter* (reference in n. 18, below).
18. Marston's preface to the first edition of *The Patrician's Daughter* (1841), as quoted by several reviewers, for example, George Henry Lewes, in "Article IV," *Westminster Review* 37 (January–April 1842):340. The first edition is not available to me. I have used the fourth edition of the play (London: C. Mitchell, 1843), whose text had been amplified and adapted for the stage (passages not used in the theatre are marked). This reprints the preface to the first edition but unaccountably omits the statement about the conflict between aristocratic and democratic pride. (The statement was later repeated, however, in Marston's *Dramatic and Poetic Works*, 1876.) I have found no promptbook of Macready's production, but Helen Faucit's promptbook, evidently used in touring, is in the Shakespeare Centre Library, Stratford-upon-Avon.
19. "Dr. Westland Marston," *Athenaeum*, 11 January 1890, p. 57.
20. See Michael Booth et al., *The Revels History of Drama in English, 1750–1880*, ed. Clifford Leech and T.W. Craik (London: Methuen, 1975), 237–38. Not only are the comments on *The Patrician's Daughter* unduly harsh, but the implication that this was Marston's most successful play is incorrect.
21. *The Diaries of William Charles Macready 1833–1851*, ed. William Toynbee, 2 vols. (London: Chapman and Hall, 1912), 2:188–89.
22. My discussion of the critical response to *The Patrician's Daughter* is based on the following: *The Times*, 8 November 1841, p. 3 (on the published play) and 12 December 1842, p. 5 (on the play in production); *Examiner*, 9 October 1841, pp. 644–45, and 17 December 1842, p. 806; *Morning Chronicle*, 12 December 1842; *Bell's Life in London*, 18 December 1842; *Observer*, 11 December 1842; *Spectator*, 17 December 1842, p. 1209; *Morning Post*, 12 December 1842; *Athenaeum*, 17 December 1842, pp. 1091–92; *Literary Gazette*, 17 December 1842, pp. 866–67; *Illustrated London News*, 17 December 1842, p. 512; Lewes, "Article IV,"

321–47; *Morning Herald*, 12 December 1842. The first four journals were largely favorable to the play; most of the others found serious faults in it, though some had praise for the production.

23. "A Crisis in Early Victorian Drama," 375, 398.

24. He encouraged George Eliot to write a conventional tragic drama with a historic setting. See his journal entry of 8 February 1864, in *The George Eliot Letters*, ed. Gordon S. Haight, 9 vols. (New Haven: Yale University Press, 1954–1978), 4:132–33.

25. For a copy of the Prologue see the *Theatrical Journal*, 17 December 1842, p. 407. My discussion of the production will be based largely on the 1842 reviews mentioned in n. 22, above. The quotation about scenery is from the *Morning Chronicle*. Quoted comments about Macready not identified in my text are from the *Morning Post* ("heroic eccentricities"); *Athenaeum* ("violence . . . utterance"); *Examiner* ("dignity and feeling"); and *Morning Chronicle* ("most delicate skill . . . grandest force"). Phelps's performance is praised in *Morning Herald*, *Morning Post*, and *Spectator*.

26. *Edinburgh Observer*, 28 November 1843.

27. My discussion of Helen Faucit owes most to *The Times* ("sparkling animation," offended dignity, "shattered frame . . . "); *Athenaeum* ("strong emotion"); *Morning Chronicle* (descriptions of the first scene, growing love, repudiation of Mordaunt, and "many tears" elicited by final scenes); *Morning Herald* ("quiet . . . despair"); *Theatrical Chronicle*, 17 December 1842, p. 274 (ineffective rejection scene, "painfully thrilling" dying scene). The effectiveness of Helen Faucit and Mrs. Warner in the confession scene is emphasized by *The Times*, *Examiner*, and *Bell's Life in London*. The *Morning Herald* mentions Mrs. Warner's "appalling" look here; *Examiner*, her "forcible and earnest" acting.

28. Macready considered twenty performances the mark of a "very successful" tragedy. See Charles H. Shattuck, ed., *Bulwer and Macready: A Chronicle of the Early Victorian Theatre* (Urbana: University of Illinois Press, 1958), 212.

29. For Manchester's Anti-Corn Law and Chartist activities, see [British Association for the Advancement of Science], *Manchester and Its Region: A Survey Prepared for the Meeting Held in Manchester August 29 to September 5, 1962* (Manchester: Manchester University Press, 1962). For the combination of idealism and self-interest among the Anti-Corn Law advocates, see John Morley, *The Life of Richard Cobden*, 13th ed. (London: T. Fisher Unwin, 1906), 140–43.

30. Shirley S. Allen, *Samuel Phelps and Sadler's Wells Theatre* (Middletown, Conn.: Wesleyan University Press, 1971), 277–78, 320; George C. D. Odell, *Annals of the New York Stage*, 15 vols. (New York: Columbia University Press, 1927–1949), 4:643–45; 5:92, 342; 6:112, 152; 7:5.

31. *Anne Blake*, another blank-verse play of modern times by Marston, is sometimes paired with *The Patrician's Daughter*, but it is not a tragedy.

32. I have used the following text of the play: J. Westland Marston, *Strathmore*:

A Tragic Play in Five Acts (London: C. Mitchell, 1849). I have found no promptbook of Kean's production, and M. Glen Wilson, authority on Charles Kean, tells me he does not believe one is extant. I am grateful to Professor Wilson for letting me read relevant portions of his biography of Kean (not yet published).

33. Marston had learned his lesson the hard way. In 1847 he had experienced the failure of his serious comedy *The Heart and the World*, which, in addition to being, as he admits (*Our Recent Actors*, 167), "so purely . . . psychological . . . as to neglect incident," was full of abstruse, undramatic speeches.

34. My comments on *Strathmore*'s reception are based on reviews in the following journals, all published in 1849: *Morning Herald*, 21 June; *Sun*, 21 June; *Morning Post*, 21 June; *Morning Chronicle*, 21 June; *The Times*, 21 June; *Examiner*, 23 June: 390; *Athenaeum*, 23 June: 652; *Literary Gazette*, 23 June: 468; *Illustrated London News*, 23 June: 426; *Era*, 24 June; *New Monthly Magazine*, 86 (Pt. 2, 1849): 517.

35. M. Glen Wilson, "Charles Kean at the Haymarket, 1839–1850," *Theatre Journal* 31 (October 1979):339.

36. My discussion of the production will be based on the reviews mentioned in n. 34, above. Quoted comments on Kean's performance not identified in my text are from the *Morning Chronicle* ("frank . . . bearing" and "emphatic earnestness"); *The Times* ("rapt appearance"); *Morning Herald* ("force and truth" in depicting struggles); *Athenaeum* ("universal plaudits" when he swooned); *Era* ("eloquent . . . touching" in final acts). Those on Mrs. Kean are from the *Morning Chronicle* ("exquisitely true," wild pleading in the farewell scene, "irresistible power" in "NO!"); *The Times* ("dreamy state," "flashes of energy"); *Sun* ("harrowing," "heart-rending pathos" when pleading for father, "sublimity" in "NO!"). For the trial scene see *Morning Chronicle* (contrast between judge and prisoner); and *Morning Herald* ("hoarse murmurs").

37. *Our Recent Actors*, 117.

38. I base these figures on the Haymarket advertisements in *The Times*. According to these, *Strathmore* had twenty consecutive performances and was given on two later nights, the last being 21 July. Kean's account book (see n. 40, below) lists *Strathmore* for twenty-eight nights, but this is evidently an error. Even so, it was acted twice as many times as *The Patrician's Daughter* had been when it was first produced.

39. John Cole, *The Life and Theatrical Times of Charles Kean, F.S.A.*, 2 vols. (London: Richard Bentley, 1859), 1:365.

40. Charles Kean, List of Receipts 1848–1850, Harvard Theatre Collection, MS. Thr. 15.2.

"Helpless and Unfriended"

NINETEENTH-CENTURY DOMESTIC MELODRAMA

Martha Vicinus

> Where can my poor girl be? I be sore afraid when she do stay so long away; a fair flower hazards the plucking at every hand, and she ha' now no protector but her old mother; my poor husband in prison, and the young hope of our days fled from us when he wur but ten years old! But that grief I can never speak of to my husband; it do almost turn his brain—but many and many a night ha' found me waking and thinking what ha' been his fate. Hey, bless me, this is a sad world for the helpless and unfriended!

It is easy now to laugh at Dame Wakefield's catalogue of woes in John Baldwin Buckstone's *Luke the Labourer* (1826) and at the fortuitous rescue of her daughter and the rediscovery of her son. As the taste for these extremes has declined, domestic melodrama has fallen into disrepute, despite its continued lively existence on television. In the nineteenth century, however, domestic melodrama served as a cultural touchstone for large sections of society who felt both in awe of and unclear about the benefits of the new industrial society being built around them. The conflict between the family and its values and the economic and social assault of industrialization were vividly dramatized on stage. The exploration of contemporary concerns about class and gender gave melodrama its immediacy, while placing these issues within the family gave them emotional force. Melodrama was a psychological touchstone for the powerless, for those who felt themselves to be "helpless and unfriended."

Melodrama and the Family

Melodrama can be seen as a cultural response to the growing split under capitalism between production and personal life. Its rise in the mid-seventeenth century coincides with the rise of the bourgeoisie and urban capitalism.[1] In increasing numbers, which became an avalanche in the nineteenth century, people no longer worked close to or in their homes, but in factories and workshops at the hours set by their masters. Even the expanded cottage industry increasingly involved an outside taskmaster. In the close-knit traditional communities, such as coal-mining villages, work remained the social, emotional, and cultural center, but elsewhere, despite unionization, the psychic center of life was separate from work. It was for all classes overwhelmingly in the family, and this became the arena for domestic melodrama. The home was the setting for passion, sacrifice, suffering, and sympathy; the workplace for action, for earning money to pay for the home comforts.[2] Within the home the powerless struggled for recognition, for their values over those of the wider world. The ideal of domestic happiness, like myths of a past golden age, assuaged fears an audience might have about being too committed to the goals of an industrializing society.[3] Melodrama provided a temporary resolution of conflicts between the home and the outside world.

The focus on the family and its emotional conflicts gives melodrama its archetypal power. Oedipal, or at least generational, conflict is central to many plots. Familiar struggles become charged with intense feeling because of their psychosexual nature. The continuous popularity of *Richard II* and *Macbeth* throughout the century was in part because of their bloody and violent portrayal of family conflict. So too, the popular temperance plays, such as *Ten Nights in a Bar-Room* (1858) or *The Drunkard's Warning* (1856), emphasize intrafamilial disasters. While the ostensible cause is liquor, the actions—beating, murders, and crazed suicides—carry an additional emotional force because they occur between family members. The father destroys the family by killing his son or casting out his daughter; he, in turn, is destroyed by his liquor-drowned grief.

Melodrama always sides with the powerless. Children are repeatedly misunderstood by their parents, and must prove themselves by extraordinary deeds. Fathers instantly banish their sons when they refuse to marry the right person, or have the wrong friends, or take a poor job. One parent or the other soon after sinks into death, calling for the lost child. Given the intensely enclosed world of melodrama, where everyone knows everyone, it is impossible to defy a family edict or impose wrongful behavior with impunity. Retribution is always at hand. Even more charged than father-son relations are those between fathers and daughters. The daughter is either a paragon of self-sacrifice and duty to her aged parent, or she is defiant of his will, and deserts him for the villain. If she is patient and obedient, a virtuous lover eventually proves himself and they can marry. If she leaves without her father's blessing, she inevitably rues the day in long apostrophes. When Duke Vivaldi refuses to marry the low-born Clari who has left her family for him, in *Clari; or, The Maid of Milan* (1823), she flees to her father, "Your unhappy child, sorrowing, imploring, returns to you!"[4] The duke then abruptly sees the error of his ways, and agrees to marry her. While a son could defy his erring father, a daughter's only salvation was humble obedience.

The emphasis upon the weak and the unappreciated made children, preferably orphans, important figures. Playwrights cast a preternaturally wise and innocent child into the role of an emotional savior. The child is most successful when he or she is most victimized. In *East Lynne* (1861), Lady Isabel's son dies in her arms, punishing her yet saving her; his timely return to a "better world" leaves him untouched by the wrongs of his family and paves the way for her own death. As the representative of complete innocence and love, the child can both punish and triumph, in heaven, if not here.

The perennial themes of family love and hatred were adopted and heightened to fit specific conditions in the nineteenth century. Playwrights, working with familiar backdrops and stock characters, could show class differences, family tensions, and an idealized past. Cornelia Carlyle, Lady Isabel's bossy sister-in-law, provides comic relief—and yet another rationale for leaving Archibald Carlyle's home. Villagers dance in the garden of Audley Court in *Lady Audley's Secret* (1863), reminding the audience of traditional country life. The original opening backdrop and staging of Douglas Jerrold's *The Rent Day* (1832) was a self-conscious imitation of David Wilkie's romantically conceived narrative painting of the rural hierarchy in happy agreement on the annual rent day.[5] Jerrold also pioneered realistic language; he prided himself on the accuracy of the sailors' speeches in *Black Ey'd Susan* (1829). While the actual speeches might be bombastic, the vocabulary was carefully drawn from life. Placed within a realistic framework, domestic melodrama was a world of wish-fulfillment and dreams.

These realistic settings are a key to understanding the popularity of domestic melodrama in the nineteenth century. Faced with cataclysmic religious, economic, and social changes, most Victorians could feel powerless on occasion, believing that all traditional values were in danger of being turned upside down. The family became the refuge from change and the sustainer of familiar values. But as melodrama so tellingly documents, it also became the arena for the most profound struggles between good and evil. The strength of the home and of domestic ties is tested under extreme conditions. Yet these struggles also reassure because they show virtue defeating villainy, and—in characteristic Victorian fashion—being rewarded with love, wealth, and security. Melodrama's focus on the passive and powerless within the family made it particularly appealing to the working class and to women, two groups facing great dangers without economic power or social recognition.

Melodrama was popular with the working class in its efforts to understand and assimilate capitalism; it appeared to offer truths not found elsewhere. Social and economic conditions were unstable during much of the nineteenth century; melodrama acknowledged this and seemed to demonstrate how difficult circumstances could be endured, and even turned to victory. Tragedy appeals to those who feel, however erroneously, that they have some control over lives ruined by personal decision and error; melodrama to those who feel that their lives are without order and that events they cannot control can destroy or save them. Happy endings tying everything together offer solace by their very nature, because they assert that unwilled events will finally bring good fortune. The virtuous Farmer Heywood in *Rent Day* is saved at the last moment, even as the bailiffs remove his furniture; a lost inheritance is discovered in the stuffing of an old chair. Heywood can do nothing to save himself but wait for justice. A happy conclusion is achieved, although the social and economic framework of the play remains unchanged; under capitalist conditions the wicked steward must demand prompt payment of the rent regardless of the loyalty and reliability of the renters. While the cash nexus prevails, the inheritance can ensure an appropriate ending, and provide a temporary reconciliation of the irreconcilable. Melodrama is concerned not with what is possible or actual, but with what is desirable.

Melodrama also appealed to women, who found it to reflect the contradictions in their own lives. Removed under capitalism from participation in essential production, the middle-class woman found all her energies focused on the family and its emotional life. As the angel in the house, she was expected to sacrifice all for the emotional, moral, and physical well-being of her husband and children. The recurrent themes of rebellion and self-sacrifice spoke to the underlying emotional tension in women's lives.

The heroine, ostensibly weaker than the hero, invariably plays a more active role, suffering greater persecution in order to confirm her moral superiority.[6] Rachel Heywood and Dame Wakefield never lose faith, even when their husbands denounce them or go mad.

The single most popular play of the nineteenth century was *East Lynne*, whose heroine, Lady Isabel Vane, combined most successfully the extremes of rebellion and self-sacrifice. Based upon a runaway best-seller by Mrs. Henry Wood, the play could fill the coffers of any flagging company with its titillating combination of guilt and remorse in high places. Lady Isabel, miserable because her colorless husband ignores her and her sister-in-law rules her house, runs away with Captain Levison. She deserts her children, only to return later in the degraded position of their governess. Audiences could luxuriate in her unending remorse, physical disfigurement, and numerous other punishments. Afy Hallijohn, who had also succumbed to the vile Captain, suffers only temporary ostracism and ends successfully married to a prosperous tradesman. Lower class and single, she did not offend against the middle-class ideal of womanhood, but Lady Isabel must suffer endlessly, deliciously guilty, yet innocent in spirit.[7]

East Lynne had an unusually somber subplot, concerning the mysterious murder of Afy's father and the disappearance of the suspect, Richard Hare. His loyal sister, Barbara Hare, inspires Lady Isabel's husband to take up his legal case when their father spurns him. The mutual commitment of Carlyle and Barbara to this secret cause not only forces Lady Isabel into Levison's arms, but also—after a decorous wait—into each other's. Carlyle's comic sister, shrewish toward Lady Isabel, reveals her heart of gold in helping Richard. Needless to say, Levison turns out to be the actual murderer, and Richard is cleared of wrongdoing. Contained within the subplot is a cross-class conflict, the repressed power of an idealistic woman who effectively influences a good man, and the reform of a sharp-tongued spinster. When these ingredients are added to the devilish machinations of Levison and the mental agony of the aristocratic Lady Isabel, the extraordinary popularity of *East Lynne* is easy to understand.[8]

An even more overt example of rebellion was another best-seller, *Lady Audley's Secret* (1862), by Mary Elizabeth Braddon, dramatized by George Roberts and C. H. Hazelwood. Lucy Graham marries Lord Audley after her first husband runs away; when he unexpectedly returns, she pushes him down a well. She never pretends to love Lord Audley, but coolly goes about securing her own position within his family and the community. Unlike earlier melodrama, Lucy is not an outsider, but a traitor within the very heart of the family. Lucy articulates the naked greed and class envy of the marginally genteel: "I live now for ambition and interest, to mould the world and its votaries to my own end. Once I was fool enough to wed for love. Now I have married for wealth."[9] While Sir Michael Audley encourages Morris dancing and other country customs, she aims to impress a wider world with her wealth and beauty, even at the price of destroying all tradition. Braddon and her dramatic adaptors reveal Lady Audley's behavior as madness, but the play vividly reminded its audience of the fragility of the old values in the face of ambition.

Lady Audley and Lady Isabel represent the extremes of rebellion and self-sacrifice. They also epitomized unresolved social problems agitating women and men during the high Victorian period. Individual morality, sexuality, and female participation in political and economic spheres are all part of the conflict within *East Lynne* and *Lady Audley's Secret*. Both Mary Elizabeth Braddon and Mrs. Henry Wood doubtless knew that many women *did* think of leaving their marriages, or derived a little too much satisfaction from watching the actresses' defiant women.

Insanity and death are the fate of Lady Audley and Lady Isabel. In T. A. Palmer's version of the novel, the severe punishment laid upon Lady Isabel is deplored, but the message for theatregoers is:

> What am I now—an outcast, whom men pity, and from whom all good women will shrink. I have abandoned my husband, children, my home, cast away my good name, wrecked my happiness for evermore, and deliberately offended heaven, for him—for *him*—oh! my punishment is hard to bear—I have deserved it, all my future life spent in repentant expiation can never atone for the past, never, never.[10]

The strength of melodrama rests in evoking emotional situations that cannot be resolved, and then offering a form of resolution by linking current values, such as a wife's fidelity, to universal hopes. An audience could have its cake and eat it too; we can enjoy Lady Isabel's superior sensitivity and still see her punished for transgressing society's laws. The central paradox of domestic melodrama is its defense of the domestic ideal against a malign society under the belief that a larger moral order will prevail, yet this moral order is actually a reflection of current social values.

Melodramatic Characterization

Character development is less important in melodrama; we must retrain our expectations and sensibilities to focus upon action and plot. The good hero or heroine confronts a variety of evil forces threatening to destroy the family, but never loses faith that justice will ultimately triumph. Throughout a play the hero is perfectly virtuous, though sometimes he may become discouraged or even destroyed by his enemies. The fault lies not in him, but in society, which must change. Actions and circumstances dominate. What is important is the emotional energy expended upon the righting of wrong, the unravelling of seemingly hopeless situations.

Both *Luke the Labourer* and *Rent Day* have passive suffering figures in Farmer Wakefield and Farmer Heywood. Wakefield, a stock minor character, spends most of the plot ineffectually grieving for his lost son, poor finances, and harried wife and daughter. Heywood, ostensibly the hero of *Rent Day*, is equally unproductive; his only important action is to accuse his wife wrongfully of being unfaithful. Martin Heywood's behavior illustrates the way in which domestic melodrama repeatedly connected larger, social villainy with family betrayal. Material poverty, even the public disgrace of losing the farm, is nothing in comparison with the loss of marital love. Indeed, part of the emotional force of the play comes from the audience's sense that trouble never comes alone. Thus, even when we know that Martin's grief is unnecessary, his suffering provides us with a measure of how deep a good man's misery can be:

> And this, then, is the end! All's gone!—I cannot carry with me even a hope of better days. Now, indeed, labour will be hard to me; for I shall work with a broken heart. Now, fortune cannot bless me; for she with whom I should have shared all good—But let me think no more of her. Think no more! Like a ghost she seems to haunt me. But she has shamed me—and may she—! No, I cannot curse her, with her children looking in my face. I will not curse her.[11]

Language fails to express his grief, and like Farmer Wakefield, Heywood falls into temporary insanity. What matters is not the irrationality of his accusations, but his emotional devastation. We watch a good man tortured, but with the knowledge that justice will triumph.

Self-sacrifice is central to melodrama, for its major characters all have hidden talents and unrecognized virtue. For powerless women and men, melodrama was a vehicle for releasing frustrated talents, unrealized because of social conditions or financial constraints. Circumstances in melodrama enable characters to demonstrate their worth to those they love. In *Rent Day*, Rachel Heywood's decisive behavior despite thieves, fears of seduction, and her husband's calumny, shows the power of true womanhood under stress. The man she saves from robbery turns out to be the long-absent squire; in gratitude he gives the Heywoods the freehold on their farm, while her husband begs her forgiveness.

Yet many of the most attractive characters find no fulfillment without radical change, whether brought about by themselves or circumstances. Lady Isabel's real life begins after her fall, when she can begin sacrificing herself for her children. Lady Audley is a poor deserted wife, like countless others; only after committing bigamy does she gain a place on stage. Yet such actions implied the need for some cataclysmic change in society, an unthinkable solution for melodrama. A fantasy ending had to be found that brought radical change without radical disruption. The lost inheritance of *Rent Day* is echoed in *Clari* and *Luke the Labourer* by the sudden change of heart on the part of the villains. In the later melodramas, such as *East Lynne* and *Lady Audley's Secret*, family happiness is never restored, but the erring women are expelled. Melodrama gave acceptable explanations for irrational behavior, thereby making unhappiness manageable. By insisting on the ultimate triumph of social and personal justice, melodrama was able to provide consolation and hope without denying the social reality that made goodness and justice so fragile.

Much of the emotional effectiveness of melodrama comes from making the moral visible. The good is made palpable in the passive suffering of the virtuous characters, while evil is embodied in the villain. The villain's greed and sensuality are outward manifestations of a desire to control others. By preying upon a beautiful woman (or foolish man), whose allegiance is or should be to her father, lover, or husband, he gains control over all the men around her. The archetypal villain robbed the father of his money, the wife or daughter of her virtue, and the hero of his manliness. He was a powerful combination of lust, violence, and avarice—three vices fraught with danger and attraction in the nineteenth century.

At the beginning of every melodrama, the villain seems to have all the power over the other characters; he is able to say and do things no one else would risk. Through the villain a playgoer could savor restrained or forbidden emotions. Fantasies of the very worst that could happen—or that was within one—could be enjoyed. The attractiveness of evil was well known to melodramatists, who used their utmost skill to work upon the contradictions in their audiences' lives. Vile as the duke in *Clari, Maid of Milan* may be, his outspoken sensuality and power over all his subjects thrilled audiences. As we watch Lady Audley work upon Sir Michael's infatuation, we can recognize the lust for power that possibly lies within all women. Men, not women, suffer when women do not fulfill their stereotypes; men, not women, have illusions. The villain or villainess embodied the unspoken sexual desires of the audience, giving temporary permission to imagine the forbidden.

The villain's greatest crime was to destroy the family. But for him or her, there would be no disruption of the loving circle. Yet a closer look often shows otherwise. For example, Lady Isabel's plight needs a villain to be resolved. If life continued without her seducer, Captain Levison, she would be left in a supposedly happy family without suffering for or developing her sensitivity. In reality, her family is not happy, but since no one but her maid believes her misery, a desperate action must be taken. Paradoxically, her fall enables her to combine good and evil—to be the worst of mothers, yet the best of mothers in her disguise as her children's governess. Her emotional fulfillment depends upon her disgrace. Only after she has fallen is she free to suffer fully and to grow in emotional stature and importance. Indeed, Lady Isabel is far more interesting after her fall than before because her passive endurance has some point to it.[12] The villain serves to strengthen the emotional family bonds, as Lady Isabel daily realizes what she has lost in fleeing her children.

For all the evil possessed by the villain, domestic melodrama rarely left his wrongdoing unexplained. At the end of *Luke the Labourer*, Luke explains that he has plotted against Farmer Wakefield and his family because "You turn'd me away, and I had no character, because you said I were a drunkard. I were out o' work week after week, till I had not a penny in the world, not a bit o' bread to put in mine nor my wife's mouth. I then had a wife, but she sicken'd and died—yes, died—all—all—along o' you."[13] Luke, it turns out, is just like Farmer Wakefield—a family man with the same hopes and fears; but his luck does not hold, and suffering makes him a villain. Wakefield's refusal to extend his social responsibility to help the weak Luke leads to Luke's moral deterioration. All men must learn to recognize their links with others. The same moral concludes *Rent Day*, when the vile steward Crumbs reveals that he had wormed his way into the young Squire's confidence in order to rob him because the Squire's father had seduced Crumbs's wife many years before. His wife's picture hanging in Grantley Hall spurs him on to further revenge. Unlike other forms of melodrama, domestic melodrama humanizes the villain. Even in the midst of describing the most vile machinations, an essentially optimistic and positive world view led playwrights to soften their portrayal of the villain. Pure lust or avarice may appear to dominate, but underneath we frequently find a monomaniac desire to revenge the loss of his family. The domestic villain shared the same values as the hero or heroine and the audience.

The villain is always kept an isolated figure, rather than being cast as part of a larger pattern of injustice. To do so would have been to call into question the ideology of an industrializing capitalist society; individual virtues conquer the world, not combined action. The villain, with his insatiable desire, is cordoned off and treated as an aberration. Yet he or she is the force behind all of the action, enabling others to test their values. Melodrama provided an arena for the struggle between virtue and wrong, pushing both villain and hero or heroine to their utmost. The very limits of what can or cannot be done, of power or powerlessness, are tested; the audience could experience vicariously the extremes of good and evil. Melodrama's very familiarity in plotting and characterization aided in the creation of a sense of reassurance, of stability in the midst of terrible or awesome changes. No matter how great the evil done, good would triumph.

Melodrama and Ideology

Even while it raises wider issues, melodrama can be a device for distancing them. Clearly, its grand gestures and simplified moral code were easily susceptible to stereotyping, moving archetypes into the commonplace. Rather than enhancing our emotional involvement in and understanding of family conflict, unsuccessful melodrama became a source of laughter and parody even in its own day. The woes of Dame Wakefield in *Luke the Labourer* lend themselves readily to comedy, given her inflated laments and their extreme complications. By the late nineteenth century the familiar gestures and characterizations had become objects of relentless humor, but even earlier they had been parodied.[14] The central problem of melodrama was that it raised serious issues and then could not resolve them.

The plight of the fallen woman, toyed with so daringly by Mrs. Henry Wood, was especially liable to false emotion. The ostensible purpose of most writers who dealt with the subject was to chastise the audience for lacking Christian forgiveness and to point out the evils which befell those who failed to sustain the all-protective family. This immediately establishes a conflict of purposes, since by definition melodrama idealizes the audience's moral view, and defines evil as alien to the social order. If the villain is Society because it refuses to support the fallen woman, then the audience must somehow be attacked for complicity. Rather than do this, *East Lynne* simply condemns Lady Isabel and allies itself with conventional morality, while indulging in pitiful scenes of suffering.

Melodrama cannot effectively run counter to the most cherished beliefs of its audience, and these included female purity. The fallen woman must be distanced. In *Clari; or, The Maid of Milan*, Clari is permitted back into the family circle because the Duke Vivaldi had failed to carry out his sexual threats after absconding with her, but we are firmly reminded, "virtue can hold no intercourse with vice."[15] Lady Isabel can never return. The melodramatic presentation of her end, complete with those famous lines on the death of her son, "And he never knew me, never called me mother!"[16] evokes pity that the audience can admire in itself and use to distance itself from her. Here again we return to the central paradox of melodrama: while defending an ideal against a vengeful society in the name of a higher moral order, in actuality this moral order reflects the current values of the society presumably being attacked. The need for reassurance amidst great social change meant an adherence to the dominant mores.

Domestic melodrama by its very nature is conservative, however subversive its underlying message. It argues for the preservation of the family and its traditional values—a binding in of the errant son or unforgiving father or wayward daughter. As these values changed beyond recognition, it had to decline or adapt. Yet for nearly a century the topical circumstances and realistic settings of domestic melodrama successfully housed the major social conflicts of the nineteenth century. We now find new truths for our times in Victorian melodrama without reviving the old beliefs. Our sympathies have shifted openly to Lady Audley, and away from those she made suffer. Lady Isabel remains an interesting artifact for studying the portrayal of the fallen woman. Yet these changes in perspective have not undermined the immense importance of melodrama as a popular literary form; it is still with us in Harlequin romances, soap operas, and movies. Victorian domestic melodrama is doubly valuable for what it tells us about the "helpless and unfriended" during a time of enormous social change, and for the insights it provides into the sources and value of sentimentality for Victorian audiences. No other form could express so powerfully familial and social hopes and fears. Rather than seeing Victorian drama as a minor genre without literary interest, we should see it as a vehicle for some of the most powerful fantasies and desires of the time. Lady Isabel's plea could apply equally to domestic melodrama: "Think of me sometimes, keep one little corner in your heart for me—your poor—erring—lost Isabel."[17]

NOTES

1. Eric Bentley, *The Life of the Drama* (New York: Atheneum, 1964), 195–218.

2. Chuck Kleinhans, "Notes on Melodrama and the Family Under Capitalism," *Film Reader* 3 (1978):42.

3. David Grimsted, "Melodrama as Echo of the Historically Voiceless," in *Anonymous Americans: Explorations in Nineteenth-Century Social History*, ed. Tamara K. Hareven (Englewood Cliffs, N.J.: Prentice Hall, 1971), 86. For different perspectives on melodrama, see Frederic V. Bogal, "Fables of Knowing: Melodrama and Related Forms," *Genre* 2 (1978):83–108; and Kurt Tetzli von Rosador, "Myth and Victorian Melodrama," *Essays and Studies* 32 (1979):97–114.

4. Howard Payne, *Clari; or, The Maid of Milan* (London: John Miller, 1824), 59.

5. For a discussion of the relationship between David Wilkie's painting, *The Rent Day* (1807), and Jerrold's play, see Martin Meisel, *Realizations: Narrative, Pictorial, and Theatrical Arts in Nineteenth-Century England* (Princeton: Princeton University Press, 1983), 147–52.

6. See Michael R. Booth, *English Melodrama* (London: Herbert Jenkins, 1965), 24–29, for a discussion of the suffering and courage of the theatre heroine.

7. For a discussion of Mrs. Henry Wood's Lady Isabel and the ideal Victorian lady, see Jeanne B. Elliott, "A Lady to the End: The Case of Isabel Vane," *Victorian Studies* 19 (1976):329–44.

8. The long-standing popularity of *East Lynne* on both sides of the Atlantic is discussed by Gilbert B. Cross, *Next Week—East Lynne* (Lewisburg, Pa: Bucknell University Press, 1975).

9. C. H. Hazelwood, *Lady Audley's Secret*, in George Rowell, ed., *Nineteenth-Century Plays* (London: Oxford University Press, 1953), 245.

10. T. A. Palmer, *East Lynne*, in Leonard R. N. Ashley, ed., *Nineteenth-Century British Drama* (Glenview, Ill.: Scott, Foresman, 1967), 379.

11. Douglas Jerrold, *The Rent Day* (London: John Dicks, n. d.), 14.

12. Margaret Oliphant noticed this incongruity in her review of the novel *East Lynne*: "The Magdalen herself, who is only moderately interesting while she is good, becomes, as soon as she is a Magdalen, doubly a heroine. It is evident that nohow, except by her wickedness and sufferings, could she have gained so strong a hold upon our sympathies. . . . Nothing can be more fatal than to represent the flames of vice as a purifying fiery ordeal, through which the penitent is to come elevated and sublimed" (*Blackwood's Magazine* 91 [1862]: 567).

13. John Baldwin Buckstone, *Luke the Labourer; or The Lost Son* (London, n.d.), 15.

14. For an excellent and thorough discussion of Victorian attitudes toward melodrama, see Kurt Tetzli von Rosador, "Victorian Theories of Melodrama," *Anglia* 95 (1977):87–114. See also the parodies of Jerome K. Jerome in *Stageland: Curious Habits and Customs of Its Inhabitants* (London: Chatto and Windus, 1889).

15. Payne, 43.

16. Palmer, 390.

17. Palmer, 396.

Historical Drama and the "Legitimate" Theatre
TOM TAYLOR AND W. G. WILLS IN THE 1870s

Stephen Watt

> The matters therefore that concern the Gods and divine things are the highest of all others to be couched in writing; next to them the noble gests and great fortunes of princes, and the notable accidents of time, as the great affairs of war and peace.
> —George Puttenham, "The Arte of English Poesie" (1589)

> There is no doubt that it [W.G. Wills's *Charles the First*] has more claim to be considered an epoch-making play than any work produced on the London stage for many years, carrying out as it does the notion started by Mr. Tom Taylor's *'Twixt Axe and Crown*.
> —*The Times*, 23 December 1872

George Puttenham's orthodox Elizabethan conception of the literary canon, one in which historical literature figures prominently among the "highest" of matters "couched in writing," foreshadows one connotation of the term "legitimate" theatre as it evolved on the Victorian stage.[1] Of course, the notion that historical drama occupies a privileged space in the order of things does not originate in sixteenth-century literary criticism; on the contrary, it seems to have persisted in western thought since Aeschylus's *The Persians*. Not surprisingly, then, throughout the nineteenth century a repertory of poetic history plays and revivals of Shakespeare confirmed the theatrical "legitimacy" of the London stage's brightest stars—and also of the lesser lights who earned their status on

[187]

provincial stages throughout England, Ireland, and Scotland.[2] The term "legitimate" continued to be used well into the twentieth century, even though nowadays, as boundaries between high art and mass culture are demolished by writers like Sam Shepard and in postmodern performance art, it seems rather meaningless. James Joyce noticed in *Ulysses*, for example, that the veteran player Mrs. Millicent Bandmann-Palmer could attract crowds to see her as Augustin Daly's Leah (or as Jane Shore or Mary, Queen of Scots) one night, and as Hamlet the next. And in London at the Lyceum Theatre for nearly thirty years, Henry Irving employed a similar formula in his repertory with immense success. Irving produced plays that were, admittedly, neither Shakespearean nor historical—Leopold Lewis's *The Bells* (1871) for instance—but his appearance in W. G. Wills's *Charles the First* (1872) led many to agree with *The Times* that they were witnessing an "epoch-making drama." In fact, Tom Taylor's earlier *'Twixt Axe and Crown* (1870) and Wills's *Charles the First* produced a widely-felt optimism in the 1870s that a new era of legitimate drama had arrived.

The connection between historical drama and the legitimate theatre was in force throughout the Victorian age, though contemporary historical events were frequently turned into far less lofty theatrical entertainments. As George Glenn in this volume and J. S. Bratton elsewhere have outlined, historical incidents soon after their occurrence served as subjects for spectacle at lesser East End houses, at Astley's, and at Drury Lane.[3] The crowds that swarmed to non-Patent houses at the beginning of the nineteenth century to see reenactments of spectacular naval battles and other military confrontations were followed in 1854 and 1855 by those who attended what Bratton estimates to be some twenty-five plays based on events in the Crimean War. Later in the century, Drury Lane, under Augustus Harris's management, indulged the popular taste for flag-waving patriotism, excitement, and spectacle in *The Armada* (1888) and *The Royal Oak* (1889). The appeal of a more restrained, literary historical drama, however, was much more limited; and by the late 1860s and early 1870s there was a widespread fear that, to quote Wills's brother Freeman, "the poetic drama was supposed to be dead" and "Shakespeare spelled ruin" for theatre managers.[4] As the *Times* review cited above heralding *Charles the First* as an "epoch-making play" makes clear, the perceived decline of the legitimate, of Shakespeare in particular, was accompanied by the disappearance of the history play: "Except when novels were dramatized, our authors, since the time of Lord Lytton's *Richelieu*, seemed almost to have forgotten the possibility of placing the really prominent figures of history upon theatrical boards. . . . As we have already said, the notion of dealing with real history on the stage . . . seemed to have faded away" (23 December 1872, p. 6). For this reviewer, as for George Puttenham's Elizabethans, "real history" was centered around the "noble gests" and "great fortunes" of well-known persons, a historical perspective seldom actualized in spectacles which more typically placed common sailors, soldiers, and occasionally their loyal wives in the midst of an exciting and well-known contemporary episode. Such "real" history became something of a rarity on the mid-Victorian stage.

In the repertory of major actors—William Charles Macready, Charles Kean, Samuel Phelps, or Henry Irving—historical drama provided roles similar in magnitude to leading roles in Shakespeare. Macready mounted Edward Bulwer's *Richelieu* (1839), a play frequently revived by Irving, and Robert Browning's *Strafford* (1837). Even the creator of "sensational melodrama" Dion Boucicault penned an occasional history play like *Louis XI* or historical romance like *The Corsican Brothers* in the 1850s. Unfortunately for the fate of legitimate drama, as Macready discovered with *Strafford* and Phelps would later with the historical dramas of James White, producing such plays was often risky business. Success with one play could be followed by failure with another. Phelps apparently learned this lesson during his tenure at Sadler's Wells (1844–62): after Macready produced White's *The King of Commons* in 1846, Phelps successfully mounted, during the following year, White's *Feudal Times* and *John Saville of Haysted*, each running in repertory for twenty-five nights. But after the weak showings of F. G. Tomlins's *Garcia; or, The Noble Error* (1849) and White's *James the Sixth* (1851), Phelps appeared in only four history plays during the last twelve years of his management of Sadler's Wells.[5] Thus, while perhaps not extinct, the legitimate historical drama was somewhat moribund in 1870, the year of Taylor's *'Twixt Axe and Crown*. This play, I shall argue, along with Wills's *Charles the First*, appealed to the tastes of a varied audience in a heretofore unprecedented way, reestablishing the history play as a viable theatrical attraction and restoring it to its position atop the canon of legitimate drama. It is also a purpose of this essay to describe the conventions which Taylor and Wills exploited so successfully, in the process refining a powerful dramatic formula which became synonymous with "legitimacy" on the late-Victorian stage.

Before 1870, Tom Taylor had written or collaborated on over seventy popular plays, perhaps the best-known of which are *Still Waters Run Deep* (1855) and *The Ticket-of-Leave Man* (1863). Taylor also contributed regularly to and was later editor of *Punch*, served as an art critic for *The Times*, and taught at the University of London.[6] He was an extremely knowledgeable man of the theatre who, as is well known, served as Ellen Terry's beloved mentor in the years before her partnership with Irving. While Nina Auerbach has insinuated recently that Taylor served as a panderer in Terry's ill-fated marriage to George Frederick Watts, there is little question, as Martin Banham emphasizes, that Terry always treasured Taylor's affection for her.[7] In the 1850s and 1860s, Taylor wrote successful farces, melodramas, comedies, and, as I have mentioned, the rather more serious social melodrama, *The Ticket-of-Leave Man*. Before 1870, and with the exception of his adaptation in 1859 of Hugo's *Le Roi s'amuse* (*The Fool's Revenge*), when Taylor turned to historical materials he usually produced "romances," which were little more than plays of intrigue that relied upon stale dramatic conventions and elaborate staging. But during the later years of his career Taylor's interest in historical drama developed, leading to *'Twixt Axe and Crown*, *Joan of Arc* (licensed as *Jeanne D'Arc* in 1871), *Lady Clancarty* (1874), and *Anne Boleyn* (1876). In the first of these dramas Taylor develops what would become a very successful dramatic formula: *'Twixt Axe and Crown* combines the aesthetic appeal of poetic drama with the quiet sentiment of domestic melodrama, satisfying both the audience's curiosity about history and also their appetite for pathos.

'Twixt Axe and Crown opened on 22 January 1870 at the Queen's Theatre, Long-acre, running for a remarkable two hundred performances. It is a five-act, blank-verse tragedy which concerns political insurrection during Mary the First's short reign (1553–1558), her unhappy marriage to Philip the Second of Spain, her conflict with Princess Elizabeth, and the fate of Edward Courtenay, a nobleman caught between political machinations and love for Elizabeth. Taylor's selection of this subject could not have been more timely. Only days before the opening of the play, the American actress Mrs. F. W. Lander played both Elizabeth and Mary Stuart at the Lyceum. At that time, too, there was a strong interest in paintings of sixteenth- and seventeenth-century political figures. The Royal Academy exhibitions regularly featured paintings of Mary Stuart, Charles I, Oliver Cromwell, and others.[8] Among the more famous depictions of Elizabeth were Paul Delaroche's *The Death of Queen Elizabeth* (1828) and Augustus Leopold Egg's *Queen Elizabeth Discovers She Is No Longer Young* (1848). Unlike the old or dying Elizabeths in these paintings, Taylor's Elizabeth is vibrant, compassionate, and ultimately firm-minded when she learns of Courtenay's execution near the end of the play. As further evidence of the popularity of Elizabethan history at this time,

on the day Taylor's play opened, the *Saturday Review* announced the publication of the fifth and sixth volumes of Froude's *History of England* from Wolsey's fall to the defeat of the Spanish armada. Amidst all this concentrated interest in earlier history, a poetic rendering of a widely-known episode from Elizabethan England—or, as Wills recognized in writing *Charles the First*, of incidents during the civil war—was likely to interest playgoers.

Taylor saw that a sentimental and tragically charged melodrama could be shaped from these historical materials, and he designed his characters to fit the genre. Taylor's most difficult task, one that Lord Tennyson was unable to achieve in his later, less successful *Queen Mary* (1875), was to create a sympathetic character from a traditionally maligned monarch. Given contemporary interest in Elizabeth, Taylor's chore was even more onerous than it might otherwise have been. In the preface to *'Twixt Axe and Crown*, he acknowledges that his history is slanted sentimentally in Mary's favor, precisely because Mary had been too "harshly judged" by historians who failed to comprehend that she was "in many respects of a loving and womanly nature—warped by evil counsels, but struggling towards the light."[9] Believing in "historical rehabilitation," Taylor averred that Mary should be redeemed from her "Bloody Mary" reputation, which is exactly what *'Twixt Axe and Crown* accomplishes. Taylor's Mary, similar in several respects to Schiller's Maria Stuart, who was seen frequently on London stages,[10] is a love-starved recluse who is first rejected by Courtenay, then abandoned by her heartless husband. This portrayal continues through to the last act when, because of the imprisoned Elizabeth's impending execution and Courtenay's beheading, the audience's sympathy for Mary might be lost. Taylor, though, precedes Elizabeth's last-minute triumph and escape from the executioner by emphasizing Mary's pitiable physical and psychological weakness. Before she dies in the play's last act, a sickly and neglected Mary is given several opportunities to elicit the audience's sympathy. For example:

> If he [Philip] but knew
> How ill all's with me here! How sore my need
> Of some kind presence—some small word of love!
> I do not look for much.
>
> (*HD*, 199)

The "bloody Mary" who sent opponents to their doom becomes, in Taylor's hands, a submissive wife whose chief desire is to please her husband:

> To work his [Philip's] will, whose will is his wife's law!
> Whom to content is to content myself.
>
> (*HD*, 201)

In this depiction, Mary becomes one of numerous devoted spouses in both domestic melodrama *and* historical drama in the 1870s: Wills's ill-fated Charles the First and Jane in *Jane Shore* (1876), and later—most notably—Taylor's own Lady Clancarty and Anne Boleyn.

Of course, Taylor needed to explain Elizabeth's and Courtenay's imprisonments, not to mention the deaths of Wyatt and his followers, in a way that would also deflect the audience's censure away from Mary. Conventional villains provide the means for such a deflection: Renard, a Spanish ambassador, and Gardiner, a Catholic zealot who would betray his country for the benefit of the Church. Gardiner especially, the hypocritical cleric who would descend to any treachery to further his power, becomes almost a prototype of historical villains in the 1870s and 1880s. Wills's Cromwell in *Charles the First* is succeeded in this role by craven Puritans in his *Buckingham* (1875) and Harris's *The Royal Oak*; Taylor's Gardiner is followed by other Catholic villains like Father Carey in Harris's *The Armada* and various diabolical persecutors in plays about Joan of Arc like Taylor's *Jeanne D'Arc*.[11] Indeed, religious figures in many of these plays are not simply power-hungry or avaricious, but overtly sexist as well. Such is the case with Wills's John Knox in *Mary, Queen O' Scots* (1874). In one despicable speech Knox announces his contemptible "understanding" of women's "natures":

> Madam [Mary], that thou art a Queen,
> Thy subjects with affection would admit;
> But I, John Knox, doth know that thou art a woman,
> And women may be faithful to their bonds
> Of credit, or allegiance, or religion;
> But without bonds, they are but lawless cattle.[12]

The principal exceptions to this portrayal of the clergy are the three clerics prominent in Irving's repertory: Bulwer's Richelieu, Shakespeare's Cardinal Wolsey, and Tennyson's Becket. But in *'Twixt Axe and Crown* little question exists about Renard's or Gardiner's motivations:

> Renard [to Gardiner]:   Give us up
> The heads of Lady Elizabeth and Courtenay

> | | And Philip shall give *you* what, until now,
> | | By my advice, he has refused—his aid
> | | To plant . . . the Inquisition
> | | Here, in your England. . . .
> | Gardiner: | Your hand on *that*!
>
> (*HD*, 174)

The opposition between protagonist and antagonist so clearly inscribed in most varieties of melodrama is made conspicuous by Renard and Gardiner's villainy—and, consequently, "Bloody Mary" becomes just another victim like her sister, Elizabeth.

Counterbalancing this evil in *'Twixt Axe and Crown* and sharing the audience's sympathy with Queen Mary are the imprisoned and separated lovers Courtenay and Elizabeth. As Taylor notes in his preface, the real Courtenay's "character, conduct, and motives" are among the "disputed questions of the time"; nevertheless, there is little question about these components of Taylor's character. Courtenay's heroism prefigures that of Lord Clancarty, Wills's Buckingham, and Harris's Vyvyan Foster (*The Armada*), to name but three of many. Courtenay embodies the physical energy, loyalty, and "manliness"—the term of approval critics at the time employed so frequently—that constituted romantic heroism in Victorian historical drama. And Elizabeth, too, like Jeanne D'Arc and Lady Clancarty after her, combines a "feminine" domesticity with the courage of her male counterpart. Isabel Markham, Elizabeth's friend and confidante in the play, furnishes a description of Elizabeth which could apply to many a heroine in the late-Victorian history play; particularly applicable is Isabel's oblivious admixture of praise tinctured with culturally constructed notions of gender:

> She's man and woman both, I think, for me.
> So manly brave, and yet so woman gentle!
>
> (*HD*, 189)

Brave women and domestic, "gentle" men serve frequently as heroes in Taylor's and Wills's histories. *'Twixt Axe and Crown* ends, after considerable suspense, with Elizabeth justifying the extravagance of her friend's praise. She faces impending death with the martyr-like fortitude of Wills's Charles, yet is saved from the executioner at the last moment. As she learns of her sister's death and her ascension to the throne, Elizabeth also hears of Courtenay's execution. She falters slightly, being, after all, so "woman gentle," but she also demonstrates her "manly" resolve to lift England out of civil turmoil and lead the country to new levels of global power.

'*Twixt Axe and Crown*, then, relies upon domesticity, a revived interest in national history, displays of both courage and cowardly villainy which forge a strong opposition between good and evil, and a suspenseful plot leading to an exciting rescue. Taylor would surely add "historical accuracy" to this list, maintaining as he did in his preface to *Historical Dramas* that, like Shakespeare in constructing the *Henry IV* plays, he had merely altered the historical record in the "compression of time." Accurate or not, he enjoyed the reputation among some critics as a responsible, even meticulous, historian. In reviewing *Lady Clancarty*, the *Times* critic remarked that it was "refreshing to observe the conscientious scruples felt by an accomplished scholar at the slightest deviation from an historical track" (11 March 1874, p. 9). Recently, Matthew H. Wikander has taken a different view of the matter, regarding *'Twixt Axe and Crown* and Tennyson's later *Queen Mary* as similarly originating in a "passivist" historiography of nostalgia and sentiment in which "History's agents are its victims." For Wikander, this view of historical process counters an "activist" historiography in which history is regarded as determined by the actions of powerful figures; and, as Wikander observes, this history of pathos and victimization dominates the London stage in the eighteenth and nineteenth centuries, even appearing frequently on the contemporary stage.[13] As persuasive as his argument is, Wikander fails to consider that not every representation of the "pathos of power," even a representation of the same historical moment, was received favorably by late-Victorian audiences. Tennyson's *Queen Mary*, which in manuscript was so bulky that it required Irving's revision before it was produced at the Lyceum in 1876, ran for only twenty-three nights.[14] Of the several reasons for this failure, Mary's harshness in refusing to spare Cranmer's life even after his recantation, her wielding of political power, and her lack of "womanly" gentleness surely were among the most significant. Representing many of the same historical conflicts and featuring many of the same characters, *'Twixt Axe and Crown*, on the other hand, was enormously successful both critically and commercially. Few plays could match its run of two hundred performances.

'Twixt Axe and Crown owed its success not only to the sentimental historiography which underlies it or the dubious attractions of melodrama, but

also to Taylor's emphasis of elevated language over sensational action, signalling to many both a return to the more ambitious drama of the Macready years on the London stage *and* the possibility of a bright future. The *Era*, for example, expressed surprise at the production of a poetic drama and believed it could bolster the lagging spirits of those playgoers who "have wearied of the modern realism and 'sensationalism' of the stage. Few . . . would have ventured to predict a few months ago that such an experiment [the production of a poetic historical drama] would have been ventured at this theatre; but it is cheering to observe that the engagement of Mr. and Mrs. Rousby [the lead actors in the 1870 production] appears to have turned the dramatic tide in favour of *the more substantial kind of theatric fare*" (23 January 1870, p. 14; my emphasis). Considering the financial risks of theatrical management at this time, such a venture was indeed hazardous. Yet, as the *Era* reviewer remarks, this "experiment" worked. It did so primarily because of Taylor's skillful blending of the "strong dramatic situations necessary to seize the attention of the present generation of playgoers with that more poetic diction which would satisfy the requirements of an intelligent taste" (23 January 1870, p. 14). The *Saturday Review* was even more enthusiastic than the *Era* in its praise of *'Twixt Axe and Crown*, not only because of Taylor's craftsmanship but because in production the play recovered the style of acting seemingly lost since the days of Macready and Kean. Moreover, the review predicted with great accuracy how plays like *'Twixt Axe and Crown* could aid a Shakespearean actor in achieving a "legitimate" success:

> The school of acting of which Mr. Macready was at one time the master . . . threatens to become extinct. There are two or three actors yet remaining on the stage who embody the tradition of the English drama as it flourished in the days of Kean and Kemble, and it seems that when they depart they will leave behind them no successors. . . . The lovers of Shakespeare are not so unreasonable as to expect that a theatre can be filled by the performance of Shakespeare's plays alone. A manager must have novelties, and we are desirous to believe that Mr. Tom Taylor has furnished to the Queen's Theatre a *new piece of the old sort*, in which actors may attain a legitimate success which may encourage them to other efforts in the same line. (29 January 1870, pp. 152–53; my emphasis)

Paradoxically then, at least in some quarters, Taylor's play did not so much "turn the dramatic tide" in a forward direction but rather recalled an ebbing tide on a nearly deserted beach. It was a "new piece of the old sort," the "sort" of play made for star-actors. For diverse audiences, the rhetorical flourishes of historical drama coupled with a restrained melodramatic action proved irresistible; especially for the more refined or "intellectual" theatregoer, it was a "more substantial kind of theatric fare" that inaugurated a new era of legitimate drama.

Though not nearly so prominent in star-actors' repertoires as were Bulwer's *Richelieu* and Boucicault's *Louis XI*, Taylor's history plays like *'Twixt Axe and Crown* offered respectability to actresses aiming toward recognition in the legitimate theatre. And, needless to say, the popularity of Taylor's plays was enhanced by these actresses. Mrs. Clara Rousby, often described by London critics as the "beautiful Mrs. Rousby," played Elizabeth in *'Twixt Axe and Crown* in both its London premiere and in a subsequent revival in 1875 at New York's Lyceum Theatre. Alternating in repertory with Shakespeare's Rosalind in New York, Mrs. Rousby's Elizabeth prompted the *New York Herald* critic to applaud the actress's "ingenuous, artless" manner and "sincere, even" demeanor, virtues which Mrs. Scott-Siddons brought to Taylor's play in New York in 1870.[15] Like Mrs. Rousby, Mrs. Scott-Siddons alternated between Rosalind in *As You Like It* and Elizabeth in her repertory. At London's Royal Olympic Theatre in 1874, Henry Neville and Ada Cavendish combined, among other plays, *Much Ado About Nothing* and *Lady Clancarty*, scoring with the latter play according to *The Times* a "decided success" (11 March 1874, p. 9). In 1876, despite some reservations, critics found Taylor's Anne Boleyn a similarly forceful addition to Adelaide Neilson's roster of mostly Shakespearean characters: "When we get a play as good as this by Mr. Tom Taylor, we should be thankful. Miss Neilson cannot be always acting Juliet and Rosalind, and here is a new part in which she is well worth seeing" (*LSR*, 12 February 1876, p. 208). Thus, when employing a dramatic formula similar to that of *'Twixt Axe and Crown*—when creating noble characters in a poetic and nonsensational context rather than merely placing a historical figure in the midst of a spectacular predicament—Taylor reaped both critical and commercial rewards.

Taylor attempted his formula again in 1871 with *Jeanne D'Arc*, but most critics thought he ventured too close to the sensational. Unquestionably he did, which is somewhat surprising: Banham reminds us in the introduction to his edition, *Plays by Tom Taylor* (1985), that Taylor vehemently denounced such excesses in his *The Theatre in England, some of its shortcomings and possibilities*. Published in the same year that *Jeanne D'Arc* premiered, Taylor's essay suggests that many playgoers of "all classes" have avoided the theatre, once a place of "intellectual resort and relaxation," because it has failed to mount plays "which will stir and enthrall without condescending to vulgar claptrap, crawling realism, or the mere physical excitement, now christened Sensation."[16] Ignoring his own astute observation, Taylor attempts to re-create Jeanne's siege of Orleans in the third act of *Jeanne D'Arc*, which amounts to little more than a series of directions on staging a spectacular battle: "Cannons on clumsy wheeled carriages are run on from the wings and fired"; the English pour through a gate between the two large towers at the fortress of the Tourelles, while the French "rally and raise ladders against the palisadoes"; several ladders, "with the men on them, are hurled into the ditch"; crossbow-men and cannoneers continue to shoot "all the time" throughout the battle, and so on (*HD*, 103–4). The play's last scene, moreover, in which Jeanne is lashed to a stake while a fire is lit beneath her finally proved too much for the critics of both the *Era* (16 April 1871) and the *Saturday Review*. While commending *'Twixt Axe and Crown* for rising above the vulgarities of sensational drama because in it Taylor "does not content himself with striking incidents but endeavors to express in language the emotions which these incidents may be expected to awaken," the *Saturday Review* found the climax of *Jeanne D'Arc* "either disgusting or ludicrous, or both combined" (22 April 1871, p. 449). The "educated public," the reviewer opines, would have been perfectly "delighted" to support *Jeanne D'Arc* as it had its predecessor—and it might have even tolerated a representation of Jeanne's martyrdom—but it could not be expected to endure the introduction of instruments of torture or a stack of burning timbers. The same reviewer even poked fun at what appeared to be the popular taste for last-act sensationalism: "It is probably by way of penance for a long course of burlesque that the British public is now going in generally for a scaffold hung with black for the last scene of a play" (22 April 1871, p. 450). "Striking" incidents and "physical excitement" in *Jeanne D'Arc* tend to overwhelm the poetic language, domesticity, and sentimental historiography that contributed so substantially to the success of *'Twixt Axe and Crown*.

Taylor appeared to learn a valuable lesson from this response and returned to more lyrical domestic histories in *Lady Clancarty* and *Anne Boleyn*. While the former ends happily with the reunion of the long-separated Clancartys, the latter concludes with Anne being ushered to a scaffold strategically located offstage. Both plays did brisk business: *Lady Clancarty*, for example, opened on March 9 and ran for the entire spring of 1874; the Olympic celebrated the play's one-hundredth performance on

June 30. The play was frequently revived, most famously perhaps by John Hare and the Kendals at the St. James Theatre in 1887.[17] And it was due in part to plays like *Lady Clancarty*, *'Twixt Axe and Crown*, and *Anne Boleyn* that legitimate drama—poetic drama, dignified prose romances, and Shakespeare—was revived in the 1870s.

This revival of both Shakespeare and contemporary legitimate drama was strengthened significantly by the formidable 180-day run of W. G. Wills's *Charles the First*, which opened on 28 September 1872 at the Lyceum Theatre. Even the most optimistic devotee of historical or poetical drama could scarcely have guessed at the success this play would enjoy and the impact on late-Victorian theatre it would exert. The theatrical strategies Taylor deployed in *'Twixt Axe and Crown*—especially the selection of a well-known historical subject, an emphasis upon domestic affairs and idealized family life disrupted by political events, and an unsensational representation of the opposition between protagonist and antagonist—were improved upon by Wills, a self-styled Irish Bohemian living and writing in London. One strong improvement, as Martin Meisel has discussed, involves the theatrical reconstruction of popular paintings through the set design and action of the play. Wills, a painter himself, carefully drew the *tableaux vivants* of several scenes to replicate well-known historical paintings, further cementing the relationship between national history, poetry, and the drama for the "educated" or refined theatregoer. Indeed, Wills helped establish the poetic history play, the Lyceum, and Henry Irving, who played Charles, as the most distinguished forces in London theatre until the rise of Bernard Shaw.

Looking back on it now from our more sophisticated, perhaps irrevocably jaded postmodern perspective, Wills's four-act, blank-verse tragedy of Charles's decline and pursuit by Oliver Cromwell's forces seems little more than a sentimental melodrama enlivened by an historical interest. Further, Wills's melodramatic reductions of Charles and Cromwell into stage-hero and utter villain seem hardly laudable and clearly unhistorical, as many reviewers at the time complained. Still, what *The Times* in December of 1872 would label an "epoch-making" play, the *Morning Post* in September called a "genuine success." And the *Post*'s reviewer plainly registered his surprise at such an unlikely turn of events: "A more genuine success has probably never been recorded; certainly, no such extraordinary scene has been witnessed in a playhouse for many years, if at all, as that [*Charles the First*] which marked the opening of the theatrical season at the Lyceum.

An astounding surprise awaits the audience.... From the first to the last there were apparent in [Irving's] impersonation dignity, and refinement, and pathos beyond praise" (*MP*, 30 September 1872, p. 2). *The Times* in September was less sanguine: the reviewer objected that the depiction of Cromwell turned history into a soppy mythology, but still on the whole he was gratified. Irving, he said, for several years known as a "promising artist," has created in Charles a "new character" whom all "can appreciate"; Isabella Bateman as Henrietta Maria "more than fulfills" the promise she has shown in the past; and Wills, "hitherto known as an adaptor only, appears [to be] an original dramatist of great power, from whom something more perfect may be expected" (30 September 1872, p. 8).[18] Interestingly prophetic of the manner in which history plays like Taylor's and Wills's would either complement in repertory or oppose revivals of Shakespeare, this same review begins with a brief summary of *Charles the First*'s most formidable "legitimate" competition, Phelps's *Othello* at the Princess's Theatre. There a crowded house applauded the "commencement" of a series of "legitimate performances" (Phelps was to play Shylock in *The Merchant of Venice* after *Othello*). Nevertheless, "everybody in town who takes a special interest in theatrical matters, and was not professionally engaged elsewhere, was present at the first performance of Mr. W. G. Wills's new play." Imperfect or not, *Charles the First* left its mark on the development of legitimate drama in late-Victorian England.

Commentators more partial to Wills hailed *Charles the First* as much more than a curious theatrical event: it was a text of far-reaching influence on the state of contemporary drama. In his preface to the 1873 William Blackwood edition, an anonymous editor places *Charles the First* "among those plays that mark a transition period in the history of drama."[19] In addition, this play, which "evidently appealed to the sympathies of the public more strongly than any new poetical work brought out within the memory of living men" (*CF*, ix), could also help revive interest in Shakespearean or other more "literate" drama. Or so Wills's brother Freeman, himself a playwright who would later collaborate in writing the enduringly popular *The Only Way* (1899) for Martin Harvey, believed. Freeman Wills recalled accurately that one of his brother's most passionate admirers was Ellen Terry, who played opposite Irving in *Charles the First* numerous times. She regarded the last five pages of the play as "perfection" and exclaimed in an effusive letter to Wills in 1891 that "never, *never* has anything more beautiful been written in English," confessing that even after having played Henrietta Maria opposite Irving's Charles for several years (her first performance in the part was in 1883) she still was "all melted" by its conclusion.[20]

Besides restoring the history play to prominence—and melting the emotions of audience and actor alike—*Charles the First* provided an impetus sufficient to launch Irving's distinguished career. Wills later became regarded by many as the "house playwright" at the Lyceum during Irving's management, joining, in Bernard Shaw's ungenerous estimation, Tennyson, Sheridan Knowles, and Bulwer-Lytton as the most conspicuous producers of "glaringly artificial high horses for the great actors of their time." Imperfect or not, artificial or not, *Charles the First* placed Irving in a position of public esteem which he had never enjoyed before the autumn of 1872, as *The Times* emphasizes: "That *Charles I* proved triumphant beyond the most sanguine expectations, that it placed Mr. Henry Irving in a new position, and that it is acknowledged to be the most remarkable drama now performed in London are facts beyond the reach of controversy" (*T*, 23 December 1872, p. 6). The "new position" Irving reached was one that would allow him, within a matter of a half-dozen years, to become the leading actor of his day. Before *Charles the First*, Irving had played comic roles successfully—Jingle in *The Pickwick Papers* and Jeremy Diddler in *Raising the Wind*—and gained critical acclaim as the guilt-ridden Mathias in Lewis's *The Bells*. After *Charles the First*, Irving still played Mathias but also Hamlet, Macbeth, Cardinal Wolsey, Richard III, and Becket. *Charles the First*, I believe, marks a turning point in Irving's career and, in fact, remained a popular attraction in his repertory for over twenty years.[21]

How did *Charles the First* create such a sensation and reestablish the preeminence of the history play on the late-Victorian stage? First, and foremost, Wills combined the eloquence of poetic language with scrupulously accurate costumes and stage pictures. Colonel H. L. Bateman, manager of the Lyceum Theatre in 1872 and producer of the play, stressed the historical accuracy of the production in the program of the play: "The scenery and appointments have been prepared with the intention of giving reality to a reproduction of the actual period during which the incidents are supposed to have taken place. The dresses with like purpose have been prepared from portraits of historical personages."[22] Of course, this concern for authenticity in pictorial representation is hardly new. In Macready's tenure at Drury Lane, accurate costuming and scenic "archaeology" were well-established principles, principles which evolved into absolutes in Charles Kean's management of the Princess's Theatre. In his preface to the 1860 edition of *Costume in England*, Frederick William Fairholt compares the imperative for "correct" costuming in the arts with the historian's concern for precision in the dating of events: "As no historian could venture to give wrong dates designedly, so no painter could falsify history by delineating the character on his canvas in habits not known until many years after his death, or holding implements that were not at the time invented."[23] If such "painted lies" could not be "tolerated" in historical painting, as Fairholt contends, then neither was it acceptable in the production of Victorian historical drama. For this reason, to cite one example, Edward Godwin, the father of Ellen Terry's two children and a reputable stage "archaeologist," was employed in 1878 to conduct research on fifth-century Roman clothing, statuary, and even saddlery for Wilson Barrett's production of Wills's *Claudian*.[24] Authenticity in the historical details of set and costume—something James Boaden had rather uncritically praised in John Philip Kemble's dictum for "punctilious exactness" in the latter's tenure at Drury Lane nearly a century before—became not just *a* concern but *the* concern in productions both of Shakespearean and historical drama on the mid- and late-Victorian stage.[25] Clearly such accuracy contributed to the success of *Charles the First*.

London critics recognized the historical correctness not only of costume and setting, but also of Irving's makeup, which was patterned after Van Dyke's portraits. The *Times* reviewer felt that at certain moments he had witnessed Van Dyke's Charles "startled living from its frame"; the *Post* echoed this observation: "It was as though one of Van Dyke's portraits had stepped out of its frame and been endowed with life." These viewers' responses merely hint at the play's larger indebtedness to well-known historical painting. As *The Times* noted, in *Charles the First* Wills "always takes care that his drop curtain shall not fall without effect." This "effect" in the cases of acts one and four was created by stage groupings which resembled well-known paintings: Frederick Goodall's *An Episode of the Happier Days of Charles I* (1853) for the act one curtain, and Sir John Everett Millais's *A Huguenot on St. Bartholomew's Day, Refusing to Shield Himself from Danger by Wearing the Roman Catholic Badge* (1852) in act four. Moreover, it is demonstrable that the provenance of Wills's conception of this ill-fated king was not only historical record, but also the highly domestic Victorian historical iconography of figures like Charles the First. As Meisel suggests, the first act of Wills's play, "ruffled only by voices and messages from the distant world of politics," emphasizes Charles in the role of dedicated father and spouse.[26] The entire first act resembles the collision of domestic sentiment and veiled political tension in Goodall's painting in which Charles and his family, assembled at the front of the royal barge, float contentedly on the Thames while a company of armed guards stands at attention in the background. Wills's stage directions—"they [Charles, his wife, and children] enter the barge, and as it moves slowly off, the curtain falls to soft music" (*CF*, 29)—reproduce the central action of Goodall's picture. As in Wills's play, Goodall's Charles is centered on the barge surrounded by his wife and young children; however, as the promptbook for the 1872 production indicates, Wills's reproduction very subtly intrudes harsh political reality into this scene by positioning two men-at-arms on the barge (far stage-left). In both Goodall's picture and Wills's play, the "distant world" of politics is clearly moving toward the blissful world of the domestic.

Throughout the first act of *Charles the First*, Charles's devotion to his family is juxtaposed to the decline of his monarchy. The play begins with two associates' (Eleanor and Huntley) ominous discussion of growing Roundhead power, then Eleanor's advice to the queen to leave the country. Charles's initial appearance marks him as the family man the iconographic tradition had depicted: Daniel Maclise's *An Interview Between Charles I and Oliver Cromwell* (1836) and Charles West Cope's *Charles I Erecting his Standard at Nottingham* (1861), for example, show Charles embracing his children even in the midst of serious political dealings. In Wills's play, Charles enters with Prince James on his shoulders and an adoring Princess Elizabeth at his side begging for another of her father's stories. As Charles complies by reciting the ballad of King Lear, Henrietta Maria rushes to her husband to inform him of unrest at Westminster. Charles will not be deterred, though, from entertaining his children before considering politics. When he does give full expression to his political convictions, it is in a speech which effectively establishes him as a benevolent ruler wronged terribly by his detractors:

> I would be call'd the King of Liberty!
> I say strike every chain from off my people;
> Let liberty, like crystal daylight, enter
> And fill each home—illume each road and highway;
> Till the king's body-guard, when he rides forth,
> On either hand be Love and Loyalty!
>
> (*CF*, 26–27)

This same speech also reveals his determination not to match evil for evil in combating his political opponents; instead, he will find "some silken fetters" for the Commons before they "manacle their King." Just as in popular painting, in Wills's play Charles is a sensitive, almost doting father and a liberal, if somewhat naive, ruler. As such, he is an ideal monarch who will inevitably be slaughtered by a sinister Cromwell. In this confrontation between the lovingly domestic and the insidiously political, melodrama and history merge, as they had so successfully in Taylor's *'Twixt Axe and Crown*.

When Cromwell appears in the second act, he is a brutal antagonist to the saintly Charles. And this depiction of a cowardly opportunist—of Cromwell as a melodramatic villain—sparked the most vocal opposition to Wills's drama. This criticism was not confined to the few hostile reviews the play received in London newspapers. In fact, a rival play—Colonel A. B. Richards's pro-Commonwealth *Oliver Cromwell: An Historical Tragedy* which opened at the Queen's Theatre, Long-acre, on 21 December 1872—not only recapitulated critical objections to Wills's Lord Protector, but also employed many of the same conventions of Wills's *Charles the First* to redeem his reputation. Although written earlier (1847) and revived to counter *Charles the First*, Richards's play seems to respond directly to the Cavalier sympathies of Wills's play. Domesticity, emphasized not only in *Charles the First* but also in Wills's *Jane Shore* and most of Taylor's histories, preoccupies Richards in *Cromwell*. The play begins with the Lord Protector on a "rustic seat" near a table covered with letters and books, presumably information relating to contemporary social tensions. Richard Cromwell sits on his father's knee, other children frolic about, and Mistress Cromwell spins on a nearby wheel. Cromwell embraces all of his children and gently sends them to bed before a group of men arrive, urging him to take a more active part in political affairs. In an aside, his wife fears that "all the good" she and her children have accomplished in keeping Cromwell *out* of public life will be destroyed by her husband's visitors—and, of course, her fear is justified by subsequent action. Even so, while Cromwell listens attentively to reports of Charles's tyranny and abuse, he maintains respect for his king, arguing that "we must defend the King against himself and England's enemies."[27] Here his motivation for action is as noble and patriotic as Charles's motives in Wills's play; and, like Charles, Cromwell cares more for his family than he does for political power. This fact is underscored when, like Taylor's Mary and Wills's Charles, Richards's Protector suffers as a passive victim of history when his daughter Elizabeth dies in the course of the play.

Also like Wills, as Meisel points out, Richards alluded to well-known paintings when constructing scenes. *The Times* strongly implies that the most moving scene that opening night in December was appropriated from a popular historical painting: Paul Delaroche's *Cromwell Gazing at the Body of Charles I* (1831). As in the painting—and just the inverse of the opportunistic Lord Protector in Wills's play—Richards's Cromwell is a mournful, contemplative figure who admires the fallen Charles and examines his own motives for participating in regicide. In effect, the stage picture replicates Delaroche's painting, and as Cromwell stands over Charles's body in act four, Richards supplies him with a soliloquy praising the monarch and expressing his own regret:

> How well he died, that lived not well. His words
> Strike cold here. Kings have died ere now, whose lives
> Were worthless, hurtful to their people's good;
> None meek as this.
>   Oh, could an angel light
> The deepest corner of my secret soul,
> And say ambition drugged not my design
> With soul-consuming poison.
>
> (C, 31)

At the end of the same soliloquy, Cromwell decides, "I am not guilty! / It was the nation's voice" that called for the "headman's axe," not his. The act ends with Cromwell suffering the death of his beloved daughter, the loss of whom is a "heavy burden. Yea, perchance too heavy / For a man." With "no thought left save for England now" (38), Cromwell embarks upon his project to "make the name of England sound / As great as glorious, with an echo full / As ever that of antique Rome of yore" (40). With more pathos and eloquence such as this—and more *tableaux vivants* resembling historical paintings—Richards's *Cromwell* might have received the popular approval Wills's play obtained; however, as the *Times* reviewer put it, the author of *Cromwell* was "not content with the daring principle adopted by Mr. Wills, of bringing his *grand pictures* sharply before the public without troubling himself about their connection." Still, even though Richards' play ran for little more than a month, closing on 26 January 1873, it replicated many Londoners' strong objection to Wills's depiction of Charles's adversary, a depiction that even the highly enthusiastic *Times* felt would spark the "greatest divergence of opinion."

Wills defended his characterization of Cromwell—and responded to the *Times* (and others') allegations that *Charles the First* was not a historical drama but a "mythical tale" contrived with the "utmost" poetic license—in a public letter to the *Morning Post* on 25 October 1872. In this letter, Wills cites the facts behind his portrait of the Lord Protector: the massacres of thousands of Irishmen at Drogheda and Wexford in 1649 and 1650 as evidence of Cromwell's cruelty; his acceptance of the confiscated estates of the Marquis of Worcester as an indication of his greed; and the authority of "numerous contemporary pamphlets" as proof of Cromwell's second-act offer of support to Charles in exchange for an earldom. Charles's response to this offer serves to highlight Cromwell's duplicity:

> Thee, who dost truckle for the wealth and title
> Which you denounce so roundly from the hustings,—
> A mouthing patriot with an itching palm,
> In one hand menace, in the other greed.
>
> (*CF*, 50)

In his letter, Wills maintains that the allegation of Cromwell's avarice is *not* a "slanderous invention" on his part and invokes historical fact to silence the "chorus of indignation" his portrayal of Cromwell had prompted: "I really supposed the matter [of Cromwell's eagerness to accept an earldom] to be familiar to all readers of history—numerous contemporary pamphlets attest the statement which I have only antedated, and they certainly warrant the dramatist, if not the historian, in accepting it as a fact" (25 October 1872, p. 3). Fact or not, Wills's detractors labelled this an irresponsibly "free" view of history; "free" view or not, this public debate did absolutely nothing to diminish the popularity of Wills's play at the Lyceum. It may even have encouraged it.

In addition, then, to the pictorial aspects of Wills's play and the performances of Irving in the title role and Isabel Bateman as Henrietta Maria, his controversial historicism also attracted spectators to the Lyceum Theatre. Frankly, though no commentator with whom I am acquainted discusses this, Wills's view of Cromwell seems hardly surprising. An Irishman conscious of his native country's political turmoil, Wills had published a three-volume novel, *The Love That Kills*, in 1867 which, as he explains in the preface, renders an account of the conditions in Ireland that led to the Great Famine and peasant rebellion of 1848. In the first volume of the novel, Father Walshe, an Irish nationalist priest, explains to a large crowd that the English government's purpose in Ireland was ever "to crush and trample down the Irish, to decimate and drive them from their native soil, to refuse them daily bread on the land they till" (84–

85).²⁸ History's chief example of England's imperialist aim was, of course, Cromwell, who, for five days at Drogheda, "massacred" the "flower of Irish chivalry" (86). Cromwell is almost always similarly vilified in Irish writing, and Wills's play proves no exception to this.

The end of the second act of *Charles the First* serves as an example both of Cromwell's villainy and the unsensational restraint that also led to its success. Here the forces of Charles and Cromwell assemble on each side of the stage, poised for a fight if it is necessary. But it is not. Similarly, in act three a Christlike Charles, in armor and resembling the Charles of Van Dyke's masterpiece, *Charles I on Horseback*, which was popularly viewed in Victorian England, is prepared to fight.²⁹ But he does not. Instead, he is surrounded by Cromwell's men, who have been aided by the traitorous Moray, who plays Judas to Charles's Christ. The act does not end sensationally with the sophisticated pyrotechnics of Boucicault's *The Octoroon* (1859) or Taylor's *Jeanne D'Arc*, but poignantly, with the anguish and eloquence of a betrayed man hurt deeply by the disloyalty of a man he loved. Appropriately, Charles alludes both to painting and Christianity to express his feelings:

> I saw a picture once by a great master,
> 'Twas an old man's head.
> 'Twas called a Judas! Wide that painter erred.
> Judas had eyes like thine [Moray], his hair of youthful gold;
> Upon his brow shone the white stamp of truth;
> And lips like thine did give the traitor kiss!
>
> (*CF*, 66)

At this point, Charles turns to Cromwell and yields to him his sword as the curtain falls "with effect." Poetry replaces action; sympathy replaces displays of martial prowess; tears replace excitement. A similarly quiet, pathetic act ends the play. Throughout much of the last act, Henrietta Maria pleads unsuccessfully for her husband's life, and the play concludes with Charles being taken from the comforts of his family and led offstage to meet his destiny. Wills gives Charles the drama's last line, "Remember," and London theatregoers did, for a very long time.

In *Charles the First* and *'Twixt Axe and Crown*, therefore, Wills and Taylor rediscovered and refined important ground rules for the late-Victorian dramatist. These include the selection of the best-known historical figures in episodes of high dramatic tension, an emphasis on domestic activity and family life, moments of sentiment calculated to touch the emotions of the audience, a melodramatic opposition between protagonist and antagonist, historically accurate costuming and decorative "archaeology," and scenes which replicated widely-viewed historical painting. In addition, as the failure of Taylor's *Jeanne D'Arc* indicates and the triumphs of Wills's *Charles the First* and *Buckingham* would seem to confirm, a rhetorical and thoroughly unsensational rendering of heroical demeanor separated, for many theatregoers, the "legitimate" from the merely "sensational." As James F. Stottlar has argued, Wills's plays seem quieter, less rambunctious than, say, Boucicault's sensation plays or the lavish spectacles of Augustus Harris later in the nineteenth century.[30] Daring theatrical effect and histrionic "opportunities" for the star-actor, Stottlar aptly observes, were replaced in Wills's dramas by quiet pathos, a marked theatrical restraint which appealed to large audiences ready for sentiment and the tears it produced.

Perhaps most important, Wills's play and those like Taylor's *'Twixt Axe and Crown* attracted audiences comprised of various social classes, a phenomenon many believed necessary if legitimate drama were to survive on the London stage. The educated classes, thought to have abandoned a theatre which catered to a less discerning clientele, returned in the 1870s, once again making Shakespeare profitable for Irving, Phelps, and actors like Barry Sullivan. At the same time, plays like *Charles the First* appealed to less sophisticated audiences as well. Surely the ideology underlying such plays, one communicated by depicting great figures of history as private men and women with easily identifiable desires and fears, had something to do with this. In this way, Wills's and Taylor's historical drama accomplished something that very few varieties of Victorian popular culture could match: a toppling of class barriers. As Hugh Cunningham postulates about Victorian popular culture, "Where the meeting of the classes was apparently on . . . equal terms and where the ideology was openly stated, the meanings attached to the experience were very different."[31] This was likely the case with the history play of the 1870s: in moments of reflection, educated theatregoers and reviewers saw plays like *Charles the First* as a return to literary refinement; conversely, the play supplied working-class theatregoers with examples of the powerlessness of great historical figures, forming analogies between these more distinguished personages and themselves. Of course, in the theatre after the last curtain those in the pit and gallery, those of all classes, could join in a more communal, less intellectual response: the shedding of sympathetic tears together.

Like Taylor, Wills continued to write historical drama throughout the 1870s. Among these are *Mary, Queen O' Scots, Buckingham, Jane Shore, Claudian* (1877), and *A Royal Divorce* (1891)—what Joyce in *Finnegans Wake* termed "the problem passionplay of the millentury." Continuing the domestic emphasis of the plays discussed above, in *A Royal Divorce* Wills depicts Napoleon's wife Josephine as the long-suffering, ever-loyal helpmate of the emperor. The formula that worked so well in 1870 was just as potent, or nearly so, twenty years later. And like *Charles the First*, many of these were among the late-Victorian theatre's most successful historical or poetic dramas. Stottlar estimates, for example, that in separate runs in 1876 and 1877 *Jane Shore* was performed 278 times and that *Olivia* (1878), Wills's extremely popular adaptation of Oliver Goldsmith's *The Vicar of Wakefield*, ran for 138 nights in its original production and 135 more in Irving's revival of 1885.[32] Many of these plays generated equal excitement in the provinces. In Dublin, for instance, *A Royal Divorce*, as performed by the W. W. Kelly Company, was a popular attraction, seen nearly every year in the last decade of the nineteenth century and several times in the first decade of the twentieth. Thus, with plays like *Charles the First* and *'Twixt Axe and Crown* both Wills and Taylor demonstrated that historical drama could attract large and diverse crowds to the theatre if the dramatist concocted the proper formula. What seems to have taken London by surprise in the early 1870s became a staple commodity, especially as cultivated by Irving during his reign at the Lyceum until the end of the century. During this time, the history play furthered the connotations of the concept "legitimate theatre" and provided well-known actors—or even lesser celebrated touring players—with something substantial to play when they weren't doing Shakespeare.

NOTES

1. For further discussion of historical drama and the literary canon, see Alastair Fowler, "Genre and the Literary Canon," *New Literary History* 11 (1979): 97–119.

2. For an interesting discussion of "legitimate" drama in mid-Victorian provinces, see Kathleen Barker, "Charles Dillon: A Provincial Tragedian," in *Shakespeare and the Victorian Stage*, ed. Richard Foulkes (Cambridge: Cambridge University Press, 1986), 283–94. Barker notes that, by the middle of the century,

the supply to the provinces of "London stars, especially performers of the so-called 'legitimate drama,' fell off sharply" (283).

3. See J. S. Bratton, "Theatre of War: The Crimea on the London Stage," in *Performance and Politics in Popular Drama*, eds. David Bradby, Louis James, and Bernard Sharratt (Cambridge: Cambridge University Press, 1980), 119–37.

4. Freeman Wills, *W. G. Wills, Dramatist and Painter* (London: Longmans, Green, and Co., 1898), 2.

5. Shirley S. Allen, *Samuel Phelps and Sadler's Wells Theatre* (Middletown, Conn.: Wesleyan University Press, 1971), 283–85.

6. For information on Tom Taylor's life, see Winton Tolles, *Tom Taylor and the Victorian Drama* (New York: Columbia University Press, 1940), especially 57–61. See also *Plays by Tom Taylor*, ed. Martin Banham (Cambridge: Cambridge University Press, 1985), 1–21. I wish to express here my thanks to Martin Banham, James Hurt, and Denis Salter for their help and encouragement with this essay.

7. See Nina Auerbach, *Ellen Terry: Player in Her Time* (New York: Norton, 1987), 82–84; Banham, 3; Ellen Terry, *The Story of My Life* (London: Hutchinson, 1908), 117, 119.

8. Roy Strong, *And When Did You Last See Your Father?* (London: Thames and Hudson, 1979), 42. I am greatly indebted to Strong's book for its informative discussion of historical painting. See also Martin Meisel, *Realizations* (Princeton: Princeton University Press, 1983), 229–46.

9. All quotations from Taylor's plays and prefaces come from his *Historical Dramas* (London: Chatto and Windus, 1877), hereafter abbreviated as *HD*. Page numbers follow quotations in the text.

10. George Rowell describes Victorian productions both of Schiller's plays and French neoclassical drama in *Queen Victoria Goes to the Theatre* (London: Paul Elek, 1978), 66–72.

11. Taylor's play spawned two rival dramas about Joan of Arc in 1871: Edwin Villiers' *Joan of Arc* in October and an anonymous *Joan of Arc* at the Garrick Theatre in November. Villiers' play is BL Add. MS 53099U and the Garrick, BL Add. MS 53099L. As I explain in "Shaw's *Saint Joan* and the Modern History Play," *Comparative Drama*, 19 (Spring 1985): 58–86, with the exception of Percy Mackaye's *Jeanne D'Arc* (1906), most Victorian plays about Joan of Arc feature villainous Catholic priests. This is true, for example, of the above accounts and of John Henderson's later *Joan of Arc* (1896), BL Add. MS 53607L.

12. W. G. Wills, *Mary, Queen O' Scots*, 11. The manuscript of this play is included in the Lord Chamberlain's Collection, Manuscript Division, British Library, London, Add. MS 53134D. The play was licensed in February 1874 by the title *Mary Stuart*. In later notes, all manuscript plays in this collection will be abbreviated BL Add. MS and followed by a catalogue number.

13. Matthew H. Wikander, *The Play of Truth & State: Historical Drama from*

Shakespeare to Brecht (Baltimore: Johns Hopkins University Press, 1986), 133. See Wikander, 86–135, for a discussion of historical drama in eighteenth- and nineteenth-century England.

14. The manuscript of *Queen Mary* was so cumbersome that Mrs. S. F. Bateman, then manager of the Lyceum Theatre, wrote to Tennyson on 9 December 1875 that "the exigencies of the stage demand that the play be reduced in length and that it may not be longer than *Hamlet* and it ought to be a half an hour shorter and not fuller of characters, *Hamlet* being well known to be the *fullest play on the stage.*" The following June Mrs. Bateman wrote to Tennyson that she hoped "our experiment" might be repeated in the future with a "more sympathetic subject and therefore certainly with a happier result" than a twenty-three-night run. I am quoting here from letters in the Lyceum Collection, Theatre Museum, Victoria and Albert Museum.

15. *New York Herald*, 5 January 1875, as quoted in George C. D. Odell, *Annals of the New York Stage*, 15 vols. (1937; reprint, New York: Columbia University Press, 1927–1949), 9: 552.

16. Taylor, as quoted by Banham, 5.

17. For further discussion of *Lady Clancarty* in the Hare-Kendal repertory, see T. Edgar Pemberton, *John Hare, Comedian* (London: George Routledge and Sons, 1895), 113.

18. For a discussion of Wills's adaptations, see James F. Stottlar, "A Victorian Stage Adaptor at Work: W. G. Wills 'Rehabilitates' the Classics," *Victorian Studies* 16 (June 1973): 401–32.

19. W. G. Wills, *Charles the First* (London: William Blackwood, 1873), vii. All further quotations from this play, hereafter abbreviated *CF*, come from this edition and will be followed in the text by page numbers. A Samuel French acting edition of *Buckingham* (1875) exists, which the British Library has foliated with pages written in Wills's own hand, catalogued BL Add. MS 53155A. The manuscript of *Mary Queen O' Scots* (1874) is cited above, and *Jane Shore* (1875) is catalogued BL Add. MS 53146Q.

20. Freeman Wills, 95.

21. For a brief discussion of the beginning of Wills's relationship with Henry Irving, see Madeleine Bingham, *Henry Irving and the Victorian Theatre* (London: George Allen and Unwin, 1978), 90–101.

22. The promptbooks and programs for several Lyceum productions during the Irving era are located in the Theatre Museum, Victoria and Albert Museum, London, England. I am grateful to the museum's staff for making these available to me.

23. F.W. Fairholt, *Costume in England* (London, 1860), as quoted in Strong, *And When Did You Last See Your Father?*, 55.

24. A letter from E.W. Godwin to Wilson Barrett on the architecture and costuming for *Claudian* is available in an untitled volume of correspondence, British Library, catalogue no. 11784g17.

25. For a brief discussion on the improvements in historically accurate representation from the Kembles to Macready, see Alan S. Downer, *The Eminent Tragedian* (Cambridge, Mass.: Harvard University Press, 1966), 19–27.

26. Meisel, 242. Not surprisingly, Wills and Taylor seemed attracted to the same paintings. Some twenty years before Wills employed Millais's *A Huguenot*, Taylor reported in *Punch* that he owed Millais "the acknowledgment of a great and enduring pleasure" at viewing *A Huguenot* and *Ophelia*, both exhibited at the Royal Academy in May, 1852. Taylor saw in the former the drama of "two fates" hanging "trembling in the balance" and found in the paintings "a deeper feeling of human emotion . . . than in all the rest of those eight hundred squares of canvas put together" (*Punch*, 22 [1852]: 216–17).

27. Colonel A. B. Richards, *Cromwell*, BL Add. MS 53114M. All quotations from this play, hereafter abbreviated *C*, will be followed by manuscript page number in the text.

28. W. G. Wills, *The Love That Kills*, 3 vols. (London: Tinsley Brothers, 1867), 1: 84–85.

29. For a discussion of Victorian interest in Van Dyke, see Roy Strong, *Van Dyke: Charles I on Horseback* (London: Allen Lane/Penguin, 1972).

30. See Stottlar, "A Victorian Stage Adaptor at Work," 428–32. See also his "'A House Choked with Gunpowder and Wild with Excitement': Augustus Harris and Drury Lane's Spectacular Melodrama" in this volume.

31. Hugh Cunningham, "Class and Leisure in Mid-Victorian England," in *Popular Culture: Past and Present*, eds. Bernard Waites, Tony Bennett, and Graham Martin (London: Croom Helm, 1982), 78.

32. Stottlar, "A Victorian Stage Adaptor at Work," 402–3.

"A House Choked with Gunpowder and Wild with Excitement"

AUGUSTUS HARRIS AND DRURY LANE'S SPECTACULAR MELODRAMA

James Stottlar

When in the fall of 1879 young Augustus Harris became the improbable lessee of London's Drury Lane Theatre, few observers gave him much of a chance to succeed. He was still only in his twenties (with less than five pounds in his pocket, one popular story goes) and he was taking over a theatre which no lessee since Garrick had been able to make pay. F. B. Chatterton had ended his long but increasingly unprofitable tenure in February, and the fact that the cavernous old building had remained without a tenant for nearly nine months—well into the fall season—is probably testimony enough that its appeal to theatrical speculators was, to say the least, limited. Of the many rumors that circulated during the spring and summer about the future of the empty building—that it would be renovated to accommodate a circus, be converted into a hippodrome, or become the home of a minstrel company—not a single one of them even whispered that it would continue as a playhouse.

But it did continue as a playhouse, as we know, and Harris did succeed, wildly and beyond all but perhaps his own most sanguine expectations. Within a year he had Drury Lane on its financial feet, and from then until his early death in 1896, his triumphs there followed one another with a predictability rivaling those of the most successful managements of the time. Harris's first decade at Drury Lane established a pattern for his success, and the so-called "Drury Lane melodramas," the pieces with which he opened each fall season from 1880 on, played a major part in this.[1]

Probably because he had little money and no clear idea of what to do at Drury Lane once he was in charge of it, Harris stayed on the sidelines for most of what was left of his first season, taking an active hand only in the production of the traditional Christmas pantomime, which that year (1879) was the veteran E. L. Blanchard's *Bluebeard*. For the first few weeks of his tenancy, just before Christmas, he sublet the theatre to George Rignold, recently back from tour, for a production of *Henry V*; the following spring, after the pantomime, Harris offered stopgap revivals of *Lady Audley's Secret* and other stock pieces for several weeks, and then for what was left of the theatrical season sublet the theatre to Marie Litton's company for a production of *As You Like It*. Although both Shakespeare productions were highly praised by the critics—*Punch* (6 March 1880, pp. 97–98), in fact, thought *As You Like It* about the best Shakespeare production seen in London in years—neither proved profitable at the Drury Lane box office. *Bluebeard*, however, was another story. Hailed as perhaps the most lavish and spectacular pantomime ever staged in London, it provided Harris with his first big success at Drury Lane, with the capital to launch the 1880–1881 season with a new piece of his own— and with an idea.

The six or eight months that Harris spent on the sidelines may well have been the most fruitful of his whole managerial life, for he apparently devoted much of his time to looking about the theatrical marketplace, analyzing Drury Lane's place in it, and devising an annual calendar of theatrical fare that he thought would prove both feasible and profitable. In the quarter-century or so between 1865 and 1888 theatrical competition became especially fierce. Sixteen new theatres were built in London's West End, and of the nine that were already in existence in 1865, seven would either be rebuilt entirely or altered extensively—which means that during this period an average of one new or rebuilt theatre was opening in the West End every year. By 1888, the seating capacity in West End theatres was more than triple what it had been in 1865, and the competition fostered by this fact alone forced some degree of specialization on virtually every playhouse in town. Theatre managers were discovering that in order to survive they had to find what kinds of pieces their companies and their buildings were best suited for and then do them better than they were being done elsewhere.

Hence Harris was forced to specialize. He could see that his theatre, the largest in London, was particularly unsuited for the newer and quieter fashions in plays and acting. Nor could he help but note that legitimate drama, even when as conscientiously staged and favorably reviewed as the Rignold and Litton productions had been, did not seem to pay any better for him than it had for his predecessors. Besides, in the early 1880s Henry Irving at the Lyceum had the legitimate market cornered, and Harris could see this, too.[2] On the other hand, the rousing success of *Bluebeard* seemed to indicate that pantomime, particularly lavish and spectacular pantomime, could be made to pay very well at Drury Lane. The massive stage that would dwarf cup-and-saucer pieces was ideal for the creation of the large-scale scenic and mechanical effects around which *Bluebeard* had been built. Besides, the vast three-thousand-seat auditorium, which swallowed even the verse of Shakespeare, provided excellent views of these large-scale effects and could seat enough patrons not only to pay for all the spectacle, but to produce almost enough profit to support the entire Drury Lane enterprise for the rest of the theatrical year.

Therefore Harris decided to make pantomime the centerpiece of his annual bill of fare, the production around which his other offerings would be oriented, and he no doubt wished that he could do pantomime all year long. In any case, this decision forced Harris into a three-part season: he now had to find a suitable offering for the fall to lead up to the pantomime, and another for the spring to follow the pantomime. The critics helped him with one of these decisions, though it might not have been help that he wanted, by reminding him that Drury Lane was, after all, one of the two so-called national theatres in London; consequently, there were certain, or uncertain, obligations to what was called "high art" that the lesseeship of Drury Lane entailed. Harris knew, of course, that these obligations were traditional and not statutory, and that in recent years, at least, they had been largely ignored. Nonetheless, he apparently felt the need to doff his hat in the direction of "high art" sometime in the course of the year, and the six or eight weeks left in the spring after the pantomime apparently seemed to him the best, or least costly, time to do it. He experimented with various kinds of "high art" in the early part of the decade, some of it imported—the Saxe-Meiningen Company one year, the Comédie Française another—but ultimately settled on the Carl Rosa Opera Company for his regular spring attraction. Although Harris did make modest profits on most of his "high art," he apparently regarded this portion of his season as little more than an obligation that he felt bound to honor.

This much decided, Harris's last scheduling problem was to find a money-maker that would carry Drury Lane from the fall opening of the theatrical season to the beginning of the pantomime run at Christmas. In many ways, this was the most crucial of the decisions, for if a successful pantomime could more or less pay his bills for the year, and if the profits from "high art" could not be counted upon to be more than modest, then the difference between a handsome profit for the year and a marginal one, or even none at all, depended finally upon the drawing power of the fall production.

As late spring turned to early summer in 1880, the nature of Harris's first fall production became the subject of increasing speculation, much of it, critics would say, fostered by Harris himself. Then, on the evening of 31 July 1880, nine months after Harris took over at Drury Lane, all of the planning, waiting, and speculating were over, and the curtain went up on the first performance of *The World*. It turned out to be an Augustus Harris production in more ways than one, for he not only stage-managed it and played one of the leading roles, but helped write it as well. His deep involvement in all aspects of the production led critics to conclude—rightly—that *The World* was more than just another new play: that for all practical purposes it was a formal announcement of the new course that Harris had chosen for Drury Lane.

No small part of this announcement was the date that Harris had chosen for his opening, for the end of July was nearly two months before the theatrical season traditionally began in the West End, a time when fashionable people were, or were supposed to be, out of town. "Few things seem less probable than Drury-lane opening its doors for the season before the month of July has run its course," confessed the surprised reviewer for the *Era* (8 August 1880, p. 5), and he was not alone in his surprise. But Harris had his reasons. For one thing, he was making plain that he was not primarily catering to fashionable society, but to what he and others would call the "public," or the "people," or the "multitude," or the "million." He was appealing to the "feelings of the public at large," he would say later, not to the "prejudice of a class."[3] This, of course, is not to say that he was trying to drive fashionable patronage from his door, but once he established that his "fall" opening would in fact take place in the middle of the summer, there could be little doubt about where Harris was looking for his primary support.

But more important to Harris were the practical advantages of an early opening, among them the extra six or eight weeks of profits before he had to close down in mid-December to prepare for the pantomime. In addition, the early opening allowed Harris to get the jump on his competition. With most of the other theatres either closed or offering stopgap summer productions, Harris had things much his own way until the rest of the playhouses opened in late September. He was offering one of the few new full-scale productions in town during this period—sometimes the only one—and this, in spite of the reduced pool of playgoers, made achieving box-office success easier than it would be in the fall when several dozen new pieces would all be competing for the public's favor. By the time the fashionable people did return, Harris could (and would) be filling the hoardings with puffs about the "unprecedented success"—never anything less—of his new piece. Aside from the profit, the early opening allowed him plenty of time to polish and prune his new production before the more critical audiences returned in autumn.

The other and more important part of Harris's announcement on 31 July 1880 was, of course, *The World* itself. It was, the staid *Times* would say of a revival of it four years later, "without exception the most stupendous play ever contrived" (15 September 1884, p. 11). And, indeed, nothing quite like it had ever been seen before. The first-night audience went wild, interrupting the action with cheers and applause, and at the end called for everybody—"including the authors," the *Era* reported (8 August 1880, p. 5)—with an enthusiasm that had not been seen or heard at Drury Lane in years. The era of "Druriolanus," as Harris would soon be dubbed, had begun.

The World is not an easy piece to describe. It had five acts divided into nine tableaux, and boasted seventeen characters with speaking parts, nine of whom, including the one played by Harris, were up to no good. On opening night it lasted nearly four hours, though its running time was reduced in subsequent performances as the stage crew got better at assembling, shifting, and striking the play's many elaborate sets, and at operating its complicated stage machinery. Its plot baffled many, including the veteran reviewer for the *Illustrated Sporting and Dramatic News*, who found himself drifting into delirium as he tried to recount it. "Miss Helen Barry," he reported, as his mind began to wander near the end, "refused to go down the lift in Mr. Augustus Harris's chambers; whereupon Miss Fanny Josephs chucked that gentleman down the well instead, for which act Mr. Poland, with whom was his friend Mr. Montague Williams, appeared for the Public Prosecutor and said that there was no possible ground for a charge of manslaughter against the doctor and that the jury would no doubt at once see that the wages of sin were followed by a fancy dress ball and a last dance." All in all, he concluded, *The World* was "as sensational and bloodthirsty a piece of dramatic network as one need desire" (7 August 1880, p. 315).

Actually, for those with text in hand, the plot is not quite that confusing. What happens, very broadly, is this: Clement Huntingford, estranged from his father through the machinations of his younger brother Harry, goes to the diamond fields of Australia to make his fortune, using the alias Charles Hartley. There, he falls in love with a governess named Mary Blythe, who is unaware of his love for her, and who, as the play opens at dockside in Australia, is boarding a passenger ship bound for England, there to marry her fiancé. Owen, another diamond hunter, and his young son Ned are also going back on the same ship to look for Owen's daughter Mabel, whom Owen has left alone and unprotected in London, and whom he fears has suffered a fate worse than death. Just before the ship is to leave, Clement, at the pier to say goodbye to Mary, receives word that his father has died, so he gets on board, too, hoping to claim his title and estates in England. Unfortunately, the ship has been marked for disaster by one of the many villains who, having consigned to it some heavily-insured but low-quality diamonds, has planted a time bomb in its hold. At sea, Clement learns from Mary that the fiancé to whom she is returning is none other than his brother Harry, but he makes no sign. The bomb goes off about this time, killing many passengers and sinking the ship, but Clement, Mary, Owen, Ned, and several villains escape in a life raft and are eventually rescued.

In England, the report of Clement's arrival is unhappy news to Harry, who, thinking his brother dead, has squandered much of the family fortune and allowed himself to fall into the hands of a money lender. He plans to murder Clement. So does another of the villains, one Bashford, once Clement's partner in the diamond fields, who has reason to know that Clement has returned to England with a fortune in diamonds. In the darkness of the hotel room where the two would-be murderers lurk, Harry mistakes Bashford for his brother and kills him instead. The next day Clement, upon meeting Harry for the first time in many years, recognizes him as the intruder in his room who murdered Bashford. Before he can notify the authorities, however, Harry connives with two doctors and a lawyer to have Clement declared legally insane and committed to a private asylum. Mary, in the meantime, has her problems, too, for she discovers among other things that her fiancé, Harry, already has a wife, a sympathetic, long-suffering, and frequently tearful young lady; she turns out to be the long-lost Mabel for whom Owen and Ned have been searching. After much anxiety and grief, Clement makes a bold and exciting escape from the asylum and manages to get warrants for the arrests of the villains. Harry, attempting to flee, falls into an elevator shaft and is crushed to death, and the rest of the villains are literally unmasked and arrested at a costume ball. Clement and Mary are to live happily ever after, and Mabel, sadder and wiser, is to spend her days in the benevolent custody of her father and her brother Ned.

What *The Times* found "stupendous" about *The World*, however, was not its plot, which, for all its flourishes, resembled a hundred other Victorian melodramas, and consisted, as the *Era* said, of "familiar characters on familiar paths to familiar destinations" (15 September 1884, p. 88). This ought not to be surprising, given the fact that Harris's collaborators were Henry Pettitt and Paul Meritt, both journeymen writers of melodramas. Pettitt was known for pieces like *Sentenced to Death* (1875) and *Snatched from the Grave* (1876), Meritt for *The New Babylon* (1878), *The Worship of Bacchus* (1879), which he wrote with Pettitt, and, what might describe them all, *Rough and Ready* (1873). But the real features of the piece, the things that audiences left the theatre buzzing about and that reviewers found themselves writing about, were the many spectacular scenic and mechanical effects. Among the most notable of them were: a passenger ship, with real passengers, seen slowly moving away from its pier to begin its ocean voyage; the same ship being blown up at sea; a boxing-ring sized raft, with survivors, seen tossing in rough waves until a passing ship comes to its rescue; an authentic promenade of fashionable people at an authentic stage replica of the London Aquarium; a more or less authentic stage replica of an unusual London hotel that is over-equipped with working elevators in every room; the plausible interior of a private mental institution, the set of which pivots during the hero's escape from it, transforming the whole into a realistic river panorama; and a lavish, full-scale fancy dress ball, which ends the play. Each of these required a new and elaborate set, and most required elaborate working machinery as well.

The critics split harshly over *The World*. A few, like the reviewer for the *Illustrated Sporting and Dramatic News*, who went delirious trying to describe its plot, and who elsewhere in his column described it as a "decalogue of crimes and casualties," took an amused view of it all. He even reported that the well-known statue of Shakespeare above the portico at Drury Lane had been seen on opening night with its head in its hands, weeping (7 August 1880, p. 315). *Punch*'s man, another lighthearted soul, described *The World* as one of those "what-shall-we-do-next-to-startle-em sorts of pieces," and airily assured those planning to attend that they need not grieve too long for those unfortunate passengers who were lost in the explosion at sea because nearly all of them would turn up "alive and well in the third act, promenading about the Aquarium in the identical dresses they had worn on that fatal day aboard the ill-starred vessel" (14 September 1880, p. 72). But other reviewers failed to see the humor either in the production itself or in what it signalled about the future of Drury Lane. From on high, the *Athenaeum* lamented that the "large class of people who like coarse fare" would certainly find their tastes "gratified" by Harris's new piece, and predicted gloomily that Drury Lane "will never again, except briefly and under special circumstances, be devoted to legitimate drama" (7 August 1880, p. 187). In between were critics like Clement Scott of the *Daily Telegraph*. He argued that *The World* was a practical solution to a practical problem—that Harris had a large auditorium to fill, and that necessarily meant offering pieces of the broadest possible appeal (2 August 1880, p. 2).

About one thing, however, there could be no difference of opinion: the huge success of *The World* at the Drury Lane box office. As planned, it played to large and excited crowds right up to Christmas when the 1880 pantomime, E. L. Blanchard's *Aladdin*, took over. The pantomime, too, was a success, as was Harris's contribution to "high art" in the spring—a scheduled four-week engagement of the visiting Saxe-Meiningen Company, which was extended to eight weeks. Drury Lane had not had a year like this in recent memory, and when it was over, young Augustus Harris had good reason to congratulate himself on the accuracy of his calculations and on the profitability of the course that he had charted for Drury Lane, a few humorists, carpers, and utopian critics notwithstanding.

It should not be surprising, therefore, that *Youth*, the piece with which Harris opened his 1881–1882 season almost two months early, would be cut from the same cloth; again Harris had a hand in writing it, and again Henry Pettitt, this time alone, was his collaborator. *Youth* had no act divisions at all, only tableaux, and to list them in order, with their subtitles, is to tell all:

I Beechley Church ("The Only Son")
II The Upper Thames: The Boating Cottage ("The Moth and the Flame")
III Frank's Lodgings ("The Serpent on the Hearth")
IV Mrs. Walsingham's House ("Sweet Revenge")
V The Convict Prison ("Gang Mates")
VI Departure of the Troop Ship ("Auld Lang Syne")
VII The Entrenchment ("Death or Glory")
VIII Beechley at Night ("For Valour")

For those still in doubt: in the first tableau, the Reverend Joseph Darlington, vicar of Beechley, turns away the flashy Mrs. Walsingham, his mistress of years ago, who wishes to give up the fast life that she has been leading in London and retire to Beechley, where she was born. Angered by his dismissal, she vows revenge on the vicar through his son Frank, whom she plans to entangle and corrupt. In tableau two she succeeds in throwing Frank into the arms of her siren-like protégée, Eve de Malvoisie. Tableau three reveals Eve and the unhappy Frank married and living in ruinously expensive quarters, and discovered there by the Reverend Darlington. In tableau four, the innocent Frank is arrested for forgery, the result of an elaborate plot hatched by Eve and her lover, Major Reckley. Tableau five depicts life in prison and, in particular, the heroics of Frank and his gang mate Gardham, another victim of the wiles of an unfaithful wife, who save the life of a warder. In tableau six, Frank and Gardham, released on tickets-of-leave, enlist in the army as privates and board a troop ship leaving for the battle zone. In tableau seven, Frank and Gardham show their valor in battle; Gardham is killed, but before he dies he hands over to Frank some personal papers. In tableau eight, Frank, back in Beechley and wearing the Victoria Cross, reveals to Eve that their marriage is invalid: the personal papers left behind by Gardham, it seems, prove that Eve was his unfaithful wife before she was Frank's. This frees Frank to marry the patient Alice, his original, angelic, and unperturbed fiancée, who somehow always knew that everything would turn out fine—if that is what happened.

Three of *Youth*'s scenic effects were greeted with such enthusiasm that the action had to be suspended while the appropriate scenic artists and stage engineers were called before the curtain to make their bows. The first of these was a boating scene in tableau two in which Frank appears to paddle a canoe past the shoreline of the upper Thames. In reality, the canoe remains stationary while the background scenery is pulled past by stage hands. Another was the departure of the troop ship in tableau six, which everyone agreed was an improvement on the similar embarkation scene in the beginning of *The World*. This time Harris showed only the bow of the ship, full size, with authentic winches, booms, and dock paraphernalia in place. At the end of the tableau, amid blasts from the steam whistle, showers of confetti, much waving and weeping by a crowd of well-wishers, and a brass band playing "Auld Lang Syne," the protruding bow of the ship is seen to move slowly backwards into the wings and presumably off to sea. Much of the success of this scene resulted from the orderly embarkation of a large detachment of authentically attired and equipped troops passing through a cheering stage crowd, the details of which Harris apparently picked up in the spring from the Saxe-Meiningen Company, renowned for its careful drilling of supernumeraries in crowd scenes and processions. The last of the big scenic effects was tableau seven, a full-scale battle scene complete with genuine Martini Henry rifles provided by the Birmingham Small Arms Company and Gatling guns supplied by Messrs. Armstrong and Company. Sandwiched around these spectacles were two much-praised exteriors of Beechley Church Yard, one by daylight and one by moonlight; two lavishly appointed interiors, one of Frank's lodgings, which embodied the latest in modern drawing room furnishings, and the other of Mrs. Walsingham's house, which was the epitome of what was often called "gilded vice"; and one supposedly authentic look at life in Her Majesty's prisons.

The critics were divided again. Those who liked *The World* liked *Youth*; those who did not, lambasted *Youth*, and for the old reasons. Most agreed, however, that the scenic and mechanical effects of *Youth* were more sophisticated and better executed than those of *The World*, and many observers, even some of the carpers who thought that elaborate scenic effects were outside the province of drama, had to concede that the embarkation and battle scenes were among the best things of their sort ever seen on the London stage. There also seemed to be more support this time around for Harris in his role of manager. He "has done everything possible to achieve success," one impressed opening-night supporter declared, "and the British public will not be ungrateful" (*Era*, 13 August 1881, p. 7). He proved to be right, for *Youth*, like *The World*, was still playing to large audiences right up to pantomime time.

It might be useful to pause here to point out what was by now becoming obvious: namely, the family resemblance between Harris's melodramas and his pantomimes. Consider, for instance, this account of one of the three "big" scenes in *Robinson Crusoe*, the 1881 Christmas pantomime that *Youth* closed to make way for. The scene begins with a ship getting under way on the Thames, its decks crowded with a crew of child sailors. Next, the *Era* reviewer reported,

> we have our eyes feasted with a beautifully painted and ingeniously contrived panorama showing both sides of the Thames. As the sea is approached the vessel begins to rock, and, when fairly in the open, the heaving billows, the dark thunder clouds, the flashing lightning, seem to

predict disaster. . . . It is all very realistic and very exciting, and we get a sense of relief when, by the aid of some lovely sirens, we are permitted to go with the wreck of the vessel to the "bottom of the deep blue sea" to be spectators of what is called the Ballet of Silver Fishes. (31 December 1881, p. 4)

Patrons who scratched their heads and wondered where they had seen something like this before did not have to look back very far, for the opening part of this scene comes, of course, right out of *Youth*. It is possible, in fact, that the very scenery pulled past the child sailors and their stationary ship to create the illusion of motion here is the same scenery, perhaps modified, that the same stage hands had been pulling past Frank and his canoe since early August. The ship itself, again modified, may well have been the one seen leaving the Australian pier in the opening tableau of *The World*, and the stormy canvas sea on whose "heaving billows" this ship tosses before sinking to the bottom may well have been the same sea on which *The World*'s raft full of survivors had tossed the year before.

Later on, the same *Era* reviewer described another of this pantomime's much-applauded scenes, one set in London in the last century. "While children dance with delight," he recounted, "and the inhabitants crowding the balconies cheer, there come marching in the representatives of a host of trades and professions." And come they do, in a long procession, all authentically attired and bearing the symbols and accoutrements of their occupations: soldiers, clockmakers, chimney sweeps, bootmakers, barbers, hatters, carpenters, tailors, candlestick-makers, millers, fishmongers, grocers, butchers, spectacle-makers, and many others march past, with the brewers, "looking rubicund and jolly as befits their calling," bringing up the rear. Even casual observers of this colorful contingent of tradesmen marching past an enthusiastic stage crowd must have recognized it as the counterpart to the rousing embarkation of the troops in *Youth*, even down to the cheering and waving crowd of well-wishers. And almost certainly, what directly inspired this procession of tradesmen was the same Saxe-Meiningen visit that had inspired the embarkation of the troops.

Some reviewers noticed the connection between Harris's melodramas and his pantomimes literally from the start. "The Captious Critic," who went delirious trying to recount the plot of *The World*, was one of them. In the very beginning of his review, in fact, he referred to that piece as a "veritable tropical pantomime, crammed to repletion with all sorts of marvelous tricks and trap-door surprises," and later observed that the "pantomime rally" in which the hero makes his escape by flooring the madhouse keeper was "really premature before the 26th of December" (*ISD*, 7 August 1880, p. 315). Another critic who noticed the connection right away was Clement Scott for the *Theatre*, part of whose review of *The World* went like this:

> No pantomime ever was known to fail. If it be dull, the goblin scene, or the ballet, or the comic business, or one particular scene, or the transformation works it up. The success comes from variety. Just so with a melodrama as conducted by our modern triumvirate. A ship is blown up, there is a mutiny on board, a raft is seen labouring on mid-ocean with dead and dying men, the sick are rescued, a man is incarcerated in a lunatic asylum on a false certificate, a villain who desires to compromise a woman's honour meets a just fate in tumbling headlong down a hotel lift. Why, one of such effects has been known to make a melodrama, and a combination of them is guaranteed success. (November 1883, p. 254)

Michael Booth, in the standard work on spectacle in the Victorian theatre,[4] examines at length the nineteenth century's near-addiction to what he calls the "pictorial ethic" and demonstrates forcefully the dominant role that spectacle came to play in the theatre of the time, particularly in melodrama and pantomime, but in poetic and historical drama as well. But the connection that Clement Scott is making here, and the one that I want to make, is not so much a connection between melodrama and pantomime in any historical or theoretical sense, but a connection between the melodramas and pantomimes that Harris actually produced at Drury Lane—and particularly between their all but interchangeable spectacular effects. For though Harris's melodramas might be shown to be mixtures of elements from many sources—panoramas, extravaganzas, *tableaux vivants*, the literature of the minor theatres, even penny dreadfuls, the *Police Gazette*, and the illustrated papers generally—it was their enthusiastic exploitation of spectacle in its many forms that accounted finally for their success, as it did for that of the pantomimes that replaced them every Boxing Night.

In fact, as Booth argues, and as one reviewer of the time verifies, no West End management, even those with pretensions to gentility, or even elegance, and whose patrons were apt to look down their noses at what was going on at Drury Lane, could even pretend to be able to do without spectacle (*LDT*, 8 August 1881, p. 3). Irving at the Lyceum, the Kendals at the St. James's, and Gilbert, Sullivan, and D'Oyly Carte at the Savoy all recognized the drawing power of spectacle and garnished their offerings with it, sometimes liberally.

But what was garnish elsewhere was very nearly the whole dish at Drury Lane, and everybody noticed it. "The hammer usurps the pen, and the dialogue is drowned in the noise of moving scenery and the explosion of burning buildings," said one reviewer of *Pluck*, Harris's 1882 melodrama (*ISD*, 12 August 1882, p. 533). Harris was not the kind of manager to let "dialogue get in the way of the scenery" (*Athenaeum*, 7 August 1880, p. 187), said another reviewer, this time of *The World*; and still another found himself wondering during a performance of *Youth* "whether it was necessary to have any dialogue or any people to speak it" (*LSR*, 13 August 1881, p. 204). Others, saying the same thing differently, observed that Harris's melodramas were essentially "exhibition[s] of clever stage carpentry and of scenic effect on the largest scale," and not "illustration[s] of characters and incidents intrinsically interesting" (*ISD*, 12 August 1882, p. 517); and that at Drury Lane everything was "mechanism," though "mechanism of unusual precision and force" (*ISD*, 20 September 1884, p. 6).

This was as true of Harris's pantomimes as of his melodramas, though it caused less stir among the critics because spectacle, after all, was *supposed* to be the main attraction of pantomime, particularly at Drury Lane. Like most pantomimes of the 1880s, Harris's were based loosely on nursery stories, fairy tales, and other children's stories. And all but the last of them were written by the aging veteran E. L. Blanchard, occasionally with collaborators, one of whom was Harris. *Robinson Crusoe* (1881), *Sinbad the Sailor* (1882), *Whittington and His Cat* (1884), *Aladdin* (1885), and *Babes in the Woods* (1888) were organized, as the melodramas were, into a dozen or so scenes or tableaux, almost all of which were selected for their scenic and/or mechanical potential, some of which had little relationship to the story being told. "The nursery legend chosen," observed a reviewer of *Puss-in-Boots*, Harris's 1887 pantomime, "is as simple as it is kindly; but what the legend is, and whence it comes, are things of little moment at Drury-lane, when it is to be regarded, first and foremost, if not entirely, as a pretext for gorgeous spectacle" (*Era*, 31 December 1887, p. 8). A reviewer of one of the melodramas shared this view, declaring that other pieces like it would continue to be written "so long as a fresh series of elaborate scenic effects could be devised and plots could be invented with new combinations of exciting incidents" (*LDT*, 7 August 1882, p. 6). Two or three, sometimes four or five, of the scenes in each pantomime were particularly elaborate, as they were in the melodramas, and were designed to be show-stoppers: eye-catching ballets, processions, and pageants; exciting descents into the sea and stunning ascents into the clouds; clever tricks with mirrors, traps, and lights; ingenious scenic transformations and impressive feats of strength and acrobatics.

Some reviewers went as dizzy trying to describe the scenic effects in the pantomimes as others did trying to describe those in the melodramas. This, for instance, is an account of what was called the "Indian Ballet," the third of the featured scenic effects in *Robinson Crusoe*; it takes place on Crusoe's island, and comes after the shipwreck of the child sailors and before the procession of tradesmen: "Curious looking people arrive upon all sorts of animals including elephants, alligators, ostriches, turtles, and giraffes. The stage is very soon crowded by a glittering throng, and the eyes become fairly dazed and the brain bewildered in the attempt to take in all the wondrous paraphernalia of this marvellous spectacle, which denotes unstinted outlay. We can safely say," he concluded, "that in the history of Drury-lane pantomimes nothing so splendid has been witnessed" (*Era*, 31 December 1881, p. 4). But that was what reviewers were saying of Harris's pantomimic spectacles the next year, and the next, and the next. Finally, as the decade waned, one seasoned reviewer of Drury Lane pantomimes had a suggestion for his colleagues. "It would be an act of wise provision for the needs of each recurring Christmastide," he said,

> if among the permanent paraphernalia of newspaper printing-rooms was included a stereotype inscribed with the words, "In this year's pantomime Mr. Augustus Harris has surpassed all previous efforts, even of his own." For, so surely as Boxing Night comes round, so surely is the Mr. Harris of this year found overtopping by a head and shoulders the Mr. Harris of the last. Some fine day the calendar will have to be altered, and the month of December rechristened August, as marking the time when Druriolanus Imperator, the master of many stage legions, drags the whole world captive at the wheels of his triumphal car. (*Era*, 31 December 1887, p. 8)

Thus it was that in the matter of spectacle, Harris's melodramas and his pantomimes went arm-in-arm through the 1880s, borrowing scenery and effects from each other, sharing ideas, outdoing each other in friendly and lucrative rivalry, and looking and sounding a great deal alike. *Pluck*, the melodrama that opened the 1882 season at Drury Lane, had a train wreck; a run on a bank, complete with the smashing of real windows; a snowstorm, meant to bring to mind the real one of the previous winter which paralyzed almost all of England; and what one critic called the "great stage fire of London," a conflagration in which a three-story building burned (*ISD*, 12 August 1882, p. 517). *Freedom* (1883), set in Egypt, featured ruined mosques and temples, and a marketplace with real animals; it was more picturesque than spectacular, which may be why it was the only one of Harris's fall productions in the 1880s that did not make it to Christmas. It was replaced in October by *A Sailor and His Lass*, which, with its seventeen scenes and forty-odd characters, quickly made amends. It featured a real cab, cabby, and horse; the dynamiting of a building; yet another shipwreck; the rescue of survivors, some of them (including Harris) dangling from masts and yardarms; an elaborately authentic court of justice in which the innocent hero is convicted and condemned; and a gallows scene that had audiences howling, as the heroine, with reprieve in hand, raced in the cab to save him. (She made it.) The next year, 1884, saw the revival of *The World*, a last-minute decision on Harris's part that was designed to take advantage of several recent and highly publicized disasters at sea, and of the publicity generated by recent investigations into abuses of the lunacy laws. Needless to say, the rescue of the raft full of survivors and the hero's escape from the private asylum were greeted with even more enthusiasm this time than they had been in 1880. *Human Nature* (1885) featured a battle scene in a desert city in Egypt and the stirring return of the British troops to a plausible replica of Trafalgar Square, again in the presence of a cheering crowd. Not to have seen the latter, one reviewer declared, "is to be ignorant of the most triumphal demonstration of the possibilities of the stage-manager's art" (*ISD*, 19 September 1885, p. 6). *A Run of Luck* (1886), written by Harris in collaboration with Pettitt, had horses early and horses late. Its big scenes included the preparation for a hunt, complete with hounds and horses, and an authentic replica of the paddock at Goodwood, where real jockeys and their equipment were weighed and real horses prepared for the race, and where crowds of race enthusiasts cheered their favorites as they thundered across the finish line. There was an earthquake on the Riviera in 1886, so in 1887 Harris worked one into *Pleasure*.[5] It was one of his two or three best effects of the decade, leaving audiences covered with dust and one critic declaring that compared to a rival earthquake in *Claudian*, it was "like wine after water" (*ISD*, 10 September 1887, p. 746).

This earthquake was meant to be educational as well as thrilling, for in this scene Harris introduced his patrons to a demonstration of the newly-patented Shaftesbury safety lamp, which extinguished itself when knocked over, as it was, nightly, during the stage earthquake. The other big scene in *Pleasure* depicted a carnival at Monte Carlo in which fashionable people in real carriages threw real flowers at each other and the audience.

Harris's last two melodramas of the decade were historical, something new for him. *The Armada* (1888) celebrated the tricentennial of the defeat of the Spanish fleet and was generally thought to be Harris's most ambitious, costly, and spectacular piece. It had fifteen scenes, several of which resolved themselves ultimately into tableaux of well-known paintings—Seymour Lucas's *Game of Bowls on Plymouth Hoe*, for instance. It also featured the thrilling rescue of the heroine from the stake in the Plaza of Cadiz, where the Inquisitors were preparing to burn her; a grand procession to Whitehall at the end; and, of course, what everybody had come to see: the famous sea battle, which, according to one surviving witness, left the "house choked with gunpowder and wild with excitement" (*Era*, 29 September 1888, p. 14). As an additional feature of this production, Harris got up an exhibit of Armada-era relics in the Grand Saloon at Drury Lane, a collection of costumes, coins, documents, and, most popular of all, instruments of torture. *The Royal Oak* (1889), which brought the decade to a close, featured the expected scene in Boscobel Wood in which Charles eludes his pursuers by hiding in a plausible tree; his thrilling escape to France by water; another near-execution, this time at the block on Tower Hill; and Charles's triumphal return to London, a procession scene that apparently really did top them all.[6]

Drury Lane pantomimes, meanwhile, were doing similar things, sometimes the same things. The great scene in E. L. Blanchard's *Sinbad the Sailor* (1882) was a long and lavishly-staged procession of England's monarchs from William the Conqueror to Queen Victoria, which ended with a review of the British troops returning from Egypt, an old friend by now. The biggest scene of Blanchard's *Cinderella* in 1883 was another procession, this time of fairy tale characters, "the whole forming an army of unsurpassed and unsurpassable magnificence," one reviewer had it, "sending the onlooker frantic with delight" (*Era*, 29 December 1883, p. 3). Blanchard's *Whittington and His Cat* (1884) featured a colorful Oriental Ballet and a Lord Mayor's Show in the Olden Time, complete, as usual, with authentic costumes and emblems. And so it went from Boxing Day to Easter at Drury Lane much as it did from midsummer to Christmas: displays of armor; processions of model British workmen, of Shakespearean characters, of fair women from real life as well as from literature; hunting scenes, cloud scenes with soaring aerialists, cavern scenes in which lounged forty thieves dressed in white silk coats, white opera hats, and black tights; an exhibition of strength by "the strongest man in the world," who nightly strode onto the stage and lifted up a horse; and, as was usually said, a host of other wonders.

The large stage at Drury Lane allowed Harris to produce his spectacles on a scale that astounded even veteran critics, who found themselves wondering how he could recoup his outlays in the hundred nights or so allotted to each of his melodramas in the fall and to each of his pantomimes in the winter. That it was not easy was made plain by Harris himself, who, in announcing in the *Era* the withdrawal of *Freedom* in October 1883, and its replacement by *A Sailor and His Lass*, estimated his nightly operating expenses at between 250 and 260 pounds, which did not, of course, include his original production costs (29 September 1883, p. 5). He often spent more on a single scene than many managements could afford to spend on a whole production, and so drove his competitors to despair. "If Augustus Harris wants a steam engine," lamented George Conquest, one competitor, "he buys a steam engine—I look round the theatre for a few tables and paint the tops like wheels."[7] It is little wonder that later attempts to revive some of Harris's pieces at theatres with small stages and smaller budgets failed.

"Bold attack, fertile resources, firm discipline, money, enterprise, and an enormous stage" (*LDT*, 8 September 1884, p. 8) were generally seen as the cards that Harris had to play, and when it came to spectacle, at least, even his detractors agreed that he played them with zest. Popular wisdom had it that you got more for your money at Drury Lane, in any season, than you did anywhere else in London, and sometimes you got too much for it—four and a half hours' worth on occasion, with resultant missed trains and long walks home. Surely, as they trudged homeward after midnight, some of the more philosophical of these victims of Harris's largesse would have endorsed the verdict of that critic of 1882 who declared that the real trouble with Augustus Harris was that "he tried to do too much, and he did it" (*ISD*, 30 December 1882, p. 382).

NOTES

1. Like most plays of this time, Harris's melodramas were never published and today remain largely unknown. The copies I examined were submitted to the

Examiner of Plays for licensing and are now part of the Lord Chamberlain's Collection, Manuscript Department, British Library.

2. Augustus Harris, "The National Theatre," *Fortnightly Review*, 1 November 1885, p. 635.

3. Harris, 635.

4. Michael R. Booth, *Victorian Spectacular Theatre, 1850–1910* (London: Routledge and Kegan Paul, 1981), 60–92.

5. *Pluck* was written by Harris in collaboration with Henry Pettitt; *Freedom*, in collaboration with George F. Rowe; *A Sailor and His Lass*, in collaboration with Robert Buchanan; *Human Nature*, in collaboration with Henry Pettitt; *Pleasure*, in collaboration with Paul Meritt.

6. *The Armada* and *The Royal Oak* were written by Harris in collaboration with Henry Hamilton.

7. Frances Fleetwood, *Conquest: The Story of a Theatre Family* (London: W. H. Allen, 1953), 147.

Edwardian London West End Christmas Entertainments, 1900–1914

J. P. Wearing

The cogency of the first fourteen years of this century as a discrete theatrical period has been demonstrated by J. C. Trewin in *The Edwardian Theatre*.[1] He rightly sees the period as being "the last surge of the Theatre Theatrical" (xiii); of course, the intellectual theatre was taking strong root, but much more peripherally than we now tend to think.[2] Popular taste embraced musical comedies and plays, comedies, farces, revues, and melodrama, if longevity of production is an accurate gauge, and it was to that popular demand that the commercial West End theatre catered very directly.[3] Moreover, the nature of the theatrical season during these years provides evidence of the sensitivity of managers to audience demands, as well as revealing the profound impact World War I had upon the London theatre.

The season began at the beginning of September each year and ran until the end of July the following year. August was a dead month theatrically; in any given year, only one out of seven West End theatres was open (and very rarely any of the fashionable ones). After the war, fully half of the theatres continued business during August, and it can be fairly said that the West End theatre had become a year-round operation.

The importance of Christmas to the 1900–1914 seasons varied with individual managerial policies, although the obviously festive, theatrical nature of Christmas itself helped shape those policies in a way no other period of the season could. Some managers hoped their opening September production would see them through the entire season (with the additional possibility of a summer tour in the provinces). A failure could be replaced in October or November, again with the hope of longevity, and if the substitute failed, December offered the chance of a Christmas work. Several managers, but most notably Arthur Collins with his spectacular melodramas at Drury Lane, produced a September work designed to run only through early December, when it would be followed by a specific Christmas piece. January through July presented the long-run managers with a second opportunity to replace autumnal offerings which were only moderately successful and which had run out of steam by the new year. Mid to late February, or thereabouts, usually marked the end of the "Christmas sub-season"; consequently, new works would be produced which were designed either to last out the season or to carry over into the next. April and May were still viable months for new productions because of the fresh interest stirred generally by the Covent Garden opera season of April/May through July, and because of the touring possibilities. (This general pattern was subject to considerable variation because an ailing work would be taken off quickly at any point in the season and, usually, something new tried.) Thus Christmas productions occupied a significant place in the overall season, a significance heightened by the paucity of the new works presented in December as managements geared up for Christmas. This phenomenon was particularly noticeable in 1901, as the *Athenaeum* observed: "The weeks immediately preceding Christmas count ordinarily among the slackest of the year. Very rarely, even at that period, has there been a dearth of dramatic novelty so complete as has this year been witnessed. Such novelties as are in preparation for Christmas are musical or pantomimic, and the closing year brings with it no event of interest purely dramatic" (14 December 1901, p. 820).

In fact, much more than pantomimes and musical pieces were offered to West End audiences, which at Christmas often included many (notably suburban family parties) who patronized the theatre only during the season. The menu included the broad category of children's/fairy/fantasy plays, farces and farcical comedies, comedies, melodramas, romances, serious plays and Shakespeare; however, as the *Athenaeum* critic rightly noted, Christmas week "has gradually become dedicated to entertainments belonging to the season" (27 December 1906, p. 842). Indeed, "King Panto" was king of the Christmas entertainments, with the most popular and traditional stories finding their place on stage. *Cinderella* led the field, being produced twice as often as the next favorites, *Aladdin* and *Sleeping Beauty* (in various guises). *Dick Whittington*, *Jack and the Beanstalk*, *The Babes in the Wood*, and *Little Red Riding Hood* were all produced twice, although each individual pantomime was eclipsed numerically by the productions given to the two most popular individual pieces—*Charley's Aunt* (twelve productions) and *Peter Pan* (eleven).[4]

Curiously, in light of its enormous popularity, pantomime was regularly attacked in the press, whose critics frequently bewailed pantomime's decline from earlier artistic standards.[5] By 1909 a critic in the *Athenaeum* could declare: "As an art-form [pantomime] is cumbrous, almost ridiculous, and it is usually a vulgarization of some of the prettiest elements of our literature—our nursery legends." No longer was pantomime a pure and unadulterated relation of a nursery or fairy tale; rather, as the same critic noted, it was a "curious hybrid . . . an amalgam of spectacle and fairy tale, ballet and farce, music-hall songs and social travesty" (2 January 1900, pp. 223–24). Max Beerbohm, in writing for the *Saturday Review*, frequently emphasized the bastardization of pantomime and thought it had become no more than a virtually plotless excuse for a series of variety acts: "In a modern pantomime the story is so deliberately neglected—is preserved, indeed, merely as a thread to connect the turns of an infinite variety show."[6] This plotlessness was such a sufficiently widespread phenomenon as to draw a leading article from *The Times*, which pointed out the obvious fact that a well-delineated plot would appeal more directly to children at whom pantomime was ostensibly directed.[7] Beerbohm thought that "what children want . . . is a show with plenty of monsters, demons, noise and buffoonery. These things are to be found at Drury Lane; but there, alas! unpleasantly overlaid with didactic processions, allegorical ballets and all the rest of it."[8]

It is doubtful, too, whether other salient features of pantomime appealed much to children. Probably very few of them attended music halls whose stars found legitimate theatrical employment in pantomime and whose songs were prominent:

> It must always be remembered that the halls of every type were still taboo to all unless they wished to be classed as bohemians or "fast," and respectable middle-class family audiences could only see the stars of music hall at Christmas time in pantomime. It was Augustus Harris who, in 1880, banished from Drury Lane the old-fashioned pantomimists who had always ruled the then so-called traditional productions and began to import comedians and serio-comics from burlesque and the halls, making the new form of Christmas production, with i[t]s manly Dame and dashingly feminine Principal Boy, which we now look on and call misguidedly "Traditional Pantomime."[9]

Nor would children appreciate all the numerous topical allusions or jokes which ranged over a wide variety of subjects more likely to appeal, as the *Times* critic implied, to adults: "But to the average sensual man [*Sinbad*] offers an abundance of agreeable opportunities. You can hear all the music-hall songs of the year without frequenting music-halls, get a fair insight into current politics and sociology without reading Parliamentary reports or other dry columns of your morning paper" (27 December 1906, p. 3). Specific examples show what kind of insight was offered. Dan Leno and Herbert Campbell sang about the shortcomings of the British War Office in *The Sleeping Beauty and the Beast* (1900), reflecting contemporary discontent with the handling of the Boer War. More personal was the satire directed at Joseph Chamberlain and his advocacy of import tariffs in *Humpty Dumpty* in 1903, as the *Times* review indicates: "Who, indeed, even in the straitest sect of the free-importers could feel seriously affronted by the spectacle of an actor in pantomime holding up a big and little loaf and calling himself the saviour of his country? Mr. Chamberlain, possibly, if he were as sensitive to caricature as some other statesmen—seeing that the actor who momentarily impersonated him for the rest of the evening figured as a scarecrow—but, assuredly, no one else" (28 December 1903, p. 10). The 1909 *Aladdin* demonstrated that the London underground could be a source of humor, as could the grisly force-feeding of suffragettes: "Topical allusions are the salt of pantomime: the Widow Twankey cannot open and close double doors without shouting 'Next station, Tottenham-court road!' and when Abanazar hears a hubbub without he says, 'They are only feeding a suffragette'" (*T*, 28 December 1909, p. 8). But it would surely take a precocious child to savor that latter sort of jibe.

More appealing, probably, would be the spectacle lavished on many pantomimes, particularly those at Drury Lane, or the numerous slapstick gags with automobiles, golf, or other similar physical props. More breathtaking were the acrobatic feats, which, along with other turns from the music hall, became a regular feature of most pantomimes, as the *Times* critic could indicate in 1902: "As usual, the Grigolati troupe hover through the air, and, for a novelty, Mme. Grigolati takes her flight right out through the auditorium, scattering flowers over the people in the stalls" (27 December 1902, p. 4). Nevertheless, these novelties, turns, gags, and topical allusions were frequently burdensome, at least in the critics' eyes: "These Drury Lane pantomimes are too long, too colossal. After three hours or so the attention flags, the eye becomes wearied of magnificence, and it is high time for the children to be in bed. As matters stand, Mr. Collins ought to call his pantomimes not 'productions,' but 'overproductions.' He should take a hint from the trade unions and limit the output" (*T*, 27 December 1901, p. 4).

Whether the critics were better arbiters of popular taste than Arthur Collins is, perhaps, questionable. However, there can be no doubt about the appeal of individual performers, most notably Dan Leno and Herbert Campbell, who dominated Drury Lane pantomimes until their deaths in the same year, 1904. Campbell, who was jolly, rubicund, and portly, performed more broadly than did the slight Leno, and so Campbell's "vast size and . . . vast method" were better suited to the expanses of Drury Lane. However, Leno (with his air of resignation, asides, convoluted tales, surprised looks, and broad smiles) was generally deemed the genuine talent, the genius, the "living classic."[10] Others would later gain popularity—Harry Randall, Walter Passmore, Marie George, Wilkie Bard, George Graves—but none would ever ascend to Leno's heights.

It should not be thought that pantomimes were of a piece and cast in the Drury Lane mold. Even Drury Lane pantomimes changed somewhat between 1900 and 1914. G. R. Sims, who wrote the books from 1912 onwards, provided a stronger, consecutive tale and, as the *Athenaeum* noted, removed "much of the blatant stupidity that a decade ago would have been deemed an indispensable element" (3 January 1914, p. 19). Other theatres attempted to gear their pantomimes to "please a special public." The Lyceum attracted a "popular audience" which enjoyed very broad effects and strong humor, while the Adelphi aimed at a "public which loves musical comedy . . . and depends on its entertaining qualities upon the personality of its chief performers" (*Athenaeum*, 4 January 1908, p. 24). Indeed, the Lyceum rivalled Drury Lane strongly, both in the quality and cost of its productions:

> The Lyceum may charge half-prices for its fare, but it certainly does not give what the *restaurateurs* [sic] call half-portions. Your plate is piled high, and good, honest, wholesome food they give you, too. It may not be the last word in the artistic subtlety of serving, but it is a meal that any normal appetite may enjoy . . . [*Little Red Riding Hood*] is almost certainly what it claims to be, a fairy pantomime, a pantomime about children and fairies, and one that children are bound to enjoy. (*T*, 24 December 1908, p. 9)

Very closely related to pantomimes, and often blurred generically with them, were "children's plays," a blend of fairy tale and fantasy. The most frequently performed example of this genre was *Alice in Wonderland* and *Alice Through the Looking Glass* (either jointly or individually). Here the intrinsic Victorian absurdist whimsy could appeal or appall, depending upon the adapter of Lewis Carroll's original. Thus Savile Clark's version elicited rapture from Max Beerbohm: "None of the most delightful incidents . . . has been omitted, and none of them has lost its savour, and all of them grow out of and into one another in the right kind of reasonably-unreasonable sequence. The result is a perfect little pantomime. Every adult must revel in it. I cannot so safely answer for children."[11] However, an adaptation offered three years later (in 1903) was really, said *The Times*, a "variety entertainment" which bore too little resemblance to the original: "The attempt to graft such entertainment (and in this case the author, Mr. Y. Knott, has shown some ingenuity) must result in the crowding out of Lewis Carroll. . . . The White Knight is obviously in a hurry to get to his 'imitations of popular actors'; Tweedledum and Tweedledee introduce football jokes" (23 December 1903, p. 11).

Other subjects in this category included *The Swineherd and the Princess*, *Bluebell in Fairyland*, *The Water Babies*, *Little Hans Andersen*, *Snowdrop and the Seven Little Men*, *Pinkie and the Fairies*, and *The Golden Land of Fairy Tales* (the titles are themselves descriptively revealing). Such productions were welcomed critically when they exhibited simplicity, refinement, and innocent appeal. Thus the 1903 *Times* critic observed that *Little Hans Andersen* was "of a delightfully refined order, playful, poetic, and easily intelligible to children and grown-up people alike" (23 December 1903, p. 5), while *The Golden Land of Fairy Tales* approached the ideal:

> At last we have a children's fairy play on the right lines—not a perfect play, but on the right lines. We are so used to pantomime and its attempts to combine attractions for a certain kind of grown-up with attractions for children—or to neglect the children altogether; to *Alice in Wonderland* with low comedians, song, and dance, and to things of that kind, that we might well despair of seeing a children's play which treats the famous stories with proper reverence and gives them a chance to show their own merits. That is what *The Golden Land of Fairy Tales* does. It takes some of the best stories in Grimm and puts them on the stage quite simply and very decoratively. (15 December 1911, p. 12)

Belonging to this children's category, but possessing an idiosyncratic quality and appeal, was *Where the Rainbow Ends*, a piece full of adventure, fairy creatures, the supernatural, dragons, and St. George. The play and its overt patriotism became increasingly popular with each revival and was a virtual paradigm by 1914: "We have had patriotic plays which made patriotism brutal, and children's plays which seemed meant to rouse braggartry and stupid passion. In *Where the Rainbow Ends* . . . we have a children's patriotic play which lifts patriotism to a level above fear and swagger, because the authors have treated their subject with a dash of poetry and cared for ideas more than party cries" (*T*, 22 December 1911, p. 9). The "patriotic note" *Where the Rainbow Ends* sounded in 1911 was, needless to say, doubly welcome in 1914—or so the *Times* reviewer reverently suggested: "Patriotism, as exploited by loud-voiced vocalists and glaring tableaux, may be sadly overdone, but the charm of *Where the Rainbow Ends* is that the patriotic chord sounded is never out of harmony with the general sentiment, and St. George is an ideal hero for every British boy and girl to revel in at the moment" (28 December 1914, p. 3). Despite the later reviewer's protestation, it would seem *Where the Rainbow Ends* did project that "peculiarly British form of moralistic patriotism, which claimed a special role for Britain as the arbiter of world affairs and the upholder of Christian civilisation" and which helped Britain to enter World War I and see it as "the proclamation of a moral crusade."[12]

The appeal of *Where the Rainbow Ends*, ultimately, was linked to the era of its genesis, a trait not discernible so readily in that most popular Christmas children's play (both then and ever since), *Peter Pan*. This (and Barrie's other) work has been written about so extensively that commentary here is almost superfluous. However, it is perhaps worth reprinting A. B. Walkley's accolade to the first production: "There has always been much of the frank and trusting simplicity of the child in Mr. Barrie's work, of the child for whom romance is the true reality and that which children of larger growth call knowledge, something divined to be not worth knowing. It was certain, therefore, in advance that when he set himself to write a play for children and about children he would give us of his very best, his most fanciful, and his most tender. To our taste *Peter Pan* is from beginning to end a thing of pure delight."[13]

Peter Pan very rapidly became a permanent feature of the Christmas scene and developed audiences which attended each revival with almost cultish fanaticism, as the following observations from contemporary critics attest:

> . . . its text is now so familiar to the audience that the favourite passages are applauded before the actors can get them uttered. (*T*, 21 December 1909, p. 10)

> The spell of *Peter Pan* in his seventh year is as potent as ever. There are several changes in the cast, but they make little difference to the delight of the audience in the familiar scenes and words which . . . the whole house, but especially the gallery and the pit, seemed to know by heart. (*T*, 27 December 1910, p. 7)

> The worship of *Peter Pan* shows no sign of abatement, for all that the performances this year have shrunk to afternoons only. Among the most ardent devotees the cult has developed a ritual, of which two important acts are pelting the players, during or after the scenes, with twopenny bunches of flowers, and accompanying the orchestra by clapping the hands very fairly in time with the music. (*T*, 24 December 1913, p. 8)[14]

This evident familiarity was not shaken, apparently, by some of the textual changes which occurred during *Pan*'s early years, such as the elimination of Columbine and Harlequin, and the conversion of the play from three to five acts. However, the fanatics would probably have derided the almost wholesale transformations injected into the Royal Shakespeare Company's 1982 revival which featured, among many things, a storyteller and a *male* Peter Pan.[15]

Indeed, transvestism—that curiously pervasive facet of Christmas entertainments—serves to link *Peter Pan* not only with pantomimes but with that other most revived work in the period, *Charley's Aunt*. This farcical comedy, which was produced originally from December 1892 through December 1896, was revived each Christmas apart from 1902, 1903, and 1906. It, too, was sometimes seen as indistinguishable in tone from other genres: "and surely no happier occasion for the revival of *Charley's Aunt* could have been found than the pantomime season, for if, frankly, it would be impossible in the present day to recapture that 'first, fine, careless rapture' which three long years were necessary to exhaust in the case of this once perennial farce, it is still impossible to be insensible to the play's appeal as pantomime" (*T*, 27 December 1905, p. 8).

Transvestism in the theatre is too broad a topic to be considered here; however, it should not be forgotten that it occurred in other popular genres, notably musical comedy. As Mander and Mitchenson point out, it became a tradition for the comedian in a musical comedy to disguise himself as a woman at some point in the plot.[16] Thus G. P. Huntley in *Lady Madcap* found himself attended by six housemaids who assisted him in dressing as an old woman. And if musical comedies shared transvestism with pantomime, they also displayed hybridism in frequently borrowing features of the music hall, variety, and revue. For example, while *Madame*

Sherry was acceptable (because it was not music hall "under another name" [*T*, 24 December 1903, p. 4]), *The Cherry Girl* was castigated by *The Times*: "We think it highly probable that children, and other logical keen-witted people, will rather resent the loss of the original story, and refuse to be charmed with the ingenuities and the undoubted humours of the variety entertainment into which Act II degenerates" (*T*, 22 December 1903, p. 5). Moreover, even an already popular musical comedy, such as *The Belle of Mayfair* (eventually performed 431 times), could be given added Christmas appeal with the addition of a star harlequinade, but which, in retrospect, serves to demonstrate how amorphous the genre could be.

Other Christmas offerings, while of a more rag-bag nature, usually had some ingredient consonant with the season. There was the adventure and romance of *The Scarlet Pimpernel*, the traditional sentiment of *The Little Lord Fauntleroy*, the Dickensian redolence of *Liberty Hall*, and even Dickens proper in *David Copperfield*. And, finally, there was Shakespeare, although only *The Tempest* of 1905, with its supernatural element, came close to what might be perceived as the Christmas spirit. However, Shakespearean productions of the period tended towards the spectacular, and so the connection between them and pantomime can be established.[17] Shakespeare could also be highly topical, as can be seen in the staging of *Henry V* in 1900 and in 1914 when the Boer War and World War I lent fresh patriotic significance to the play. The 1900 *Henry*, *The Times* observed, had a "brilliant crowd headed by Mr. Lewis Waller in the foreground of some admirable stage-pictures by Messrs. Banks and Hawes Craven. The causes underlying the present popularity of this trumpet-call to patriotism are sufficiently obvious; they are the causes which have brought khaki comedy to the Haymarket and military ballet to Leicester-square" (24 December 1900, p. 10). The 1914 *Henry* was, *The Times* thought, perhaps even more appropriate to the season: "Not only does it breathe in every line the ancient, inbred integrity, piety, good nature, and good humour of the people of England, but it gives passionate utterance to what has always been the Englishman's pride in the English small Army—'We few, we happy few, we band of brothers'" (28 December 1914, p. 3).[18] And that same season, on the "home front" as it were, there was the ominous birth of spy-plays, such as *The Man Who Stayed at Home* and *On His Majesty's Service* (really topical melodramas which were to develop later into the popular thriller plays of the twenties).

Although numerous other individual productions have been omitted in this rather sweeping survey (Shaw's *Arms and the Man* and *John Bull's Other*

Island, not to mention such genres as school-life plays and melodramas), it is clear that Christmas entertainments offered the Edwardian theatregoer a wide variety of genre and subject. What these productions, perhaps, had in common was the potential to stimulate (and even overwhelm) the imagination with spectacle, fantasy, and make-believe. Nor did managers and writers hesitate in adopting generic theatrical features which would further their endeavors. And that, surely, was entirely appropriate to a season which celebrates a virgin birth, angels singing to shepherds, and three kings/wise men from the East bearing gifts, and which has adopted Christmas trees and shining baubles, and combines Santa Claus, sleighs, and reindeer encompassing the rooftops of the world. The Christmas season, in every sense, was and is eclectic.

NOTES

1. J. C. Trewin, *The Edwardian Theatre* (Oxford: Blackwell, 1976). For general accounts of the "Edwardian" period which also justify the chronological extension beyond the reigns of individual monarchs, see Samuel Hynes, *The Edwardian Turn of Mind* (Princeton: Princeton University Press, 1968), and *The Edwardian Age: Conflict and Stability, 1900–1914*, ed. Alan O'Day (London: Macmillan, 1979).

2. For example, the Barker-Vedrenne seasons of 1904–1907, which did much to establish Shaw in London, took place at the Court Theatre which lay outside the West End.

3. See Trewin's long-run list in *The Edwardian Theatre*, 155–60.

4. Full details of these and other Christmas productions can be found in J. P. Wearing, *The London Stage, 1900–1909: A Calendar of Plays and Players* (Metuchen, N.J.: Scarecrow Press, 1981), and *The London Stage, 1910–1919: A Calendar of Plays and Players* (Metuchen, N.J.: Scarecrow Press, 1982).

5. A Drury Lane pantomime usually ran approximately 120 performances on a twice daily basis. Assuming full houses, it would be seen by over 300,000 people; certainly a quarter of a million actual patrons would not be an exaggeration. The history of pantomime is interestingly related in R. J. Broadbent, *A History of Pantomime* (1901; reprint, New York: Benjamin Blom, 1964); David Mayer, *Harlequin in His Element: The English Pantomime 1806–1836* (Cambridge, Mass.: Harvard University Press, 1969); and Raymond Mander and Joe Mitchenson, *Pantomime: A Story in Pictures* (London: Davies, 1973). The text of the 1900 Drury Lane pantomime, *The Sleeping Beauty and the Beast*, is printed in Michael R. Booth, *English Plays of the Nineteenth Century*, 5 vols. (Oxford: Clarendon Press, 1969–76), 5:379–449. The latter work also contains a useful introduction as well as information on pantomime production and rehearsal.

6. Max Beerbohm, *More Theatres* (New York: Taplinger, 1969), 95. See also his *Last Theatres, 1904–1910* (New York: Taplinger, 1970), 117.

7. "But they [children] would be still better pleased if there were more attention to [plot], for they like some relation to reality even in their games" ("Pantomime," *Times*, 29 December 1908, pp. 7–8).

8. Max Beerbohm, *Around Theatres* (New York: Knopf, 1930), 66.

9. Raymond Mander and Joe Mitchenson, *British Music Hall*, rev. ed. (London: Gentry, 1974), 55. This quotation refers to the late 1890s, but circumstances had not changed radically at the opening of the century.

10. See Beerbohm's moving tribute to Leno in *Around Theatres*, 448–52.

11. Beerbohm, *Around Theatres*, 139.

12. Colin Nicolson, "Edwardian England and the Coming of the First World War" in O'Day, 157.

13. *The Times*, 28 December 1904, p. 4; reprinted in A. B. Walkley, *Drama and Life* (1908; reprint, Freeport, New York: Books for Libraries, 1967), 209. Of the numerous works on Barrie, the following two are particularly apposite to *Peter Pan*: Roger Lancelyn Green, *Fifty Years of "Peter Pan"* (London: Davies, 1954), and Andrew Birkin, *J. M. Barrie & the Lost Boys* (London: Constable, 1979).

14. One of the period's Peter Pans, Pauline Chase, published a collection of letters from some of her/his admirers; see Pauline Chase, *Peter Pan's Postbag: Letters to Pauline Chase* (London: Heinemann, 1909).

15. See *Fifty Years of "Peter Pan,"* 102–20, and *London Theatre Record* 2(1982): 695–700.

16. See Raymond Mander and Joe Mitchenson, *Musical Comedy: A Story in Pictures* (New York: Taplinger, 1970).

17. For a cogent discussion of spectacle in Shakespeare, melodrama, and pantomime, see Michael R. Booth, *Victorian Spectacular Theatre 1850–1910* (London: Routledge and Kegan Paul, 1981).

18. There is probably an echo in this last line of the fact that the British Expeditionary Force (i.e. the army) numbered only 100,000 at the outbreak of the war. Even England fighting France in *Henry V* is not too anomalous when Britain's diplomatic ambivalence towards France in the years prior to the war is considered (see Colin Nicolson, "Edwardian England" in O'Day, 144–68).

PART THREE

Comedy and Social Drama

The Image of Fashionable Society in American Comedy, 1840–1870

Tice L. Miller

Public interest in New York society was paramount in the 1840s and 1850s. The old prerevolutionary Knickerbocker families with names such as Brevoort, Schermerhorn, Bleeker, Rhinelander, Van Rensselaer, and Stuyvesant found their exclusive circle challenged by such upstart vulgarians as the Astors, the Vanderbilts, the Belmonts, and the Jeromes.[1] As the *nouveaux riches* jockeyed for position on Gotham's social ladder, they sought ways to authenticate their newly acquired status. On a scale never before witnessed in New York, they made an art of ostentatious living: elaborate mansions on Fifth Avenue, daily shopping trips to A. T. Stewart's department store, an endless round of parties and balls (especially when foreign dignitaries such as Charles Dickens were in town), summer vacations at Saratoga Springs, the patronage of cultivated poets and Italian tenors, and for the Sabbath, the expenditure of up to $1400 for a pew at Grace Church.

Manners had to be cultivated, manifesting at least the outward appearance of good breeding on all occasions. Tongues wagged and doors closed when John Jacob Astor ate peas and ice cream with a knife at a dinner party given by the Albert Gallatins.[2] With no social traditions of their own, polite society imitated those of aristocratic Europeans—especially the French after Louis-Napoleon became emperor in 1852. Uncertain about who belonged in Gotham society, they indulged the whims of Isaac Hull Brown, sexton of Grace Church and social arbiter over Fifth Avenue society for two generations. Brown inspected guest lists and presided over $50,000 weddings. He even greeted guests at the most fashionable parties.[3]

Such comings and goings of New York's elite invited the attention of the press and stage. James Gordon Bennett's *New York Herald* began covering the social scene in the late 1830s, offering lightly satirical and at times tasteless treatments of the Upper Ten.[4] After its initial shock, society became a willing accomplice in making certain that its stories were reported in the press.[5] And by midcentury, satirizing New York's better families had become a favorite pastime of the city's journalists. George W. Curtis's *The Potiphar Papers* (*Putnam's Monthly Magazine*, 1853) introduced such fascinating creatures as Gauche Boosey, Minerva Tattle, and the Reverend Cream Cheese.[6] At the same time, Fitz-James O'Brien in *The Lantern*, *Putnam's*, and *Young America* lampooned the social strivings of the new rich. His "Brown Studies" and "About the Sexton Bumble-Bee" drew attention to the relationship which had developed among the liberal society ministers, the young-men-about-town, and the society matrons.[7] Later in the decade, Edward G. P. Wilkins in *Harper's Weekly* and *Saturday Press* satirized the same crowd for their illiteracy and pretentiousness.[8] He assumed the persona of a silly young society belle and wrote letters to the editor about the doings of fashionable society.

Playwrights faced a slightly different problem than journalists. Discriminating theatregoers were no more interested in local plays than in local fashion or art. They wanted to see what had been popular at Covent, not Castle, Garden. Managers were reluctant, therefore, to spend money on American comedy when New York audiences wanted the London stamp of approval. Thus it was simply business as usual when Henry Placide imported *London Assurance* to the Park Theatre in 1841, shortly after its success in London.

The lack of an adequate international copyright law also did little to encourage American playwrights. Wilkins complained in the *Saturday Press* (10 March 1860) that Laura Keene preferred foreign plays to native ones because she could obtain the former free of charge. The majority of playwrights in the 1850s and 1860s also worked as journalists, and Wilkins believed that comic writers were "too well paid elsewhere to think of writing for the theatres, the managers of which fancy that paying money to authors is equivalent to throwing it out the window."[9]

There is evidence also that aristocratic patronage of the arts favored Italian opera in the 1840s and 1850s. Joseph N. Ireland blames the demise of the Park Theatre in 1848 upon society's neglect: "having voted the theatre a vulgarity and the opera the only entertainment for people of taste, [a society clique] carefully abstained from countenancing even the most refined and elevating dramatic productions of their mother tongue."[10] G. C. D. Odell notes that the Astor Place Opera House was the fourth house built for Italian opera in the city. And in spite of the failure of each attempt, there always seemed to be wealthy investors waiting to try again.[11]

The greatest obstacle to the acceptance of native social comedy, however, lay in the age itself—an age of Andrew Jackson and the common man—an age which believed that a man should be judged by his actions, not by his rank or title.[12] Since New York society had no widely accepted code of manners, a requisite for true social comedy, the playwright had to establish the social situation immediately by what his characters said and did. In contrast, British and French authors could assume that their social situations and characters would be received in a certain way by the audience.

Even with such unfavorable conditions, a growing number of social comedies were written between 1840 and 1870. Strictly speaking, they are more farcical than comic, and burlesque more than they delineate character; yet they provide an image of fashionable life in New York which, if not entirely accurate, is vivid and colorful.[13] Mrs. Mowatt's *Fashion* (1845), recognized by Poe as a minor masterpiece, dealt with American adulation of European manners. Although never acted in its day, James K. Paulding's *The Bucktails; or, Americans in England* (1847) made a claim for America as a place of high society. Extant social comedies from the 1850s include Charles Pardey's *Nature's Nobleman* (1851), Cornelius Mathew's *False Pretences* (1856), Edward Wilkins's *Young New York* (1856), Mrs. Sidney Bateman's *Self* and *The Golden Calf* (both 1857), William Henry Hurlburt's *American in Paris* (1858), and D. W. Wainwright's *Wheat and Chaff* (1858). Odell mentions several popular works which have not survived, including *Saratoga Springs* at Mitchell's Olympic Theatre (1841) and O. E. Durivage's adaptation of *The Potiphar Papers and Lower Twenty* (1854). Short plays were used as curtain raisers. Two extant pieces seem representative of this genre: Charles M. Walcot's *A Good Fellow* (1854), and Wilkins's *My Wife's Mirror* (1856). Public taste demanded more sensational fare in the war-torn 1860s, although Irving Browne's *Our Best Society* (1868) from *The Potiphar Papers*, and Bronson Howard's *Saratoga* (1870) carry on the tradition. While all of these plays would seem excessively sentimental to modern tastes, the best—especially Mrs. Mowatt's *Fashion*—offer wit and humor in the classical tradition. And they were warmly greeted by critics who were bored with the traditional repertory. Fitz-James O'Brien in *Putnam's* (October 1854) asked for a "good comedy of American life" which would touch upon "the various shades of our very peculiar and somewhat anomalous society."

The complexity of American life, however, did not interest playwrights as much as the world of the *nouveaux riche* family. They observed a class of Americans who practiced conspicuous consumption while they preached such middle-class values as virtue, thrift, generosity, modesty, loyalty, and honesty. Arthur Beaufort in *Wheat and Chaff* explains that true aristocrats are those who give willingly to the poor and need no outward show of rank to "herald their munificence." The wealthy Caroline in *Nature's Nobleman* "sings, plays, talks French and is a rare hand at verse making"; in addition, she "can tuck up her sleeves and go into the dairy, and is firstrate at preserves." Such sentiments suggest that to remain sympathetic onstage, wealthy characters must behave as if they were no better than the lowest servant. Madames Tiffany in *Fashion* and Apex in *Self* prove unwise in hiding their humble origins. Mrs. Tiffany's life as a milliner in upstate New York and Mrs. Apex's wood-cutting grandfather remain sources of embarrassment to ladies wishing to be accepted as pedigreed aristocrats. Zachary Westwood in *Nature's Nobleman* provides the last word on the subject: "Aristocrats! It riles me to hear the word—it hadn't ought to pass American lips; we are borrowing the notions as well as the fashions of foreigners."

Mrs. Tiffany and Mrs. Apex are not unique to the genre but are closely related to Mrs. Milledollar in *False Pretences*, Mrs. Ten-per-cent in *Young New York*, Mrs. Sunnysides in *A Good Fellow*, and Mrs. Potiphar in *Our Best Society*. In attempting to rise in society, they threaten the financial and moral stability of the family. Mrs. Milledollar is determined to give a party, even as her husband faces ruin. Mrs. Ten-per-cent is "addicted to four parties a week." Mrs. Sunnysides gives parties and furnishes her new mansion with items of luxury even as the creditors foreclose on the property. In the end, these matrons of society will be treated with little sympathy. Mrs. Tiffany will be bundled off to the country where she will learn "economy, true independence, and home virtues instead of foreign follies." Mrs. Apex will give up "parties, balls, dress and extravagance and will, in turn, darn her husband's stockings, nurse her grandchildren, and 'live as a middle-aged woman should do!'" Mrs. Umbraton in *A Good Fellow* will admit that thrift and hard work are preferred to shopping trips and expensive parties. The bald heads at Wallack's Theatre must have all nodded in agreement at such sentiments.

If the stage painted a less-than-flattering portrait of the ladies of society, it did little better with their husbands. Mr. Tiffany, Mr. Apex, Mr. Milledollar, Mr. Ten-per-cent, and the rest are not titled aristocrats but merchant princes and bank presidents. The majority are millionaires (a new term in 1850) with the stereotype already set of the Scrooge-like business tycoon who spends all his time making money. Mr. Tiffany has "melted down [his] flesh into dollars, and mortgaged . . . [his] soul in the bargain." Peter Funk in *False Pretences* characterizes a millionaire as someone who "turns every man into money," who "shaves notes," joins churches, "squeezes" his best friends, and "grinds" the fine edge off of every man he meets. Jacob Milledollar must call in a bank note knowing that it spells ruin for his best friend, Adam Crockery.

The children of the best families fare no better. Seraphina Tiffany behaves exactly like her mother. Her worship of foreign titles prompts her to run off with the fake Count Jolimaître because she wants to be a "Countess." Adolphus Washington Ten-per-cent is a "chip off the old block," addicted to "billiards, brandy and water, and the 'corps de ballet.'" Balaam Milledollar has no vocation and no real interests. He is joined in these pursuits by Paul Potiphar and Gauche Boosey in *Our Best Society*. Herbert Vane in *Wheat and Chaff* has gambled away his fortune at Paris, Baden-Baden, and Deuce's in New York.

The image of the family which begins to emerge from these plays is that of husbands preoccupied with making money, their wives obsessed with obtaining social position, and their children adrift in the corrupting influence of the big city. Playwrights seem especially critical towards society matrons for neglecting the home and allowing children to grow up without proper moral teachings.

Normal restraints upon such actions by the *nouveaux riches* also have become casualties of city life. Friends of long standing have been pushed aside for those considered more fashionable. Mrs. Tiffany, for instance, does not welcome the old farmer Adam Trueman because he evokes memories of less prosperous times. Instead, she and her fellow society matrons fill up the front parlor with the "crème de la crème" of society together with prominent artists and poets. The "crème de la crème" for Mrs. Apex includes Mrs. Codliver (a wealthy vulgarian addicted to patent medicines), Sallie Simper, Ida Indolence, Dorothea Dumpling, and Fanny Fortuna. All suggest the superficial qualities associated with the "upper crust," although they are borrowed from older English models. In *Young New York*, the Ten-per-cents are visited by Miss Cerulia Sawin from Boston, who is addicted to Ralph Waldo Emerson, astronomical observations, and other intellectual fads of the day. Mr. Augustus Fogg from Mrs. Tiffany's parlor has no other ambition than to talk bosh and eat. Mrs. Tiffany's pet poet, Twinkle, preaches that velocity is the true measure of a poet, which means that the quality of a poem is measured by the speed of composition. Italian opera tenors such as Apollo in Boucicault's *Apollo in New York* (December 1854)[14] and Signor Patrici Skibberine in Wilkins's *Young New York* are also necessary in "well-stocked" parlors.[15] In *False Pretences*, Mrs. Eyeball is accused of having her parlor filled "once a week with talented people who talk about everything they don't understand, and understand everything which they don't talk about."

If the family members are corrupted by social ambition then, of course, their religious beliefs and moral values deteriorate. In place of the stern old Calvinist preacher of earlier times, the *nouveaux riches* want a more cultivated society minister with a more liberal and secular theology. The Reverend Cream Cheese in *Our Best Society* knows all the gossip, the latest liberal religious theories, and the special tastes of his rich society matrons. The Reverend Needham Crawl in *Young New York* is more concerned with "Bible Societies, religious anniversaries, Christian associations, Oxford Prayer Books, and two percent a month" than with the spiritual needs of his "flock." Liberal ministers are in such demand in new Fifth Avenue mansions, that the Smashers in *False Pretences* are accused of looking up all the fresh clergymen who come to town.[16]

The wealthy are depicted as extravagant and tasteless, not only in their homes, but also on their summer vacations at Saratoga Springs. This resort area, popular for its hot baths and horse racing, became a favorite setting for social comedies in the mid-nineteenth century. J. H. Hackett's *The Moderns; or, A Trip to the Springs* (1831) and William Mitchell's *Saratoga Springs* (1841) were but two early plays to trade upon the reputation of the resort as a summer playground for New York society. The first act of *Nature's Nobleman* is set in Saratoga. When asked later how her vacation went at Cape May (New Jersey), Caroline replies: "Much the same as at Saratoga. Killed time in fifty foolish ways, and endeavored to convince myself I was very amused." In *Young New York*, Mr. Ten-per-cent found the comforts at Saratoga less than desirable: "Fashion keeps us out of our comfortable homes three months in a year, and sends us here to Saratoga, where we pay two hundred dollars a-week, for a dog-kennel, which they call a parlor, and three dry-goods boxes, impudently termed bed-rooms; get nothing to eat—drive over dusty roads—and drink water, flavored with old iron, bootheels, and brimstone—bah!" Bronson Howard would continue this practice by setting one act of his *Saratoga* (1870) at the Congress Inn in that resort city. Extravagant summer vacations in Saratoga Springs were to the "best society" in the period, 1840–1870, what Newport would become in the 1880s and 1890s.

The image of the Upper Ten which emerges is unflattering to all aspects of that society. While the obligatory sentimental ending of each play might suggest that the rich are at heart good people, the rest of the play condemns a moneyed class of Americans who are vain, selfish, pretentious, extravagant, and silly. Not content to live in an egalitarian society, its members import European culture to advertise their newly acquired status. Fashions, books, leading actresses, paintings, plays, and words themselves were borrowed, mainly from the French. The plot of *False Pretences* turns on the inability of the Milledollars to understand Monsieur Boquet's letter of introduction. Unwilling to admit that they cannot read a word of French, they "have a go at it" through trial and error. They conclude that Monsieur Boquet is the son of the emperor. In reality, he is only a barber. Mrs. Milledollar has studied French at Madame Parleyvou's School but is as ignorant as the rest. And in *Fashion*, Mrs. Tiffany tells her maid to say "fauteuil" instead of "arm-chair" because the former "has a foreign—an out-of-the-wayish sound that is perfectly charming—and so genteel! There is something about our American words decidedly vulgar." Finally, Cypher Cynosure, in *Self*, cannot talk about New York without telling everyone how much better everything is in Paris.

Money—having it, spending it, losing it—is the measure of everything in this society. Interestingly, these money-conscious, fashionable people run up debts and don't pay their bills. Herbert Vane in *Wheat and Chaff* states what must have been regarded as a cliché: "Tradesmen take it kindly when owed by a man of fashion." Mr. Umbraton in *A Good Fellow* reports that the spendthrift Sunnysides furnished their house on credit without any concern about paying: "All the world applauded their fine taste; within a twelve month the upholsterer failed—the sum they owed him would have saved his credit. Who thought of the upholsterer?" Money also determines friendship; Mrs. Milledollar states the obvious: "When friends lose money—out they go." And in John Brougham's 1856 comedy, *The Game of Life*, the same point is made that "fashionable friends will do nothing to save you from ruin."

The "best society" has only a mercantile appreciation of art and literature. Jacob Milledollar describes a painting in the only way he can: "There's one picture is nine feet long and five feet broad, and it costs me seventy-five dollars." Wealthy vulgarians in Mrs. Bateman's *The Golden Calf* want to buy old masters while they are in Europe but they cannot pronounce the artists' names nor understand anything but the price. In Irving Browne's 1868 adaptation of *The Potiphar Papers*, Mrs. Potiphar points with pride to the family library: "Books are enormously high now-a-days, and so I had these blocks made, and painted. And lettered in imitation. They'll answer every purpose. Of course nobody ever takes books down, and for that matter we can hide the key if necessary." The fashionable people waste money on homes and furniture they do not know how to use. Mr. Ten-per-cent sums up the problem: "I've got a great house in Madison Avenue; got the furniture of the parlors out from Paris—cost a cool ten thousand. Parlor's always shut up, unless my wife gives a splurge."

The image of society manifested in these plays struck some critics as inaccurate. A letter to the editor of *Atlas* (30 November 1856) complained that the writers of "these local plays" have no actual knowledge of the upper classes. Thus their presentation of fashionable frailties and follies were purely imaginary. Yet several playwrights had more than a casual knowledge of fashionable society. Mrs. Mowatt was the daughter of Samuel Ogden, a wealthy member of New York's elite. She had grown up accustomed to wealth and social position. Edward Wilkins wrote *Young New York* with firsthand knowledge of Fifth Avenue society through his friendship with Cora Withers.[17] The majority of writers, however, could have had little intimate contact with the Upper Ten. They gave the public what they wanted with all the intellectual honesty of the *New York Herald* or *New York Sun*. It is interesting to consider that the *New York Times* (13 May 1856) praised Wilkins's *My Wife's Mirror* for avoiding the clichés of fashionable plays including "monstrous parvenues in Fifth Avenue drinking blacking for claret, or British bricklayers mistaken for Neapolitan Princes." The farcical treatment of society's follies would suggest a largely unsympathetic and unsophisticated audience.

While lampooning the *nouveaux riches* remains a constant element in social comedies of the period, another more subtle but more important motif suggests the underlying cause of the problem. The Tiffanys, Apexs, Milledollars, Ten-per-cents and the rest have left the simple rural life for that of the city. They have abandoned rural values for the mad pursuit of money and pleasure. At the beginning of the play, they face moral as well as financial bankruptcy. But by act five they have saved both their souls and their cash by returning, at least spiritually, to the farm. Mrs. Tiffany will physically leave the city. The others who must remain give up city life: balls, parties, extravagant shopping, gossip. All will find salvation in family life, not in Fifth Avenue salons or parties, or on vacation at Saratoga Springs.

Even when the moral collapse of the family seems imminent, one member of the younger generation usually makes an appearance to serve as a model of virtue and honor for the rest. In *Self*, a dutiful daughter, Mary Apex, sacrifices her own happiness to save her father. Rose Ten-per-cent defies her father and marries for love; her spunk and honesty pay off in a happy family reconciliation in act five. Franklin Whittemore, a young lawyer, remains a true friend in *False Pretences*, as does Arthur Beaufort in *Wheat and Chaff*. Or the regeneration of the family can be the work of an old friend of the family who is visiting from the country. The role is vintage stage Yankee. Adam Trueman in *Fashion*, John Unit in *Self*, and Zachary Westwood in *Nature's Nobleman* wander through the scenery with no other function than to mouth rural wisdom and rescue the family from corrupting city influences. And in *Nature's Nobleman*, the artifice of the resort areas—Saratoga Springs and Cape May—is contrasted with the natural beauty of Zachary's old farm. It is only in the country that false faces can be dropped and each character reveal his own true self. The themes of rural innocence and purity pitted against urban corruption run through the entirety of American literature and no more so than in nineteenth-century comedy. While these plays are rough sketches with little pretension to being fine literature, they provided the public with an image of upper-class life in New York. And these images will grow more vivid when handled with greater expertise by William Dean Howells, Henry James, and Edith Wharton.

NOTES

1. See Henry Collins Brown, *Brownstone Fronts and Saratoga Trunks* (New York: E. P. Dutton, 1935); Alan Churchill, *The Upper Crust: An Informal History of New York's Highest Society* (Englewood Cliffs, N.J.: Prentice-Hall, 1970); Lloyd Morris, *Incredible New York* (New York: Random House, 1951); Edward K. Spann, *The New Metropolis: New York City, 1840–1857* (New York: Columbia University Press, 1981).

2. Churchill, *Upper Crust*, 49.

3. Morris, *Incredible New York*, 21; Churchill, *Upper Crust*, 40–41.

4. Charles Astor Bristed gave society the name of "Upper Tendom" or the "Upper Ten-thousand."

5. Frank Luther Mott, *American Journalism*, rev. ed. (New York: Macmillan, 1950), 233.

6. See Gordon Milne, *George W. Curtis: The Genteel Tradition* (Bloomington: Indiana University Press, 1956).

7. See Francis Wolle, *Fitz-James O'Brien: A Literary Bohemian of the Eighteen-fifties*, University of Colorado Studies, series B, *Studies in the Humanities*, vol. 2, no. 2 (Boulder: University of Colorado Press, 1944).

8. See Tice L. Miller, *Bohemians and Critics: American Theatre Criticism in the Nineteenth Century* (Metuchen, N.J.: Scarecrow Press, 1981).

9. The *Saturday Press* was published in New York by Henry Clapp, Jr., between 1858 and 1860, and resurrected briefly in 1865–1866.

10. Joseph N. Ireland, *Records of the New York Stage*, 2 vols. (New York: T. H. Morrell, 1866), 2:464.

11. George C. D. Odell, *Annals of the New York Stage*, 15 vols. (New York: Columbia University Press, 1931), 5:381. The failure of wealthy New Yorkers to establish Italian opera in the city proved embarrassing, especially after the failure of the Astor Place Opera House in 1847. William Mitchell burlesqued this fiasco at the Olympic Theatre in December 1847, in a piece called the "Upper Row House in Disaster Place," which ran for seventeen consecutive performances.

12. See John Geoffrey Hartman, *The Development of American Social Comedy from 1787 to 1936* (Philadelphia: University of Pennsylvania Press, 1939); Daniel F. Havens, *The Columbian Muse of Comedy: The Development of a Native Tradition in Early American Comedy, 1787–1845* (Carbondale: Southern Illinois University Press, 1973); Montrose J. Moses, *The American Dramatist*, 2d ed. rev. (Boston: Little, Brown, 1917); Arthur Hobson Quinn, *A History of the American Drama from the Beginning to the Civil War*, 2d ed. (New York: F. S. Crofts, 1943).

13. For an index to locating the plays mentioned in this paper, see Don L. Hixon and Don A. Hennessee, *Nineteenth-Century American Drama: A Finding Guide* (Metuchen, N.J.: Scarecrow Press, 1977). All but two of the plays may be found in Readex Corporation's microprint collection, "American Plays, 1831–1900," a portion of its series of English and American plays of the nineteenth century. *The Golden Calf* and *The Game of Life* may be found in the American Culture Series, II, on microfilm.

14. Odell, *Annals*, 5:352.

15. Miller, *Bohemians and Critics*, 53–55.

16. For a discussion of the rise of the liberal minister in America, see Ann Douglas, *The Feminization of American Culture* (New York: Avon Books, 1978).

17. See William Winter, *Old Friends* (New York: Moffat, Yard, 1914), 80–82.

Dion Boucicault's Comic Myths

James Hurt

There are a number of possible paths through the tangled undergrowth of the hundred and fifty or so plays of Dion Boucicault, that extraordinary confusion of art and opportunism. I would like to follow only one for a short distance, that of comedy, and to outline two comic myths, one embodied by his early so-called Regency comedies—*London Assurance* (1841) and *Old Heads and Young Hearts* (1844)—and the other expressed in his Irish melodramatic comedies—*The Colleen Bawn* (1860), *Arrah-na-Pogue* (1864), and *The Shaughraun* (1874).[1] And I would like to suggest that his creation of the comic myth of the "shaughraun" left its mark upon the drama not only of his native land of Ireland but also upon that of his adopted land of America.

For Robert Hogan, the shape of Boucicault's career is simple: it was a steady decline. The early Regency comedies are the best; thereafter, Boucicault sold out to the commercial theatre and compromised his gift for hard, glittering social comedy by yielding to the popular demand for stereotyped farces, mostly translated from the French, and for cheap, sensational melodrama. Hogan writes, "Had he been able to continue writing in the strain in which he began, English dramatic literature of the late nineteenth century might have been inestimably richer. Instead, he was deflected into the commercial theater, and poured out his great mass of crowd-pleasing entertainment."[2] David Krause's judgment is less harsh. He sees the progress from *London Assurance* to *The Shaughraun* not as a mere deterioration into cynical commercialism but as a movement away from an exhausted and hackneyed comic form to a new, richer one. Krause finds in Boucicault's mixed forms and his tragic-comic protagonists a major source of the mature Irish theatre of Shaw, Synge, O'Casey, and even Yeats, in a play such as *The Pot of Broth*: "It was in his creation of this distinctly Irish yet universal character—as Myles-na-Coppaleen, Shaun the Post, or Conn the Shaughraun—that Boucicault finally transcends the Victorian world. And it is part of this triumph that Irish drama as we know it today had its origins in Boucicault" (Krause, 13).

I believe Krause's view is the more illuminating, and I would like to develop it further by considering not only the shaughraun figures of the Irish plays but the comic myth they embody, in contrast to the comic myths of the Regency plays.

London Assurance is a polished and skillful imitation of Restoration comedy. Sir Harcourt Courtly, correctly described in the acting edition's synopsis as a "superannuated old lady-killer," is preparing to marry eighteen-year-old Grace Harkaway. Grace is being forced into the marriage by her father's will, which provided that mortgages on Sir Harcourt's estate, taken to finance his youthful dissipations, would revert to Sir Harcourt if Grace, on attaining the age of nineteen, were to marry him and thus unite the Courtly and Harkaway estates. Sir Harcourt has a son, Charles, whom he believes to be an innocent child but who is in reality a roistering prodigal. The London characters—Sir Harcourt, Charles, his profligate friend Dazzle, and his valet Cool—go to the Gloucestershire estate of Max Harkaway, where Charles falls in love with Grace himself. In an incredibly complicated plot, Sir Harcourt is displaced as Grace's intended by his son, who in the process also acquires the estate.

The plotting of *London Assurance*, despite its complexity, is smooth and clear, the dialogue is smart and witty, and it is not surprising that it not only was a considerable success as a vehicle for Charles Mathews in its original production but held the stage regularly through the rest of the century. And yet *London Assurance* is basically anachronistic. It imitates the form of Restoration comedy in the absence of a social context that would give it meaning, and so it tumbles finally into the mechanical and incoherent. The play, as the title suggests, is about "London assurance," a certain urban glibness and self-confidence that contrasts with a genuine aristocracy of manners. Sir Harcourt makes this theme explicit in the curtain line:

> Barefaced assurance is the vulgar substitute for gentlemanly ease; and there are many, who, by aping the *vices* of the great, imagine that they elevate themselves to the rank of those, whose faults alone they copy. No, sir! The title of gentleman is the only one *out* of any monarch's gift, yet within the reach of every peasant. It should be engrossed by *Truth*—stamped with *Honor*—sealed with *Good-feeling*—signed *Man*—enrolled in every true young English heart. (66–67)

The problems with this noble sentiment are that it is spoken by the character in the play who has most made a mockery of it and that the entire action of the play contradicts it. The world of *London Assurance* is one of naked self-interest, and the winners are those who manifest not "gentlemanly ease" but at best a crude vitality. The play lacks even an implicit moral center, no matter how unconventional, and as a result it seems trivial and mechanical; Boucicault seems unwilling to confront the full implications of his potentially disillusioned world.

Some of the same generalizations apply, perhaps less extremely, to *Old Heads and Young Hearts*, which similarly follows the comedy-of-manners formula. Two young couples, Littleton Coke and Alice Hawthorn and Charles Roebuck and Kate Rocket, are in love but are frustrated by fathers and by prudential considerations. The plot is, if anything, more complicated than that of *London Assurance*, but it similarly involves a trip into the countryside where, after a number of complex intrigues, fathers are overthrown and the couples are properly united. The play does provide a moral perspective outside that of the main characters in the persons of Littleton's bluff country brother Tom and the genial, bumbling country parson Jesse Rural, but they hardly succeed in altering the generally cynical and predatory tone of the main action.

Regarded as social comedy, both *London Assurance* and *Old Heads and Young Hearts* have blurred, uncertain focuses. Their Restoration models were firmly grounded in a real social class. Audiences came to see themselves on the stage, and the thrust of the comedy was toward defining and reaffirming class values: "true wit" and "true gentility" as opposed to false versions. In his Regency comedies, the youthful Boucicault tried to recreate these comedies in a radically changed social situation. But in the exploits of a Sir Harcourt Courtly, Boucicault's Victorian popular audience would have seen not their own behavior but that of a stage aristocracy which had little to do with ordinary experience.

To move from the Regency comedies to the Irish plays is to leapfrog sixteen years of Boucicault's career, from 1844 to 1860, the date of *The Colleen Bawn*. The crucial event in Boucicault's personal life in this period was his removal to America in 1853. *Old Heads and Young Hearts* was written for an English audience, *The Colleen Bawn* for an American one. The story of Boucicault's study of the American theatre and his restless campaign to suit American tastes has been thoroughly and amusingly told by Richard Fawkes in his brilliant biography of Boucicault.[3] The campaign was finally won with *The Octoroon* (1859), a play which in its combination of comedy and melodrama, its treatment of a society divided against itself, and its use of an exotic outsider figure to resolve the conflicts anticipates the Irish melodramatic comedies.[4]

The Irish plays are comedies, despite the emphasis that has been placed upon their famous "sensation scenes": Myles-na-Coppaleen's dive into the lake, Shaun the Post's scaling of the prison walls, and the shooting of Conn the Shaughraun. David Krause has perhaps best captured their tone: "At last Boucicault seemed to have found the confidence and abandon to enjoy a good-natured laugh at the expense of the romantic melodrama that he himself had made so popular; . . . he combined farce with melodrama in such a way that, for all the 'hair-raising' suspense and 'death-defying' deeds, the comic tone produced something close to mock-melodrama" (Krause, 31).

But the Irish plays are comic not merely in tone but in structure and meaning as well, although their comic structure is very different from that of *London Assurance* and *Old Heads and Young Hearts*. The early Regency comedies, beneath their comedy-of-manners surface, follow the New Comedy myth in which youthful wooing against parental opposition expresses vital rebellion against a rigidly authoritarian and hierarchical society. The Irish melodramatic comedies (and Boucicault's adaptation of *Rip Van Winkle* as well) express a different comic myth and one arguably more meaningful in societies more open and less hierarchically ordered than England. The crucial action in these plays is not Jack getting Jill (although love figures heavily in the plays) but the confrontation of warring elements in a divided society and their ultimate, or at least provisional, reconciliation. The crucial figure in this reconciliation is a clown—in Boucicault's terminology a "shaughraun"—who stands somewhat apart from the society but who hovers over the action, directing it to a restoration of harmony.[5] The shaughraun figure may be read in different ways, as the "spirit of comedy" itself, as an embodiment of a natural morality superior to the codes of society, or more naturalistically as a nonviolent political rebel. In any case he is a "carnivalesque" clown figure who functions to dissolve social conflict and restore a "natural" harmony.[6]

Boucicault's Ireland is admittedly an idealized, picture-postcard Ireland; Shaw, in an 1896 review of *The Colleen Bawn*, thought Boucicault was "blarneying the British public" by presenting a "conception of Ireland as a romantic picture, in which the background is formed by the Lakes of Killarney by moonlight, and a round tower or so."[7] Regarded, though, not as realism but as dramatic myth, Boucicault's theatrical Ireland is fissured by conflicts darker and more urgent than the courtship quarrels of

New Comedy. The fundamental conflict in *The Colleen Bawn* is between the values of the Anglo-Irish society of the great houses and those of the native Irish, a conflict that not only separates the characters but also is internalized in the character of Hardress Cregan, secretly married to Eily O'Connor, the Colleen Bawn, but ashamed of her peasant ways, and impelled by circumstances and his own snobbishness toward a "legitimate" marriage to Anne Chute. In his treatment of Cregan and of his fanatically devoted boatman Danny Mann, Boucicault is barely able to overcome the brutality of the ultimate source of his story, an 1819 murder case in which the prototype of Eily was savagely murdered and the prototypes of Cregan and Danny Mann were hanged. Gerald Griffin had softened and moralized the story in his novel *The Collegians* (1829), and Boucicault further displaced the evil in turning the story into a romantic comedy. But Hardress Cregan, with his repressed violence that led him as a boy to cripple Danny Mann, Cain-like, in a fit of temper, his snobbish rejection of his wife Eily, and his half-unwitting acceptance of Danny's offer to kill Eily, is far from the stereotyped young rascals of *London Assurance* and *Old Heads and Young Hearts*. Cregan's redemption through suffering, when he believes that Eily has been murdered through his unwitting agency, has an emotional depth that would be too heavy for comedy if it were not balanced by the witty love-combat and misunderstandings of Kyrle Daly and the sparkling Anne Chute.

The counterforces to the native Irish society in *Arrah-na-Pogue* and *The Shaughraun* are at once simpler and more dangerous. They are the English. *Arrah-na-Pogue* is set in the County Wicklow in the midst of the Rising of 1798, while *The Shaughraun* takes place against the background of the Fenian raids of the 1860s. *Arrah-na-Pogue* turns around the fate of Beamish Mac Coul, an exiled rebel who has secretly returned to Ireland to claim the hand of his fiancée, Fanny Power, while *The Shaughraun* deals with the adventures of a young Irish gentleman, Robert Ffolliott, transported to Australia, who similarly returns to seek amnesty and the hand of Arte O'Neill.

Characters are defined in the three plays in relation to the conflicts of their divided societies. There is a certain similarity in the character configurations of all three. These groupings owe a great deal, of course, to the "line roles" in the nineteenth-century stock company, and as a matter of fact coincide with the character organization of the Regency comedies. But a close study of how Boucicault realizes his basically stock characters is a lesson in the range and flexibility of characterization possible to a fine craftsman even within a formulaic structure. All three plays double the romantic interest by having two pairs of lovers, and in each Boucicault carefully balances one pair against the other. Both pairs of lovers in *The Colleen Bawn*, for example, are tested by misapprehensions and misunderstandings, and Cregan's remorse and reform under the pressure of grief over Eily's presumed death are comically echoed in Anne Chute's misunderstanding of the object of Kyrle Daly's affections. The parallel romances of Beamish Mac Coul and Fanny Power and Shaun and Arrah in *Arrah-na-Pogue* and Robert Ffolliott and Arte O'Neal and Harry Molineux and Claire Ffolliott in *The Shaughraun* are similarly linked in a number of ways.

Despite our conception of melodrama as a black-and-white pitting of good against evil, the three Irish plays contain a good bit of moral complexity in their treatment of their central conflicts. The major antagonists in the plays are decent people. The Irish values of Eily O'Connor, for example, are balanced by the Anglo-Irish virtues of Anne Chute, and when they first meet, they feel an instant kinship:

Anne: We are rivals.
Eily: I am sorry for it.
Anne: So am I, for I feel that I could have loved you. (*CB*, 78)

The English Secretary in *Arrah-na-Pogue* behaves with magnanimity toward Colonel O'Grady and Fanny Power, intervenes to save Shaun's life, and gives Beamish Mac Coul a safe-conduct out of the country. Harry Molineux, in *The Shaughraun*, similarly blurs the line between the good Irish and the bad English. Perhaps in these characters, Boucicault is demonstrating the same tact that enabled him to please both North and South in America in *The Octoroon* in 1859. But the implication of this evenhandedness is that human decency can transcend political and social divisions.

The wholly negative characters in the Irish plays—Corrigan in *The Colleen Bawn*, Feeny in *Arrah-na-Pogue*, Harvey Duff in *The Shaughraun*—are so not because they belong to a particular faction, but because they lack any loyalty and are ready to betray either side in their own interest. All are what Mrs. Cregan in *The Colleen Bawn* calls "middle-men":

Mrs. Cregan: I hate this man; he was my husband's agent, or what the people here call a middle-man—vulgarly polite, and impudently obsequious.
Hardress: Genus squireen—a half sir, and a whole scoundrel.

Anne: I know—a potatoe on a silver plate: I'll leave you to peel him. (*CB*, 53)

The most memorable characters in the Irish plays, though, apart from the shaughrauns, are the ingenues—the Colleen Bawn, Arrah, and, to a lesser extent, the trio of Arte O'Neal, Claire Ffolliott, and Moya in *The Shaughraun*. In the latter play, the grace and wit, the earthiness and determination, of the earlier characters are divided among the three. But *The Colleen Bawn* and *Arrah-na-Pogue* revolve largely around a fascination with their title characters. Both Eily and Arrah combine a mythic resonance with a down-to-earth humanity. Both are simple and loving and yet capable, under stress, of great strength and determination. Curiously androgynous in some ways, both could be described in Arrah's curtain line:

> It is when a man is in trouble that the breast of his girl grows bowld agin misfortune. When *he's* wake, *she's* sthrong, and if he can purtect her wid his arm, she can cover him wid her heart. It's then she is full of sinse an' cuteness—for her heart gets into her head, and makes a man of her entirely. (*A*, 169)

The idealization of Eily and Arrah, their identification by epithets, and their roles in their plots suggest that they are both incarnations of Ireland, versions of the Dark Rosaleen. The competition of Myles-na-Coppaleen and Hardress Cregan for Eily in *The Colleen Bawn* suggests that the ultimate object of their rivalry is Ireland itself. It is hardly a competition. Eily, like Ireland, is firmly in the hands of the Anglo-Irish Cregan, but he is unworthy of her, and it is only through the faith and the bravery of the native Irish Myles that she can be saved from Danny Mann, the shadow of Cregan's own shallow selfishness. Similarly, in *Arrah-na-Pogue*, it is their love for Arrah (Ireland) that saves both her foster-brother Beamish Mac Coul and her lover Shaun, as her kiss, passing a message of escape from her lips to his, had saved Beamish once before (in a scene that Joyce loved and returned to again and again in *Finnegans Wake*). It is not that these simple plays are consistent allegories—allegory was hardly Boucicault's intention—but they take on a distinct coloring from Irish patriotic symbolism.

The shaughraun figures in the Irish romances are also touched with the symbolic. The shaughrauns owe something to the Tony Lumpkins of English social comedy and perhaps even more to the Jonathans and Moses of the American stage. But they transcend their origins in buffoonery to become moral touchstones of their plays. Boucicault's progressive development of this character is reflected in his titles, moving from the plays named for their heroines to the simple *The Shaughraun*. The shaughrauns play increasingly important roles in the three plays, ultimately constituting a symbolic male figure to balance the feminine personifications of Ireland. Myles-na-Coppaleen is a secondary though fascinating figure in *The Colleen Bawn*. Boucicault picked up the character and his name ("Miles of the Little Horses") from Griffin, but he gave him an altogether original function in the plot, not only to save Eily from Danny Mann in the water cave but also to stage-manage Eily's disappearance and providential reappearance in time to save Cregan. Myles, like his successors, is a creature of nature, ill at ease in the village but perfectly at home on the rocky mountain above the action: his bed, he says, is "on the mountain above—the bolster is stuffed wid rocks, and I'll have a cloud round me for a blanket" (95). A moonshiner by trade, he has his still in an eerie water cave, where Danny Mann tries to kill Eily and where Myles is able to save her. George Rowell's comments on the integral nature of Boucicault's sensation scenes are to the point here: the fundamental conflicts of the play are enacted here in the clash between Myles and Danny for the soul and life of Eily in an elemental, dreamlike environment.[8]

Shaun the Post, in *Arrah-na-Pogue*, is a very different shaughraun; indeed, as Krause points out, he is hardly a shaughraun at all. He is a "fairly respectable mailman, and only too eager to become a domesticated husband. . . . It is only after Shaun is hauled off to prison and treated like a subversive rogue that he fortunately begins to act like one, resorting to such a display of guile and comic bravado that the play quickly comes alive with spontaneous mirth" (Krause, 34). His trial scene (2.5) is so brilliant a confrontation of established tyranny and anarchistic good sense that Shaw paid it the compliment of imitation in *The Devil's Disciple*.[9] Again as in *The Colleen Bawn*, it is in the sensation scene that the fundamental conflicts and images of the play reach their clearest expression. Stone walls literally cannot hold Shaun as he escapes from his death cell and scales the walls of the prison tower, following the sound of Arrah's singing. Like Myles, he seems half a creature of nature, a mountain goat climbing the rocks to freedom. And his defiance of established authority, like Myles's moonshining and hunting, brings about a truer justice.

The touch of otherworldliness in Myles-na-Coppaleen and the solid earthiness of Shaun the Post meet in the title figure of *The Shaughraun*. Conn O'Kelly is on the one hand a lazy, trifling Stage Irishman not even a mother can fully approve of:

Mrs. O'Kelly: Conn niver did an honest day's work in his life—but dhrinking', and fishin', and' shootin', an' sportin', and love-makin'.
Moya: Sure, that's how the quality pass their lives.
Mrs. O'Kelly: That's it. A poor man that spoorts the sowl of a gentleman is called a blackguard. (*S*, 187)

On the other hand, Conn is an almost mythical figure who can stow away on a boat to Australia to "poach" his transported master back to Ireland, draw the fire of his Irish-turncoat pursuers, without serious injury, in order to save his friend, and attend his own wake and drink all the liquor (in another scene that impressed Joyce and that was recalled in *Finnegans Wake*).

The Shaughraun marks the full attainment of Boucicault's mature conception of melodramatic comedy. The world of the melodramatic comedies is no longer the smart, cynical world of the neo-Restoration comedies, in which the sole action turns around a glib young aristocrat winning a wealthy heiress. The Irish plays are incomparably broader in their background, incorporating political and social divisions as well as personal and romantic ones. And resolution comes not through ingenious trickery within the value system of the society but through the agency of figures outside the society—the shaughrauns. In the Regency comedies, we see voracious idlers in competition; when sons overthrow fathers, the only prospect is the perpetuation of the same values by another generation. In the Irish melodramatic comedies, the values of the society itself are brought into question and reformed in the direction of such human values as love, tolerance, and courage. The Regency comedies are powerfully paternal; the significant conflicts are between fathers and sons. The Irish comedies are just as powerfully maternal. Hardress Cregan resolves to marry Anne Chute against his better judgment in order to save his mother from a forced marriage with Corrigan, Arrah-na-Pogue is as much a maternal figure to Shaun the Post as a romantic one, intervening to protect him from authority, and Conn is a fatherless young man whose fecklessness is a sort of perpetual childhood under the protection of his loving but censorious mother. One element in the transition from the Restoration imitations to melodramatic comedy is perhaps the feminization of the comic spirit.

That Boucicault's conception of melodramatic comedy was not confined to Irish subjects is demonstrated by his adaptation of *Rip Van Winkle*, which he did for Joseph Jefferson in 1865, between *Arrah-na-Pogue* and

The Shaughraun. We lack reliable texts of the version of the play Jefferson was using before Boucicault's revision or of Boucicault's revision itself; the surviving text is generally agreed to have been much altered over the years by Jefferson himself. But it seems clear that Boucicault's major contribution to the play was to shift the emphasis from Rip as an old man to Rip as a young, lovable, irresponsible scamp. Here is Boucicault's own account of the revision:

> "Joe," I said, "this old sot is not a pleasant figure. He lacks romance. I daresay you make a fine sketch of the old beast, but there is no interest in him. He may be picturesque, but he is not dramatic. I would prefer to start him in a play as a young scamp, thoughtless, gay, just a curly-headed, good-humored fellow such as all the village girls would love and the children and dogs would run after." Jefferson threw up his hands in despair. It was totally opposed to his artistic preconception. But I insisted and he reluctantly conceded. Well, I wrote the play as he plays it now. It was not much of a literary production, and it was with some apology that it was handed to him. He read it, and when he met me I said: "It is a poor thing, Joe." "Well," he replied, "it is good enough for me." It was produced. Three or four weeks afterward he called on me, and his first words were "You were right about making Rip a young man. Now I could not conceive and play him any other way."[10]

Boucicault, in other words, made Rip into an American shaughraun.

The definitive history of American theatrical comedy remains to be written. But the American theatre does not appear to have carried the model of *Rip Van Winkle* and the Irish melodramatic comedies into the twentieth century. The most significant comic movements of the twentieth-century American theatre—the social comedy of the thirties, for example, musical "comedy," or Neil Simon's machine-made comic hits—seem to owe little to Boucicault's yoking of comedy and melodrama.

Melodramatic comedy, on the Boucicault model, did survive into the twentieth century in America in one place, however: in film. The theatrical origins of American film comedy have never been very fully studied; film historians have tended to emphasize the background of the early film comic actors in music hall and vaudeville. But short vaudeville sketches, though they could provide a model for individual routines and gags, provided no model for the extended structure of narrative comedy. Nicholas

Vardac's excellent study of the passing of the torch from theatrical to film melodrama might well be paralleled by a similar study of the theatrical sources of early film comedy. Boucicault died in 1890, on the threshold of the film era; the first screenings of the Edison-Armat vitascope took place in 1895 and 1896. Boucicault's plays were natural material for the earliest films. Joseph Jefferson in *Rip Van Winkle* was filmed "in eight episodes" in 1896, and Kalem Studios, between 1911 and 1913, filmed *The Colleen Bawn, Arrah-na-Pogue, The Shaughraun,* and *The Octoroon*.[11]

The combination of melodramatic incident and comic tone, focused around an outsider figure, characteristic of the films of Buster Keaton, Harold Lloyd, Harry Langdon, and preeminently Charlie Chaplin, are in many ways pure Boucicault. All four comedians, in their own inimitable ways, are "shaughrauns," and the richness of their social criticism depends upon the slant perspectives they take upon the societies through which they pass, as Conn the Shaughraun's view from the mountains gives him a perspective outside the divided societies he sees. The mixture of comedy, pathos, and thrills in early film comedy is thoroughly Boucicaultian as well. Chaplin's return to the road at the end of *The Tramp* and his reunion with Jackie in *The Kid* are scenes Boucicault would have recognized as similar to his own inclusive vision of life. And even Boucicault's sensation scenes found a place in early American film comedy. What, after all, are Harold Lloyd clinging to the parapet of a skyscraper high above the street or Buster Keaton clinging to the cowcatcher of a careening locomotive but Boucicault sensation scenes made even more sensational by the magic of the movies?[12]

Just before his death, Boucicault wrote an essay, published posthumously, "The Future American Drama." In many ways, it is a surprising statement to come from the master of sensation drama.

> Tragedy and high comedy will always be held in respect on the future American stage, but it seems probable that the drama of modern life, the reflex of the period, will prevail over every other kind of entertainment. This drama will present a character or a group of characters, not a complicated or sensational action, affording a physiological study by way of illustration, not by way of description. The ingenious comedy of intrigue and the drama of incident, the artifice of which resembles a mechanical contrivance, rather than the simple outcome and result of incidents flowing naturally to their catastrophe, has surfeited the audience with dramas and com-

edies that are really more like tricks on the cards, than exhibiting the game of life. Of this legerdemain, the French stage of the present century affords numerous examples. We are done with it.[13]

It may be that the creator of the onstage exploding steamboat and the onstage burning tenement was not altogether ingenuous in calling for a drama that deemphasized sensational action in favor of character. But history has been kinder to Boucicault's sensations than he himself was. His American legacy, like his Irish one, was a rich, inclusive popular comedy of both character and action that anticipated the impure dramatic forms of a complex and most impure age.

NOTES

1. Citations of Boucicault plays are to the following texts: *London Assurance* (New York: Dick and Fitzgerald, 1889); *Old Heads and Young Hearts* in *Plays by Dion Boucicault*, edited with an introduction and notes by Peter Thomson (Cambridge: Cambridge University Press, 1984); *The Colleen Bawn, Arrah-na-Pogue*, and *The Shaughraun* in *The Dolmen Boucicault*, ed. David Krause (Dublin: Dolmen Press, 1965); all hereafter cited in the text.

2. Robert Hogan, *Dion Boucicault* (New York: Twayne, 1969), 116.

3. Richard Fawkes, *Dion Boucicault* (London: Quartet Books, 1979), 78–111.

4. For a thoughtful interpretation of *The Octoroon* along these lines, see Gary A. Richardson, "Boucicault's *The Octoroon* and American Law," *Educational Theatre Journal* 34 (1982): 155–64.

5. For the term "shaughraun," Boucicault apparently nominalized the Irish participle *seachran* ("wandering"). A "shaughraun" is thus a wanderer or tramp—an outsider. See Krause, 37.

6. My reading of the Irish melodramatic comedies is indebted to Stephen M. Watt, "Boucicault and Whitbread: The Dublin Stage at the End of the Nineteenth Century," *Éire-Ireland* 18 (Fall 1983):23–53. Watt reads the plays, as I do, as myths, but emphasizes their fantasized treatments of the conflict between England and Ireland rather than their comic structures. Significantly, he refers to the plays as "comic melodramas" rather than "melodramatic comedies."

7. Bernard Shaw, "Dear Harp of My Country!" in *The Portable Bernard Shaw*, ed. Stanley Weintraub (New York: Viking, 1977), 111.

8. George Rowell, *The Victorian Theatre, 1792–1914* (Cambridge: Cambridge University Press, 1978), 57.

9. For a detailed study of Shaw's debt to Boucicault, see Martin Meisel, *Shaw*

and the Nineteenth-Century Theater (Princeton: Princeton University Press, 1963), 184–223 and 269–89.

10. Quoted in Philip C. Lewis, *Trouping: How the Show Came to Town* (New York: Harper and Row, 1973), 125–26.

11. A. Nicholas Vardac, *Stage to Screen: Theatrical Method from Garrick to Griffith* (Cambridge, Mass.: Harvard University Press, 1949), 169 and 187.

12. Thomson also notes Boucicault's affinities with cinema, 14.

13. "The Future American Drama," *The Arena* 2 (November 1890):650–51.

Society in Transition
FROM MANUSCRIPT TO PERFORMANCE

Daniel Barrett

T. W. Robertson's *Society* has long been considered a landmark in nineteenth-century English theatre, although it is more often cited than studied. The story of its production is briefly told. Robertson originally wrote the play for the Haymarket, where he intended it to succeed *David Garrick* (1864), his first London hit. But the manuscript was abruptly rejected by J. B. Buckstone, the Haymarket manager, and later turned down at several other West End theatres. Finally, through the intercession of his friend H. J. Byron, Robertson had the play accepted first at the Prince of Wales's Theatre in Liverpool, and with this production as a recommendation, at the rechristened and refurbished Prince of Wales's Theatre in London. There *Society* opened on 11 November 1865, marking the first of Robertson's six successful collaborations with Marie Wilton, which continued over the next five years with *Ours*, *Caste*, *Play*, *School*, and *M.P.* Given this checkered series of events, one might expect the original play to have undergone substantial changes before ever reaching the stage. Instead, a study of the various manuscripts, acting editions, and published reports shows that Robertson was adamant in seeing that his play, with some adjustments, remained faithful to his original conception.

Besides the matter of authorial intentions and alterations, *Society* poses other questions. Why, for instance, did Buckstone reject the manuscript in the first place? Also, if Robertson did not tinker much with the play, how was it performed so successfully at a theatre whose acting and production methods differed considerably from the Haymarket's? And most important, why did *Society* succeed at all? Recent critics have shown that many of the characters, themes, and stage conventions Robertson employed had been common fare in the Victorian theatre for the past thirty years.[1] However, reviewers and audiences alike felt they were seeing something new and stimulating, and contemporary impressions cannot be totally negated by our own perspective. To understand the appeal of *Society*, we must go beyond the text itself to visualize its full potential as a stage piece performed by a select company in a perfectly appropriate theatre. Only when placed in this sort of theatrical context can Robertson's achievement be appreciated or even understood.

Why did *Society* face such opposition? The story of Buckstone, who wrote "Rubbish" or some other profanity (illegible now) on the manuscript and predicted the play must fail wherever it was produced, is laughable in hindsight, but it is also quite incredible given the circumstances. Robertson had just supplied the Haymarket and its famous comedian, E. A. Sothern, with a comedy that had run for over two months, and a few weeks after it closed he was back with an original comedy that bore many resemblances to the *David Garrick* plot. In both plays, the main character has fallen in love with a woman whose family raises strong objections to his profession and social status—Garrick, after all, is an actor, and Sidney Daryl in *Society* is a poor journalist and "literary barrister." As a result, the rejected suitors indulge in drunken scenes—Sothern found these especially appealing—yet remain gentlemen in principle if not in fact. After some rather contrived complications, the family prejudices are resolved, although Daryl must win a parliamentary election, a baronetcy, and a substantial fortune to turn the trick.

Given these similarities, one must ask why Buckstone chose not to accept *Society* or suggest revisions, but to dismiss the play outright. Three possible reasons come to mind:

1. Buckstone disliked his role of John Chodd, Sr. Granted, the part offered little scope for Buckstone's talents in low comedy. But by 1864, Sothern had become the undisputed kingpin of the Haymarket company through his renowned impersonation of Lord Dundreary in *Our American Cousin*. Indeed, his celebrity had altered the chemistry of the Haymarket company, transforming it from a veteran ensemble troupe specializing in traditional English comedy to a company supporting one star.[2] It seems doubtful, then, that Buckstone would have refused the play solely because of dissatisfaction with his own part.

2. The play was ahead of its time. This is an attractive solution, especially in light of Robertson's later, more characteristic, plays at the Prince of Wales's. Certainly a few of the scenes in *Society* (such as the quiet love scene between Daryl and Maud Hetherington in act one) are more re-

strained and modern than one finds in most contemporary drama. But the play is also a formula comedy with many traditional comic types, absurd coincidences, strong curtains, and a romantic happy ending. Overall, *Society* is too much a mixture of old and new for anyone to suppose that a manager would consider it a radical departure in playwriting.

3. The "Owl's Roost" episodes were too controversial. Although he recommended the play to Marie Wilton, H. J. Byron told her that the London managers "were chiefly afraid of it . . . on account of a scene which the journalistic world would take offence at, and the critics would, beyond all doubt, condemn, as it contained sketches of men well known to the author and in 'Bohemia.'"[3] Byron's fears were well founded: many critics reacted harshly to what they saw as a gross caricature. Buckstone and his colleagues may well have viewed these scenes as theatrical poison. Since the Owl's Roost was too integral a part of the plot to cut or patch, the only solution was to reject the play. Although other factors may have contributed, the Owl's Roost seems to have been a major obstacle to managerial approval.

Robertson must have known this, but an examination of the play's progress in manuscript shows he was resolute in retaining the Owl's Roost scenes—and practically everything else he had written. Indeed, the most striking fact that emerges from comparing the original manuscript, dated 12 August 1864, with the license copy submitted to the Lord Chamberlain's office over a year later, is how little the play was revised prior to its London premiere.[4] Characters, scenes, dialogue, even detailed stage directions—most appear in the earliest draft exactly as they were executed in 1865 and finally published in the *Principal Dramatic Works* in 1889. One gets the feeling that Robertson had been contemplating this play for some time, knew what he wanted to say, and was determined to see the play through to production exactly as he wrote it. Miraculously, he found a manager, company, and theatre that let him do precisely that.

We have regrettably little information about how Robertson and Marie Wilton worked out their amiable partnership that permitted Robertson in effect to direct his own plays. No correspondence exists on the order of the Bulwer-Macready-John Forster letters so admirably collected and edited by Charles Shattuck in *Bulwer and Macready*. Robertson said nothing on the matter, and Marie Wilton wrote only that "my views of acting so entirely agreed with Mr. Robertson's that we encountered no difficulties whatever, and everything went smoothly and merrily" (*Bancrofts* 1:201). In any case, Robertson seems to have been a collaborative, not an autocratic, director.

Although he had definite ideas of how his comedy should be performed, he also trusted the actors' instincts and seems to have encouraged their suggestions. For their part, the young company regarded Robertson as an experienced playwright (although he had actually had few plays produced) and were more than willing to heed his instructions.[5] Squire Bancroft, for one, later acknowledged, "I would like to note how much the success I was fortunate enough to achieve was due to the encouragement and support I received from the author, who spared no pains with me, as with others, to have his somewhat novel type of characters understood and acted as he wished" (*Bancrofts* 1:202).

The text itself presented few problems. Marie Wilton had been charmed with Robertson's initial reading of the script, and she gives no hint that she objected to any of it—even to her own role of Maud Hetherington, a rather tame heroine by her standards. Yet it was probably her moderating influence that caused Robertson to revise some of the harsher or more satirical passages.[6] For instance, in the first of the two scenes in the Owl's Roost (2.1), Sidney Daryl leads the club members in a merry drinking song that includes, at least in the original manuscript, a verse entitled "Journalistic":

> When papers speak with puff and praise
> Of things and people now-a-days
> Of kings, quack-medicines, railroads, plays
> Old laws, inventions new
> Alliterative words, and fuss
> Big adjectives, terms curious
> Sound, fury, what's all this to us
> But cock-a-doodle doo.
>
> (2.1, f.19)

This verse may have been sung in the opening production (it also appears in the license copy), but it was replaced soon after by the "Commercial" verse that appears in all the printed versions. The manager or author may well have decided to delete this overt though mild piece of satire, thus hoping to appease those journalists who felt offended by the Owl's Roost scenes.

The most interesting excision, however, occurs in act three, when Daryl confronts Maud over her decision to marry the contemptible John Chodd, Jr. Daryl scolds Maud for her apparently mercenary pursuit of

Chodd's fortune, but as the manuscript shows, Robertson had a much more abrasive speech in mind:

> How can two beings live in a first floor over a shop, with but two bonnets a year and neither page, groom, or footman? Society requires those joys in plush [,] those beautiful boys in buttons. Some must have its comforts, its equipage, and opera. Go—attend them—chase him to his garret where the starveling mechanic and his wife lie, hungry in each other's arms. (3.3, ff. 58–59)

The depths of Daryl's sarcasm seems inappropriate for this scene, and might be a reflection of Robertson's own bitterness at the privation he and his family had suffered in the years before *David Garrick*. Certainly Robertson must have regarded the reception of *Society* as a bittersweet triumph, for his wife had died three months earlier from illness brought on and exacerbated by overwork and exhaustion. Robertson often has a great deal to say in his plays about the debilitating effects of poverty, but these particular lines were never spoken in the theatre.

Another alteration in the script involved shifting the location of act two, scene two, from the home of Sir Farintosh Fadileaf to that of Lord and Lady Ptarmigant. In the process, the roles of Fadileaf and his friend Colonel Browser were eliminated. This was a simple cost-cutting measure by the Prince of Wales's management, since the set for the Ptarmigants' house in 3.2 could be reused, and two extra and rather superfluous roles need not be cast. Still, Robertson must have been reluctant to let the characters go, for the printed acting edition preserves the Fadileaf-Browser scenes in quotation marks, with the author's instructions that "The lines between inverted commas can be omitted."[7] Robertson obviously felt the characters were important, but why? William Tydeman includes them in his recent edition of the play, believing that they "add a further stratum to Robertson's portrait of 'society.'"[8] They also inform us that the present ministry has been defeated and an election is imminent, preparing us for the events of act three. But in this case, plot development yielded to finances: judging from the playbills and notices, Fadileaf and Browser were never performed, either in the premiere or in revivals.

Aside from the loss of Fadileaf's house, Robertson must have been pleased with the scenery and appointments at the Prince of Wales's. In the seven months her theatre had been open, Marie Wilton had already gained a reputation for tasteful and appropriate stage decoration. Acting as his own director, Robertson probably worked closely with set designer Charles S. James to realize the scenes described in the manuscript, particularly the London square of 1.2 and the Owl's Roost. Not all reviewers were satisfied, of course, and in an oft-quoted passage, the *Pall Mall Gazette* had particular fun in pointing out the deficiencies.[9] But these remarks were hardly typical. Critics generally felt that the play's mounting was much better than average, and certainly superior to what Robertson would have received at the Haymarket.[10]

Even more significant was the size of the playhouse itself, one of the smallest in London, with a seating capacity of only 814. Visual effects like a sunset being reflected in windows of houses or the Owl's waiter delivering orders were greatly intensified by the proximity of every spectator to the stage. Moreover, the rendezvous between Sidney and Maud in act one, scene two, had an engaging air of romantic intimacy, as if the audience were eavesdropping on a private conversation. Robertson soon learned to exploit the unique atmosphere of this theatre and became the master of small, realistic scenes that could be best appreciated by spectators close to the action.

No perusal of the manuscripts or acting editions can reveal the single greatest adjustment Robertson faced in staging his play: the casting. Having written *Society* for the veteran Haymarket company, Robertson probably imagined Buckstone as Chodd, Sr., William Chippendale as Lord Ptarmigant, Henry Howe (or Henry Compton) as Tom Stylus, Nelly Moore as Maud, and Sothern as Sidney Daryl.[11] When rehearsals began at the Prince of Wales's, he faced a much younger and less experienced but also a more receptive and adaptable company. Marie Wilton and Sophie Larkin (who had created Lady Ptarmigant at Liverpool and was the sole holdover) were the only actors Robertson knew well, so he had to trust Marie Wilton's judgment for most of the cast assignments. Sometimes she chose poorly, as when she gave the part of Daryl to Sydney Bancroft (as he was then billed). Romantic leads were never Bancroft's forte. Rather, his worldly, ironic, cynical air would have made him a perfect choice for Tom Stylus, the part he always took in revivals and, by his own admission, gave him more pleasure to act than any other.[12] Despite the apparent mismatch between character and actor, Bancroft brought off the part well, although critics would soon tire of his rather stiff attempts at romantic passion and enjoy him far more in his "Bancroft parts" of Captain Hawtree, Jack Poyntz, Hugh Chalcot, and others.

With only one exception, the other roles were logically cast. John

Clarke, another refugee from Strand burlesque who had fled with Marie Wilton to the Prince of Wales's, embraced one of his few opportunities in straight comedy with the part of Chodd, Jr. Chodd has his slapstick moments, but the character as Robertson conceived him is a callous and vulgar soul vainly trying to cloak his true nature with genteel manners. Clarke impressed everyone by the subtlety of his performance. According to the *Daily Telegraph* (14 November 1865, p. 3), "Nothing could be better conceived than the illustration thus afforded of a boorish youth striving to ape the appearance of excessive gentility, and the numberless little touches by which the innate want of refinement was exhibited beneath the garb of constrained courtesy showed how carefully the actor had studied all the details that could give reality to the impersonation." Two experienced actors, Sophie Larkin and Fred Dewar, played the parts of Lady Ptarmigant and Tom Stylus with spirit and restraint. And everyone agreed that only Marie Wilton could have made Maud Hetherington an interesting heroine. Wilton must have been desperate indeed to stage a comedy that offered her so limited a starring vehicle. Yet reviewers unanimously praised the delicacy and poignancy of her performance, qualities far removed from the boisterous high spirits that would be her trademark in Robertson's later plays.[13]

The only conflict between Robertson and his new manager occurred over her wish to entrust Lord Ptarmigant to 21-year-old John Hare. "Tom did not like the idea *at all*, so young a man playing so old a one," she wrote years later to Clement Scott (*Yesterday* 1:604). Stubborn as he was with most production details, Robertson gave in this time. That was fortunate, for Hare succeeded not only in looking the part, but in turning an apparently one-dimensional character into a memorable personality. Almost every reviewer commented on the excellence of his performance, and one declared it entitled him "to rank with the masters of his profession."[14] One feels that because of his youth and inexperience, Hare might have been particularly eager to follow Robertson's instructions. Eventually he became the quintessential Robertsonian actor, playing a wide range of roles with the same meticulous attention to detail in makeup, costume, voice, and expression.

At a distance of well over a century, we can easily view the association of Robertson and the Prince of Wales's as an incredibly fortunate union, as if *Society* should have been written for that company and theatre in the first place. Robertson must have felt quite differently. Instead of opening at the Haymarket, the home of English comedy, the play would first appear at a small, out-of-the-way theatre still trying to find an identity, reputation, and audience. Instead of hearing his lines spoken by Sothern and the venerable Haymarket corps, he found himself directing a largely unknown and untested group of actors. One must remember, too, his bitter disappointment at being turned down at the Haymarket, no doubt aggravated by subsequent rejections elsewhere. A less flexible or resourceful playwright would simply have tossed the manuscript aside and gone back to journalism, or at the most, relegated it to the Prince of Wales's with no hope for its success and the deepest regret at what might have been. Instead, Robertson saw the opportunity that this unusual theatre and company presented, and thus reinvented the play in his own mind—not in the lines themselves, but in how they were delivered, how the characters appeared, and how the stage was decorated. Robertson deserves credit for adapting his art to theatrical circumstances so that eventually he would be called "a pre-Raphaelite of the theatre," a title peculiarly suited to his later comedies at the Prince of Wales's, but not to *Society*.[15]

Why, then, did *Society* prosper in the theatre of 1865? Critics from E. B. Watson to Michael Booth have discussed how Robertson's plays, both as texts and as stage performances, are in some ways highly derivative, owing a considerable debt to earlier plays and an evolving style of realistic acting and stage presentation. Booth has culminated this reaction to the old "revolutionary" view of Robertson by concluding "that Robertson confirmed existing trends rather than created new ones, that his comedies represented the exhaustion of an established tradition of writing rather than a new approach to comedy."[16] That Robertson drew on earlier character types, plots, and themes cannot be denied. In fact, this is only what one would expect. No innovative dramatist, at least one who hopes to get performed, can be a complete iconoclast in such a conservative institution as the theatre. But to proceed from this fact to the assumption that Robertson only completed what had already evolved is, in my opinion, a distortion of history. Contrary to George Rowell's belief that Robertson's work "was by no means seen as the milestone in English drama it now often appears," critics and audiences alike recognized in *Society* the start at least of something different, refreshing, and provocative.[17]

For one thing, the play represented a stunningly successful challenge to the supremacy of sensation drama in the London theatre of the 1860s. This fact is generally ignored, yet anyone who reads the *Report from the Select Committee on Theatrical Licenses and Regulations* (1866) can observe the universal acclaim given to sensation drama and its chief purveyor, Dion

Boucicault. Several witnesses stated they had found sensation drama the surest theatrical drawing card, not always to their satisfaction.[18] More than one manager echoed the opinion of E. T. Smith that "for a person to bring out a merely talking drama, without any action in it, or sensational effects, is useless; the people will not go to that theatre; they will go where there is scenic effect, and mechanical effects to please the eye" (Question 3865). Nobody stressed this theme more than Boucicault himself, as he grandly claimed he could easily supply all the West End theatres with his innovation of contemporary melodrama deftly constructed around a climactic sensation scene (Questions 4180–4181, 4195–4196). In the midst of such testimonies, one committee member asked Smith, "[I]s there not a piece which has been acted lately for a great many nights, called 'Society'? . . . Are you aware that that is as entirely a 'talking drama' as you can possibly put together? . . . That there is not a sensation scene from beginning to end, and that that piece has drawn for a great many nights?" Smith said he had never seen it, but the query shows that *Society* was indeed an exception to the existing theatrical rule (Questions 3901–3903).

Reviewers noted this same phenomenon. *The Times* (14 November 1865, p. 7) wrote that while sensation drama should not be condemned, neither should it enjoy a monopoly on the public. *Society* was one of those rare plays that could "entertain an audience with a style of drama that depends greatly on character, wit, and humour, and never goes beyond the tone of comedy for the sake of exciting pity or terror." Sensation drama could never have found a home at the Prince of Wales's in any case. The small stage and limited backstage area precluded the kind of special effects—fires, explosions, drownings, shipwrecks, earthquakes—that the genre required as its stock-in-trade. But Robertson, though not averse to attempting sensation drama himself, seems to have written in conscious reaction to its typically convoluted plots, unrealistic characters, and exploitation of spectacle and emotion.[19] Because of his own emphasis on lifelike characters and conversational dialogue, *Society* impressed its viewers as an intellectual comedy that required a finer sense of appreciation than most contemporary drama called for.[20]

If the lack of spectacle marked *Society* as a bold departure from theatrical fashion, the Owl's Roost represented its most unconventional element. In fact, the play seems to have been constructed around these two scenes, as though Robertson above all wished to pay tribute to the Bohemian society that had nurtured and supported him in the years before his success.

Nothing quite like the Owl's Roost had been seen on stage before. Robertson affectionately modeled the club and its denizens on his own favorite watering holes, the Arundel and Savage clubs. Clement Scott remembered watching the first performance with a friend, and as each member was introduced, they immediately recognized what person had served as the unwitting original for that character (*Yesterday*, 1:504–505). Moreover, Robertson's portrayal of club life was unvarnished and lightly satirical, with the members appearing to be social misfits who follow only two rules: moneymaking and fame are to be scorned, and drunkenness is an unmistakable sign of genius. In his edition of Robertson's plays, Michael Booth writes that journalists were delighted with the Owl's Roost.[21] Actually, the journalists hated it; the general public was delighted. Several reviewers seconded the feelings of one colleague who thought this portrayal, besides being absurd, "might well be left to be dealt with by those whom the dramatist has so unprovokedly and unworthily endeavoured to insult."[22] Robertson's supporters tried to soft-pedal the satire, but even their attempt to defend Robertson shows that Byron's original fears about these scenes were not misplaced. The critical outcry, if it had any effect at all, only served to make the scenes more enticing to the public. And over the years, it was the Owl's Roost that kept the play fresh and humorous, even as some of its other elements firmly dated the play.[23]

If the appeal of *Society* could be summarized in one word, however, it would be its *modernity*. This is not to say that the comedy was realistic, that audiences felt they were seeing a perfectly authentic representation of London high (and low) life, as critics have sometimes assumed. Rather, *Society* struck playgoers as a sophisticated, witty, charming comedy thoroughly in tune with its time. Partly this had to do with its originality of composition: not only was it free from sensational elements, but it was not even loosely based on a French original—a rare find indeed for 1865.[24] Partly the modern tone derived from the characters, the best of whom (Sidney Daryl, Tom Stylus, Chodd, Jr., the club members), although "sketched by a free and somewhat bold hand, are at least not the conventional beings who have so often figured on the boards, but are fresh studies from new models" (*LDT* 14 November 1865, p. 3). And partly the effect was a matter of the eye-pleasing stage decor and costuming. In Marie Wilton's words, "the elaborate and careful *dressing* of our plays astonished theatregoers, and was admitted by the critics to be a revelation"—at least by those young or ignorant enough to have forgotten Madame Vestris in her prime (*Bancrofts*, 1:203).

Most of all, *Society* seemed delightfully modern because of its terse, colloquial, sometimes biting dialogue, always one of Robertson's strengths as a playwright. Some of the lines are worthy of Wilde, as when Lady Ptarmigant rebukes Maud for detesting Chodd, Jr.: "What on earth has that to do with it? You wouldn't love a man before you were married to him, would you? Where are your principles?" More often, the memorable lines are tinged with anger, as when Sidney says of the Ptarmigants' fashionable soirée:

> Why man, this is a flesh market where the matchmaking mammas and chattering old chaperons have no more sense of feeling than drovers—the girls no more sentiment than sheep, and the best man is the highest bidder; that is, the biggest fool with the longest purse. (2.2)

Audiences found such lines daring and (to use the preferred term) cynical. One critic surmised that the "hollow tone of cynicism" was probably due to "a morbid condition of the writer's own mind,"[25] a fair assumption for anyone who knew Robertson.

People could forgive these outbursts, however, because for the most part Robertson's language ranged from funny to brilliant. Clement Scott gives the most graphic description of the mood in the theatre on opening night:

> When the curtain drew up, all fell back in their seats as usual, and seemed prepared for something good, perhaps, but still something of the old sort. But MR. ROBERTSON'S bright, sparkling dialogue, his home truths, his kindly affectation of cynicism, his similes, and his keen appreciation of the little weaknesses of the world we live in, soon woke up the audience from its conventional apathy, and then all appeared to bend forward in their seats, and after one look all round to see if the impulse was general, their faces seemed to say, "We have got some good stuff here!"[26]

Certainly the effect of the dialogue had much to do with the actors' well-trained delivery. But clearly Robertson had an excellent instinct and ear for humorous conversation, and for the next few years, his characters' speech gave the plays their tart, funny, thoroughly contemporary tone.

In the past, readers have come to *Society* expecting a revolution and finding only pleasant conformity. The reputation of the play has endured, rather than the play itself. Clement Scott, despite his obvious enjoyment, thought it "Not much of a play as plays went" (*Yesterday*, 1:489). Archer believed it inaugurated one of the three dramatic epochs he had witnessed in the nineteenth century; yet he found a revival in 1881 "melancholy," the play "a curiosity."[27] Even Robertson sensed the play's limitations, writing in 1868 that "'Society' is a piece only for London. It was a complete failure in America, and has been anything but a success in the provinces, except at Newcastle. It is a thoroughly 'Contrary' comedy requiring special acting and a special audience."[28] By that time, Robertson had improved on it as he grew more accustomed to the actors, atmosphere, and audience at the Prince of Wales's. But the later comedies only confirmed the principles that the first represented: a rejection of spectacle and burlesque in favor of original plots, unconventional characters, intelligent humor, and social satire. His well-deserved reputation as a challenging and innovative dramatist began with his refusal to compromise where *Society* was concerned. He simply outlasted the opposition until he could find a Marie Wilton who believed that "danger was better than dulness" (*Bancrofts*, 1:201), and together they fashioned a production remarkably faithful to the play that Robertson first envisioned.

NOTES

1. Martin Meisel, *Shaw and the Nineteenth-Century Theater* (Princeton: Princeton University Press, 1963), 71–74; Michael R. Booth, *English Plays of the Nineteenth Century*, 5 vols. (Oxford: Clarendon Press, 1969–1976), 3:33–43; Errol Durbach, "Remembering Tom Robertson (1829–1871)," *Educational Theatre Journal* 24 (1972):284–88; Michael R. Booth, "T. W. Robertson," in Robertson, *Six Plays* (Ashover: Amber Lane Press, 1980), vii–xxiii.

2. Although Buckstone refused to admit that Sothern's ascendancy had detracted from the Haymarket's emphasis on "a well-acted play, with every part well sustained," this fact was abundantly clear to those testifying before the Select Parliamentary Committee in 1866. The committee, convened to review licensing procedures for theatres and music halls, received testimony from thirty-three witnesses on practically every theatre-related topic, including the current state of acting. E. T. Smith, referring to the monetary success of London managers, said, "Mr. Buckstone is particularly lucky; he has got Mr. Sothern, and people run after him." The effect on acting standards was less salutary, according to Frederick Tomlins. When asked why there were no more wonders of the stage, he replied, "We have got Mr. Sothern and his Lord Dundreary" (*Report from the Select Committee on Theatrical Licenses and Regulations* [1866; reprint, Shannon: Irish University Press, 1970], Questions 3531, 3896, 6902). Further references to this report will be identified in the text by question number.

3. Squire and Marie Bancroft, *Mr. & Mrs. Bancroft On and Off the Stage*, 2 vols. (London: Richard Bentley, 1888), 1:200. All quotations from this text, hereafter abbreviated *Bancrofts*, will be followed by volume and page numbers in the text.

4. The holograph manuscript now resides at the Shakespeare Birthplace Trust, Stratford-upon-Avon, as MSS.82.5 ROB, having been presented to the Shakespeare Memorial Library by T. Edgar Pemberton in 1898. The question arises whether this is *the* manuscript or simply a later draft of the play. But several pieces of evidence—the date, the blotted-out "Rubbish" (apparently opposite f. 2), commentary by Robertson's contemporaries—all testify to this being the only draft Robertson ever wrote or submitted to managers. This fact nearly had disastrous consequences when the play was temporarily misplaced just before Robertson showed it to Alexander Henderson, who first produced it in Liverpool. (See T. W. Robertson, "Memoir," in *The Principal Dramatic Works of Thomas William Robertson*, 2 vols. [London: Sampson Low, 1889], 1:xli.) The license copy is in the Lord Chamberlain's Collection, Department of Manuscripts, British Library (Add. MS. 53046/E).

5. Daniel Barrett, "T. W. Robertson's Plays: Revisions to Nicoll's Handlist," *Nineteenth Century Theatre Research* 11 (1983):93–103.

6. We have no evidence that Marie Wilton actually intervened in this way, and she stated that "[Robertson] and I never once during the whole of our acquaintance knew what it was to have an angry word." However, in her "Personal Notes on Robertson" published in the Bancrofts' memoirs, she dwelled almost entirely on Robertson's spiteful nature and acerbic sense of humor, both of which were entirely alien to her own buoyant personality (*Bancrofts*, 1:321–24). One can easily imagine her quietly insisting that anything too insulting or sarcastic be revised or excised from a script.

7. *Society* (1866). Lacy's Acting Edition of Plays, vol. 71, no. 1060:28. All subsequent quotations are taken from this edition.

8. *Plays by Tom Robertson* (Cambridge: Cambridge University Press, 1982), 36.

9. "[O]ne does not expect to find in Tottenham-court-road the elegance which Madame Vestris exhibited at the Lyceum; but we may reasonably expect to see a fashionable drawing-room in the 'noble mansion' of Lord Ptarmigant furnished with more than one chair, and with a carpet of visible proportions. . . . The scarcity of furniture, by the way, is the only explanation of the fact that his lordship returns to the stage in one scene for the purpose of carrying off the one chair above mentioned" (17 November 1865, p. 10).

10. Recalling the Haymarket and Adelphi theatres of 1860, Clement Scott wrote, "The scenery at their theatres was poor, the wardrobes hopelessly inefficient, and the casting of a play a matter of apparent indifference" (*The Drama of Yesterday and To-day*, 2 vols.[London: Macmillan, 1899], 1:360). All quotations from this text, hereafter abbreviated *Yesterday*, will be cited by volume and page numbers in the text. See also the *Era*, 12 November 1865, p. 15; *Morning Star*, 13 November 1865, p. 3; *Observer*, 12 November 1865, p. 6.

11. Robertson, "Memoir," xxxix.

12. Marie and Squire Bancroft, *The Bancrofts: Recollections of Sixty Years* (1909; reprint, New York: Benjamin Blom, 1969), 84.

13. See, for example, the *Morning Star*, 13 November 1865, p. 3; and *Illustrated Times*, 18 November 1865, p. 311.

14. *Illustrated Sporting News and Theatrical Review*, 18 November 1865, p. 582.

15. William Archer, *The Old Drama and the New* (1923; reprint, New York: Benjamin Blom, 1972), 260.

16. *English Plays of the Nineteenth Century*, 3:42.

17. George Rowell, *Theatre in the Age of Irving* (Totowa, N.J.: Rowman and Littlefield, 1981), 54.

18. *Report from the Select Committee*, Questions 3706, 4553, 4944, 5089–5090, 6245–6246.

19. Daniel Barrett, "T. W. Robertson [1829–1871]: The Dramatist as Critic," *Victorian Periodicals Review* 14 (1981):144–49.

20. *New-York Daily Tribune*, 26 February 1866, p. 8.

21. "T. W. Robertson," ix.

22. *Morning Post*, 13 November 1865, p. 2. See also *Era*, 12 November 1865, p. 15; *Observer*, 12 November 1865, p. 6; *Daily News*, 13 November 1865, p. 2; and *Sunday Times*, 19 November 1865, p. 3.

23. William Archer, *English Dramatists of To-Day* (London: Sampson Low, 1882), 22–24.

24. As noted in *Daily Telegraph*, 13 November 1865, p.3; *Sunday Times*, 19 November 1865, p.3; and *Saturday Review*, 23 December 1865, p.785.

25. *Illustrated Sporting News and Theatrical Review*, 18 November 1865, p.582.

26. *Fun*, 25 November 1865, p.101. Scott is identified through the Proprietor's Copy of *Fun* at the Huntington Library.

27. Archer, *The Old Drama and the New*, 338; Archer, *English Dramatists of To-Day*, 22.

28. ALS, Robertson to (?), 13 October 1868 (?), Harvard Theatre Collection.

W. S. Gilbert

THE COMEDIC ALTERNATIVE

Judith L. Fisher

Eight years after T. W. Robertson produced *Society* at the Prince of Wales, his cup-and-saucer, sentimental style had attained as much popularity as sensation drama. This more realistic style was pushing comedy and melodrama closer together, eventually to produce the "problem" plays of Arthur Wing Pinero and Henry Arthur Jones. Pure comedy, tempered by Robertson's realism, still mixed sentiment, pathos, broad humor, and melodrama. Gimmicks such as Irish or cockney dialects, sensation scenes, and low physical comedy characterized the funny subplot which accompanied the sentimental main plot. During the 1860s comedy became increasingly domestic and realistic but still emphasized love, marriage, and occasionally, as in Robertson's plays, social class conflict.

By the 1870s, William Schenk Gilbert could use these well-entrenched conventions to create his own kind of comedy. Gilbertian "topsy-turvy-dom," characteristic of the Gilbert and Sullivan operettas, turned familiar character types and sentimental plots upside down. "Little Buttercup," for instance, in *H.M.S. Pinafore* is a rosy English beauty who sells "tobaccy" to the sailors and hides "a canker worm . . . slowly but surely eating its way into [her] heart" (102).[1] Or, in the same operetta, "Deadeye Dick" claims that only his name makes him a villain. Pooh-Bah in *The Mikado* is under treatment for his exorbitant snobbery—but doesn't let it keep him from serving the tailor Koko for money. The same contradictions characterize Yum-Yum, the modest little school girl who admits, "Yes I am indeed beautiful! Sometimes I sit and wonder in my artless Japanese way, why it is that I am so much more attractive than anybody else in the whole world" (373). And, by way of a final example, *Ruddigore*, itself a send-up of gothic melodrama, has "professional bridesmaids" and eight "Bad

Barons of Murgatroyd" who are ghosts, and also turns the innocent hero into the villain. All these absurdities pervert standard character types just as the Gilbertian plot parodies the "logic" of the sentimental love plot by extrapolating from an unbelievable premise. In the midst of a ridiculous world, the characters move perfectly unconscious of any absurdity.

Engaged, produced in 1877, anticipates the topsy-turvydom of the operettas. The play uses stock characters from sentimental comedy and melodrama to produce hilarious comedy instead of sentimental sympathy.[2] The resulting play combines melodramatic extravagance, cup-and-saucer realism, character satire, and farce. In short, *Engaged* manipulates dramatic conventions as conventions instead of using them to tell a story.

The premise in *Engaged* is the Scotch marriage law. Cheviot Hill, the romantic lead, and Belinda Treherne, the romantic heroine, announce they are husband and wife to protect her from her now-unwanted fiancé. The problem centers on *where* they make their proclamation—England or Scotland—because they are standing in the garden of a cottage on the border. If in England, then their intended ruse *is* a ruse because English marriage required an officiating priest; however, in Scotland, a man and woman could simply announce that they were married. This opening premise snowballs into confusion when we meet Minnie Symperson and Maggie Macfarlane, Cheviot's other romantic interests. Maggie also has a lover, Angus Macalister, and Belvawney, the "villain," is not only in love with Belinda but has a vested interest in keeping Cheviot unmarried. Since this accidental plot device does not depend on any personality trait of the characters, no character "learns" anything; no moral stance is challenged. The only human motivation is Cheviot's tendency to fall in love with every woman he meets, which Gilbert reduced to a mechanical reaction. Cheviot's and Belinda's "marriage" in act one is purely an artificial "what if" problem, typical of farce.

Nineteenth-century farce relied upon a mechanical movement from a simple situation to a snowballing of complication upon complication. Individuals are powerless in farce; they are driven by the comic plot contrivance. However, farce's humor depends upon unreal caricatures, sometimes sporting ludicrous wigs and absurd names such as Patter and Clatter or Box and Cox, and overt gagging with the audience in asides and comic exposition. Gilbert used the license of farce—the audience expected farce to ridicule theatrical performance—to distance his audience, instead of creating sympathy as in Robertsonian comedy. A farce plot allowed him to play with the verbal and visual language of the stage—acting style, costuming, and speech—all signs to the audience of specific emotional traits, moral positions, and patterns of behavior. He kept the signs but eliminated the "Idea" which would have made the signs meaningful to his audience. Moreover, the characters are all delightfully unaware that there is the slightest inconsistency in their behavior or dialogue. In fact, Gilbert included an admonitory note to the cast which explicitly forbade the self-conscious style common to farce. "It is absolutely essential to this piece that it should be played with the most perfect earnestness and gravity throughout. There should be no exaggeration in costume, make-up, or demeanor, and the characters, one and all, should appear to believe, throughout, in the perfect sincerity of their actions."[3]

Engaged's standard procedure introduces the audience to a familiar character type who is played "straight" but who also manifests the character traits of an incongruous type. The conventions contradict each other and of course confound the audience's expectations. In addition, all the characters are overtly self-seeking and unconscious of any disparity between their cupidity and their theatrical rhetoric. Gilbert used the rural dialect of his virtuous peasants to suggest, then deny, their wholesomeness; the innocent twaddle of his ingenue, Minnie, does not disguise her financial acuity; and the inflated romantic rhetoric of his hero, heroine, and villain is deflated by their mundane greed. The conventional settings and farce structure accentuate these distortions.

Such parody naturally demands both an existing catalogue of conventional characters and an audience experienced in theatregoing. The familiarity of character types is suggested by Robertson's ten-part series, "Theatrical Types" (*Illustrated Times*, January–August 1864). His descriptions of dress, manner, and private life of the ingenue, romantic leads, and villain provide a key to Gilbert's parody. In addition, Gilbert made his own precedent for using the theatre to satirize itself and other art forms. Two of the pieces he wrote for the German Reed Gallery of Illustration and a farce preceding *Engaged* overtly parody artistic conventions. *Our Island Home* (1870), for example, put the Reeds' company onstage as themselves but also inverted their real personalities. The audience had to rely upon its knowledge of the Reeds to "supply the necessary implicit contrast to what was explicit on the stage."[4]

The German Reed production of *A Sensation Novel* (1871), the year after *Our Island Home*, also played this aesthetic game. Gilbert called each act of *A Sensation Novel* a "volume," the scenery the "frontispiece," the performances "vignettes," and German Reed's score "musical notes." Again, anticipating *Engaged*, the play assumed the audience would recognize the conventions Gilbert travestied. Jane Stedman summarizes Gilbert's aesthetic parodies:

> The first "volume" of *A Sensation Novel* opens with an Author, whom the Demon of Romance enables to turn out fifty books a year. The Demon supplies him with stereotyped characters: former human beings now expiating trivial faults by impersonating "those stock characters of the sensation novelist which are most opposed to their individual tastes and inclinations." At the end of each "volume" they are permitted to step out of their roles temporarily and to try and discuss or try and alter the plot whose unwilling subjects they are. (34–35)

The characters called "accepted types" by the Demon are the virtuous governess, the unemployed Sunday school teacher, the sensation detective, the wicked baronet, and Lady Rockalda—"the beautiful fiend with the yellow hair and the panther-like movement" (Stedman, 35). This emphasis on Lady Rockalda's blonde hair illustrates one way Gilbert undercut conventions: fair hair was usually reserved for the hero and heroine.[5] Villainesses wore raven tresses or red hair after the 1863 success of C. W. Hazlewood's adaptation of *Lady Audley's Secret*. But even this reversal is complicated because Rockalda's blonde hair actually suited the virtuous nature of the woman *forced* to play the role—but the hair was obviously a wig.

As *A Sensation Novel* illustrates, sentimental didacticism was an early victim of topsy-turvydom. *Engaged* strayed from the moral path of Robertsonian comedy even more distinctly because it was a direct parody of the conventions of sentimental comedy. To the *Athenaeum* this omission of the moral lesson resulted in "one of the most mirthful and original" plays of recent years.[6] The *Theatre*, on the other hand, complained that all Gilbert's early work was "very symmetrical, and very neat; but it is never very sincere, and in consequence, it can rarely, if ever, bring home to us any sincere conviction."[7] Some critics did in fact discover a strong strain of morality in *Engaged* and other of Gilbert's pre-operatic work and compared him to Aristophanes.[8] But a vague moral tone did not mean the plays taught morality—a crucial difference in nineteenth-century art. Consequently, even these critics censured Gilbert's "misanthropy" and "heartless cynicism," condemning his failure to have his characters reform themselves—the essence of didacticism. The *Illustrated London News*, for example, acknowledged the "vehement laughter" provoked by *Engaged*, but admonished Gilbert for omitting all virtue from the characters and ignoring his dramatist's duty to "correct certain faults or frailties."[9] But by ignoring this "duty" Gilbert paved the way for a new, parodic comedy of wit.

Gilbert's parody rose with the curtain. A "humble but picturesque cottage" (*Engaged*, 331) introduces the cliché of the virtuous but struggling peasant lad and lassie, personifying Jerome K. Jerome's claim that on stage, "all the virtuous people lived in cottages" (Jerome, 59). Maggie Macfarlane, "a pretty country girl," and Angus Macalister, "a goodlooking peasant lad," are apparently the picture of rural Scottish affection.

> *Angus:* Forgive me, Meg, for I speak honestly to ye. Angus Macalister is not the man to deal in squeaming compliments. Meg, I love thee dearly, as thou well knowest. I'm but a puir lad, and I've little but two braw arms and a straight hairt to live by, but I've saved a wee bit siller—I've a braw housie and a scrappie of gude garden-land.
> *Meg:* Angus, I'll be fair and straight wi'ee. Thou askest me for my hairt. . . . If thou, gude, brave, honest man, will be troubled wi' sic a puir little humble mousie as Maggie Macfarlane, why she'll just be the proudest and happiest lassie in a' Dumfries. (*Engaged*, 331–32)

Superficially, then, Angus and Maggie seem an exaggerated version of the pastoral hero and heroine, but their own words undercut these stereotypes.

Like any worthy sentimental hero, Angus is prone to tears. Seven times in the play, Angus is weeping or wiping his eyes and drawing attention to it by a line of dialogue. This sensitivity parodies a standing convention of the romantic dramatic character whose "sensibility to outward impressions" was the "true mark of the noble mind," according to Joseph Donohue.[10] But Angus's weeping bedews unconventional situations. His "honest tears" lubricate his willingness to sell Maggie to Cheviot for two pounds. His tears of joy are also an ironic accompaniment to his way of life as, weeping, he says to Maggie's mother:

> I'm a fairly prosperous man. What wi' farmin' a bit land, and gillieing odd times, and a bit o' poachin' now and again and what wi' my illicit whiskey

still—and throwin' trains off the line, that the poor distracted passengers may come to my cot, I've mair ways than one of making an honest living. (*Engaged*, 332)

The irony of "honest" is unmistakable, because "honest" has already been used five times to describe Angus. His demeanor and delivery present him as the worthy peasant hero, but the audience recognizes his similarity to a rural rascal like Luke the Labourer. The parody would be even more obvious to an audience of 1877 already familiar with the name: Robertson's Angus MacAlister in *Ours* (1866) was a brave Scottish officer played by Bancroft as a straightforward, sentimental role with no dialect.

Like Gilbert's Angus, Maggie starts out true to her heroine type—the virtuous peasant girl like Boucicault's Irish beauty, the Colleen Bawn. But Gilbert stretches Maggie's self-avowed modesty until it becomes vanity. She is the prototype for Rose Maybud in *Ruddigore*, but where Rose consults her etiquette book to justify her selfishness, Maggie's own "honest" nature rationalizes her cupidity. Maggie describes herself as a "puir-brown hill-side lassie" who dislikes flattery. True to the type of the village heroine, she is beset (she thinks) by designing aristocrats. Conventionally, Belvawney as the villain should try to seduce Maggie and she should resist, so she assumes that "he means her harm" when all he wants is the answer to the simple question, "What constitutes a Scotch marriage?" Maggie imagines the seduction, insisting "I canna be your bride." Maggie's willful misunderstanding destroys her credibility as a serious heroine and distances the audience.

Gilbert completely reverses this convention when Cheviot Hill, the "hero," arrives. Cheviot not only tries to seduce Maggie, but her very "gudeness" leads her into the flirtation. Since the opening scene has established "puir humble" Maggie as a "verra gude girl" (*Engaged*, 334), we expect her assent to Cheviot's "You *are* a good girl, are you not?" But while Maggie is explaining that she is "a much better girl than nineteen out of twenty in these pairts" [all "gude girls too"], Cheviot gets his arm around her waist, kisses her, and she thanks him (*Engaged*, 334). The audience naturally wonders what Maggie and her friends are good *at*. Maggie's modest "I canna tell a lie" manner also "forces" her to admit she is "remarkably pretty, and I've a verra neat figure" (*Engaged*, 341). Her protestations of modesty and fear of seduction dissolve in her practicality: she advises Angus to sell her for two pounds and later sues Cheviot for breach of promise. She is, moreover, remarkably ready to change affections, saying to Cheviot immediately after parting from Angus, "Oh sir, my happiness is in your hands noo; be kind to the puir lassie who loves ye sae weel" (*Engaged*, 345).

Maggie's urban counterpart, Minnie Symperson, at first seems just as angelic. True to the stereotype of the ingenue, Minnie dresses in light colors (usually white) and wears her hair down her back. The common epithets and titles applied to her are "lamb," "little Dickey-bird," "wren," "robin," and "little bird." Minnie's description of herself as "simple little Minnie" gives us the same kind of clue to the nature of her inconsistency as "honest" applied to Angus and "gude" applied to Maggie. Minnie is anything but simple. Her baby-talk delivery is contradicted by her sophisticated knowledge of finance and shrewd manipulative ability:

> Papa, dear, Cheviot is an all but perfect character, the very type of knightly chivalry; but he *has* faults and among other things he's one of the worst-tempered men I ever met in all my little life. Poor simple little Minnie thought the matter over very carefully in her silly childish way, and she came to the conclusion, in her foolish little noodle, that, on the whole, perhaps she could work it [getting a financial settlement] better after marriage, than before. (*Engaged*, 351)

Minnie also knows exactly how much money Cheviot has—"£2000 a year from shares in the Royal Indestructible Bank." When Cheviot is supposedly ruined, this innocent announces to her Papa,

> Unless your tom-tit is very much mistaken, the Indestructible was not registered under the Joint-Stock Companies Act of sixty-two, and in that case the shareholders are jointly and severally liable to the whole extent of their available capital. Poor little Minnie don't pretend to have a business head, but she's not *quite* such a donkey as *that*, dear Papa. (*Engaged*, 374)

When Cheviot is found not to have been ruined, "poor little Minnie" demands proof positive. And, in a perversion of dramatic convention, the ingenue is renounced by the romantic lead because she is mercenary.

Minnie and Maggie share the conventions of the innocent virgin. While Maggie is the country belle, Minnie is the sheltered upper-middle-class sentimental heroine. Their similar names emphasize their similar types. The "ie" diminutive suggests their vulnerability and innocence. "Minnie," in particular, suggests smallness and frailty, while "symper" brings to mind any number of Victorian child-women (Dickens's Dora in

David Copperfield). A general examination of nineteenth-century drama indicates a naming pattern which alerted audiences to the degree of a character's sophistication. Innocent heroines usually have simple one- or two-syllable names, often ending in phonetic "a" or "i" (that is, "i," "y," or "ie"). They are known throughout the play by their Christian names as if to underscore their childlike natures. T. W. Robertson's heroines are cases in point. Maud (*Society*, 1865), Mary (*Ours*, 1866), Eva (*Progress*, 1869), and Bella and Naomi (*School*, 1869) are all "white muslin" types, to use Robertson's term from his *Illustrated Times* series (4:107). Young, innocent, sometimes preyed upon, but always naive, girls named May (*The Ticket-of-Leave Man*, 1863), Ida or Lotty (*Two Roses*, 1870), or Lucy (*A Pair of Spectacles*, 1890) never come to harm in comedy and usually end up with the hero.

The more sophisticated heroine has a more elaborate name (often French), such as Gilbert's Belinda Treherne. Often, as is also the case in *Engaged*, she is referred to as "Miss" or "Mrs." for at least part of the play. A heroine named Georgina (*Money*, 1840), Valeria (*All That Glitters Is Not Gold*, 1851), Mrs. Montressor (*An Unequal Match*, 1857), Blanche (*Ours*, 1866), Mrs. Eddystone (*The Woman of the World*, 1868), Seraphina or Amanda (Robertson, *Illustrated Times*, 4:107) is likely to have romantic pretensions or be worldly wise, and, in either case, to be more experienced. Gilbert played on this tradition in earlier plays, naming his villainess in *A Sensation Novel* Lady Rockalda and contrasting in *Tom Cobb* (1875) the sentimental Caroline with the down-to-earth Matilda—called 'Tildy. This naming convention leads naturally to the suspect "Mmes" of Jones and Pinero, Mrs. Dane, Mrs. Tanqueray, and Mrs. Ebbsmith. Wilde also uses the convention with Gilbert's ironic twist in *The Importance of Being Earnest*, playing the urban sophisticate Miss Gwendolyn Fairfax against the not-so-innocent ingenue Cecily.

Belinda Treherne, called Miss Treherne in act one, lives up to the pretensions suggested by her name. We meet her when she is running away from one suitor with another suitor, Belvawney. She marries yet a third, Cheviot Hill. Belinda travesties that "stately creature, with high forehead, haughty mien, and thrilling voice"—the Leading Lady (as described by Robertson). In tragedy she is "clad" (Robertson claims she is never "merely dressed") in either "heavy, massive black velvet, or white, aerial, floating, breezy muslin" (4:107). As expected, Belinda, having literally "lost" Cheviot, enters in act two, "dressed in stately and funereal black."

Belinda's character introduces the second variety of Gilbert's theatrical parody. While Angus, Maggie, and Minnie undercut the conventions of "character parts," and light comedy, Belinda, Cheviot, and Belvawney travesty melodrama conventions which developed from the more extravagant romantic style. Their characters combine romantic excess with more mundane Robertsonian realism. The antithetical styles are not only devalued through this contrast, but also debased by Gilbert's addition of a strong streak of greed. As with the comedic parodies, it is not a case of one type triumphing over another, but both types being ridiculed.

Speaking style again plays a large part in this aesthetic game. Instead of dialect or baby-talk, romantic poetic diction was Gilbert's target. Belinda, Cheviot, and Belvawney all spout Gilbert's version of melodramatic rhetoric which stemmed from romantic tragedy. The exaggeration of both diction and delivery was expected of romantic characters because poetic drama, according to Dion Boucicault, "assumes that the dialogues are uttered by beings larger than life, who express ideas that no human being could pour out."[11] Alan S. Downer noted one actor's recollection that romantic diction became so pervasive that actors offstage greeted each other with "Let me grasp that manly hand" instead of "How are you?"[12] The bombastic effects of such exaggeration when integrated into "cup-and-saucer" comedy may be imagined.

Gilbert satirized not just the style but also the substance of the Romantic Heroine and Hero. Love was the endless topic of the Leading Lady in melodrama. Her passion is summed up by Laura, the heroine of Augustin Daly's *Under the Gaslight* (1867):

> Let the woman you look upon be wise or vain, beautiful or homely, rich or poor, she has but one thing she can really give or refuse—her heart. Her beauty, her wit, her accomplishments she may sell to you—but her love is the treasure without money and without price.[13]

Laura's is the battle cry of hundreds of Victorian heroines. Their love, even if at the risk of remaining untold, is never to be tainted with mercantilism. Such scruples keep Clara, in one version of *Money*, from true happiness—temporarily:

> You know how fearful is my character . . . yet I would lay this hand upon the block—I would walk barefoot over the ploughshare of the old ordeal—to save Alfred Evelyn one moment's pain. But I have refused to share his poverty, and I should die with shame if he thought I had grown enamoured of his wealth. (*Money*, 70–71)

Resembling these heroines, and modeled after Gilbert's Caroline Etherington of *Tom Cobb*, Belinda lives by excessive passion. Compare, for instance, Caroline's discussion of her lover's soul with Belinda's passionate speech to Belvawney.

> *Caroline:* . . . [His soul is] Like the frenzied passion of the antelope! Like the wild-fire of the tiger lilly! Like the pale earnestness of some lovesick thundercloud that longs to grasp the fleeting lightning in his outstretched arms! (*Tom Cobb*, 270)

Belinda's prose is less nonsensical, but Gilbert made her typicality more apparent by paradoxically linking her passion to her pecuniary interest and by reducing her speeches to formulae:

> I love you madly, passionately; [she says to Belvawney] I care to live but in your heart; I breathe but for your love; yet, before I actually consent to take the irrevocable step that will place me on the pinnacle of my fondest hopes, you must give me some definite idea of your pecuniary position. I am not mercenary, heaven knows, but business is business. (*Engaged*, 335)

Every protestation of love for Belvawney descends abruptly from the heights of Romance. Belinda's "impetuous passion" (335), "imperishable ardour" (336), her "rapture that thrills every fibre of [her] heart" (347), concludes, mock heroically, in a question of "business."

Belinda's sorrow is equally poetic and mocked in a similar formula. Dressed in her "funereal black," her tones become stately and slightly Shakespearean. To tell Minnie's father that she wants to see Minnie (mistaking him for the butler), Belinda intones, "Say that one on whose devoted head the black sorrows of a long lifetime have fallen, even as a funeral pall, craves a minute's interview with a dear old friend" (*Engaged*, 352). Her poetic pretensions are destroyed by the ensuing tart-eating scene wherein Belinda's indescribable sorrow at losing Cheviot is comically punctuated by her gluttony. This ludicrous contrast was the model for Wilde's voracious Algernon in *The Importance of Being Earnest*. Belinda eats constantly during the scene, playing tag with the tarts around the room as Minnie moves them out of her reach. Between nibbles, Belinda uses—or overuses—the standard tragic device of the rhetorical question. The collision between rhetorical excess and tart-eating reduces the traditional situation of the distraught, deserted heroine to absurdity.

> Maybe he [Cheviot] is dead; in that case I am a widow. Maybe he is alive; in that case I am a wife. What am I? Am I single? Am I married? Am I a widow? Can I marry? Have I married? May I marry? Who am I? Where am I? What am I? What is my name? What is my condition in life? If I am married, to whom am I married? If I am a widow, how came I to be a widow, and whose widow came I to be? Why am I his widow? What did he die of? Did he leave me anything? If anything, how much, and is it saddled with conditions? Can I marry again without forfeiting it? Have I a mother-in-law? Have I a family of step-children, and if so, how many, and what are their ages, sexes, names, and dispositions? These are the questions that rack me night and day, and until they are settled, peace and I are not on terms! (*Engaged*, 354)

Gilbert punctured the idealized morality of the Heroine when he confronted her with Cheviot and Belvawney, both of whom she has professed to love forever. As a Heroine she cannot be false, so she is indeed true—to both.

> Cheviot, I love you with an irresistible fervour that seems to parch my very existence. I love you as I never loved man before, and as I can never hope to love man again. But in the belief that you were ruined I went with my adored Belvawney before the registrar, and that registrar has just made us one. (*Engaged*, 382)

She reverses the position but keeps the terms equal when she discovers that she is in fact married to Cheviot.

> Belvawney, I love you with an intensity of devotion that I firmly believe will last while I live. But dear Cheviot is my husband now; . . . Cheviot—husband—my own old love—if the devotion of a lifetime can atone for the misery of the last few days, it is yours, with every wifely sentiment of pride, gratitude, admiration, and love. (*Engaged*, 383–84)

Belinda is not even true to her rhetorical type, because greed undercuts her romanticism. Further, the cup-and-saucer heroine who eats tarts leaves the impression that her romantic protestations are only a role. Belinda is like the characters in *A Sensation Novel* who, through no fault of their own, are forced to play antithetical roles. Regardless of the situation, Belinda must speak according to type even though her typical speeches contradict themselves.

Cheviot Hill, a type of the romantic hero, echoes Robertson's description of the Walking Gentleman: "a well-dressed young fellow, always in love. With him 'circumstances over which he has no control' . . . invariably make the course of true love run as rough as can be" (6:187). Gilbert took Robertson and the tradition literally. Cheviot is the pawn of the farcical marriage vow, Belvawney's mesmeric eyes, and of his own mechanical love-at-first-sight habit. This last is a Gilbertian parody of the convention wherein one sight of the heroine immediately enraptures either the hero or the villain. A classic early example of the syndrome is Crosstree, the villain in Douglas Jerrold's *Black Ey'd Susan*. Crosstree has tried to accost Susan, not knowing her, and the result is inevitable: "The wife of a sailor! wife of a common seaman! why she's fit for an admiral. I know it is wrong, but I will see her—and come what may, I must and will possess her" (*Susan*, 21). Even Robertson the "realist" used this convention. In *School*, Lord Beaufoy and Bella experience spontaneous combustion, although Robertson ignites the fires through stage business instead of overt declamation.

Like his predecessors, Cheviot is swept off his feet—but by every woman he sees. Gilbert used the same formulaic technique, emphasized by recurring capitals for important words.

> I love that girl, madly, passionately, irresistibly. She is my whole life, my whole soul and body, my Past, my Present, and my To Come. I have thought for none but her; she fills my mind, sleeping and waking. (*Engaged*, 338)

This eloquent description of Cheviot's passion for Minnie also applies to Maggie five minutes after they meet. And, of course, Belinda becomes Cheviot's "light of my future life, the essence of every hope, the tree upon which the fruit of my heart is growing—my Past, my Present, my Future, my own To Come" (364). Cheviot's flights of rhetoric recall many sentimental heroes like Alfred Evelyn in *Money* who rhapsodizes with similar fervor over his lost love, Clara:

> Look you, this is life! The eyes that charmed away every sorrow—the hand whose lightest touch thrilled to the very core—the presence that, like moonlight, shed its own hallowing beauty over the meanest things: a little while—a year, a month, a day, and we smile that we could dream so idly. All—all—the sweet enchantment, known but once, never to return again, vanished from the world! (*Money*, 84)

Cheviot's "once" is often. His proclivity is ironic because he actually has difficulty getting himself married. The farcical situation so entangles him that by the last scene of the play, Maggie is suing him, he has rejected Minnie, and Belinda has married Belvawney. Cheviot feels "cursed" and with the "deadly calm" of heroic resolve prepares to shoot himself.

The clearest example of the Gilbertian technique in *Engaged* is Belvawney, a masterpiece of rhetorical and "typical" parody. In the first place, his name would have sounded familiar to his audience, recalling Charles Dickens' Belvawney in *Nicholas Nickleby*: "Miss Belvawney, who seldom aspired to speaking parts, and usually went on as a page in white silk hose, to stand with one leg bent and contemplate the audience."[14] Gilbert's Belvawney travesties the Heavy Man who in turn is modeled on the tragedian of the romantic stage. Unlike those of the rest of the cast, Belvawney's costume departed from the ordinary. As the engraving of Harold Kyrle as Belvawney shows, he was immediately typed as a villain by his black greatcoat, black hat, black trousers, black hair, and black moustaches.

This "black" villain has a respectable history, originating in the dark Byronic hero. The image was so familiar that Dickens could parody the type in *Nicholas Nickleby* in 1839. Mr. Lenville, Dickens's "first tragedy," was "a dark-complexioned man, inclining indeed to sallow, with long black hair, and very evident indications . . . of a stiff beard, and whiskers of the same deep shade" (297). The type also resembles Edwin Booth and Henry Irving as either brooding hero (Hamlet) or dark-dyed villain (Iago). Irving "wore his blue-black hair in a lumpish thatch" to set off his "pale, pronounced profile." Booth had the same dark hair, pale face, and intense eyes.[15] Belvawney adds green spectacles to increase his mystery. The spectacles cover his mesmeric eyes with which he controls Cheviot, anticipating George DuMaurier's *Trilby* (1894).

Belvawney's dark costume and supernatural power are only two exaggerations of the "villain"—his acting is also larger than life. Kyrle muffles his black cloak around his chin, hiding his hands as if to glide off the stage with the traditional demonic laugh. When he woos Belinda, Belvawney, in the best Richard III manner, stoops to leer up into her face. He typically observes the action peering out from underneath the lowered brim of his hat. And when he threatens Cheviot with his mesmeric power in act two (*Engaged*, 363), his doubled posture, outstretched arms, and claw-like hands suggest Count Dracula hovering over his latest victim. Belvawney uncovers his eyes "with melodramatic intensity," taunts Cheviot "with

Harold Kyrle as Belvawney, *Engaged*, act 1. (From the *Illustrated Sporting and Dramatic News*, 20 October 1877. By permission of Michael Booth and the Victoria and Albert Museum.)

The end of act 1 and a collage of scenes from *Engaged*. (From the *Illustrated Sporting and Dramatic News*, 3 November 1877. By permission of Michael Booth and the Victoria and Albert Museum.)

fiendish exultation," and caps the scene, "Ha, ha, ha, ha, . . . with a Satanic laugh" (*Engaged*, 363). (Robertson had written in the *Illustrated Times* series, "'Ha! ha! ha! ha!' villains always laugh four times, only four," 10:411.) Altogether, Belvawney is as stylistically dastardly as Sir Giles Overreach.

Such a villain would be incomplete without the appropriate rhetorical flourish. Belvawney uses suitable asides to inform the audience of his schemes (*Engaged*, 336, 337). His speech is littered with appropriate archaisms: "Methinks" (336), "Come hither, maiden" (337), "Farewell" (334). Moreover, he even has a melodramatic entrance in act two, where, in true villain style, he tries to halt Cheviot's marriage.

> *Symperson:* . . . Tell me all about it
> *Cheviot:* (In despair.) I cannot!
> Enter Belvawney
> *Belvawney:* I can!
> *Symperson:* Belvawney!
> (*Engaged*, 367)

However, unlike his role models, Belvawney's villainy, like Belinda's and Cheviot's passion, is all symbol and no substance. His actual impotence and pathos counteract his "black villainy." Belvawney's not-so-fiendish plot to trap Belinda exists only in his two asides while Cheviot and Belinda trap themselves unknowingly. Belvawney mopes comically in act two, pining for Belinda. His mesmeric power has in the past controlled Cheviot, but when we meet him, his eyes are so inflamed that he cannot take his glasses off, and when he does exert his power in act two, nothing comes of it. He ineffectually pleads with Cheviot not to marry and finally loses Belinda anyway after he thinks he has safely married her. His own scruples interfere with his scheming. After telling everyone that Cheviot is ruined so that Belinda will marry him, he betrays his own trick to keep Cheviot from killing himself. In the snarled plot, Belvawney would be ruined even if Cheviot did kill himself. So Belvawney is just as driven by his type and the farce plot as are the other characters. Belvawney, Belinda, and Cheviot, coerced by their stylistic imperatives and the screwball comedy plot, suggest Michael Booth's description of the predicament of farce characters: "the harassment of the ordinary individual beyond the bounds of reason, his entrapment in an incomprehensible and absurd situation, his unwilling involvement in an apparently mad world."[16]

By 1877, of course, the stock characterizations which are the source of *Engaged* existed mainly in melodrama. As Alan S. Downer pointed out, "passions which can be analyzed, classified, and broken up into component gestures and set expressions will be of little use to the more delicate natural portraiture demanded by Robertsonian comedy and the new realism" (Downer, 575). But it was precisely this incongruity which made these outmoded gestures serve Gilbert so well in comedy. An example from later in Gilbert's career suggests what he learned from experiments such as *Engaged*. A Philadelphia *Times* reporter observed Gilbert rehearsing the *Pirates of Penzance*: "[Gilbert] by word and gesture showed the unprotected females [the women's chorus] how to express their horror, first by starting with hands uplifted, then retreating a yard or two by the use of only one foot, and finally looking back affrighted to see what the terrible fellow was going to do to them."[17] This posture was documented as early as 1822 in Henry Siddons's *Practical Illustrations of Rhetorical Gesture*,[18] under the title "Horror. no. 24." This standard handbook for actors illustrated all the passions in sixty-seven woodcuts followed by narrative descriptions of the stances in action. That the same expression would appear over fifty years later suggests just how long-lived and familiar was the stage iconography with which Gilbert worked.

The notable consequence of this compound of comedy, melodrama, and farce is an acerbic wit unlike that which informs the sentimental comedies of Robertson, H. J. Byron, and James Albery. Chalcot and Mary finding true love over a roly-poly pudding during the Crimean War (*Ours*, 1866), Polly Eccles fending off Captain Hawtree with a ham in *Caste* (1867), Ida and Lotty nuzzling each other over their roses (*Two Roses*, 1870)—these scenes invite mawkish sentiment. Gilbertian topsy-turvydom is an antidote for such plays. The familiar conventions encourage us to make the error of watching *Engaged* as this or that "type" of play and so to look for a dramatic commitment of some sort: the real love affair is this one, marrying for money is wrong, etc. However, the play's consistent inconsistencies deny any commitment, effectively reminding us that we are watching a play. In this does *Engaged* differ most from Robertsonian comedy and anticipate Wilde. Robertson depends on the audience to imaginatively participate and so absorb his moral lessons. Gilbert demands that we see the play as artifact—and any recognition then forces us to accept the artifice in our own lives. We must admire *Engaged* for its own precision and dexterity; Gilbert's art is a finely balanced mechanism that effectively separates the audience from the artwork.

Lines such as Belvawney's "I knew that the unselfish creature loved you for your wealth alone" (*Engaged*, 378) anticipate Wilde's epigrammatic style which, unlike Gilbert, is based on the characters' consciously acting. Witness Algernon subverting the traditional view of love and marriage, deliberately posing:

> It is very romantic to be in love. But there is nothing romantic about a definite proposal. Why, one may be accepted. One usually is, I believe. Then the excitement is all over. The very essence of romance is uncertainty.[19]

Wilde may have been thinking of Belvawney's declaration to Minnie and Belinda, which is almost schizophrenic in its uncertainty.

> One of you will be claimed by Cheviot; that is very clear. To that one I do not address myself—but to the other (whichever it may be), I say I love you (whichever you are) with a fervour which I cannot describe in words. If you (whichever you are) will consent to cast your lot with mine, I will devote my life to proving that I love you and you only (whichever it may be) with a single-hearted and devoted passion, which precludes the possibility of my entertaining the slightest regard for any other woman in the whole world. (*Engaged*, 370)

Both wits twisted conventions: Wilde played with life, Gilbert with art. Wilde recalled the mannerist world of Jane Austen where the social form is all, but *Engaged* recalls the plots and characters of seventy-seven years of British drama.

NOTES

1. This and the following examples from the operettas are from W. S. Gilbert, *Plays and Poems* (New York: Random House, 1932). All citations are indicated by page number in the text.

2. Sidney Dark and Rowland Grey quote Gilbert's tribute to Robertson, made to William Archer, in *W. S. Gilbert: His Life and Letters* (1923; reprint, New York: Benjamin Blom, 1972), 59.

3. In Michael Booth, *English Plays of the Nineteenth Century*, 5 vols. (Oxford: Clarendon Press, 1969–76), 3:385–94. All citations from *Engaged* are from this edition. Citations from Gilbert's *Tom Cobb* are from Booth, vol. 4. Citations from Edward Bulwer-Lytton's *Money* and Douglas Jerrold's *Black-Ey'd Susan* (abbrevi-

ated *Susan*) are from *Nineteenth-Century Plays*, 2d ed., ed. George Rowell (New York: Oxford University Press, 1972). All references to Robertson's ten-part series are cited by part and page number.

4. Jane W. Stedman, *Gilbert Before Sullivan* (Chicago: University of Chicago Press, 1967), 32. All references to *Our Island Home* and *A Sensation Novel* are from this edition, hereafter abbreviated as Stedman and followed by page number.

5. Jerome K. Jerome was one of many who noted the automatic equation of goodness with fair hair: "'Be virtuous and you will have hair the color of tow' seems to be the basis of the whole theatrical religion." *On the Stage and Off: The Brief Career of a Would-Be Actor* (New York: Henry Holt and Co., 1891), 134. Referred to as Jerome in the text.

6. "Drama: The Week," *Athenaeum*, 13 Oct. 1877, p. 475.

7. "Mr. Gilbert as Dramatist," *W. S. Gilbert: A Century of Scholarship and Commentary*, ed. John Bush Jones (New York: New York University Press, 1970), 14. Michael Booth catalogues this critical debate in his afterpiece to his edition of *Engaged*.

8. For specific comparisons to Aristophanes, see Walter Sichel, "The English Aristophanes," 69–110, and Edith Hamilton, "W. S. Gilbert: A Mid-Victorian Aristophanes," 111–34, in *A Century of Scholarship and Commentary*.

9. "Theatres," *ILN*, 13 Oct. 1877, p. 303.

10. Joseph W. Donohue, Jr., *Dramatic Character in the English Romantic Age* (Princeton: Princeton University Press, 1970), 52. Referred to as Donohue in the text.

11. Dion Boucicault, "The Art of Acting," in *Laurel British Drama: The Nineteenth-Century*, ed. Robert W. Corrigan (New York: Dell, 1964), 30. First delivered as a talk in the Lyceum Theatre, London, 26 July 1882, this speech was an effort with Henry Irving to establish a School of Dramatic Art.

12. Alan S. Downer, "Players and the Painted Stage: Nineteenth-Century Acting," *PMLA*, 61 (June 1946):546.

13. Augustin Daly, *Under the Gaslight*, in Michael Booth, ed., *Hiss the Villain* (New York: Benjamin Blom, 1967), 326.

14. Charles Dickens, *Nicholas Nickleby* (New York: Signet, 1981), 299. *Nickleby* was so imbued with contemporary English drama that Dickens dedicated it to W. C. Macready. All citations from *Nicholas Nickleby* are from this edition.

15. Both descriptions are from Eleanor Ruggles, *Prince of Players* (New York: W. W. Norton, 1953), 275.

16. Michael R. Booth, *English Plays of the Nineteenth-Century: Farce*, 4:23.

17. Jane W. Stedman, "Gilbert's Stagecraft: Little Blocks of Wood," in *Gilbert and Sullivan: Papers Presented at the International Conference*, ed. James Helyar (Lawrence: Kansas University Libraries, 1971), 209–10.

18. Henry Siddons, *Practical Illustrations of Rhetorical Gesture and Action* (1822; reprint, New York: Benjamin Blom, 1968), 24.

19. Oscar Wilde, *The Importance of Being Earnest* (New York: Avon, 1965), 30.

Charles Wyndham in
Mrs. Dane's Defence

George Rowell

In the company of late Victorian actor-managers, Charles Wyndham could make at least one claim: when he wasn't doing Shakespeare, he was playing his usual repertoire. Like all performers trained in "stock" companies, he had undertaken Shakespearean roles at Manchester or Liverpool, and as late as the 1870s he still helped out in Shakespeare when directing the Crystal Palace matinées, a little known and undervalued chapter in the annals of the Victorian theatre. But the parts he played—Gratiano, Mercutio—reveal the light comedian in the making, and suggest that neither tragedy nor poetic drama was likely to prove his province. In fact, he never tackled a single Shakespearean role in London.

What he did tackle—to such effect that he commanded the Criterion Theatre for more than forty years and built his own theatre (still bearing his name) as well as the New Theatre (now the Albery)—was comedy. He first achieved West End success as an "electric light" comedian in "sophisticated" farce (*Brighton* [1875]; *Pink Dominos* [1877]), then, in the 1880s, graduated to "Old English" comedy, notably *The School for Scandal*, *She Stoops to Conquer*, and above all *David Garrick* (a Victorian play but retrospective in both theme and technique). In his maturity he became the *raisonneur* of Society comedy, who was due to stage *The Importance of Being Earnest* (1895) before surrendering it to George Alexander, and did stage five of Henry Arthur Jones's major pieces.[1] On his standing as a performer the most impartial (since they never worked together) witness is probably Bernard Shaw, who declared of *The Philanderer*: "I had written a part which nobody but Charles Wyndham could act in a play which was impossible at the Criterion Theatre,"[2] and inscribed a presentation copy of his plays: "Ah! si les autres pouvaient, ou si Charles Wyndham voulait."[3]

The five Jones plays he staged were decidedly uneven in quality. *The Bauble Shop* (1893) and *The Physician* (1897) both suffer from that strain of inflated melodrama which their author unhappily misconceived as serious literature, but *The Case of Rebellious Susan* (1894), *The Liars* (1897), and *Mrs. Dane's Defence* (1900) form as significant a triptych of late Victorian society as its theatre could offer. Moreover, they provide (perhaps unwittingly) a stimulating study in Victorian attitudes as well as Victorian stagecraft. Lady Susan Harabin was intended as a practicing rebel against the "dual" morality. Only Wyndham's caution as master of Society ceremonies discouraged Jones from drawing a wife who paid out her unfaithful husband in kind. Lady Jessica Nepean in *The Liars*, when similarly slighted, teeters on the verge of flight to Africa with her explorer-admirer, but has to agree that "it won't work." To Mrs. Dane, however, her creator shows no mercy. Seduced by her employer and seeking to protect her child's good name as well as her own by necessary deception, she is browbeaten into surrendering the love of an honourable man because the "rules of the game are severe. If you don't like them, leave the sport alone." In pronouncing sentence Wyndham in the role of Sir Daniel Carteret was speaking not only as master of Society ceremonies but also as moderator of Society morals.

The first production of *Mrs. Dane's Defence* in 1900 marked a climax in both Jones's and Wyndham's careers. Neither was to achieve such a triumph again, though both had their later successes. For Wyndham, the taste was particularly sweet, since the play brought his first real reward in his own theatre (and had been preceded by undeniable failure in *Cyrano de Bergerac* [1900]). It was also his first—and perhaps last—major success in an entirely serious role. The comedy of *Mrs. Dane's Defence* is restricted to the secondary characters; even Mary Moore, his Lady Susan and Lady Jessica, took the supporting part of Lady Eastney, who knows Sir Daniel is being unjust but marries him notwithstanding. At sixty-three, Wyndham could not hope to continue in leading roles. The ten years which followed *Mrs. Dane's Defence* saw a necessary but poignant adjustment in his and Mary Moore's responsibilities. The three comedies by Hubert Henry Davies which provided their final successes (*Mrs. Gorringe's Necklace* [1903], *Captain Drew on Leave* [1905], and *The Mollusc* [1907]) were really Mary Moore's plays, with Wyndham gracefully filling in (admittedly important) corners. But *Mrs. Dane's Defence* was a triumph for the prosecution.

Like most of Wilde's *femmes fatales*—Mrs. Erlynne, Mrs. Arbuthnot, and presumably Mrs. Cheveley—Mrs. Dane has no right to that name. She is in fact a Miss Felicia Hindemarsh, who was employed as a governess to the children of a wealthy English family. She allowed her employer to press his attentions on her, and during the family's stay in Vienna his wife discovered the relationship and committed suicide. Her husband then became deranged, leaving the governess to fend for herself and the child she was expecting. She was lucky enough to find shelter and anonymity with a married cousin in Montreal, and, when both the cousin and her husband conveniently and quickly died, inherited their substantial fortunes and assumed the cousin's identity. Back in England, she establishes herself in the desirable district of "Sunningwater" (evidently a distillation of Sunningdale and Virginia Water), and rapidly attracts the envy of its womenfolk and the admiration of its men. Amongst the former is the malicious Mrs. Bulsom-Porter; among the latter both Mr. Bulsom-Porter and young Lionel Carteret, who proposes marriage. But a relation of Mrs. Bulsom-Porter, who was on the staff of the British consulate at Vienna when the scandal broke, sees and recognizes Mrs. Dane, and is ill-advised enough to comment on the resemblance. Mrs. Bulsom-Porter has thus the motive and the means to denounce her.

The play thereupon develops into an investigation, and although audiences are early aware that Mrs. Dane is Felicia Hindemarsh, they are not only disposed to take her part but intrigued by her convincing assumption of Mrs. Dane's identity. More than one critic pointed admiringly to Jones's emulation of Wilkie Collins's use of two cousins in *The Woman in White*. The investigation is undertaken chiefly by Sir Daniel Carteret, a prominent judge living in the district and Lionel's adoptive father. The play reaches its climax in act three, set in Carteret's library, with what amounts to his cross-examination of Mrs. Dane. It has sometimes been objected that this results in a courtroom drama without a court, but the effect is that Sir Daniel can act as both judge and counsel for the prosecution, which no legal arena would allow. Despite her familiarity with her cousin's past history, the accused gradually falls into inconsistency. Although claiming to be an only child, she states: "We had governesses," and has therefore to admit to the cousin's existence. More seriously, Sir Daniel's library provides a reference book in which the vicar of her old home is listed as the Reverend Francis Hindemarsh, and her only recourse is to acknowledge that cousin as Felicia. Finally her story is shattered, and in a somewhat lame last act she agrees to withdraw to North Devon (would Ilfracombe be less curious or more charitable than "Sunningwater"?), and

Lionel's immediate future is settled as building Egyptian railways, although his ultimate fate seems to be in the arms of an earlier love, Janet Colquhoun. Meanwhile Sir Daniel persuades Lady Eastney, young, wealthy, and a widow, to marry him. The Carteret cup runneth over.

To a Victorian moralist, Mrs. Dane was guilty of both adultery and deception, and Sir Daniel's prosecution and sentence might have seemed justified. But early in the play he has revealed that as a young barrister he fell in love with the wife of one of his clients, and persuaded her to leave her husband and child and flee abroad. Passages and a rendezvous at Liverpool were fixed, but at the last moment she sent word that the boy was gravely ill and the opportunity was lost. Both she and her husband died in due course, and Carteret was allowed to adopt the son, Lionel (improbably, since he is a bachelor and no relation). But, as he unwisely tells Lady Eastney:

> I've been successful and happy after a fashion; but there has never been a moment since I lost her when I wouldn't have cheerfully bartered every farthing, every honour, every triumph I've scored in my profession, to stand again on that platform at Liverpool and know that she was coming to me.[4] (*MD*, 362)

It is hard to discriminate between his behaviour towards Lionel's mother and Mrs. Dane's employer's towards her, except that, as she bitterly observes: "We mustn't get found out. I'm afraid I've broken that part of the law" (*MD*, 426). Even Lady Eastney perceives the injustice of her fate, commenting:

> Oh, aren't you Pharisees and tyrants, all of you? And don't you make cowards and hypocrites of all of us? Don't you lead us into sin and then condemn us for it? Aren't you first our partners and then our judges? (*MD*, 416)

to which Sir Daniel lays down inexorably (but inaccurately): "The rules of the game are severe. If you don't like them, leave the sport alone. They will never be altered."

Jones took great pains to present Mrs. Dane as not merely pretty but gentle and appealing (unlike Paula Tanqueray, on whose temper and coarseness Pinero laid some stress), and the wardrobe seconded his efforts. The *Era* sketched her first-act dress: "An evening gown in white mousseline, all hand-painted with encircling trails of great pink roses and with insertions of cobwebby lace let into its clinging softness. . . . Trailing from one bare shoulder almost to the hem of the shirt, shaded pink roses are entwined with leaves and thorny stalks to form one long spray whose last little bud peeps out over a foamy bordering of tulle rosettes, alternately pink and white" (13 October 1900, p. 12). To make Sir Daniel tolerable, therefore, posed a challenge, yet Wyndham's interpretation was not merely tolerable but positively triumphant. He had, of course, had useful training in playing Sir Richard Kato in *Rebellious Susan* and Sir Christopher Deering in *The Liars*. They, however, set out to save marriages, not prevent them; Lady Susan never saw her encounter with Lucien Endensor as more than solace for her wounded pride under the spell of the Egyptian moonlight, and though Lady Jessica is genuinely drawn to her strong, silent empire-builder, she comes to realize that (since her husband has not given her grounds for divorce under the then-existing law) elopement would ruin Edward Falkner and probably leave them both miserable. As Carteret, on the other hand, it took all Wyndham's authority and persuasiveness to impose on his audience the *dictat*

> Whatever I've done, whatever I've been myself, I'm quite resolved my son shan't marry another man's mistress. (*MD*, 416)

Lena Ashwell, an actress of some experience who nevertheless achieved her greatest success as Mrs. Dane, records her anxiety in undertaking the role: "I was a dark horse, and Mrs. Dane was a woman with a murky past, and heroines should have a virtue on their side. Even if for a time circumstances were against them, they should be proved innocent in the end. I felt encouraged when I heard two scene-shifters discussing Mrs. Dane, and one said: 'Love her! Why, I'd marry her myself.'"[5] But of course it was one thing for a stagehand to marry a dark horse, quite another for a judge's son.

In spite of this, and although staged in Victoria's reign, the play was not universally endorsed. That it offered a dramatic anticlimax was accepted, but the critic of the *Illustrated London News* strikes a surprisingly radical note in considering the author's moral position: "The conclusion of the play is of necessity the conventional one of separation for the lovers, and its general tone reflects only too exactly the sordid materialism which is the outlook of our modern society" (13 October 1900, p. 12). The charge of "sordid materialism" is unexpected, since Mrs. Dane, who seems as richly endowed and much better dressed than the rest of "Sunningwater," is not dismissed for her financial inadequacy, but perhaps this critic believed her deeply in debt and marrying Lionel to pay her bills. Moreover, it was not solely the weakness of act four that aroused some comment on the play's construction. The *Stage*, for example, while hailing "a brilliant but unsatisfactory, clever but perverse, unequal but successful play," censured the "indiscretion" of the diplomat Risby in "blurting out" his recognition of the likeness between Mrs. Dane and Felicia Hindemarsh (13 October 1900, p. 13). He also dismissed the end of act two as "absurdly illogical," since it hinges on Sir Daniel's acceptance of the detective's "bare word" that Mrs. Dane is "not in the least like her," an unfair verdict from an apparently inattentive juror, since Sir Daniel's reply is, "We shall want fuller information, but that will do for the present." At least one critic also affirmed that act two "is laid in the chambers of a kindly Judge" rather than in his private library (*ILN*, 13 October 1900, p. 12). Generally the press reaction was a grudging awareness, still widely familiar, that the audience had performed their task for them, of recognizing a winner.

What did gain universal approval was the writing and acting of the cross-examination scene. *The Times* summed up the universal shout: "It is by this act and for this act that the play exists" (10 October 1900, p. 3). Such unanimity is all the more remarkable, since Jones subsequently made it clear that the basis of the plot (and of this scene in particular) was a more mundane civil suit of the mid-1890s, the Osborne jewel case, when Sir Charles Russell, interrogating his client out of court, concluded: "Woman, you are lying!"[6] Moreover, the first draft of the exchange between the detective and Sir Daniel in act two gave away too much although the documentation of this error is less than precise. The author's daughter claims her father told her: "I made the mistake of allowing the judge to get the better of Risby, the detective, and when I came to the big scene—Sir Daniel knew already she was guilty, so there was no big scene." Either Henry Arthur or daughter Doris made a slip over the detective's name, Fendick. But the same source adds: "My father knew he had not got the play right, and he went away to Switzerland. Suddenly one morning at Ragatz the correct construction flashed into his brain, and he wrote the whole of the third act in four hours at white heat. There was one small interruption; the funeral procession of the Burgomaster passed under my father's window, and he got up to watch it pass by."[7] Wyndham's recent

Scene from *Mrs. Dane's Defence*, act 2: "Is this lady Miss Hindemarsh?" (Drawing by S. Begg. From the *Illustrated London News*, 13 October 1900. Photograph by Theatre Museum. Courtesy of the Trustees of the Victoria and Albert Museum.)

Scene from *Mrs. Dane's Defence*, act 3: "Woman, you're lying!" (Drawing by Bernard Partridge. From *Sphere*, October 1900. Photograph by Theatre Museum. Courtesy of the Trustees of the Victoria and Albert Museum.)

biographer Wendy Trewin tantalizes by quoting this passage and adding: "Literary detectives will look for the point in the script where this occurred," but confuses the issue by claiming "he [Jones] had let the audience [not Sir Daniel] know the woman was guilty," a state of things which obtains in the published text.[8]

No ambiguity existed or exists about the success of the scene or its triumphant interpretation. The wisdom of casting Lena Ashwell, an actress who had played Shakespeare under both Irving and Tree, was overwhelmingly endorsed. The *Era* (13 October 1900, p. 13) referred to "Miss Ashwell's nervous style, so easily adaptable to the expression of revolt, anguish, and terror," and claimed: "There was sufficient in her reading of the fascination which the text undeniably attributes to the adventuress." When, for a New York revival in 1906, the management sought publicity by alternating Margaret Anglin and Lena Ashwell in the parts of Lady Eastney and Mrs. Dane, Jones summed up simply: "God made Lena Ashwell for Mrs. Dane, just as He made Mrs. Pat Campbell for Mrs. Tanqueray" (D. A. Jones, 210).

The tributes to Wyndham as Sir Daniel are even more remarkable, since the "line" and the player were both entirely familiar. Yet the actor-manager brought to Carteret an authority apparently exceeding even that with which he had endowed Kato and Deering. Above all, his orchestration of the cross-examination scene satisfied all heads and touched all hearts, earning praise for "his blending of grieved resentment with tenderness and chivalry" (*Era*, 13 October 1900, p. 13), and an acknowledgement that "the Judge's alternations of mood—earnest belief, puzzled bewilderment, vague suspicion, and outraged discovery—make up a subtle dialogue, most impressive in its keen fencing, its constant changes, its suppressed emotion" (*ILN*, 13 October 1900, p. 12).

The reception of this scene (for which, as in opera, the principals took an interpolated "call") was tumultuous. Doris Arthur Jones reports her father saying of the applause: "You could lean up against it" (D. A. Jones, 209), and the *Stage* (11 October 1900, p. 13) is more specific: "Miss Ashwell . . . shared with Mr. Wyndham the four tempestuous calls after the third act." As so often in his career, Wyndham's vocal quality stretched the descriptive powers of his reporters. After his death W. L. Courtney asserted: "Nine men out of ten would tell you that Wyndham's voice was harsh and unmusical; nineteen women out of twenty would tell you that it was the most compelling and seductive thing in the world."[9] On this particular occasion the author recognized "a distinctive penetrating voice whose slightly raucous edge was secretly tuned and guided to every accent of tenderness and persuasion and caress,"[10] and later in life told his daughter that "He'd only two notes in his voice, but he could do anything with them" (D. A. Jones, 209–10). A quarter of a century afterwards the Lady Eastney of the evening, a partial witness but a vastly wise judge, summed up their achievement: "The play proved to be one of our greatest triumphs; but if it lives—as it deserves to—there will no doubt be other "Lady Eastneys" and other "Mrs. Danes," though I doubt whether there will ever be such a fine "Sir Daniel" as Mr. Wyndham. I do not mean only from the acting point of view, but from the personal also. His beautiful silver hair, fine bearing, and graceful figure made him a most distinguished and dignified picture of middle age, not easily to be forgotten" (Moore, 141–42). The plaudits of the first-night audience and the predictions of the critics were confirmed by the play's popularity. It ran for 209 performances, and survived the death of Queen Victoria on 22 January 1901 (an event fatal to many London productions) until, in accordance with theatrical practice, the season concluded with some reminder of earlier favorites, still in the actor-manager's repertoire: in this case a brief revival of *Rebellious Susan*.

The later history of Wyndham and *Mrs. Dane's Defence* is less stirring and even sad. There was a brief revival in June 1902, with most of the original cast, but London did not see him as Sir Daniel again until 1912, by which time he was almost seventy-five and suffering increasingly from a form of memory loss known as "aphasia" (inherited from his father but aggravated by overwork in "stock" companies during his apprenticeship), which was marked by an inability to associate words with the subject intended. Of the many blackly comic stories told in this context, perhaps the blackest and most comic is his hailing a cab and telling the astonished driver: "I forget the name of the theatre I want to go to, but it's the one named after me. *Take me there*."[11]

The rehearsals confirmed that Wyndham, who had acted less and less frequently, was likely to be lost for his lines. On the appointed day, 16 May, he determined to run through his part with his son, Howard (by this time his right-hand man in managing the three family theatres), who tells the sorry tale:

> On the morning of the first night, he said to me, "Howard, come down with me to Hampton Court, I want you to hear me say my part." In the quiet of the grounds we walked about and went through his part. He was by

no means perfect, so suggested we went through it again. The second time was much worse and the old man got quite worried. Once more we tried it and the third time it was tragic. He could hardly remember a word. What was to be done? I suggested telegraphing to the manager to have a message which I had written printed and slipped into the programme asking for the indulgence of the audience for any lapse of memory as Sir Charles had suddenly become ill, but did not want to disappoint everybody by postponing the performance. He read it over, I was about to send it off, when he said, "No, I have never done such a thing in my life—I will go through it. You stand one side of the stage with the book and the prompter in the other and between you I shall get through."

The play started and all went fairly well until he came to the very long speech in the first act. He managed the first few lines, then I found him leaving the author's lines and wandering in a morass of words with neither meaning nor sense. Neither I nor the prompter could help him. His voice meanwhile was getting lower and more indistinct every second. How I suffered! What could possibly be the end?

Suddenly a man in the gallery shouted out, "Speak up, Charlie." That was too much for him. He, with his wonderful resonant voice which the whole world admired, to be told to speak up was more than he could stand. He seemed to shake himself like an old war horse and miraculously picked up the missing lines, delivering them with such artistry and effect that at the end of the speech the house rose to him.

So far so good, but two more acts to get through and I, bathed with perspiration, was little more than a limp rag.

In the play there is a scene where my father, playing the part of a K.C., cross-examines, in his chambers [sic], the heroine.

It's a long examination and every question when answered is followed by another question. There is a certain sequence in ordinary dialogue, but none in cross-examination.

By this scene I was very frightened, so, as he sits all the time at his desk, I saw no reason why he should not have a brief in front of him to refer to.

This brief I had had typed in large capitals with his questions heavily underlined and the replies in smaller type except the last few words which would give him his cue.

I was very proud of my handiwork and knew he couldn't possibly go wrong.

It worked splendidly but having often seen barristers either looking back in their briefs or turning over leaves ahead, he had to add that little touch of realism himself with the obvious result he lost his place. There again I was helpless. I could only prompt him each sentence as, alas, he never found his place again.[12]

Others confirm his struggles that night at the New Theatre. Doris Arthur Jones recalled him asking a startled Lena Ashwell: "Let me see, your father was the Vicar of Wakefield?" (D. A. Jones, 209). Athene Seyler is at the time of writing a revered ninety-six-year-old. She was then a twenty-two-year-old ingenue playing Janet Colquhoun, though soon to be one of London's best-loved leading ladies, who stood horrified in the wings as the climactic line: "Woman! You are lying! Your name is Felicia Hindemarsh!" emerged as "Woman! You are lying! Your name is Felicity Tittlemouse!"[13] Mary Moore, powerless to help even in those scenes she shared with Wyndham, writes ruefully: "There was an undeniable something that seemed to be wafted over the footlights to us, something that told us they were doubting Sir Charles's powers. Sir Charles felt this very keenly, and referred to it for some time afterwards with some bitterness, which was not like him" (Moore, 200). In fact the revival had a disastrous effect on both leading ladies: Lena Ashwell developed shingles, Mary Moore suffered a breakdown, and both were out of the cast for spells during the brief run.

When the play closed, Wyndham accepted the inevitable. His only later appearances were single performances in his favorite part, David Garrick, at matinées staged for the good of the Actors' Benevolent Fund, of which he had become president in 1905 when Irving died. Even these were "terribly pathetic" according to his Ada Ingot, since Wyndham would spend the whole morning with the prompter, going through a role he had played hundreds, perhaps over a thousand, times. In his very last performance, at the New Theatre on 16 December 1913, however, he was blessedly "perfect."

This account must not end on a note of distress, but return to the claim with which it opened. Wyndham was a non-Shakespearean actor who endowed the mostly ephemeral roles he played, whether as "electric light" comedian, poised interpreter of period style, or *raisonneur* of Victorian problem plays, with a near-Shakespearean substance. This can be finally illustrated from the moment in Mrs. Dane's cross-examination when, after she has broken down, she makes an agonized mention of her son. Sir Daniel's response—There was a child?—suggests in cold print all the pathos and sentimentality often sneeringly imputed to Victorian melodrama. At the premiere Wyndham transmuted these base metals, if such they are, into theatrical gold. His speaking of the four words wrung his listeners' hearts (D. A. Jones, 210). Two years later Sir Daniel Carteret's creator was himself created Sir Charles Wyndham, and the audience's accolade was given royal recognition by Edward VII. Honor was satisfied.

NOTES

1. See George Rowell, "Wyndham of Wyndham's," in *The Theatrical Manager in England and America*, ed. Joseph W. Donahue, Jr. (Princeton: Princeton University Press, 1971), 207.
2. Bernard Shaw, "Preface," *Plays Unpleasant* (London: Constable, 1925), xiii. *The Philanderer* was written in 1903 but not performed until 1905.
3. Mary Moore, *Charles Wyndham and Mary Moore* (London: Privately printed, 1925), 123. All further quotations from this text, hereafter abbreviated Moore, will be followed by page citations in the text.
4. The text has been reprinted by Michael R. Booth in *English Plays of the Nineteenth Century: Dramas, 1850–1900.* 5 vols. (Oxford: Clarendon Press, 1969–76), and in his *The Magistrate and Other Nineteenth-Century Plays* (Oxford: Oxford University Press, 1974). All further quotations from the play, hereafter abbreviated *MD*, come from the former edition and will be followed by page citations in the text.
5. Lena Ashwell, *Myself and My Friends* (London: Michael Joseph, 1936), 117–18.
6. On Jones's use of this case, see R. A. Cordell, *Henry Arthur Jones and the Modern Drama* (New York: Long and Smith, 1932), 162–63, where his account to Archibald Henderson is cited; and William Archer, *The Old Drama and the New* (London: Heinemann, 1923), 302.
7. Doris Arthur Jones, *The Life and Letters of Henry Arthur Jones* (London: Gollancz, 1930), 208. All further quotations from this text, hereafter abbreviated D. A. Jones, will be cited by page in the text.
8. Wendy Trewin, *Charles Wyndham and the Alberys* (London: Harrap, 1980), 153.
9. W. L. Courtney, *The Passing Hour* (London: Hutchinson, 1925), 202–3.
10. Dedication "To Sir Charles Wyndham" in Macmillan edition, 1905.
11. Percy Hutchison, *Masquerade* (London: Harrap, 1936), 29.
12. Unpublished TS, now in Bristol University Theatre Collection.
13. George Rowell, conversation with Athene Seyler, 1956.

Works Cited

References below are only to books, plays, and articles in scholarly or important popular periodicals, and manuscripts of full-length works. References to newspaper reviews or to shorter manuscript materials are given in the text and notes accompanying each chapter.

Adams, W. Davenport. *A Dictionary of the Drama*. London: Chatto and Windus, 1904.
Alger, William R. *The Life of Edwin Forrest, the American Tragedian*. 2 vols. Philadelphia: J. B. Lippincott, 1877.
Allen, Shirley S. *Samuel Phelps and Sadler's Wells Theatre*. Middletown, Conn.: Wesleyan University Press, 1971.
Anderson, James R. *An Actor's Life*. London: Walter Scott, 1902.
Anderson, Mary. *A Few Memories*. New York: Harper Brothers, 1869.
Archer, William. *English Dramatists of To-Day*. London: Sampson Low, 1882.
──── . *The Old Drama and the New*. 1923; reprint, New York: Benjamin Blom, 1972.
──── . *William Charles Macready*. London: Kegan Paul, 1890.
Ashley, Leonard R. N., ed. *Nineteenth-Century British Drama*. Glenview, Ill.: Scott, Foresman, 1967.
Ashwell, Lena. *Myself and My Friends*. London: Michael Joseph, 1936.
Atkinson, Brooks. *Broadway*. New York: Macmillan, 1974.
Auerbach, Nina. *Ellen Terry: Player in Her Time*. New York: Norton, 1987.
Baker, Henry Barton. *History of the London Stage and Its Famous Players (1576–1903)*. 1904; reprint, New York: Benjamin Blom, 1969.
Bancroft, Marie, and Squire Bancroft. *The Bancrofts: Recollections of Sixty Years*. 1909; reprint, New York: Benjamin Blom, 1969.
──── . *Mr. & Mrs. Bancroft On and Off the Stage*. 2 vols. London: Richard Bentley, 1888.
Banham, Martin, ed. *Plays by Tom Taylor*. Cambridge: Cambridge University Press, 1985.
Barker, James Nelson. *The Indian Princess*. In *Representative Plays by American Dra-*

matists, edited by Montrose J. Moses, pp. 565–628. New York: E. P. Dutton, 1918.
———. *Marmion*. New York: Longworth, 1816.
———. *Superstition*. In *Representative American Plays from 1767 to the Present Day*, 7th ed., edited by Arthur Hobson Quinn, pp. 109–40. New York: Appleton-Century-Crofts, 1957.
———. *Tears and Smiles*. In Paul H. Musser, *James Nelson Barker*, pp. 140–207. Philadephia: University of Pennsylvania Press, 1929.
Barker, Kathleen. "Charles Dillon: A Provincial Tragedian." In *Shakespeare and the Victorian Stage*, edited by Richard Foulkes, pp. 283–94. Cambridge: Cambridge University Press, 1986.
Barrett, Daniel. "T. W. Robertson [1829–1871]: The Dramatist as Critic." *Victorian Periodicals Review* 14 (1981): 144–49.
———. "T. W. Robertson's Plays: Revisions to Nicoll's Handlist." *Nineteenth-Century Theatre Research* 11 (1983): 93–103.
Barrett, Lawrence. *Charlotte Cushman*. New York: The Dunlap Society, 1889.
———. *Edwin Forrest*. American Actor Series. Boston: James R. Osgood, 1881.
Beckett, Samuel. *Three Novels*. New York: Grove Press, 1958.
Beerbohm, Max. *Around Theatres*. New York: Knopf, 1930.
———. *Last Theatres, 1904–1910*. New York: Taplinger, 1970.
———. *More Theatres*. New York: Taplinger, 1969.
Bentley, Eric. *The Life of the Drama*. New York: Atheneum, 1964.
Bernheim, Alfred. *The Business of the Theatre: An Economic History of the American Theatres, 1750–1932*. 1932; reprint, New York: Benjamin Blom, 1964.
Bingham, Madeleine. *Henry Irving and the Victorian Theatre*. London: George Allen and Unwin, 1978.
Birking, Andrew. *J. M. Barrie and the Lost Boys*. London: Constable, 1979.
Bogal, Frederic V. "Fables of Knowing: Melodrama and Related Forms." *Genre* 2 (1978): 83–108.
Booth, Michael R. "The Acting of Melodrama." *University of Toronto Quarterly* 34 (1964): 31–48.
———. *English Melodrama*. London: Herbert Jenkins, 1965.
———. *Prefaces to English Nineteenth-Century Theatre*. Manchester: Manchester University Press, 1980.
———, ed. *English Plays of the Nineteenth Century*. 5 vols. Oxford: Clarendon, 1969–76.
———, ed. *The Magistrate and Other Nineteenth-Century Plays*. Oxford: Oxford University Press, 1974.
——— et al. *The Revels History of Drama in English, Vol. 6: 1750–1880*, edited by Clifford Leech and T. W. Craik. London: Methuen, 1975.
———. *Victorian Spectacular Theatre, 1850–1910*. London: Routledge and Kegan Paul, 1981.

Boucicault, Dion. "The Art of Acting." In *Laurel British Drama: The Nineteenth Century*, edited by Robert W. Corrigan, pp. 25–42. New York: Dell, 1964.
———. *The Dolmen Boucicault*, edited by David Krause. Dublin: Dolmen Press, 1965.
———. "The Future of American Drama." *The Arena* 2 (November 1890): 650–51.
———. *London Assurance*. New York: Dick and Fitzgerald, 1889.
———. *Plays by Dion Boucicault*, edited by Peter Thomson. Cambridge: Cambridge University Press, 1984.
Bratton, J. S. "Theatre of War: The Crimea on the London Stage." In *Performance and Politics in Popular Drama: Aspects of Popular Entertainment in Theatre, Film, and Television, 1800–1976*, edited by David Bradby, Louis James, and Bernard Sharratt, pp. 119–37. Cambridge: Cambridge University Press, 1980.
Brereton, Geoffrey. *Principles of Tragedy: A Rational Examination of the Tragic Concept of Life and Literature.* Coral Gables, Fla.: University of Miami Press, 1968.
British Association for the Advancement of Science. *Manchester and Its Region: A Survey Prepared for the Meeting Held in Manchester August 29 to September 5, 1962.* Manchester: Manchester University Press, 1962.
Broadbent, R. J. *A History of Pantomime*. 1901; reprint, New York: Benjamin Blom, 1964.
Brooks, Peter. *The Melodramatic Imagination*. New Haven: Yale University Press, 1976.
Brown, Eluned, ed. *The London Theatre, 1811–1866: Selections from the Diary of Henry Crabb Robinson*. London: The Society for Theatre Research, 1966.
Brown, Henry Collins. *Brownstone Fronts and Saratoga Trunks*. New York: E. P. Dutton, 1935.
Bulwer-Lytton, Edward. *Money*. In *Nineteenth-Century Plays*, edited by George Rowell, pp. 45–120. 2d. ed. New York: Oxford University Press, 1972.
Burnham, Charles. "Stage Indecency Then and Now: A Play That Made Our Daddies Blush Could Be Read in Sunday School Today." *Theatre Magazine*, September 1925, p. 16.
[Calcraft, John William]. "How The Theatre Royal in Hawkins' Street Came To Be Built, With A Cursory Glance At What Has Been Done There During Thirty Years . . . ," *Dublin University Magazine* 39 (1852): 284.
Callis, Anne Everal. "Olga Nethersole and the *Sapho* Scandal." Master's thesis, Ohio State University, 1974.
Carlisle, Carol J. "Passion Framed by Art: Helen Faucit's Juliet." *Theatre Survey* 25 (November 1984): 177–92.
Chase, Pauline. *Peter Pan's Postbag: Letters to Pauline Chase*. London: Heinemann, 1909.
Churchill, Alan. *The Upper Crust: An Informal History of New York's Highest Society*. Englewood Cliffs, N. J.: Prentice Hall, 1970.

Clapp, Henry Austin. "Edwin Booth." *Atlantic Monthly* 72 (September 1893): 312.
———. "Edwin Booth in Some Non-Shakespearean Parts." *Outing* (June 1885): 349.
———. *Reminiscences of a Dramatic Critic*. Boston: Houghton Mifflin, 1902.
Clarke, Asia Booth. *The Elder and the Younger Booth*. Boston: James R. Osgood, 1882.
Cole, John. *The Life and Theatrical Times of Charles Kean, F.S.A.*, 2 vols. London: Richard Bentley, 1859.
Coleman, John. *Fifty Years of an Actor's Life*. 2 vols. London: Hutchinson, 1904.
Cordell, R. A. *Henry Arthur Jones and the Modern Drama*. New York: Long and Smith, 1932.
Corrigan, Robert W., ed. *The Laurel British Drama: The Nineteenth Century*. New York: Dell, 1964.
Courtney, W. L. *The Passing Hour*. London: Hutchinson, 1925.
Cross, Gilbert B. *Next Week—East Lynne*. Lewisburg, Pa.: Bucknell University Press, 1975.
Cunningham, Hugh. "Class and Leisure in Mid-Victorian England." In *Popular Culture: Past and Present*, edited by Bernard Waites, Tony Bennett, and Graham Martin, pp. 66–91. London: Croom Helm, 1982.
Daly, Augustin. *Under the Gaslight*. In *Hiss the Villain*, edited by Michael Booth, pp. 271–341. New York: Benjamin Blom, 1967.
Daly, Joseph Francis. *The Life of Augustin Daly*. New York: Macmillan, 1917.
Dark, Sidney, and Rowland Grey. *W. S. Gilbert: His Life and Letters*. 1923; reprint, New York: Benjamin Blom, 1972.
Dibdin, Thomas. *The Hermione; or, Retaliation*. Larpent MSS. 1288.
———. *The Mouth of the Nile; or, The Glorious First of August*. London: J. Barker, 1798.
Dickens, Charles. *Nicholas Nickleby*. New York: Signet, 1981.
Donohue, Joseph W., Jr. *Dramatic Character in the English Romantic Age*. Princeton: Princeton University Press, 1970.
———, ed. *The Theatrical Manager in England and America*. Princeton: Princeton University Press, 1971.
Dormon, James H. *Theatre in the Antebellum South, 1815–1861*. Chapel Hill: University of North Carolina Press, 1967.
Douglas, Ann. *The Feminization of American Culture*. New York: Avon Books, 1978.
Downer, Alan S. "Early American Professional Acting." *Theatre Survey* 12 (November 1971): 79–96.
———. *The Eminent Tragedian: William Charles Macready*. Cambridge, Mass.: Harvard University Press, 1966.
———. "Players and Painted Stage: Nineteenth Century Acting." *PMLA* 61 (June 1946): 522–26.

Dunlap, William. *History of the American Theatre*. 1832; reprint, New York: Burt Franklin, 1963.
Durbach, Errol. "Remembering Tom Robertson (1829–1871)." *Educational Theatre Journal* 24 (1972): 284–88.
Eich, L. M. "The American Indian Plays." *Quarterly Journal of Speech* 30 (1944): 212–15.
Elliott, Jeanne B. "A Lady to the End: The Case of Isabel Vane." *Victorian Studies* 19 (1976): 329–44.
Emerson, Ralph Waldo. *The Collected Works of Ralph Waldo Emerson*. 4 vols. Cambridge: Belknap Press, 1971–87.
Falk, Robert. "Shakespeare in America: A Survey to 1900." *Shakespeare Survey* 18 (1965): 102–18.
Faucit, Helena. *On Some of Shakespeare's Female Characters*. National Library of Scotland, Department of Manuscripts. MS. 16433 f. 3637 v.
Fawkes, Richard. *Dion Boucicault*. London: Quartet Books, 1979.
Fitzsimmons, Raymond. *Edmund Kean: Fire from Heaven*. New York: The Dial, 1976.
Fleetwood, Frances. *Conquest: The Story of a Theatre Family*. London: W. H. Allen, 1953.
Fletcher, Richard M. *English Romantic Drama, 1795–1843: A Critical History*. New York: Exposition Press, 1966.
Ford, Richard. *Dramatizations of Scott's Novels: A Catalogue*. Oxford: Oxford Bibliographical Society, 1979.
Foulkes, Richard, ed. *Shakespeare and the Victorian Stage*. Cambridge: Cambridge University Press, 1986.
Fowler, Alastair. "Genre and the Literary Canon." *New Literary History* 11 (1979): 97–119.
Franklin, Andrew. *A Trip to the Nore: A Musical Entertainment in One Act*. London: British Library, 1797.
Genest, John. *Some Account of the English Stage from the Restoration in 1660 to 1830*. 10 vols. Bath: H. E. Carrington, 1832.
Gilbert, W. S. *Engaged*. In *English Plays of the Nineteenth Century: Comedies*, edited by Michael R. Booth, pp. 325–94. Oxford: Oxford University Press, 1980.
———. *Our Island Home*. In *Gilbert Before Sullivan*, edited by Jane W. Stedman, pp. 107–28. Chicago: University of Chicago Press.
———. *Plays and Poems*. New York: Random House, 1932.
———. *A Sensation Novel*. In *Gilbert Before Sullivan*, pp. 129–66.
———. *Tom Cobb*. In *English Plays of the Nineteenth Century: Farces*, pp. 255–98.
Green, London. "'The Gaiety of Mediated Success': The Richard III of William Charles Macready." *Theatre Research International* 10, 2 (Summer 1985): 107–28.
Green, Roger Lancelyn. *Fifty Years of "Peter Pan."* London: Davies, 1954.
Grimsted, David. "Melodrama as Echo of the Historically Voiceless." In *Anony-

mous Americans: Explorations in Nineteenth-Century Social History, edited by Tamara K. Hareven, pp. 80–98. Englewood Cliffs, N. J.: Prentice Hall, 1971.

———. *Melodrama Unveiled: American Theatre and Culture, 1800–1850*. Chicago: University of Chicago Press, 1968.

Grose, B. Donald. "Edwin Forrest, *Metamora*, and the Indian Removal Act of 1830." *Theatre Journal* 27 (May 1985):181–91.

Grossman, Edwina Booth. *Edwin Booth: Recollections by His Daughter and Letters to His Friends*. London: Osgood, McIlvaine and Company, 1894.

Haight, Gordon S., ed. *The George Eliot Letters*. 9 vols. New Haven: Yale University Press, 1954–78.

Hamilton, Edith. "W. S. Gilbert: A Mid-Victorian Aristophanes." In *W. S. Gilbert: A Century of Scholarship and Commentary*, edited by John Bush Jones, pp. 111–34. New York: New York University Press, 1970.

Hapgood, Norman. *The Stage in America, 1897–1900*. New York: Macmillan, 1901.

Harris, Augustus. "The National Theatre." *Fortnightly Review* 1 (November 1885): 635.

Hartman, John Geoffrey. *The Development of American Social Comedy from 1787 to 1936*. Philadelphia: University of Pennsylvania Press, 1939.

Havens, Daniel F. *The Columbian Muse of Comedy: The Development of a Native Tradition in Early American Comedy, 1787–1845*. Carbondale: Southern Illinois University Press, 1973.

Hawthorne, Edith G., ed. *Memoirs of Julian Hawthorne*. New York: Macmillan, 1938.

Hazelwood, C. H. *Lady Audley's Secret*. In *Nineteenth-Century Plays*, edited by George Rowell, pp. 233–66. London: Oxford University Press, 1953.

Heilman, Robert Bechtold. *Tragedy and Melodrama: Versions of Experience*. Seattle: University of Washington Press, 1968.

Hixon, Don L., and Don A. Hennessee. *Nineteenth-Century American Drama: A Finding Guide*. Metuchen, N. J.: Scarecrow Press, 1977.

Hogan, Robert. *Dion Boucicault*. New York: Twayne, 1969.

Hugo, Victor. *The King's Amusement*. Trans. Frederick L. Slous. In *The Works of Victor Hugo*, vol. 1, pp. 276–356. Boston: Little, Brown, 1901.

Huston, Hollis W. "Macready's *Richelieu* Promptbooks: Evolution of the Enclosed Setting." *Theatre Studies* 21 (1974–75): 41–51.

Hutchison, Percy. *Masquerade*. London: Harrap, 1936.

Hynes, Samuel. *The Edwardian Turn of Mind*. Princeton: Princeton University Press, 1968.

Ireland, Joseph N. *Records of the New York Stage*. 2 vols. New York: T. H. Morrell, 1866.

Jerome, Jerome K. *On the Stage and Off: The Brief Career of a Would-Be Actor*. New York: Henry Holt and Company, 1891.

———. *Stage-land: Curious Habits and Customs of Its Inhabitants*. London: Chatto and Windus, 1889.
Jerrold, Douglas. *Black Ey'd Susan*. In *Nineteenth-Century Plays*, 2d. ed. Edited by George Rowell, pp. 3–43. New York: Oxford University Press, 1972.
———. *The Rent Day*. London: John Dicks, n. d.
Johnson, Edgar. *Sir Walter Scott: The Great Unknown*. 2 vols. New York: Macmillan, 1970.
Jones, Doris Arthur. *The Life and Letters of Henry Arthur Jones*. London: Gollancz, 1930.
Jones, Henry Arthur. "On Playmaking." In *The Renascence of English Drama: Essays, Lectures, and Fragments Relating to the Modern English Stage, Written and Delivered in the Years 1883–94*, pp. 226–55. 1895; reprint, Essay Index Reprint Series. Freeport, N. Y.: Books for Libraries Press, 1929.
Jones, John Bush, ed. *W. S. Gilbert: A Century of Scholarship and Commentary*. New York: New York University Press, 1970.
Kirk, John Foster. "Shakespeare's Tragedies on the Stage." *Lippincott's Magazine of Popular Literature and Science*. o. s. 35, n. s. 7 (June 1884): 613.
Kleinhans, Chuck. "Notes on Melodrama and the Family Under Capitalism." *Film Reader* 3 (1978): 40–47.
Krause, David, ed. *The Dolmen Boucicault*. Dublin: Dolmen Press, 1965.
Leach, Joseph. *Bright Particular Star: The Life and Times of Charlotte Cushman*. New Haven: Yale University Press, 1970.
Leech, Clifford, and T. W. Craik. *The Revels History of Drama in English, Vol. 6: 1750–1880*. London: Methuen, 1975.
Levi, Primo. *The Drowned and the Saved*. Trans. Raymond Rosenthal. New York: Summit Books, 1988.
Lewes, George Henry. "Article IV." *Westminster Review* 37 (January-April 1842): 321–47.
———. *On Actors and the Art of Acting*. 1875; reprint. New York: Grove Press, 1957.
Lewis, Philip C. *Trouping: How the Show Came to Town*. New York: Harper and Row, 1973.
Lockhart, John G. *Memoirs of the Life of Sir Walter Scott*. 2 vols. Philadelphia: Carey, Lea, and Blanchard, 1838.
Loewenberg, Alfred. *Annals of the Opera, 1597–1940*. Cambridge: Cambridge University Press, 1943.
McManaway, James G. "Shakespeare in the United States." *PMLA* 79 (December 1964): 513–18.
Macready, William Charles. *Macready's Reminiscences and Selections from His Diaries and Letters*. 2 vols. Edited by Sir Frederick Pollock. London: Macmillan, 1876.
Mander, Raymond, and Joe Mitchenson. *British Music Hall*. Rev. ed. London: Gentry, 1974.
———. *Musical Comedy: A Story in Pictures*. New York: Taplinger, 1970.

———. *Pantomime: A Story in Pictures*. London: Davies, 1973.
Marston, [John] Westland. *Our Recent Actors: Being Recollections Critical, and, in Many Cases, Personal, of Late Distinguished Performers of Both Sexes*. 2 vols. Boston: Roberts Brothers, 1888.
———. *The Patrician's Daughter*. London: C. Mitchell, 1843.
———. *Strathmore: A Tragic Play in Five Acts*. London: C. Mitchell, 1849.
Martin, Sir Theodore. *Helena Faucit (Lady Martin)*. London: William Blackwood and Sons, 1900.
Mason, Hamilton. *French Theatre in New York: A List of Plays, 1899–1939*. New York: Columbia University Press, 1940.
Matlaw, Myron. "English and American Dramatizations of *Le Comte de Monte-Cristo*." *Nineteenth-Century Theatre Research* 7 (1979): 39–53.
Mayer, David. *Harlequin in His Element: The English Pantomime 1806–1836*. Cambridge, Mass.: Harvard University Press, 1969.
Meeks, Leslie Howard. *Sheridan Knowles and the Theatre of His Time*. Bloomington, Ind.: Principia Press, 1933.
Meisel, Martin. *Realizations: Narrative, Pictorial, and Theatrical Arts in Nineteenth-Century England*. Princeton: Princeton University Press, 1983.
———. *Shaw and the Nineteenth-Century Theater*. Princeton: Princeton University Press, 1963.
Meyers, Marvin. *The Jacksonian Persuasion: Politics and Belief*. 1960; reprint, Stanford: Stanford University Press, 1970.
Miller, Tice L. *Bohemians and Critics: American Theatre Criticism in the Nineteenth Century*. Metuchen, N. J.: Scarecrow Press, 1981.
Milne, Gordon. *George W. Curtis: The Genteel Tradition*. Bloomington: Indiana University Press, 1956.
Moody, Richard. *Edwin Forrest: First Star of the American Stage*. New York: Alfred A. Knopf, 1960.
———, ed. *Dramas from the American Theatre*. New World Literature Series. 1966; reprint, Boston: Houghton Mifflin, 1969.
Moore, Mary. *Charles Wyndham and Mary Moore*. London, privately printed, 1925.
Morley, Henry. *The Journal of a London Playgoer*. London: George Routledge, 1891.
Morley, John. *The Life of Richard Cobden*. 13th ed. London: T. Fisher Unwin, 1906.
Morris, Lloyd. *Incredible New York*. New York: Random House, 1951.
Moses, Montrose J. *The American Dramatist*. 2d. ed. Revised. Boston: Little, Brown and Company, 1917.
———. *The Fabulous Forrest: The Record of an American Actor*. Boston: Little, Brown and Company, 1929.
———. "History of Famous Plays: *The Fool's Revenge*." *Theatre Magazine* 8 (June 1908): 169–70; v.

——, ed. *Representative Plays by American Dramatists*, 3 vols. 1918–25; reprint, New York: Benjamin Blom, 1964.

——, and John Mason Brown. *The American Theatre as Seen by Its Critics, 1752–1934*. New York: Norton, 1934.

Mott, Frank Luther. *American Journalism*. Rev. ed. New York: Macmillan, 1950.

Muller, Herbert J. *The Spirit of Tragedy*. New York: Alfred Knopf, 1956.

Murray, Christopher. "*Richelieu* at the Theatre Royal, Dublin, 1839." *Theatre Notebook* 37 (1983): 128–31.

Musser, Paul H. *James Nelson Barker*. Philadelphia: University of Pennsylvania Press, 1929.

Nicoll, Allardyce. *A History of English Drama, 1660–1900*. 6 vols. Cambridge: Cambridge University Press, 1940–59.

Nicolson, Colin. "Edwardian England and the Coming of the First World War." In *The Edwardian Age: Conflict and Stability, 1900–1914*, edited by Alan O'Day, pp. 144–68. London: Macmillan, 1979.

O'Day, Alan, ed. *The Edwardian Age: Conflict and Stability, 1900–1914*. London: Macmillan, 1979.

Odell, George C. D. *Annals of the New York Stage*. 15 vols. New York: Columbia University Press, 1927–49.

O'Neill, Patrick. *James O'Neill*. San Francisco: Works Progress Administration in Northern California, 1942.

Oxberry, William, ed. *New English Drama*. 25 vols. Boston: Wells and Lilly, 1823.

Palmer, T. A. *East Lynne*. In *Nineteenth-Century British Drama*, edited by Leonard R. N. Ashley. Glenview, Ill.: Scott, Foresman, 1967.

Patterson, Ada. "James O'Neill—The Actor and the Man." *Theatre Magazine* 8 (April 1908): 101–4; ix.

Payne, Howard. *Clari, or the Maid of Milan*. London: John Miller, 1824.

Pearce, Roy Harvey. *The Savages of America*. Baltimore: Johns Hopkins University Press, 1953.

Pearce, William. *Arrived at Portsmouth*. London: Printed by G. Woodfall for T. N. Longman, 1794.

——. *The Death of Captain Faulknor; or, British Heroism*. London: Glindon, 1795.

Pemberton, T. Edgar. *John Hare, Comedian*. London: George Routledge and Sons, 1895.

Phelps, W. May, and John Forbes-Robertson. *The Life and Life-Work of Samuel Phelps*. London: Sampson Low, Marston, Searle, and Rivington, 1886.

Piave, Francesco Maria. *Rigoletto*. In *Seven Verdi Librettos*, trans. William Weaver, pp. 7–77. New York: Norton, 1975.

Pollock, Sir Frederick, ed. *Macready's Reminiscences and Selections from His Diaries and Letters*. New York: Harper & Brothers, 1875.

Pollock, Lady Juliet. *Macready As I Knew Him*. 2d. ed. London: Remington, 1885.

Quinn, Arthur Hobson. *A History of the American Drama from the Beginning to the Civil War*. 2d. ed. New York: F. S. Crofts, 1943.
———, ed. *Representative American Plays*. 7th ed. New York: Appleton-Century-Crofts, 1957.
Rankin, Hugh F. *The Theater in Colonial America*. Chapel Hill: University of North Carolina Press, 1965.
Raphael, D. D. *The Paradox of Tragedy*. Bloomington: Indiana University Press, 1960.
Recklies, Karen Adele. "Fashion Behind the Footlights in England from 1878 to 1914." Ph.D. dissertation, Ohio State University, 1982.
Reignolds-Winslow, Catherine Mary. *Yesterday with Actors*. Boston: Cupples and Hurd, 1887.
Reilly, Joy Harriman. "From Wicked Woman of the Stage to New Woman: The Career of Olga Nethersole (1870–1951); Actress-Manager, Suffragist, Health Pioneer." Ph.D. dissertation, Ohio State University, 1984.
Report from the Select Committee on Theatrical Licences and Regulations. 1866; reprint, Shannon: Irish University Press, 1970.
Reynolds, Ernest. *Early Victorian Drama (1830–1870)*. 1936; reprint, New York: Benjamin Blom, 1965.
Richards, Colonel A. B. *Cromwell*. British Library, Manuscript Division. BL Additional MS 53114M.
Richardson, Gary A. "Boucicault's *The Octoroon* and American Law." *Educational Theatre Journal* 34 (1982): 155–64.
Robertson, T. W. *Plays by Tom Robertson*. Edited by William Tydeman. Cambridge: Cambridge University Press, 1982.
———. *The Principal Dramatic Works of Thomas William Robertson*. 2 vols. London: Sampson Low, 1889.
———. *Six Plays*. Ashover: Amber Lane Press, 1980.
———. *Society*. Lacy's Acting Edition of Plays, vol. 71, no. 1060.
Rowell, George, ed. *Nineteenth-Century Plays*. London: Oxford University Press, 1953. 2d. ed. New York: Oxford University Press, 1972.
———. *Queen Victoria Goes to the Theatre*. London: Paul Elek, 1978.
———. *Theatre in the Age of Irving*. Totowa, N. J.: Rowman and Littlefield, 1981.
———. *The Victorian Theatre, 1792–1914*. Cambridge: Cambridge University Press, 1978.
———. "Wyndham of Wyndham's." In *The Theatrical Manager in England and America: Player of a Perilous Game*, edited by Joseph W. Donohue, Jr., pp. 189–213. Princeton: Princeton University Press, 1971.
Royle, Edwin Milton. "Edwin Booth as I Knew Him." *Harpers* 132 (1916): 839–49.
Ruggles, Eleanor. *Prince of Players*. New York: W. W. Norton, 1953.
Sachs, Murray. *The Career of Alphonse Daudet*. Cambridge, Mass.: Harvard University Press, 1965.

Sanders, Norman. "American Criticism of Shakespeare's History Plays." *Shakespeare Studies* 9 (1976): 11–23.
Scott, Clement. *The Drama of Yesterday and To-day*. 2 vols. London: Macmillan, 1899.
Scott, Sir Walter. *The Fortunes of Nigel*. 3 vols. Edinburgh: A. Constable, 1822.
———. *Guy Mannering; or, The Astrologer*. Boston: DeWolfe, Fiske, n.d.
Sewall, Richard B. *The Vision of Tragedy*. New Haven: Yale University Press, 1959.
Shattuck, Charles H., ed. *Bulwer and Macready: A Chronicle of the Early Victorian Theatre*. Urbana: University of Illinois Press, 1958.
———. *The Hamlet of Edwin Booth*. Urbana: University of Illinois Press, 1970.
———, ed. *Mr. Macready Produces As You Like It: A Prompt-Book Study*. Urbana: The Beta Phi Mu Chapbook Five/Six, 1962.
———. *Shakespeare on the American Stage*. 2 vols. Washington: Folger Shakespeare Library, 1976, 1987.
———, ed. *William Charles Macready's King John: A Facsimile Promptbook*. Urbana: University of Illinois Press, 1962.
Shaw, Bernard. *Autobiography, 1856–98*. Selected by Stanley Weintraub. London: Max Reinhardt, 1969.
———. "Dear Harp of My Country!" In *The Portable Bernard Shaw*. Edited by Stanley Weintraub, pp. 111–16. New York: Viking, 1977.
———. *Plays Unpleasant*. London: Constable, 1925.
Sichel, Walter. "The English Aristophanes." In *W. S. Gilbert: A Century of Scholarship and Commentary*, edited by John Bush Jones, pp. 69–110. New York: New York University Press, 1970.
Siddons, Henry. *Practical Illustrations of Rhetorical Gesture and Action*. 1822; reprint, New York: Benjamin Blom, 1968.
Skinner, Otis. *The Last Tragedian*. New York: Dodd Mead, 1939.
Spann, Edward K. *The New Metropolis: New York City, 1840–1857*. New York: Columbia University Press, 1981.
Stebbins, Emma C. *Charlotte Cushman: Her Letters and Memories of Her Life*. Boston: Houghton, Osgood, 1878.
Stedman, Jane W. *Gilbert Before Sullivan*. Chicago: University of Chicago Press, 1967.
———. "Gilbert's Stagecraft: Little Blocks of Wood." In *Gilbert and Sullivan: Papers Presented at the International Conference*, edited by James Helyar, pp. 195–211. Lawrence: Kansas University Libraries, 1971.
Steiner, George. *The Death of Tragedy*. London: Faber and Faber, 1961.
Stottlar, James F. "A Victorian Stage Adaptor at Work: W. G. Wills 'Rehabilitates' the Classics." *Victorian Studies* 16 (June 1973): 401–32.
Strang, Lewis C. *Famous Actors of the Day*. Second series. Boston: L. C. Page, 1902.
Strong, Roy. *And When Did You Last See Your Father?* London: Thames and Hudson, 1979.

———. *Van Dyke: Charles the First on Horseback*. London: Allen Lane/Penguin, 1972.
Taylor, Tom. *Historical Dramas*. London: Chatto and Windus, 1877.
Terry, Daniel. *Guy Mannering; or, The Gipsey's Prophecy*. French's Standard Drama Series, no. 77. New York: Samuel French, 186?
Terry, Ellen. *The Story of My Life*. London: Hutchinson, 1908.
Thomson, Fred C. "A Crisis in Early Victorian Drama: John Westland Marston and the Syncretics." *Victorian Studies* 9 (June 1966): 377–88.
Tolles, Winton. *Tom Taylor and the Victorian Drama*. New York: Columbia University Press, 1940.
Toynbee, William, ed. *The Diaries of William Charles Macready, 1833–1851*. 2 vols. London: Chapman and Hall, 1912.
Trewin, J. C. *The Edwardian Theatre*. Oxford: Blackwell, 1976.
Trewin, Wendy. *Charles Wyndham and the Alberys*. London: Harrap, 1980.
Tyler, George C., and J. C. Furnas. *Whatever Goes Up—The Hazardous Fortunes of a Natural Born Gambler*. Indianapolis: Bobbs-Merrill, 1934.
Vandenhoff, George. *Dramatic Reminiscences; or, Actors and Actresses in England and America*. Edited by Henry Seymour Carleton. London: Thomas W. Cooper, 1860.
Vardac, A. Nicholas. *Stage to Screen: Theatrical Method from Garrick to Griffith*. Cambridge, Mass.: Harvard University Press, 1949.
von Rosador, Kurt Tetzli. "Myth and Victorian Melodrama." *Essays and Studies* 32 (1979): 97–114.
———. "Victorian Theories of Melodrama." *Anglia* 95 (1977): 87–114.
Walkley, A. B. *Drama and Life*. 1908; reprint, Freeport, N.Y.: Books for Libraries, 1967.
Ward, John William. *Andrew Jackson: Symbol for an Age*. 1955; reprint, New York: Oxford University Press, 1971.
———. "Jacksonian Democratic Thought: A Natural Charter of Privilege." In *The Development of an American Culture*, edited by Stanley Coben and Lorman Ratner, pp. 44–63. Englewood Cliffs, N. J.: Prentice-Hall, 1970.
Ware, Ralph Hartmann. "American Adaptations of French Plays on the New York and Philadelphia Stages." Ph.D. dissertation, University of Pennsylvania, 1930.
Watermeier, Daniel J. "Edwin Booth's Richelieu." *Theatre History Studies* 1 (1981): 1–19.
Watson, Ernest Bradlee. *Sheridan to Robertson: A Study of the Nineteenth-Century London Stage*. 1926; reprint, New York: Benjamin Blom, 1963.
Watt, Stephen. "Boucicault and Whitbread: The Dublin Stage at the End of the Nineteenth Century." *Éire-Ireland* 18 (Fall 1983): 23–53.
———. "Shaw's *Saint Joan* and the Modern History Play." *Comparative Drama* 19 (Spring 1985): 58–86.

Wearing, J. P. *The London Stage, 1900–1909: A Calendar of Plays and Players*. Metuchen, N. J.: Scarecrow Press, 1981.
——. *The London Stage, 1910–1919: A Calendar of Plays and Players*. Metuchen, N. J.: Scarecrow Press, 1982.
Wells, Henry W. *Three Centuries of Drama: English*. New York: Readex Microprint, 1953–.
White, Henry A. *Sir Walter Scott's Novels on the Stage*. Yale Studies in English, No. 76. New Haven: Yale University Press, 1927.
Wikander, Matthew H. *The Play of Truth & State: Historical Drama from Shakespeare to Brecht*. Baltimore: Johns Hopkins University Press, 1986.
Wilde, Oscar. *The Importance of Being Earnest*. New York: Avon, 1965.
Wills, Freeman. *W. G. Wills, Dramatist and Painter*. London: Longmans, Green, and Company, 1898.
Wills, W. G. *Charles the First*. London: William Blackwood, 1873.
——. *The Love That Kills*. 3 vols. London: Tinsley Brothers, 1867.
——. *Mary, Queen O' Scots*. British Library, Manuscript Division. BL Additional MS 53134D.
Wilson, Garf B. *A History of American Acting*. Bloomington: Indiana University Press, 1966.
Wilson, M. Glen. "Charles Kean at the Haymarket, 1839–1850." *Theatre Journal* 31 (October 1979):328–42.
Winter, William. *The Life and Art of Edwin Booth*. New York: Macmillan, 1893.
——. *The Life of David Belasco*. 2 vols. New York: Moffat, Yard, 1918.
——. *Old Friends*. New York: Moffat, Yard, 1914.
——. *Other Days: Being Chronicles and Memories of the Stage*. New York: Moffat, Yard, 1908.
——. *The Wallet of Time*. 2 vols. New York: Moffat, Yard, 1913.
Wolle, Francis. *Fitz-James O'Brien: A Literary Bohemian of the Eighteen-Fifties*. University of Colorado Studies, Series B, *Studies in the Humanities*, vol. 2, no. 2. Boulder: University of Colorado Press, 1944.
Wood, Lawrence Ashby, Jr. "John Westland Marston, LL.D.: Neo-Elizabethan Dramatist in the Victorian Era." Ph.D. dissertation, Case Western Reserve University, 1955.
Yeater, James Willis. "Charlotte Cushman: American Actress." Ph.D. dissertation, University of Illinois, 1959.
Young, William C. *Famous Actors and Actresses on the American Stage*. 2 vols. New York: R. R. Bowker, 1975.

Contributors

DANIEL BARRETT was a product manager at Digital Equipment Corporation in Colorado Springs, Colorado, and taught in the English Department at the University of Colorado at Colorado Springs. He has contributed articles to *Theatre Notebook*, *Theatre Research International*, and *Nineteenth-Century Theatre Research* and is the author of *T. W. Robertson and the Prince of Wales's Theatre*.

CAROL J. CARLISLE, at the time of the original publication of this book, was a professor emerita of English at the University of South Carolina. Her research interests are Shakespearean interpretation and stage history. She has published *Shakespeare from the Greenroom*; an essay in *Shakespeare and the Victorian Stage*, edited by Richard Foulkes; and articles in a number of journals. She is engaged in a book-length biography of the Victorian actress Helen Faucit and is co-editing *The Two Gentlemen of Verona* for the Shakespeare Variorum.

LORRAINE COMMERET received her Ph.D. in Theatre from the University of Illinois and, at the time of the original publication of this book, held the position in Dramatic Theory and Criticism at the University of Northern Iowa. She has taught at Schiller College in Germany, the University of Wyoming, SUNY-Plattsburgh, and Culver-Stockton College. She has delivered papers at the American Theatre Association and Mid-America Theatre Conference in the areas of Shakespeare in performance, directing, modern German drama, and feminist theory and criticism.

JUDITH L. FISHER is professor of English at Trinity University. In addition to articles on Thackeray, Dickens, and Victorian periodicals, she is the author of *William Makepeace Thackeray* in the Lives of Victorian Literary Figures series, *Thackeray's Narrative Skepticism and the Egoism of Authorship*, and *Annotations of the Art Criticism of William Makepeace Thackeray* in *The Annotations for Thackeray's Art Criticism*.

GEORGE D. GLENN is a professor emeritus of theatre at the University of Northern Iowa. He received his Ph.D. from the University of Illinois. With

Richard L. Poole he co-authored *The Opera Houses of Iowa* and the Iowa chapter in *Opera Houses of the Midwest.*

JAMES HURT is a retired actor and professor emeritus of English at the University of Illinois at Urbana-Champaign. He is the author of *Catiline's Dream: An Essay on Ibsen's Plays* and *Writing Illinois: The Prairie, Lincoln, and Chicago*; and editor or co-editor of numerous textbooks including the popular anthology *Literature of the Western World.*

MYRON MATLAW, a professor emeritus of English, Queen's College, City University of New York, is the author of *Modern World Drama: An Encyclopedia, Pro and Con,* and many articles on literature and the theatre. He edited *Nineteenth-Century American Plays, American Popular Entertainment,* and other books. He was working on a biography of James O'Neill when he died in 1990.

BRUCE A. MCCONACHIE's essay on Edwin Forrest for this anthology was soon followed by *Melodramatic Formations: American Theatre and Society, 1820–1870.* Since then, he has written other books on U.S. theatre and also *Theatre Histories: An Introduction* with three coauthors. McConachie is presently the co-editor of the Cognitive Studies in Literature and Performance series for Palgrave Macmillan, in which he has published *Engaging Audiences: A Cognitive Approach to Spectating in the Theatre.*

TICE L. MILLER, a professor emeritus of theatre at the University of Nebraska-Lincoln, is the author of *Bohemians and Critics* and *Entertaining the Nation: American Drama in the Eighteenth and Nineteenth Centuries*; co-editor of and contributor to *Cambridge Guide to American Theatre,* and co-editor of *The American Stage*; advising editor and contributor to *The Cambridge Guide to World Theatre*; and contributor to and associate editor of *Shakespeare around the Globe.* He is a Fellow of the Mid-America Theatre Conference and of the College of Fellows of the American Theatre.

JOY HARRIMAN REILLY, a native of Great Britain and Ireland, received her Ph.D. in theatre history from the Ohio State University, where she is an associate professor. At Ohio State, Reilly serves as director of the Introduction to Theatre Program. Her research interests range from the history of action, Irish dramatic literature, and Theatre and Age—to devising new works.

GARY A. RICHARDSON is Benjamin W. Griffith, Jr., Professor and Chair of the English Department at Mercer University. He is the author of *American Drama: From the Colonial Period through World War I* and co-editor, with Stephen Watt, of *American Drama: Colonial to Contemporary.* He has written widely on both British and American drama in the eighteenth and nineteenth centuries for journals including *American Drama* and *Theatre Journal.* He is currently writing articles on Richard Brinsley Sheridan and American antebellum art plays.

GEORGE ROWELL was Reader in Theatre History at Bristol University until his retirement in 1987. He wrote widely on the Victorian and Edwardian stage. Among his many publications are *William Terriss and Richard Prince: Two Players in an Adelphi Melodrama*, *The Victorian Theatre: A Survey*, *Queen Victoria Goes to the Theatre*, *Theatre in the Age of Irving*, and with Anthony Jackson, *The Repertory Movement: A History of Regional Theatre in Britain*. He edited numerous volumes of Victorian drama and adapted several plays for the professional stage. He died in 2001.

DENIS SALTER has taught theatre at McGill University since 1987 and has published widely on modern drama, dramaturgy and criticism, performance theory, Victorian and Edwardian stage history, the history of Shakespeare in performance, and Canadian/Quebecois/First Nations theatre. He is the associate editor of *alt. theatre: cultural diversity and the stage*, a quarterly magazine published by Teesri Duniya Theatre, Canada's only professional theatre magazine concerned with politics, cultural plurality, social activism, and the stage. A two-time winner of the Richard Plant best essay in English prize awarded by the Canadian Association for Theatre Research, he is an Honorary Member of the Henry Irving Society in the United Kingdom.

JAMES STOTTLAR is a professor emeritus at the University of Illinois at Urbana-Champaign. His publications include articles on Victorian stage censorship and Victorian drama generally.

MARTHA VICINUS, Eliza M. Mosher Distinguished University Professor of English, Women's Studies and History Emeritus, has written on working-class literature, Victorian women, Victorian theatre and theatricality, and the history of sexuality. Her recent publications include *Intimate Friends: Women Who Loved Women, 1778–1928*, which surveys the different forms of same-sex desire among women, based on unpublished archival materials, literature, court cases, and autobiographies.

STEPHEN WATT is a professor of English at Indiana University in Bloomington. He is the author of *Joyce, O'Casey, and the Irish Popular Theater*, *Postmodern/Drama: Reading the Contemporary Stage*, and *Beckett and Contemporary Irish Writing*. He is the author, with Gary Richardson, of *American Drama: Colonial to Contemporary*; and with Cary Nelson, of *Academic Keywords: A Devil's Dictionary for Higher Education* and *Office Hours: Activism and Change in the Academy*.

J. P. WEARING, a professor emeritus of English at the University of Arizona, is the author of seventeen books including *The Shakespeare Diaries: A Fictional Autobiography*, *Bernard Shaw and Nancy Astor*, *G. B. Shaw: An Annotated Bibliography of Writings about Him*, *Bernard Shaw: On War*, the sixteen-volume *London Stage 1890–1959*, *The Collected Letters of Sir Arthur Pinero*, *American and*

British Theatrical Biography: A Directory, English Drama and Theatre, 1800–1900 (with L.W. Conolly), and editions of Pinero's *The Second Mrs. Tanqueray* and Shaw's *Arms and the Man*.

GARY JAY WILLIAMS is the author of *Our Moonlight Revels: A Midsummer Night's Dream in the Theatre*, winner of the Theatre Library Association's 1998 George Freedley Award. He is a co-author and editor of *Theatre Histories: An Introduction*, and was the editor of *Theatre Survey* from 1995 to 2001. His works on Shakespeare in performance include a stage history of *Timon of Athens* and a forthcoming essay on Edwin Booth's *Hamlet* that reflects on the changes in the field since Charles Shattuck's work. Professor Williams has received fellowships from the Folger Shakespeare Library, Harvard's Houghton Library, Yale University, and the National Endowment for the Humanities. He taught theatre history and criticism for thirty years in the Washington, D.C., area and is an emeritus professor of drama.

Index

Plays are indexed under the author's name or, when the author is unknown, under the title. Pantomimes are indexed under "Pantomime."

Abbotsford, 19
Achurch, Janet, xvi
Acting: characterization, xiv; ensemble, xiv, 45; naturalism in, xx; changes in style, 34. *See also* Characterization, Comedy, Farce, Tragedy, names of individual actors
Actor: source of roles, xiv–xvii; ascendance over playwright, xvii; social responsibilities of, xvi–xvii. *See also* names of individual actors
Actor-managers, xiv–xv, xvii, 44, 299; control of stage, xiv; relations with playwright, xiv–xv, xvii–xix. *See also* Bulwer-Lytton, Edward; Forrest, Edwin; Macready, William Charles; Nethersole, Olga; Wyndham, Charles
Actress-manager, 106, 108
Addison, Laura, 162
Aeschylus: *The Persians*, 187
Adamesque style, 124
Ainsworth, William Harrison, xx
Albery, James, xv, 296; *Two Roses*, xv, 296
Albery Theatre, 299, 310

Alexander, George, 299
America: theatre and politics in antebellum, 12–13; comedy in, 243–52. *See also* Barker, James Nelson; Forrest, Edwin
American culture: anglicized, 123
American Revolution, 123. *See also* Barker, James Nelson; Forrest, Edwin
American stage: anglicized character of, 124–26. *See also* Barker, James Nelson
Anderson, James R., 49
Anderson, Mary, 34, 104
Anglin, Margaret, 307
Arch Street Theatre, 67
Archer, William, xxii, 48, 276–77
Arnold, Matthew, 155
Artaud, Antonin, 35
Arundel Club, 275
Ashwell, Lena, 303, 307, 310
Astley's Theatre, 188
Astor, John Jacob, 243
Astor family, 243
Astor Place Opera House, 245
Athenaeum, 219, 231, 232, 283

Atlas, 29
Atwood, Thomas, 24
Audiences, xx, 244. See also Drama, Theatre, names of individual actors and playwrights
Austen, Jane, 297

Baillie, Joanna, 24; *The Family Legend*, 24
Bancroft, Sidney, 269, 271, 285
Bancrofts, xx
Bandmann-Palmer, Millicent, 188
Bangs, F. C., 91
Bard, Wilkie, 234
Barker, James Nelson, 123–36; political career, 126–27; career as a playwright, 127; *Tears and Smiles*, 127; *The Embargo*, 127; *The Indian Princess*, 127; *The Armourer's Escape*, 127; *How to Try a Lover*, 127; *A Court of Love*, 127; dramatic criticism, 127–29; *Marmion*, 127–32, 134; *Superstition*, 127, 129, 132–34; attacks Sir Walter Scott, 128
Barker, John, 126
Barrett, Lawrence, 67, 83
Barrie, J. M.: *Peter Pan*, 232, 236–37. See also Children's plays, Pantomime
Barton, James, 29
Bateman, H. L., 200
Bateman, Isabella, 199, 205
Bateman, Sidney Frances, 245, 250; *The Golden Calf*, 245, 250; *Self*, 246, 249, 251
Beckett, Gilbert à, *Open Sesame*, xviii
Beerbohm, Max, 232, 235
The Belle of Mayfair, 238
Belot, Adolphe, 113
Bennett, James Gordon, 244
Bentley's Miscellany, xv

Bernhardt, Sarah, xvi, 109
Bird, Robert Montgomery, 3, 5, 94; *The Gladiator*, 3–18, 94. See also Forrest, Edwin
Bishop, Sir Henry Rowley, 24
Bizet, Georges, 109; *Carmen*, 109
Blackwood's Magazine, 23
Blanchard, E. L., 213, 219, 224, 227; *Bluebeard*, 213, 214; *Aladdin*, 219, 224, 231, 233; *Robinson Crusoe*, 224, 225; *Sinbad the Sailor*, 224, 227; *Whittington and his Cat*, 224, 227, 231; *Cinderella*, 227, 231. See also Harris, Augustus
Blanche (ship), 144
Bluebell in Fairyland, 235
Boaden, James, 201
Boer War, 238
Booth, Edwin, xvi, 34, 59, 64–87, 292; *The Fool's Revenge*, xvi, 64–87; *Richelieu*, 59; critical reaction to FR, 73, 76, 80–83. See also Taylor, Tom
Booth, Junius Brutus, 126
Booth, Mary Devlin, 67
Booth's Theatre, 68, 80, 90, 95, 104
Boston Advertiser, 70
Boston Transcript, 80
Boucicault, Dion, xviii, 189, 253–65, 273–74, 278; *The Corsican Brothers*, xvi, 90, 92, 189; *Louis XI*, 189, 196; *The Octoroon*, 206, 255, 258, 263; *London Assurance*, 244, 253–55, 257; *Apollo in New York*, 248; Regency comedies, 253, 254, 255, 261; *The Colleen Bawn*, 253, 255, 256–59, 260, 263; *Old Heads and Young Hearts*, 253, 255–56, 257; myth of the shaughraun, 253, 256; *Arrah-na-Pogue*, 253, 257–61, 263; *The*

[332]

Shaughraun, 253, 257–61, 263; career, 253–54; comic myths, 253–65; Irish plays, 256, 257–59; *Rip Van Winkle*, 256, 261; progressive development, 259–61; conception of melodrama not limited to Irish plays, 261–62; in film, 262–63; "The Future of American Drama," 263–64

Bowery Theatre, 95

Braddon, Mary Elizabeth, xx; *Lady Audley's Secret*, 178–79

Bradley, H., 99

Braham, John, 30, 149

British Navy, 137

Broadway Theatre, 107

Brooke, Gustavus Vaughan, 153

Brougham, John, 249; *The Game of Life*, 249

Brown, Isaac Hull, 243

Browne, Irving, 135, 245, 250; *Our Best Society*, 245, 246, 247, 248; *The Potiphar Papers*, 250

Browning, Robert, xviii, 189; *Strafford*, 189

Buchanan, Robert; *A Sailor and his Lass*, 226, 228

Buckstone, John Baldwin, xvii, 174, 266, 267, 271; *Green Bushes*, xvii; *A Husband at Sight*, xvii; *Luke the Labourer*, xvii, 174, 180, 181, 182, 183

Bulwer-Lytton, Edward, xiv, 39–63, 64, 188, 189, 192, 196; *Richelieu*, 39–63, 64, 189, 196; critical response to *R*, 41–44, 49; *The Lady of Lyons*, 159; *Money*, 288, 291

Bunn, Alfred, xviii; *Guillaume Tell*, xviii

Burlesque, xviii. *See also* Extravaganzas, Farce, Pantomime

Burnand, F. C., 20; *Here's Another Guy Mannering; or, The Original Heir Restorer*, 20

Burnett, Frances Hodgson; *The Little Lord Fauntleroy*, 238

Burnham, Charles, 112, 113

Byron, George Gordon Lord, 4, 11; *Childe Harold*, 11; Byronic hero, 11. *See also* Tragedy

Byron, H. J., xxi, 266, 268, 296

Calcraft, John William, 45, 59; *Richelieu*, 59

Campbell, Herbert, 233, 234–35

Campbell, Mrs. Patrick (Stella), xvi, 109, 307

Carl Rosa Opera Company, 214

Carlyle, Thomas, 125

Carte, D'Oyly, 94, 224

Carter, Mrs. Leslie, 109

Cavendish, Ada, 196

Cazauran, A. R.: *A Parisian Romance*, 94

Chamberlain, Joseph, 233

Champaigne, Philippe de, 45

Characterization, xiv–xvii, 280–98. *See also* Drama, names of individual actors and playwrights

Chartist, 162

Chatterton, F. B., 212

Cheney, Arthur, 91, 98

The Cherry Girl, 238

Chicago Tribune, 92

Children's plays, 235–36; *Bluebell in Fairyland*, 235; *The Golden Land of Fairy Tales*, 235; *Little Hans Andersen*, 235; *Pinkie and the Fairies*, 235; *Snowdrop and the Seven Little Men*, 235; *The Swineherd and the Princess*, 235; *The Water Babies*, 235; *Where the Rainbow Ends*, 235–36; productions, 235; critical reception, 235. *See also* Pantomime

[333]

Index

Chippendale, Alfreda, 30
Chippendale, William, 271
Christmas Entertainments, 230–40.
　See also Harris, Augustus;
　Pantomime
The Chronicle Telegraph, 70
Cibber, Colley, xv, 125, 129;
　adaptation of *Richard II*, xv;
　adaptation of *Richard III*, 125, 129
Clapp, Henry Austin, 34, 70, 76
Clare, Joseph, 92
Clark, Savile, 235; versions of Alice
　stories, 235
Clarke, John, 271–72
Cobb, James, 138; *The Glorious First of
　June*, 138
Cole, John, 168–69
Coleman, John, 48, 58
Collins, Arthur, 234
Collins, Wilkie, 301; *The Woman in
　White*, 301
Comédie Française, 214
Comedy, xix–xxii, 256, 280; "high,"
　xix; "low," xix; affinities with social
　drama, xx; influence of novelists,
　xx–xxi; modernizing tendencies in,
　xxi; screwball, xxii; cup-and-saucer,
　214, 280, 281, 288; in U.S.,
　243–52; sentimental, 281. See also
　Boucicault, Dion; Drama; Gilbert,
　W. S.; Robertson, T. W.
Conquest, George, 228
Conrad, Robert S., 3, 5; *Jack Cade*,
　3–18. See also Forrest, Edwin
Cooke, Thomas, 44
Cooper, James Fenimore, 135
Cooper, Thomas Abthorpe, 129
Cope, Charles West, 202; *Charles I
　Erecting his Standard at Nottingham*,
　202
Copley, John Singleton, 123

Cork, Ireland, 168
Cosmopolitan Theatre, 95
Covenant, 162
Covenanter, 162, 163
Covent Garden Theatre, 19, 24, 28,
　39, 40, 137, 138, 140, 146, 149,
　150, 231, 244
Craven, Banks, 238
Craven, Hawes, 238
Crimean War, 188
Criterion Theatre, 299
Critic, 3
Cromwell, Oliver, 198; depiction in
　drama, 203–5. See also Richards,
　A. B.; Wills, W. G.
Crystal Palace matinees, 299
Cumberland, Richard, 149, 150;
　Nelson's Glory, 149, 150
Curtis, George W., 244; *The Potiphar
　Papers*, 244
Cushman, Charlotte, xv, 19–39; *Guy
　Mannering*, 19–39; acting style, 29;
　debt to Macready, 29; critical
　reactions to *GM*, 33–44

The Daily Advertiser, 124
Daily Graphic, 102
Daily Telegraph, 219, 272
Daly, Augustin, xvi, 188, 288; *Under
　the Gaslight*, 288
Daly's Theatre, 94
Damala, Jacques, 113
Daudet, Alphonse, 106, 113; *Sapho*,
　113
Davenport, E. L., 95
Dazey, C. T., 90, 92; *The American
　King*, 90, 92
Delaroche, Paul, 190, 204; *Cromwell
　Gazing at the Body of Charles I*, 204;
　The Death of Queen Elizabeth, 190
Democratic Review, 14

Index

Dewar, Fred, 272
Dibdin, Thomas, 138–40, 146–48; *The Hermione; or, Retaliation,* 146–48; *The Mouth of the Nile,* 138–40
Dickens, Charles, xv–xx, 160, 238, 243, 286–87, 292; *David Copperfield,* xv, 238, 286–87; *Oliver Twist,* xv; *The Pickwick Papers,* 200; *Nicholas Nickleby,* 292
Diderot, Denis, 73–74; *Paradox of Acting,* 73–74
Dillon, Charles, 153
Disraeli, Benjamin, xviii; *The Tragedy of Count Alarcos,* xviii
Dithmar, Edward A., 108, 115, 116–17
Donat, Robert, 95
Doré, Gustave, 29
Drama: fallen women in, xvi, xxi, 108, 109, 120; genres of, xviii–xix; as literature, xix; contemporary life in, xix–xx; social issues in, xix, xxi; conventions of, xx; *pièce bien faite,* xxi; *fin-de-siècle,* xxii; historical accuracy in, 40, 45, 200–201; stock characters in, 48, 281; decline of, 153; state of, 153, 154; archetypes in, 183; "legitimate," 188, 207. *See also* Acting, Actors, Characterization, Comedy, Historical Drama, Melodrama, Playwrights, Tragedy, names of individual actors and playwrights
Dramatic Copyright Act, xv
Dramatic Mirror, 112
Dramatist. *See* Playwright
Drew, John, 94; *The Squire,* 94
The Drunkard's Warning, 175
Drury Lane Theatre, 19, 28, 30, 137, 138, 149, 150, 188, 200, 201, 212, 214, 219, 227, 228, 232, 233
Dublin, Ireland, 168, 208
Duff, Mary Ann, 28
Dumas, Alexandre, 91, 95, 106; *Camille,* 78, 106; *Count of Monte Cristo,* 88–105
DuMaurier, George, 292; *Trilby,* 292
Duncan, Admiral, 139, 141
Dunlap, William, 127, 129
Durivage, O. E., 245; adaptation of *The Potiphar Papers and Lower Twenty,* 245
Duse, Eleonora, xvi, 109

Eddy, Edward, 95
Edinburgh Evening Courant, 168
Egerton, Mrs. Sarah, 30
Egg, Augustus Leopold, 190; *Queen Elizabeth Discovers She Is No Longer Young,* 190
Eliot, George, 155
Elliston, Robert William, 149
Elton, William, 49
Emerson, Ralph Waldo, 123, 125
Emmet, J. K., 95; *Write in England,* 95
Empire, 33
Empire Theatre, 109
Era, 168, 195, 197, 215, 216, 218, 222, 228, 307
Euclid Avenue Opera House, 107
Evening Post, 102
Examiner, 44, 45, 49, 53, 56, 58, 59, 167
Extravaganzas, xviii, xix, 223. *See also* Farce, Pantomime

Fairholt, Fredrick William, 200–201; *Costume in England,* 200–201

[335]

Farce, xviii, xix, 281, 282, 292; self-consciousness of, 282. *See also* Comedy; Extravaganzas; Gilbert, W. S.; Pantomime
Faucit, Helen, xvi, 48, 49, 153, 161–62; *Richelieu*, 48–49; *The Patrician's Daughter*, 160–62
Fechter, Charles, 91, 95, 96, 98, 103; *Count of Monte Cristo* script, 91, 95
Fifth Avenue Theatre, 78, 80
Figaro (London), 82
Fiske, Stephan Ryder, 80
Fitch, Clyde, 106, 113; *Sapho*, 106–20
Forrest, Edwin, xiv, 3–18, 34, 59, 67, 94; playwrighting contest, 3; political activities, 4; attack on aristocratic privilege in roles, 4–5; heroic roles, 6–7, 8–11; and Jacksonian virtues, 6–7, 12–13; acting style, 11–12; and conventions, 11–12; personal characteristics, 11–12; Shakespearean roles, 12; as a star, 13–14; Astor Place Riot, 14; public image, 14; *Richelieu*, 59. *See also* Melodrama, Tragedy
Forster, John, 41, 59
Forster Collection, 51
Franklin, Andrew, 140; *A Trip to the Nore*, 141–44; critical reception of *TN*, 143–44
French Revolution, 137
Frohman, Charles, 109
Frohman, Daniel, 109
Froude, James Anthony, 191; *History of England*, 191
Frou-Frou, 90

Gainsborough, Thomas, 124
Gallatin, Albert, 243
George, Marie, 234
George III, 141
German Reed Company, 282–83
German Reed Gallery of Illustration, 282
Gilbert, W. S., xviii, xxii, 94, 224, 280–98; social satire, xxii; "topsy-turvydom," xxii, 280, 283, 296; *Engaged*, xxii, 280–98; *Iolanthe*, 94; *H.M.S. Pinafore*, 280; *The Mikado*, 280; *Ruddigore*, 280, 285; manipulation of dramatic convention in *Engaged*, 281; *Our Island Home*, 282; *A Sensation Novel*, 282–83, 290; critical reaction to *E*, 283–84; *Tom Cobb*, 289; *Pirates of Penzance*, 296
Godwin, Edward, 201
Globe Theatre (Boston), 91
Gluck, Christoph Willibald, 44
Goethe, Johann Wolfgang von, 125
The Golden Land of Fairy Tales, 235
Goldsmith, Oliver, 208; *The Vicar of Wakefield*, 208
Goodall, Fredrick, 201; *An Episode of the Happier Days of Charles I*, 201
Gothic novel, 19–24
Grand Opera House, 94
Graves, George, 234
Greenwich Hospital, 150
Grétry, Andre Ernest, 44
Griffin, Gerald, 257; *The Collegians*, 257
Grundy, Sydney, xx
Gymnase, 113

Hackett, J. H., 248; *The Moderns; or, A Trip to the Springs*, 248
Hading, Jane, 113
Halévy, Jacques François, 109
Hamilton, Edward, 146–47
Hamilton, Henry, 106, 109; *Carmen*, 106; *The Armada*, 188, 192, 193,

[336]

227; *The Royal Oak*, 188, 192,
  227. *See also* Harris, Augustus
Hapgood, Norman, 113, 115
Hare, John, 198, 272
Harper's Weekly, 244
Harrigan, Edward, 94; *McSorley's
  Inflation*, 94
Harris, Augustus, 188, 192, 193,
  212–29; *The Armada*, 188, 192,
  193, 227; *The Royal Oak*, 188,
  192, 227; and audience, 215; *The
  World*, 215, 216–19, 221, 222,
  224, 226; *Youth*, 219–22, 224;
  Robinson Crusoe, 221, 224, 225;
  resemblance between melodramas
  and pantomimes, 221–22; *Aladdin*,
  224; *Babes in the Woods*, 224; *Puss-
  in-Boots*, 224; *Sinbad the Sailor*,
  224; *Whittington and His Cat*, 224;
  Pluck, 224, 226; pantomimes,
  224–25; *Claudian*, 226; *Human
  Nature*, 226; *Pleasure*, 226; *A Run
  of Luck*, 226; *Freedom*, 226, 228; *A
  Sailor and His Lass*, 226, 228
Hart, Tony, 94; *McSorley's Inflation*,
  94
Harvey, Martin, 199
Haverley's Theatre, 94
Hawthorne, Julian, 32
Haymarket Theatre, 49, 166, 168,
  238, 266, 267, 271, 272
Hazlewood, C. H., 178, 283; *Lady
  Audley's Secret*, 176, 178, 181, 213,
  283
Hazlitt, William, 125
Head (costume designer), 44
Henry VIII, 129
Herald, 117
Heroines: naming, 286–87
Historical Drama, 187–211;
  domesticity in, 194, 201–202;
  actresses in, 196; iconography in,
  201; ideology of, 202–7;
  characteristics of, 206–7. *See also*
  Drama; Macready, William Charles;
  Marston, John Westland; Tragedy
Howard, Bronson, *Saratoga*, 245,
  248–49
Howard Atheneum, 67
Howe, Henry, 271
Howe, Lord Richard, 138, 139
Howells, William Dean, 251
Hubris, 152
Hugo, Victor, 68, 69, 190; *Le Roi
  S'Amuse*, 68, 190; *Hunchback of
  Notre Dame*, 76
Huntley, G. P., 237; *Lady Madcap*,
  237
Hurlburt, William Henry, 245;
  American in Paris, 245

Ibsen, Henrik, xvi, xxi–xxii
Idler and Breakfast Table Companion,
  48, 49
Illustrated London News, 82, 284, 303
Illustrated Sporting and Dramatic News,
  xv, 82, 216, 218, 222–23
Illustrated Times, 282, 287
International copyright law, 244
Irish patriotic symbolism, 259
Irish Shield, 12
Irving, Henry, xiv, xv, xvi, 59, 80,
  81, 188, 189, 190, 194, 198, 199,
  200, 205, 207, 214, 224, 292,
  307, 310; *Becket*, xiv; *Hamlet*, xv;
  Macbeth, xv; *Much Ado about
  Nothing*, xv; *Two Roses*, xv
Irving, Washington, 135

Jackson, Andrew, 4–8, 13–16
Jacksonian democracy, 4–16
Jacksonian melodrama, 16
James, Charles S., 271
James, Henry, 251

Index

James IV, 129, 131
Jefferson, Joseph, 67, 261–63; *Rip Van Winkle*, 261–63
Jerome, Jerome K., 284
Jerrold, Douglas, 176, 291; *Black Ey'd Susan*, 176, 291; *Rent Day*, 176, 177, 180, 181, 182
John Bull, 43, 49
Jones, Henry Arthur, xvi, xix, xx, xxi, xxii, 280, 299–311; "problem play," xxi; *Mrs. Dane's Defence*, xxi, 299–311; *The Bauble Shop*, 300; *The Physician*, 300; *The Liars*, 300, 303; *The Case of Rebellious Susan*, 300, 303, 308
Joyce, James, 188, 259, 261; *Ulysses*, 188; *Finnegan's Wake*, 259, 261

Kean, Charles, xiv, 167–68, 189; *Strathmore*, 167–68
Kean, Charles and Ellen, 153, 167
Kean, Edmund, xiv, 47, 125, 126, 195
Kean, Ellen, 167–68; *Strathmore*, 167–68
Kean, Thomas, 125
Keene, Laura, 244
Kemble, John Phillip, 24, 47, 126, 138, 201; *Macbeth*, 24
Kembles, xvii, 137, 150
Kendals, 198, 224
Kenny, James: *Raising the Wind*, 200
Knowles, Sheridan, xiv, 4, 19, 200; *Virginius*, xiv, 4; *The Vision of the Bard*, 19

Lady Madcap, 237
Lamb, Charles, 125
Lamennais, Hughes Félicité Robert de, 155
Lander, F. W., 190
Landi, Elissa, 95
Langtry, Lillie, 107

Language: theatrical, xviii, xix, 288–90; verbal humor, xix; romantic poetic diction, 288–90. *See also* Acting, Characterization, Comedy, Drama, names of individual actors
La Pique (ship), 144
Larkin, Sophie, 271, 272
Leggett, William, 4
Lemon, Mark, xviii; *Open Sesame*, xviii
Leno, Dan, 233, 234–35
Leslie, Amy, 104
Lessing, Gotthold, 125
Lester, John, 95
Lewes, George Henry, xviii, 159
Lewis, Leopold, 188, 200; *The Bells*, 188, 200
Liberty Hall, 238
"Line roles," 257
Liston, John. xv. 28
Little Hans Andersen, 235
Litton, Marie, 213
Locke, John, 5, 16; state of nature, 5, 16
Lockhart, John Gibson, 24
London Observer, 29
London season, 230
London theatres, 213, 214, 230–31. *See also* names of individual theatres.
Lord Chamberlain's office, 268
Lowell, James Russell, 125
Lucas, Seymour, 227; *Game of Bowls on Plymouth Hoe*, 227
Lyceum Theatre (London), 188, 198, 200, 214, 224, 234
Lyceum Theatre (New York), 80, 196

Mackay, Charles, 28
Maclise, Daniel, 202; *An Interview Between Charles I and Oliver Cromwell*, 202
Macready, William Charles, xiv, xv,

[338]

Index

xvi, xviii, 14, 39–63, 153, 159, 160–61, 162, 189, 195; *Richelieu*, xiv, 39–63; *The Merchant of Venice*, xv; *Marmion*, xviii; Astor Place Riot, 14; *Macbeth*, 24; *Coriolanus*, 39; *Julius Caesar*, 39; and Shakespeare, 39–40, 60; relations with Bulwer-Lytton, 41–43, 45; critical reaction to *R*, 46–47, 56, 58; *The Patrician's Daughter*, 160–61

Madame Sherry, 237–38
Maeterlinck, Maurice, 106; *Mary Magdalene*, 106
Manchester Courier, 162
Mansfield, Richard, 94
The Man Who Stayed at Home, 238
Marshall, Charles, 44, 53
Marston, John Westland, xvii, xviii, 46, 47, 48, 55, 152–73; *Strathmore*, xviii, 152–53, 162–70; *The Patrician's Daughter*, 152–53, 155–62; *Philip of France and Marie De Meranie*, 153; critical reaction to *PD*, 159–60; critical reaction to *S*, 166–67, 168–69; and tragic hero, 169–70. See also Tragedy
Martini, Giovanni Battista, 44
Martyr, Mrs. Margaret, 144, 145
Matthew, Cornelius, 245; *False Pretenses*, 245, 246, 247, 248, 249, 251
Matthews, Charles, 254
Mayer, Marcus, 112, 117
Meilhac, Henri, 109; *Carmen*, 109
Melodrama, xix, 6–11, 20, 24–28, 35, 48, 174–86, 189, 239, 258, 280, 281, 310; conventions of, 6; hero in, 6–11; Andrew Jackson and, 7; gothic, 20, 35; music in, 26–28; language of, 35; romantic, 48, 106; domestic, 174–86; archetypal power of, 175; and family, 175–79; popularity with working class, 177; characterization in, 179–83; self-sacrifice as theme, 180; ideology, 183–85; spectacular, 212–29. *See also* Acting; Characterization; Cushman, Charlotte; Drama; Forrest, Edwin; Jones, Henry Arthur; Nautical docudrama; Pinero, Arthur Wing; Tragedy

Merimée, Prosper, 109; *Carmen*, 109
Meritt, Paul, 218; *The New Babylon*, 218; *Rough and Ready*, 218; *The Worship of Bacchus*, 218; *Pleasure*, 226
Millais, Sir John Everett, 201; *A Huguenot on St. Bartholomew's Day, Refusing to Shield Himself from Danger by Wearing the Roman Catholic Badge*, 201
Mitchell, William, 248; *Saratoga Springs*, 248
Mitford, Mary, 4; *Rienzi*, 4
Modjeska, Helena, 83, 90; *Frou-Frou*, 90; *Odette*, 90
Moore, Edward, 154; *The Gamester*, 154
Moore, Mary, 300, 310
Moore, Nelly, 271
Morgann, Maurice, 125
Morley, Henry, 33
Morning Chronicle, 44–45, 51, 53, 58, 59, 143, 160, 166
Morning Herald, 40, 160
Morning Post, 40, 149, 160, 198, 201, 205
Morning Post and Gazetteer, 140, 144
Morris, Clara, 109
Morton, Thomas, 129
Moss, Theodore, 117
Mowatt, Anna Cora, 245, *Fashion*, 245, 246, 249, 251
Music Hall, xxii, 232

Index

Napoleonic Wars, 137
National Theatre, 30
Nautical docudrama, 137–51; conventions of, 138–39; portrayal of French military, 139, 147–48; and British sense of fair play, 140, 141, 142; portrayal of Dutch, 142; spectacle, 148–49; and death of Nelson, 149; critical reaction to, 150; political importance, 150–51
Neilson, Adelaide, 153, 196
Nelson, Lord Horatio, 139, 149, 150; Aboukir Bay, 139; effect of death on drama, 149. *See also* Nautical docudrama
Nethersole, Olga, xvi, 100–120; *Sapho*, xvi, 106–120; career, 106, 107–8; trial about *Sapho*, 106, 117–19; critical reaction to *S*, 107, 115–16; as manager, 108; "Nethersole Kiss," 108, 109, 112; *Carmen*, 109; physical appearance, 109; critical reaction to *C*, 111; self-publicity, 112; *Sapolio*, 119
Neville, Henry, 196
New Theatre, 299, 310
New York Albion, 47, 58
New York Daily Tribune, 93, 102
New York Dramatic Mirror, 111, 115–16
New York Herald, 32, 73, 196, 244, 250
New York society, 243–44, 249
New York Sun, 250
New York Times, 29, 67, 80, 93, 102, 103, 109, 116, 119, 250
New York Tribune, 70, 107
New York World, 79, 101, 102, 107, 113, 115, 116, 117
Niblo's Garden, 67
Nym Crinkle (Andrew C. Wheeler), 79, 80

O'Brien, Fitz-James, 244, 245–46; "About the Sexton Bumble-Bee," 244; "Brown Studies," 244; *The Lantern*, 244; *Putnam's*, 244; *Young America*, 244
Observer, 82
O'Casey, Sean, 253
Odette, 90
Olympic Theatre, 245
O'Neill, Eugene, 98
O'Neill, James, xvi, 88–105; *Count of Monte Cristo*, xvi, 88–105; *A Celebrated Case*, 92; preparation of CMC, 93, 102; critical reaction to CMC, 102–4
On His Majesty's Service, 238
Orczy, Baroness: *The Scarlet Pimpernel*, 238
Otway, Thomas: *Venice Preserved*, 162
Oxbury, William, 28
Oxenford, John, 159

Palladian style, 124
Pall Mall Gazette, 271
Palmer, T. A., 179; *East Lynne*, 176, 178, 179, 181
Pan, 82
Panoramas, 223
Pantomime, xviii, xix, 72, 213–14, 230–40; transformation scene, 72; at Christmas, 213, 214, 230–40; *The Babes in the Wood*, 231; *Jack and the Beanstalk*, 231; *Little Red Riding Hood*, 231; *Sleeping Beauty*, 231; attacked in the press, 232–33; *Humpty Dumpty*, 233; *The Sleeping Beauty and the Beast*, 233; spectacle, 233; topical allusions, 233; *Lady Madcap*, 237. *See also* Blanchard, E. L.; Extravaganzas; Farce; Harris, Augustus; Stage effects

Index

Pardey, Charles, 245; *Nature's Nobleman*, 245, 246, 248, 251
Parker, Sir Peter, 147
Park Theatre, 244
Passmore, Walter, 234
Paulding, James K., 245; *The Bucktails; or, Americans in England*, 245
Payne, Howard: *Clari; or, The Maid of Milan*, 176, 181, 184
Pearce, William, 140; *Arrived at Portsmouth*, 140–41; *The Death of Captain Faulknor; or, British Heroism*, 144–46
Penny dreadfuls, 223
Pettitt, Henry, 218, 226; *The Silver Falls*, 106; *Sentenced to Death*, 218; *Snatched from the Grave*, 218; *The Worship of Bacchus*, 218; *Pluck*, 224, 226; *Human Nature*, 228
Phelps, Samuel, 49, 59, 67, 72, 79, 153, 162, 189, 199, 207; *Richelieu*, 49, 59; *The Fool's Revenge*, 67, 72, 79; *The Patrician's Daughter*, 162; *Othello*, 199
Picturesque style, 51, 53, 59. See also Acting; Characterization; Drama; Historical Drama; Macready, William Charles
Pinero, Arthur Wing, xvi, xix, xx, xxi, xxii, 106, 280; problem play, xxi; *The Notorious Mrs. Ebbsmith*, xxi; *The Second Mrs. Tanqueray*, xxi, 106, 118
Pinkie and the Fairies, 235
Placide, Henry, 244
Playwrights, xvii–xix; status, xvii; relations with actor, xvii–xix. See also Bulwer-Lytton, Edward; Forrest, Edwin; Jones, Henry Arthur; Pinero, Arthur Wing; Robertson, T. W.

Police Gazette, 223
Pollock, Lady Julia, 55
Pond, Anson, 94; *Her Atonement*, 94
Powers Theatre, 111
Pratt, William: *Ten Nights in A Bar Room*, 175
Price, Lizzie, 103
Prince of Wales Theatre (Liverpool), 266
Prince of Wales Theatre (London), xx, 266, 267, 270–71, 272; appointments of, 270–71
Problem plays. See Jones, Henry Arthur; Pinero, Arthur Wing
Punch, xviii, 190, 213, 218
Puttenham, George, 187, 189; *The Arte of English Poesie*, 187

Queen, 116
Queen's Theatre, 203

Randall, Harry, 234
Reece, Robert, 19; *Guy Mannering in New Guise*, 19
Referee, 81
Regency Comedies, 254, 257
Rehan, Ada, xvi, 94, 109; *The Squire*, 94
Reignolds-Winslow, Catherine Mary, 30
Rejane, 113
Report from the Select Committee on Theatrical Licenses and Regulations, 273
Revelle, Hamilton, 117
Reynolds, 73
Reynolds, Miss, 167, 168
Reynolds, Sir Joshua, 124
Richards, A. B., 203; *Oliver Cromwell: An Historical Tragedy*, 203–4
Rignold, George, 213

[341]

Robertson, T. W., xiv, xix, xx–xxi, 266–79, 280, 282, 283, 287, 291, 296, 299; influence of W. M. Thackeray, xx–xxi; *Caste*, xxi, 256, 266, 296; *Ours*, xxi, 266, 285, 296; control of production, xxi, 270–71; comedy, xxii, 266–79, 281, 283; *M. P.*, 266; *Play*, 266; *David Garrick*, 266, 267, 270, 299; *School*, 266, 291; critical reaction to *S*, 266–67, 271; *Society*, 266–79; *Principal Dramatic Works*, 268; and Marie Wilton, 268–69; language, 276; "Theatrical Types," 282, 291; heroines, 287

Robson, Fredrick, 67

Robson, May, 119; *Sapolio*, 119

Rogers, Katherine, 99

Romantic heroine and hero, 288–91. See also Melodrama, Tragedy

Romantic style, 288–95. See also Melodrama, Tragedy

Romantic villain, 292. See also Melodrama

Rossini, Giacomo, xviii; *Guillaume Tell*, xviii

Rousby, Clara, 195, 196

Rousseau, Jean Jacques, 154

Rowe, George F.: *Freedom*, 226, 228

Royal Olympic Theatre, 196

Royal Shakespeare Company, 237

Sadler's Wells Theatre, 67, 162, 189

St. James Theatre, 198, 224

St. Vincent, Admiral, 139

Salvini, Tommaso, 94

Saratoga Springs, 245

Satirist, 48

Saturday Press, 244

Saturday Review, 70, 191, 195, 197, 232

Saunder's Newsletter, 60

Savage Club, 275

Savoy Theatre, 224

Saxe-Meiningen Company, 214, 219

Schiller, Friedrich, 23, 35; *Wallenstein*, 23

Schlegel, August, 125

School-life plays, 239

Scott, Clement, 81, 82, 219, 223, 272, 275, 276

Scott, Sir Walter, xv, xviii, 19–24, 33, 34, 128, 162; *Rob Roy*, xv, 19; *Guy Mannering*, xv, 19–39; *Old Mortality*, xv, 162; *Marmion*, xviii; *The Heart of Midlothian*, 19; *Ivanhoe*, 19; *Kenilworth*, 19; *The Antiquary*, 22; *Waverley*, 22; *Waverley Novels*, 22; attitude toward stage adaptations, 24; *The Lady of the Lake*, 24

Scott-Siddons, Mrs. Sarah, 196

Sensation drama. See Boucicault, Dion; Melodrama

Seyler, Athene, 310

Shakespeare, William, xiv, xv, 4, 28, 44, 60, 125, 126, 187, 188, 194, 199, 207, 238, 299; *King Lear*, xiv, 60, 71, 94, 155; revivals in the nineteenth century, xvii; sacrifice of literary to scenic, xviii; *Coriolanus*, 4; *Macbeth*, 28, 60, 82, 175; history plays, 44; *Othello*, 60, 71, 73, 78, 83, 94; *Romeo and Juliet*, 68; *Hamlet*, 73, 78, 83, 155; *The Tempest*, 76, 238; *The Merchant of Venice*, 83, 199; romantic aesthetics, 125; stage history, 125–26; political importance in the U.S., 126; *Richard II*, 175; *Henry IV*, 194; *Much Ado About Nothing*, 196; *As You Like It*, 196, 213; *Henry V*, 213, 238

Shakespearean criticism, 125
Shaw, George Bernard, xv, xvi, xviii, xxi–xxii, 108, 198, 200, 238–39, 253, 256, 260, 299; reviews of Irving's productions, xviii; *Arms and the Man*, 238; *John Bull's Other Island*, 238; *The Devil's Disciple*, 260; *The Philanderer*, 299
Shepard, Sam, 188
Sheridan, Richard Brinsley, 138; *The Glorious First of June*, 138
Sherwood, Benson, 78; stage plan book, 78
Siddons, Henry, 24, 296; *The Family Legend*, 24; *Practical Illustrations of Rhetorical Gesture*, 296
Siddons, Sarah, 29
Simon, Neil, 262
Sims, G. R., 234; *The Silver Falls*, 106
Smith, Col. Hamilton, 44
Snowdrop and the Seven Little Men, 235
Social drama, xx; restraint, xx. *See also* Comedy; Drama; Jones, Henry Arthur; Pinero, Arthur Wing
Society comedy, 299. *See also* Comedy
Sothern, E. A., 153, 267, 271
Speaking style, 288. *See also* Language, names of individual actors
Spectacular melodrama. *See* Melodrama
Spectator, 45–46
Spirit of the Times, 102
Spy-plays, 238; *The Man Who Stayed at Home*, 238; *On His Majesty's Service*, 238
Stage, 82, 304
Stage effects, xviii, xx, 39–40, 72, 198, 204, 223, 227; historical verisimilitude, 39–40; *tableaux vivants*, 198, 204, 223, 227; *trompe l'oeil*, 72. *See also* Boucicault, Dion; Harris, Augustus; Theatre; names of individual actors
Standard, 82
Stetson, John, 90, 91, 93, 98
Stewart, A. T., 243
Stone, John Augustus, 3; *Metamora, or the Last of the Wampanoags*, 3–18. *See also* Forrest, Edwin
Strachen, J., 19–20; *Such a Guy Mannering*, 19–20
Stuart, Gilbert, 123
The Swineherd and the Princess, 235
Sullivan, Arthur, 94, 224; *Iolanthe*, 94; *H.M.S. Pinafore*, 280; *The Mikado*, 280; *Ruddigore*, 280, 285; *Our Island Home*, 282; *Pirates of Penzance*, 296
Sullivan, Barry, 153
Sully, Thomas, 29
Sun, 166
Sunday Times, 48
Syncretics, 152, 154
Synge, John M., 253

Tallis's Dramatic Magazine, 29
Tate, Nahum, xv; *King Lear*, xv
Taylor, Tom, xvi, xix, 64–87, 188–98, 199, 207, 208, 267; *The Fool's Revenge*, xvi, 64–87; *Ticket-of-Leave Man*, xix, 189, 190; critical reaction to *FR*, 70, 73, 74; *'Twixt Axe and Crown*, 188, 189–98; *Still Waters Run Deep*, 189; *Jeanne D'Arc*, 190, 192, 196, 206; *Lady Clancarty*, 190, 196, 197; *Anne Boleyn*, 190, 197; *Historical Dramas*, 194; critical reaction to *TAC*, 195; *The Theatre in England, some of its shortcomings and possibilities*, 196; critical reaction to

Taylor, Tom (*continued*)
J D'Arc, 197; *Our American Cousin*, 267
Tennyson, Alfred Lord, xiv, xviii, 76, 191, 192, 194, 200; *Becket*, xiv, 192; "The Last Tournament," 76; *Queen Mary*, 191, 194
Terry, Daniel, 19, 24–28, 33; *The Antiquary*, 24; *The Heart of Midlothian*, 24; *Guy Mannering*, 24–28. *See also* Cushman, Charlotte; Scott, Sir Walter
Terry, Ellen, xv, xvi, 190, 199, 201; *Much Ado About Nothing*, xv
Thackeray, William Makepeace, xx; *Vanity Fair*, xxi
Theatre, 223
Theatre: legitimate, xv; male dominance of English, xvi; physical changes in, xx; Elizabethan, xxi; romantic, 35; *mise-en-scène*, 39, 49, 53, 72, 78; proscenium arch, 39, 51; pictorial ethic, 223; U.S., 245–51. *See also* Acting; Characterization; Comedy; Drama; Stage effects; names of individual actors
Theatre bill, xx
Théâtre Comique, 94
Theatres Act of 1843, 162
Thomas, Denman, 94; *Joshua Whitcomb*, 94
Thomas, Walter Brandon; *Charley's Aunt*, 232, 237
Thorne, Charles, Jr., 90
Thriller plays. *See* Spy-plays
The Times, 45, 81, 139, 140, 141, 144, 149, 159, 161, 166, 187, 188, 190, 194, 196, 198, 199, 200, 201, 204, 216, 218, 232, 233, 235, 236, 238, 274

Tomlins, F. G., 189; *Garcia; or, The Noble Error*, 189
Towers, Edward, xvii; *The Demon Doctor*, xvii
Trafalgar, Battle of, 149
Tragic actors, 154–55. *See also* Acting; Characterization; Historical drama; Tragedy; names of individual actors
Tragedy, 3, 4, 6–11, 16, 152, 154–55, 292; romantic, 3, 4, 6–11, 16, 292; poetic, 152; bourgeois, 154; theory of, 154–55. *See also* Barker, James Nelson; Characterizations; Forrest, Edwin; Historical drama; Macready, William Charles; Marston, John Westland
Transvestism in the theatre, 237
Tree, Henry Beerbohm, 307
Tyler, Royall, 124; *The Contrast*, 124

Union Square Theatre, 94

Vandenhoff, George, 47
Vanderbilts, 243
Van Dyke, Sir Anthony, 201, 206; *Charles I on Horseback*, 206
Verdi, Guiseppi, 68; *Rigoletto*, 68
Vestris, Madame Lucia, xvi, 275
Vigny, Alfred de, 41, 59; *Cinq-Mars*, 41

W. W. Kelly Company, 208
Wainwright, D. W., 245; *Wheat and Chaff*, 245, 246, 247, 249, 251
Walcot, Charles M., 245; *A Good Fellow*, 245, 246, 249
Walkley, A. B., 236
Wallace, General Lew; *Ben Hur*, 117
Wallack Dynasty, 95

Wallack's Theatre, 106, 112, 113, 117
Waller, Emma, 28
Waller, Lewis, 238
Ward, Genevieve, 28
Warde, James, 48
Warner, Mrs. Mary Amelia, 161
The Water Babies, 235
Watts, George Fredrick, 190
Weekly Reviewer, 77
West, Benjamin, 123–24
Wharton, Edith, 251
Wheeler, Andrew C. (Nym Crinkle), 79, 80
Where the Rainbow Ends, 235–36
White, James, 189; *Feudal Times*, 189; *James the Sixth*, 189; *John Saville of Haysted*, 189; *The King of Commons*, 189
Whitman, Walt, 125
Wilde, Oscar, xxii, 289, 297, 300–301; epigrammatic style, 297; *femmes fatales*, 300–301; *The Importance of Being Earnest*, 289, 299
Wills, Freeman, 188, 199; *The Only Way*, 199
Wills, W. G., xix, 187, 188, 189, 192, 198, 208; *Charles the First*, 188, 189, 191, 192, 198–208; *Buckingham*, 192, 207, 208; *Mary, Queen O' Scots*, 192, 208; *Jane Shore*, 197, 203, 208; critical reaction to *CF*, 198–201; *Claudian*, 201, 208; *The Love That Kills*, 205; *A Royal Divorce*, 208; *The Vicar of Wakefield*, 208
Wilkins, Edward G. P., 244, 245, 246, 248, 250; *My Wife's Mirror*, 245, 250; *Young New York*, 245, 247, 248, 250
Wilton, Marie, 266, 268–69, 270, 271, 275; partnership with Robertson, 266, 268–69
Winter, William, 70, 76, 95, 107
Winter Garden Theatre, 67, 80
Wit, 296. *See also* Comedy; Gilbert, W. S.
Women's Christian Temperance Union, 107
Wood, Mrs. Henry, xx, 183
Wood, William, 129
World. See New York World
World War I, 238
Wyndham, Charles, xiv, 299–311; *Mrs. Dane's Defence*, 299–311

Yates, Mrs., 28
Yeats, William Butler, 253; *The Pot of Broth*, 253